Join the Recommended Country Inns® Travelers' Club and

The Recommended Country Inns® guides are the preeminent guidebooks to the finest country inns in the United States. Authors personally visit and recommend each establishment listed in the guides, and **no fees are solicited or accepted for inclusion in the books.**

Now the Recommended Country Inns® guides offer a special new way for travelers to enjoy extra savings: through the Recommended Country Inns® Travelers' Club. Member benefits include savings such as:

- Discounts on accommodations
- Discounts on food
- Discounts on local attractions

How to Save: Read the profile for each inn to see if it offers an incentive to members. For participating establishments, look for information at the end of the inn's profile or in the index at the end of the book. Simply mention that you are a member of the Recommended Country Inns® Travelers' Club when making reservations, and show your membership card when you check in. All offers are subject to availability.

How to Join: If you wish to become a member of the Recommended Country Inns® Travelers' Club, simply fill out the attached form and send it by mail to:

Recommended Country Inns® Travelers' Club
c/o The Globe Pequot Press
PO Box 833
Old Saybrook, CT 06475
Or fax to: 860–395–2855

A membership card will be mailed to you upon receipt of the form. Please allow 4-6 weeks for delivery.

**Sign up today and start saving as a Recommended Country Inns®
Travelers' Club member!**

(All offers from participating inns expire November 30, 1998, unless otherwise mentioned.)

Recommended Country Inns® Travelers' Club
Membership Form

Name: _____

Address: _____

City _____ State _____ Zip _____

Phone _____ Fax _____ E-mail _____

Age: 18–35 _____;   36–50_____;   over 50_____

Sex: Male ____   Female ____   Marital Status: Single _____   Married_____

Annual Household Income:
    under $35,000 _____; $35,000–$75,0000 _____;   over $75,000_____

Credit cards: Mastercard_____; Visa _____; Amex _____; Discover _____; Other _____

Book purchased at: Store Name: _____; City _____, State _____

Mail completed form to:
Recommended Country Inns® Travelers' Club
c/o The Globe Pequot Press
PO Box 833
Old Saybrook, CT 06475
Or fax to: 860–395–2855

MA

Recommended
Country Inns®
MID-ATLANTIC AND CHESAPEAKE REGION

"Romance seekers couldn't do better than the nearly 200 inns herein, combining the best of past and present. . . ."
—*New York Daily News*

"The real joy in this guide is its lyrical prose; you find yourself reading about the inns for sheer delight."
—*AAA World*

"Among the most helpful guides to country inns."
—*Washington Post*

"Just sitting back in a favorite chair and browsing through this delightful volume comes close to enjoying a relaxing and pleasurable vacation. . . . The variety of inns profiled is astonishing."
—*Amtrak Express*

"Information includes who the owners are, when it is open, number of rooms, rates, facilities, settings, directions, and what makes each a special place."
—*Travel & Leisure*

"Each inn has been visited personally by the author, and descriptions include substantial details about the inns and their settings."
—*Inn Review*

"A not-to-miss guide, especially if you are planning a vacation or business trip."
—*Hudson Valley* magazine

Recommended Country Inns® Series

"These guides are a marvelous start to planning the leisurely trek, romantic getaway, or time-off for reflection."
—*Internet Book Review*

The Recommended Country Inns® series is designed for the discriminating traveler who seeks the best in unique accommodations away from home.

From hundreds of inns personally visited and evaluated by the author, only the finest are described here. The inclusion of an inn is purely a personal decision on the part of the author; no one can pay or be paid to be in a Globe Pequot inn guide.

Organized for easy reference, these guides point you to just the kind of accommodations you are looking for: Comprehensive indexes by category provide listings of inns for romantic getaways, inns for the sports-minded, inns that serve gourmet meals, inns for the business traveler . . . and more. State maps help you pinpoint the location of each inn, and detailed driving directions tell you how to get there.

Use these guidebooks with confidence. Allow each author to share his or her selections with you and then discover for yourself the country inn experience.

Editions available:

Recommended Country Inns®
New England • Mid-Atlantic and Chesapeake Region
The South • The Midwest • West Coast
The Southwest • Rocky Mountain Region
also
Recommended Romantic Inns
Recommended Island Inns

Recommended Country Inns®

MID–ATLANTIC AND CHESAPEAKE REGION

Delaware ❦ Maryland ❦ New Jersey
New York ❦ Pennsylvania ❦ Virginia
Washington, D.C. ❦ West Virginia

Seventh Edition

by Brenda Boelts Chapin
edited by Suzi Forbes Chase
illustrated by Olive Metcalf

A *Voyager* Book

The Globe Pequot Press

Old Saybrook, Connecticut

ISBN 0-7627-0000-9
ISSN 1078-5523

Cover photo: The Oaks Victorian Inn, Christiansbug, VA   p. 284

Cover design: Mullen & Katz
Map design: Nancy Freeborn
Text design: Saralyn D'Amato-Twomey

Manufactured in the United States of America
Seventh Edition/First Printing

It is a morsel of certainty, snatched from the midst of the uncertainties of life; it is a sunny moment gleaming out kindly on a cloudy day; and he who has advanced some way on the pilgrimage of existence knows the importance of husbanding even morsels and moments of enjoyment.

—Washington Irving,
The Sketch Book of Geoffrey Crayon, 1820

Contents

Indexes

A Few Questions Asked about This Book

What qualifies you to write this book? There are no degrees for inn reviewing. For the past ten years, however, I've amassed a bundle of experience by personally visiting over 200 inns biennially.

What is the goal of this book? To match the right person with the right inn—to make a happy fit. To point out unusual places, delicious foods, and kind hosts.

What happens at country inns? It depends on you and what you want to happen. Trying to define a country inn experience is like trying to define happiness. Everyone has a different idea of what constitutes a pleasurable visit.

What's your favorite country inn? Inns are wonderful for different reasons. That's the point. Would you pick a favorite child?

How did you get this job? Kismet. I was in the right place at the right time talking to the right person—and I demonstrated a writing familiarity with the Mid-Atlantic region.

What is a country inn? Country inns are an expression of an innkeeper's personality and perception of hospitality; therefore the diversity in style and ambience reflects the diversity of people.

Country inns are a physical place—a Victorian mansion, a former stagecoach stop, perhaps a new architecturally designed inn. Located in a village, city, or country setting, you find them at the seaside, on mountain tops, in the woods, and along tree-lined streets. Whether you seek private, elegant gourmet dining or the social camaraderie that occurs around communal tables, inns share the focus of delicious foods.

A country inn is a series of perfect moments that will never exist again, that assure you the world is a fine, civilized place to live in the late twentieth century.

How to Use This Inn Guide

The inns are listed alphabetically by town within each state. The states are also arranged alphabetically: Delaware, Maryland, New Jersey, New York, Pennsylvania, Virginia, and West Virginia. Preceding each state listing are a map and an index, and at the back of the book is an alphabetical index to all the inns in the book as well as special-category indexes.

Abbreviations:

EP: European Plan—room without meals.

EPB: European Plan—room with full breakfast.

AP: American Plan—room with all meals.

MAP: Modified American Plan—room with breakfast and dinner.

BYOB: Bring Your Own Bottle

The inclusion of an inn is purely a personal decision on the part of the author. Please address any questions or comments to Brenda Boelts Chapin, The Globe Pequot Press, P.O. Box 833, Old Saybrook, Connecticut 06475.

Caveats:

Rates: Inns may change their rates without notice. We have given the high–low figures to approximate the price range. They will give you a good indication of the prices to expect, but it is a good idea to call ahead.

Children: Please consult the "Inns Especially Suited to Families" index in the back of the book.

Pets: Pets generally aren't allowed at the country inns in this region. Inns that do permit pets are designated in their description.

Credit cards: Visa and MasterCard are accepted unless otherwise specified in the rate section. Many inns accept other cards, too.

Reservations and deposits: These are required with such regularity that they're not mentioned in each description. With exceptions, expect to pay a deposit or use a credit card to reserve a room. This is usually nonrefundable.

Minimum stay: A minimum stay of two nights on weekends and three or more on holidays is required at some inns, as noted. If you're anticipating a vacation during busy seasons, plan ahead.

A sound night's sleep: Rooms are often assigned on the basis of bed size. If you prefer a queen-sized, twin, or double bed, please ask before you make your reservations.

Vegetarians: The majority of inns serve meat, fish, and fowl, but most inns will prepare a vegetarian dish if given advance notice.

Meal prices: Estimated prices are for single entrees, except where stated.

Fly-ins: Where appropriate, I've mentioned the nearest airport for the convenience of private pilots.

Menus: Suggested menus may change.

Smoking: When inns do not allow smoking, we have identified them as "No smoking inns" in the "rooms" section of an inn's description. If an inn allows smoking in guest rooms, we have also identified those that set aside certain rooms specifically for nonsmokers. Some other inns prohibit smoking in rooms but allow it elsewhere in the inn. If the inn's smoking policy is important to you, inquire about it when you call for a reservation.

Wheelchair access: If you need a room with wheelchair access, look for this information in the "rooms" section or in the index in the back of the book.

Tips for Selecting an Inn

Common area? Does the inn have one, and is it customarily used by guests?

Specific things to do? Ask ahead of time and you might get to do or see something unique to the area that will occur during your visit, or you could plan your visit to coincide with a special event.

Pay in advance? Most inns require advance payment, which is usually nonrefundable. Please add state and local taxes to all prices.

Arrival? Let the innkeeper know when you're arriving; if it's a small inn and you're going to be late, please call.

Recommended Country Inns® Travel Club: I state the discount, free night's stay, or other value offered by inns welcoming club members. Note that all discounts listed refer to room rates only, not to meals, and that a number of offers are subject to availability.

Recommended Country Inns®

Mid-Atlantic and Chesapeake Region

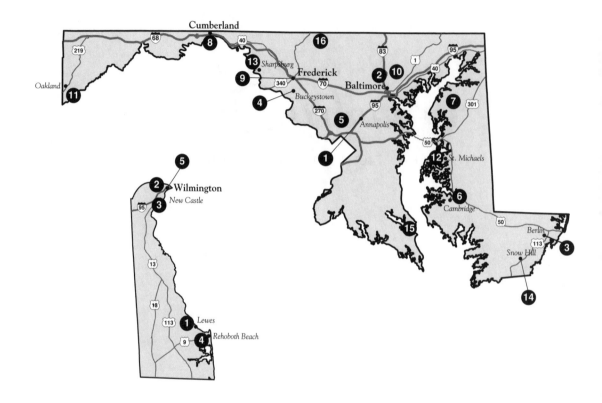

Cumberland

68

219

Oakland ·

11

8

40

13 Sharpsburg

9

340

4 Buckeystown

270

70

16

Frederick

Baltimore

2 10

83

1

40

95

95

50

7

301

12 St. Michaels

5

1

Annapolis

15

6 Cambridge

50

Berlin

113

3

Snow Hill

14

5

2 Wilmington

3 New Castle

95

13

18

113 1 Lewes

9 4 Rehoboth Beach

Delaware &
Maryland

Delaware and Maryland

Numbers on map refer to towns numbered below.

The Inn at Canal Square
LEWES, DELAWARE 19958

Your day might begin with no particular purpose, and sometimes these are the best of days. First, step onto your private balcony overlooking the canal; a sailboat moves slowly up the waterway. Later you drink coffee, enjoy croissants, and visit with other guests. You are in a quiet, professionally run hotel that buffers you from the village. Yet you know that outside the door lie a bevy of shops and things to do. And you'll do them. But for now the day is rich with expectation.

The night before you tucked yourself into a room furnished with fine traditional eighteenth-century reproduction furniture, with a queen- or king-sized bed. Perhaps you chose Number 301, which has a water view and a town view. All the rooms have modern comforts in this recently restored little hotel.

The inn has a gray-shingled facade that's reminiscent of those found in a New England seaside village—perhaps on Nantucket or Cape Cod. The boatyard next door and the sounds of seagulls calling and rigging gently slapping against masts heighten this impression.

Continental breakfast is served in the lobby, but guests may fix a tray, pick up a complimentary copy of the *Wall Street Journal,* and take everything up to the patio to read and relax.

For something different, there's a two-story houseboat docked out front, which is very stylish and offers total privacy. It includes a small kitchen, where you can fix coffee and meals, should you like. There's a lovely living room for relaxing, with the patio doors thrown wide open to the water breezes in the summertime. From the living room you have a view of the canal. The houseboat is not well suited to children under fourteen.

Lewes has changed since I first visited here. You can still catch the ferry to Cape May, which lands you about 5 miles from the heart of down-town, but it's more likely you'll stay in Lewes to tour the shops, bike ride to the beach, walk to dinner, visit the local museum, and keep a low profile for the weekend.

How to get there: Take Route 9 into Lewes, turn left at the traffic light onto Front Street, and go 1 block to the inn, which is on the right. Parking is available adjacent to the inn and across the street.

Innkeeper: Bill Lucks

Address/Telephone: 122 Market Street; (302) 645–8499 or (800) 222–7902, fax (302) 645–7083

Rooms: 21, including 4 suites; all with private bath, air conditioning, telephone, cable television, and most with private balcony. Two-bedroom houseboat with kitchen also available. Designated nonsmoking rooms.

Rates: $65 to $165, double occupancy, continental breakfast. Houseboat for 4, $175 to $225, continental breakfast. Children under 12, free; over 12, $15. Two-night mini-mum weekends in season; 3-night minimum holiday weekends.

Open: All year.

Facilities and activities: Elevator. Nearby: restaurants, beach, bicycling, small museums, an-tiquing, Cape Henlopen State Park.

Business travel: Telephone and desk in room; waterfront conference room.

New Devon Inn

LEWES, DELAWARE 19958

There isn't a dizzying array of things to do in Lewes, and that's exactly why I like it. You might meander through the shops, visit Cape Henlopen Lighthouse, or, in warm weather, lie on the beach—these are the kinds of things you can do in Lewes.

New Devon Inn, which Dale named for Devon, the mythical island in James Michener's *Chesapeake*, is located downtown on the main street, Second Street. Dale, who has a background in real estate, said that, over the years, you see buildings that speak to you—and this one spoke to her.

The inn is entered through a wide hall framed by an antiques shop and an art studio. In the lobby, you face two ornately carved elephant chairs that were brought back from Thailand by Dale's partner, Bernard Nash. There's also a large guest parlor furnished in the Art Nouveau style of the 1920s. A grand piano fills one corner of the room. In the morning, you come down here, fetch your freshly baked pastries or muffins along with cereals, make a place for yourself at the coffee table or in a great chair, and read the morning paper, gradually acquiring momentum for the day's activities.

A sitting area downstairs holds the inn's television. Along the stairway is a small music room with an antique bellows-operated organ.

The rooms have hardwood floors and antiques and pretty linens. My favorites are the two suites, one of which overlooks the town cemetery. Another favorite is the corner room (108), overlooking Second Street. The suites have queen-sized beds.

The innkeepers are good with directions in the area. If you wish, you can rent a bicycle nearby and bike out to the beach for the day. Or plan ahead. The inn participates in a midweek bicycling package for $270 per person that includes lodging for three nights and three breakfasts and dinners. Each night you stay in a different inn.

The Zwaanendael Museum, which is a block from the inn, is a copy of the town hall in Hoorn, Holland, where the first settlers departed from in 1631.

How to get there: From points west, take Route 9 east (becomes Savannah Road) into Lewes. In town, turn left onto Second Street; inn is 1 block on the left at the corner of Second and Market streets.

Innkeepers: Suzanne Steele and Judith Henderson; Dale Jenkins and Bernard Nash, proprietors

Address/Telephone: 142 Second Street (mailing address: P.O. Box 516); (302) 645–6466 or (800) 824–8754, fax (302) 645–7196

Rooms: 26, including 2 suites; all with private bath, air conditioning, and telephone. Designated nonsmoking rooms.

Rates: Seasonal: $45 to $170, double occupancy, continental breakfast. Two-night minimum, holiday weekends. Request special packages.

Open: All year.

Facilities and activities: Nearby: Cape Henlopen State Park, Zwaanendael Museum, Lewes Bay Beach, restaurants, shops, biking.

Business travel: Desks, meeting rooms, and fax available.

Recommended Country Inns® Travelers' Club Benefit: Stay two nights, get third night free, subject to availability.

Olive Metcalf

The Inn at Montchanin Village
MONTCHANIN, DELAWARE 19710

Let me be perfectly honest. This is the one inn I have not stayed in. Why? It wasn't quite complete on my last visit. Nevertheless, it opened in May 1996, and I was so charmed by the setting, the furnishings, the guest rooms and baths, the gardens, the common rooms, and the prospects for the restaurant that I didn't want to wait another year to share it with you.

Montchanin is a tiny hamlet named for Anne Alexandrine de Montchanin. She was the grandmother of Eleuthère Irénée duPont, founder of the DuPont Gunpowder Company. The inn is located in a cluster of buildings built in the early 1800s to house laborers from the nearby DuPont powder mills. The complex in-cludes several houses, a cluster of cottages, a for-mer blacksmith shop, a schoolhouse, and a mas-sive stone and post-and-beam barn.

The restoration is the ambitious undertak-ing of local preservationists Missy and Daniel Lickle. When they acquired the property, they sought an adaptive use that would preserve the quaint buildings in their original setting. They achieved this goal admirably.

The restoration is so true to the village's ori-gins that even the original tiny concrete out-houses remain. Connected to the cottages by gardens, these now house mainentance equip-ment. Privy Lane leads guests from the restaurant (in the former blacksmith shop) to the cottages.

The rebuilt barn houses the reception room and a giant reading room with a cathedral ceiling and a massive fieldstone fireplace. The entire six acres are on the National Register of Historic Places.

The guest rooms are luxuriously furnished with antique four-poster and canopy beds, armoires, and painted blanket chests. There are chain-stitched rugs on hardwood floors, graceful moldings, and sponged walls. Eight of the units have fireplaces, and almost all have either a private garden, porch, balcony, or terrace. The beds are swathed in pretty fabrics and dressed in Frette sheets, and the marble baths have every possible luxury, including oversized whirlpool tubs in some.

The blacksmith shop now houses Krazy Kat's Restaurant, which is likely to set records of its own for fine dining. One of the area's top chefs is at its helm; he designed the kitchen as well as the menu. You'll find such dishes as grilled rack of veal chops served with herb-crusted shallots roasted in olive oil, Gorgonzola-whipped Yukon potatoes, sautéed jumbo lump Maryland crab cakes, and shrimp mousseline served with whole-grain mustard cream and accompanied by sweet-potato fries.

The inn is in the Brandywine Valley, where the Wyeth family has been painting for years. It's close to Winterthur Museum and Gardens, Longwood Gardens, Brandywine River Museum, and Wilmington. Although there are no sports facilities on the premises, a golf course is located 2 miles away, and this is a terrific area for bicycling.

How to get there: From I–95 take the Concord Pike/Route 202 exit. Travel north on Route 202 to Route 141. Turn left onto Route 141, continuing to the Rockland Road intersection. Turn right onto Rockland Road, passing the DuPont Country Club. Continue on Rockland Road over the Brandywine River and bear left at the fork, just past the river. At the corner of Rockland Road and Route 100, turn right onto Route 100 north. Travel approximately 500 feet and turn into the entrance at Kirk Road and Route 100.

Innkeeper: Brooke Johnson; Daniel and Missy Lickle, proprietors
Address/Telephone: Route 100 and Rockland Road (mailing address: P.O. Box 130);
(302) 888-2133 or (800) COWBIRD, fax (302) 888-0389
Rooms: 22 (will increase to 37 in 1997), including 12 suites; all with private bath, air conditioning, telephone, television, and wet bar, 8 with fireplace, 2 with whirlpool. No smoking inn.
Rates: $125 to $350, double occupancy, EPB. Two-night minimum weekends; 3-night minimum holidays and special events.
Open: All year.
Facilities and activities: Dining room open for dinner daily 5:30–10:00 P.M., entrees $17–$23. Nearby: museums and gardens.
Business travel: Dataport and dual-line telephone in all rooms; 7 with desk; fax available; meeting space for 25 people.

Armitage Inn
NEW CASTLE, DELAWARE 19720

New Castle is one of my favorite towns. It's so authentically Colonial that I have no difficulty imagining myself walking along the narrow brick sidewalks, lighted by flickering street lamps, garbed in a dress with a voluminous skirt, a bonnet securely fastened over my curls, and my gloved hand gently resting on the arm of a handsome gentleman wearing a tall hat and tails. Perhaps we've been to a party at the home of Revolutionary War hero Zachariah Van Leuvenigh, whose handsome brick house still stands on The Strand, a greensward that rolls down to the banks of the Delaware River. Peter Stuyvesant laid out New Castle in 1651, when the area was still under Dutch rule, and it was

near here that William Penn first landed in 1681.

Today Van Leuvenigh's gracious house with its fine views is known as the Armitage Inn. It was a delightful surprise on a recent trip to discover that Stephen and Rina Marks had spent almost a year polishing the wide-plank, red-pine floors of this center-hall Colonial, with the splendid staircase that reaches to the second floor. To the right a gracious dining room waits for us to sample a scrumptious gourmet breakfast, but for now the elegant parlor, with its fire glowing in the hearth, beckons us.

We looked through the extensive library, selected a book, and spent a toasty winter afternoon in pure relaxation. Beyond the library the oldest room in the house, which dates to the 1600s, contains its original massive brick cooking fireplace and beehive oven. Beyond that are a screened porch and a walled garden.

The guest rooms have canopy beds so high that they require a step stool. Some are draped in filmy fabric, and one has a hand-crocheted canopy. Televisions are tucked into period furniture. The marble-and-tile baths are spacious; they all have hair dryers, and some have whirlpool tubs. Our favorite room is the White Rose Room, which has a little nook that overlooks The Strand and the Delaware River. During the day the river is alive with traffic, but at night we were lulled to sleep by foghorns. In the morning a flock of geese called overhead.

Stephen and Rina directed us to The Arsenal on the Green for dinner, and it was an excellent choice. Located on the village green, The Arsenal is true to its origins. It was built as an arsenal for the War of 1812. Don't miss the house specialty, crab cakes with fresh local crab, or the delectable raspberry cream pie. It's a combination of cream cheese, sour cream, and fresh raspberries on a pool of raspberry sauce.

The next day we walked through the streets admiring the handsome courthouse with its ornate cupola and browsed in the excellent antiques and crafts shops. At the foot of Delaware Street, we watched the river traffic from Battery Park. Later we visited the Amstel House, a 1730s gem that was the home of Governor Van Dyke. Wilmington is only minutes away, as are such attractions as Winterthur, Longwood Gardens, and the Hagley Museum, which describes the rise of the DuPont company.

How to get there: Traveling on I–95 take exit 5A (if coming from the south, take I–295 toward New Jersey and take exit 5A) onto Delaware Route 141 south. At the intersection of Routes 9 and 273, turn north on Route 9 and travel for ½ mile. Bear right to New Castle via Delaware Street. Continue on Delaware Street through the village to The Strand. The inn is on the right.

Innkeepers: Stephen and Rina Marks
Address/Telephone: 2 The Strand; (302) 328–6618, fax (302) 324–1163
Rooms: 4; all with private bath, air conditioning, telephone, and television, 2 with fireplace, 2 with whirlpool. No smoking inn.
Rates: $95 to $135, double occupancy, EPB. Two-night minimum weekends April–June and September–December.
Open: All year.
Facilities and activities: Tennis courts and a public park accessible through the garden gate. Nearby: playhouse, concert hall, dinner theater, Winterthur, Longwood Gardens, Brandywine Valley.

Corner Cupboard Inn
REHOBOTH BEACH, DELAWARE 19971

The summer lighting is special. The sun filters through the tall, old shade trees onto the inn's cozy patios and creates a mood of total leisure. You mix yourself a drink on the cocktail patio and chat with friends.

Around dinnertime on a summer Saturday night, your waiter opens a fine wine, the one you brought in a little brown bag. The ceiling fans turn. Dinner begins: crab imperial with just a touch of green pepper, or beautifully fried soft-shell crab, homemade bread, and more. After dinner go for a moonlit stroll on the beach.

This inn is in a lovely residential neighborhood. You find comfortable parlors and sun-

porches. I do like the former attic room with an appealing private deck nestled in the treetops. Eastwind is a small cottage with a private brick patio. Each room is different. One is small, with white walls, green-and-blue curtains, and green iron beds.

The rooms change according to the season. During summer the inn is carpeted with grass mats; these are exchanged for Oriental carpets in winter. In the inn some rooms have antiques and wooden or iron beds. Two queen-sized beds are available.

Elizabeth's decorating is a tasteful, homey blend of family heirloom and eclectic furnishings. The antique corner cupboard is in the living room. The long porch room, called the hat room because of all the straw hats on the wall, is paneled and breezy in summer. A good selection of magazines and newspapers lines the parlor tables.

In the winter guests return from a brisk walk on the beach and meet around the fireplace, sipping brandies and discussing everything but what they do for a living. Here the cares of the world are washed away.

How to get there: From Route 1A exit into Rehoboth, cross canal bridge, take first left onto Columbia Avenue, and continue to Second Street. Turn right. Go 1 block to Park and turn left; inn is located in the middle of Park.

Innkeeper: Elizabeth G. Hooper; Leslie Vining, manager

Address/Telephone: 50 Park Avenue; (302) 227–8553, fax (302) 226–9113

Rooms: 18; all with private bath, 5 with television and air conditioning. Pets allowed with charge.

Rates: Memorial Day weekend–mid-September: $145 to $245, double occupancy; $130 to $210, single; MAP. Rest of year: $90 to $180, double occupancy, EPB.

Open: All year.

Facilities and activities: Reservations for breakfast and dinner (prices start around $12.50) a must. BYOB. Nearby: beach, tennis, bicycling, golf, historic town of Lewes (15 minutes away).

The Boulevard Bed & Breakfast
WILMINGTON, DELAWARE 19802

We couldn't understand exactly what they meant to say, these beautiful ceramic tiles that surrounded the fireplace in the paneled library, where we were immersed in the glow of the fire that rainy morning in late summer. The exquisitely fashioned Meullers—the tiles are named for the tile company that made them—seemed to me to represent the Ages of Man. I decided that the adjacent tiles in card suits—clubs, spades, hearts, and diamonds—are the cards of life that we are dealt and with which we must play. The true meaning of the tiles lies with their maker, but guests at The Boulevard spin their own interpretations.

Drawn by the scent of chocolate-zucchini bread coming from the kitchen, we rose and went into the dining room, where breakfast assumes expansive proportions. Charles and Judy entice you by reciting the menu. "French toast," Charles announces, "made with a sweet cinnamon-swirl bread and bathed in maple syrup." "Or a three-cheese omelet," Judy suggests, "with either bacon or sausage on the side." Once you've decided what you'd like and how you'd like it prepared, you decide where you'd prefer to sit—the parlor or porch. For business travelers hustling to catch an early bus into central Wilmington, just a mile away, Judy serves a homemade granola and fruits and coffee.

The Boulevard provides a placid, homey oasis

from the hustle of Wilmington. This eclectically designed bed and breakfast, built in 1913, lures you in as soon as you enter the front door, with its uniquely angled pilasters and wide transom. The crimson carpeted staircase leads to the dramatic landing. Glancing from the formal dining room to the screened porch furnished in wicker, you envision a chance to repose and reenergize amidst the comforts of this mansion, now listed on the National Register of Historic Places.

Charles and Judy, early retirees from the corporate world, have owned The Boulevard since 1986. They are a ready source of information about the area and will guide you to its many sights and activities, including the Hagley, Winterthur, Nemours, and Brandywine River museums as well as Longwood Gardens. They will also direct you to local festivities found in this historic region throughout the year and to restaurants that will suit you.

My favorite room is the Peach Room with its queen-sized bed. Various queen, double, and twin beds are found in the other rooms. All rooms have cable television, and four have a telephone. The furnishings, which span the decades, include family antiques and are an eclectic mix of varied pedigree.

The architect took care to design shelves and corner cupboards and my favorite place—the long window seat on the landing, covered in original burgundy plush fabric, where you can sequester behind the pillars with a book and a cup of tea.

How to get there: From the south take I–95 north to exit 8 or Concord Pike (Wilmington 202 South). Proceed to second traffic light and turn right on Baynard Boulevard and continue to 1909 Baynard; inn is on right, on the corner of Twentieth Street.

Innkeepers: Charles and Judy Powell
Address/Telephone: 1909 Baynard Boulevard; (302) 656–9700, fax (302) 656–9701
Rooms: 6, including 1 suite; 4 with private bath, all with air conditioning and television, 4 with telephone, 1 with Jacuzzi. No smoking inn.
Rates: $60 to $75, double occupancy; $55 to $70, single; EPB. Two-night minimum holiday weekends.
Open: All year.
Facilities and activities: Nearby: Winterthur Museum, Brandywine River Museum (Wyeth art collection), Longwood Gardens, Hagley Museum, Nemours Mansion, Delaware Natural History Museum, Delaware Art Museum.
Business travel: On bus line, 1 mile to central Wilmington. Telephone in 4 rooms; desk in all rooms; fax available; laundry facility; corporate rates.

William Page Inn
ANNAPOLIS, MARYLAND 21401

Less than a block from the William Page Inn is the quadrangle where the U.S. Naval Academy's "plebes" (first-year students) meet at noon for daily drill. Walk over, observe the ritual, climb the steps to their dormitory, Bancroft Hall, and admire the Spartan orderliness of their living quarters. Then retreat happily to the posh comforts of civilian life in this inn, conveniently located in the heart of the Annapolis historic district.

Rob and Greg quickly perceive the needs of their guests. There's a patient kindness in their innkeeping style, enhanced by a knowledgeable enthusiasm about the area where they live. The decor is both soothing and traditional; the innkeepers have chosen thick beige carpeting, vanilla-colored walls, and tasteful nineteenth-century reproductions and antiques in Queen Anne and Empire styles. In the parlor, before the fireplace, is a white brocade couch framed by two wing chairs; the windows are exquisitely draped.

A crystal chandelier hangs above the stairway in the foyer. The architecture of this brown-shingled inn is vernacular family home, circa 1908.

Upstairs the towels are lush, the soaps fragrant, and the rooms spotlessly clean. All of them except "Marilyn's Room" are named for characters from *Charlotte's Web*. The rooms have queen-sized beds, and most of them have rooftop views of historic Annapolis. The spacious top-floor suite offers a skylight and a whirlpool bath worthy of a lingering soak.

Breakfasts consist of fruits, cereals, and egg casseroles or individual quiches. Occasionally, Rob cooks his Colonial Egg Casserole, which bakes at a low temperature for one and a half hours. (This recipe was written in Middle English when Rob first saw it and required much time and effort to perfect.) The breakfasts are served on trays in the living room, which allows guests a certain amount of autonomy. Following the first savory cup of coffee, someone invariably strikes up a conversation, and soon all are comparing their impressions of Annapolis.

The U.S. Naval Academy sponsors a mod-estly priced tour. A short block from the inn, you will find the William Paca Mansion and Gardens.

Inn guests find strolling to dinner from the inn a pleasure. Annapolis has many tempting nearby restaurants. Watching the people and the boats in the harbor area provides first-class entertainment.

How to get there: From Route 50 exit Rowe Boulevard. Follow Rowe past 3 traffic lights to stop sign. Turn left onto College Avenue. At light turn right onto King George Street. Continue to Gate 1 of Naval Academy and turn right onto East Street. Turn right at stop sign at Martin Street. Pull into driveway of inn.

Innkeepers: Robert Zachelli and Greg Page

Address/Telephone: 8 Martin Street; (410) 626–1506 or (800) 364–4160, fax (410) 263–4841

Rooms: 5, including 1 suite; 3 with private bath, all with air conditioning, 2 with whirlpool, 1 with television. No smoking inn.

Rates: $85 to $175, double occupancy, EPB. Two-night minimum weekends mid-March–November.

Open: All year.

Facilities and activities: Off-street parking. Nearby: restaurants, U.S. Naval Academy, William Paca Mansion, boating tours, guided tours of Colonial Annapolis, State House, historic mansions.

Business travel: Located in the heart of Annapolis. Fax available, computer rentals, valet service.

Mr. Mole Bed & Breakfast
BALTIMORE, MARYLAND 21217

Why would someone name a lovely urban inn after a mole? One guest named the inn "Monsieur Molet"—implying that grace and style marked Paul and Collin's bed and breakfast. Of course, many of you have known Mr. Mole since your mother read you the children's book *Wind in the Willows*.

Located in a nineteenth-century brick townhouse in Baltimore, the inn has 14-foot ceilings in three contiguous parlors painted a brilliant yellow that complements the innkeepers' collections: Collin's porcelains and Paul's ecclesiastical antiques and small boxes. An appreciation for the comforts of friends, a delicious hot breakfast, and a knack for storytelling characterize the innkeepers.

Breakfast is served buffet style at the hour you choose the night before. You'll find yourself gathering up rich Amish cake made with walnuts and apples, fresh breads, perhaps a fragrant country cheese, and juices and meats. Then you select a small table for two and compose yourself for the day.

"Guests," admits Paul, "seem to prefer this time for privacy. Most don't really wake up until after they've had their morning coffee and tea. Of course, spontaneous friendships occasionally form, and sometimes we hear total strangers making dinner plans together. Everyone has their own preference."

Each bedroom has a distinctive personality.

The innkeepers obviously had fun developing themes with treasures collected in Amsterdam, Brussels, London, and local markets. Hand-painted wooden fish hang above the fireplace in the Explorers Room, history books and English porcelains are in the London Suite, and stuffed moles of various sizes and descriptions in the Mr. Mole Suite. In the Garden Room a sunporch is filled with flowers and white wicker furniture.

Tucked off to the corner of one parlor is the guest's pantry, with a fridge for storing a bottle of wine and a kettle for preparing yourself a cup of Earl Grey.

Located 5 blocks from Baltimore's light rail, the inn is convenient for touring or business in this easy-to-negotiate city. Should you wish to sequester yourself for the weekend, you might amble up to the coffee shop on the next block and enjoy the urban mix that characterizes the neighborhood.

I love to walk among the bountiful stalls of Baltimore's famed Lexington Market, where some family-owned businesses are a century old, catch a matinee at the Mechanic Theater, and still have time for a sumptuous Italian meal in Little Italy. The next morning I dawdle over breakfast until the nearby antiques shops open.

Where else but at Mr. Mole would you have eighteenth-century antiques and a rubber ducky propped on the rim of the bathtub? Mr. Mole made them do it. Mr. Mole makes them do it all. He's the alter ego of the place. Like him, Paul and Collin had fun collecting all their treasures. The result is an indulgent inn appropriately named for a creature in a book.

How to get there: From I–95 take exit 53 to I–395. Exit onto Martin Luther King, Jr., Boulevard, bearing right, and continue 2 miles. Turn left on Eutaw Street, go 6/10 mile, turn right at fourth stop light, onto McMechen Street. Go 1 block to stop sign at Bolton Street. Inn is diagonally across intersection.

Innkeepers: Paul Bragaw and Collin Clark
Address/Telephone: 1601 Bolton Street; (410) 728–1179, fax (410) 728–3379
Rooms: 5, including 2 suites; all with private bath, air conditioning, and telephone. No smoking inn.
Rates: $97 to $125, double occupancy, EPB. Two-night minimum on weekends March to mid-December.
Open: All year.
Facilities and activities: Enclosed parking. Nearby: Mechanic Theater, Myerhoff Symphony Hall, Lyric Opera House, Antique Row, Walters Art Gallery, Lexington Market, Orioles Park at Camden Yards, Babe Ruth Birthplace, Inner Harbor: Science Museum, National Aquarium.
Business travel: Five blocks from train. Telephone and desk in room; fax available.

Olive Metcalf

Merry Sherwood Plantation
BERLIN, MARYLAND 21811

As we drive under the canopy of sugar maple trees that line the circular driveway, the magnificent seafoam green plantation mansion, trimmed with darker shades of green and sparkling white, looms ahead. A fanciful cupola crowns the confection. We imagine we see Elizabeth Henry Johnson—the young girl for whom the 8,500-square-foot, twenty-seven-room house was built in 1859—surveying her lands while waiting for her husband.

The restoration of the mansion, which is listed on the National Register of Historic Places, was the dedicated work of local businessman Kirk Burbage, whose family has lived in Berlin for some 200 years. He spent two years re-viving the former ruin, and his painstaking attention to detail is apparent throughout.

We arrived in time for iced tea, which was being served in the front parlor. In the ballroom creamy, arched marble fireplaces gleam, heavy damask drapes frame doorways, and lace panels cover windows. Priceless antiques include Victorian settees, a square grand piano, and a massive carved chair with lion's-head arms and bearing a brass portrait of Queen Victoria. It's said to have been made for an anticipated visit to the United States by the queen, which never took place. We sat and sipped, talking to the other guests while we all thoroughly enjoyed Stacy's narrative about the house's history and its restoration.

The house contains impressive furnishings and decor throughout. There's a magnificent chandelier in the dining room, the parlor has an organ, and the library has polished paneled walls. There are nine elegant fireplaces. We were especially impressed by several bookcases in the library that open to reveal closets. Some of the books are leather-bound first editions. Beyond the library an inviting side porch contains wicker and rattan furniture and we sat here imagining how gorgeous the gardens must be during the summer. *Southern Living* magazine has been assisting in the development of the gardens and landscaping on the eighteen-acre property. We wished we had been able to come at a time when the flowers and trees were in bloom.

The guest rooms are equally impressive, furnished with museum-quality antiques and lush fabrics. In the Harrison Room, for example, there's a massive Gothic Revival bed and a Victorian fainting couch that can be converted into a double bed. The Chase Room has an unusual bed with 5-foot posts carved into beehive finials. The Johnson Room has a carved canopy bed.

Before going out to dinner, we climbed the mahogany stairs to the cupola, lined with windows, to survey the estate's domain. Later, in the library, we spent a pleasant evening finishing a jigsaw puzzle.

We breakfasted regally the next morning in a formal dining room that boasts a brass chandelier. We were seated at a mahogany Empire-style table with Victorian rosewood chairs. If you're lucky perhaps you, too, will have oatmeal-butterscotch muffins followed by puffed apple-cinnamon pancakes, as we did.

How to get there: From Baltimore and Washington, D.C., follow Route 50 east to Berlin (it's 6 miles before Ocean City). Take the Route 113 exit and travel south for 2½ miles. Merry Sherwood Plantation will be on the right.

Innkeeper: Stacy Kenny; Kirk Burbage, proprietor
Address/Telephone: 8909 Worcester Highway; (410) 641–2112 or (800) 660–0358
Rooms: 8, including 1 suite; all with air conditioning, 6 with private bath, 3 with wood-burning fireplace, 1 with Jacuzzi. No smoking inn.
Rates: $120 to $175, double occupancy, EPB. Two-night minimum weekends.
Open: All year.
Facilities and activities: Nearby: Assateague Island National Seashore, 8 miles away; golf, horseback riding, bird-watching, bicycling; historic Berlin.

The Inn at Buckeystown
BUCKEYSTOWN, MARYLAND 21717

Enter an old-fashioned setting that emits aromatic scents and tender feelings from the moment you step inside. Dan Pelz's general good-naturedness influences the ambience while his cuisine influences the palate; both inspire conversation (either bring a great story or come prepared to hear one).

It's customary to glance at the menu on top of the hall bureau. Dinner begins at 7:30 P.M. with Dan's award-winning soups. Among his eighty-seven soup creations is the famed Jack O'Lantern Soup, a creamy pumpkin soup.

Here's the weekly scenario: Saturday, expect to find a savory veal or beef dish; Wednesday, it's a perfectly baked German duck; Thursday is for beef, as in London broil; and Friday, it's seasonal fish. It's fowl every Sunday, early and by reservation. Each night of the week, a multicourse dinner appears upon antique china around candelit oak tables. Dinner is a single entree served at one shared seating, and it's a bundle of fun.

Buckeystown is a nationally registered historic village on the Monocacy River. In the spring pink and purple azaleas, lilacs, and forsythia accent the lawn. The eighteen-room inn is an Italianate Victorian with two parlors and a wraparound front porch; the woodwork is chestnut and oak, and the floors are heart-of-pine. Sitting on a bureau in your room is Dan and Chase's guide, 'Inn' Joying. It directs you to the best in

Civil War sites, antiquing, golf, walking and cycling tours, orchards, and restaurants.

The inn is filled with collections that reflect Dan and Chase's appreciation for art. The parlors are softly lit with Art Nouveau and Tiffany lamps. There are Phoenix glass and Van Briggle pottery to admire along with Dan's clown collection, which grows as a result of guests' thoughtfulness and generosity. Chase, who has a fine-arts degree, works in oils; when a spare moment appears, he retreats to his studio and paints. It's his green thumb that's nurtured the gardens and makes the orchids flourish throughout the inn.

The attractive rooms are furnished with antiques, and the antique beds have been rebuilt to accept larger mattresses. You find everything from cozy pillows, dolls, Indian paintings, and finely carved jade to handmade quilts and rockers. The honeymoon suite, St. John's Cottage (formerly a chapel), is a gentle walk down the hill. Outside the door is a hot tub graced by wisteria. The loft bedroom, which overlooks the parlor and fireplace, makes you feel sybaritic.

The inn pets include Chagny, the French Briard, and his dear friend Mr. Stubbs, the Scotty dog.

This inn weaves a rich tapestry of friendship, ambience, and cuisine. You bring the wine. The only choice you have to make is the choice to come, and that's the best one of all.

How to get there: From I–270 north of Washington, D.C., exit Route 85 south to Buckeystown. The inn is on the left in town.

Innkeepers: Daniel Pelz, owner/chef; Chase Barnett, partner; Rebecca Smith, manager

Address/Telephone: 3521 Buckeystown Pike (mailing address: General Delivery, Buckeystown); (301) 874–5755 or (800) 272–1190

Rooms: 7, including 2 suites and 2 cottages, all with private bath and desk, 3 with fireplace, 2 with telephone, 3 with television. No smoking inn.

Rates: $230 to $309, per couple per night (gratuity and tax included), MAP.

Open: All year, but closed Mondays and Tuesdays except holidays and month of December.

Facilities and activities: Dinner Wednesday through Sunday, public invited by reservation ($31 daily except holidays, $35 holidays), BYOB. Two acres of land with pre–Civil War graveyard. Nearby: shops, antiquing, canoeing, bicycling, Antietam Battlefield, Harper's Ferry.

Upstream at Water's Gift
BURTONSVILLE, MARYLAND 20866

If you could package contentedness, this is where you'd like to gather it up. Upstream is one of Maryland's premier horse farms; Trakehner thoroughbreds are bred and trained in the art of dressage. But you need not be a horse lover. The bucolic views and the quiet are reason enough to come.

The inn was built in 1974 as a private residence; yellow pine that had been saved from local historic barns forms the interior walls in the great room. Larrine warmly invites you inside to this contiguous living-kitchen-dining space with its cathedral ceiling and views of the meadows and paddocks. She shows you the kitchen, where you can help yourself to soda, tea, or freshly baked

cookies. After your walk you might sit in one of the rocking chairs before the fireplace and visit or take a glass of tea out to the large deck. There are several works of Oriental art, plants, and oil paintings.

Initially, Larrine gives everyone a private tour of the farm; she doesn't want you to miss anything. We saw the foaling stable (a yellow-breasted swallow sat on the railing); the colts, who live outdoors since it makes them sturdier; the stables and paddocks, where thirty-two horses live; and the arena where guests are invited to watch lessons or special events that might be occurring.

We passed through the boxwood garden, which Russell planted, to the Abolts' 1753 log cabin home. Larrine pointed out the soapstone fireplace made by an Italian mason. This was a history lesson in itself. You might come here for afternoon tea, if you wish, or choose a nook in the garden.

On the way back to the inn, Larrine pointed out the walking paths. The only rule is to leave gates as you find them: open if they are open, closed if closed. The farrier had arrived that morning, so we watched while he began the process of shoeing a magnificent horse. There's always something interesting happening around the barns or arena.

You will have no trouble sleeping here. Hand controls let you make your half of the bed as hard or as firm as you wish. Inside the mattress is an air pocket that form-fits the body; the beds are state-of-the-art because Russ directs the Better Sleep Council. The sheets are pressed, a final lovely touch.

The Hunt Suite is decorated with a hunt theme, since Larrine and Russ both ride in the hunt. It's a short distance to the small greenhouse from the sunny garden room, which is lovely in the spring.

For dinner there are several restaurants nearby, or you might arrange with the inn's caterer for dinner. The caterer will prepare whatever you like. On a pleasant summer evening, you might even have dinner on the deck. Or bring along friends and reserve the entire inn for a special celebration together.

Breakfast is served elegantly in a casual way. You might have French toast hot from the oven—stuffed with Canadian bacon or turkey sausage. That could be preceded by a ginger-baked banana.

The inn is a good base for touring Washington, D.C., Baltimore, and Annapolis, but some guests come from the surrounding areas. They wish to experience the beauty and tranquillity of this lovely place.

How to get there: From the intersection of Routes 198 and 29 in Burtonsville, go 1 mile north on Route 29 and turn left at Dustin Road. Follow to the end and enter gates of Water's Gift Farm. Upstream is the first driveway on the right.

Innkeepers: Larrine and Russell Abolt
Address/Telephone: 3604 Dustin Road (mailing address: P.O. Box 240); (301) 421–9562
Rooms: 2; each with private bath, air conditioning, and television. No smoking inn.
Rates: $85 to $105, single or double, EPB.
Open: All year.
Facilities and activities: Inn is 53-acre horse farm (no guest riding). Nearby: restaurants 2 miles; Amish market, herb farm, antiques shops; equidistant from Washington, D.C., Baltimore, and Annapolis, Maryland.

Glasgow Inn Bed & Breakfast
CAMBRIDGE, MARYLAND 21613

Memory, a young guest of about fifteen, had just arrived with her parents. I listened while Louise gave directions to the Trinity Church, St. Michaels Maritime Museum, and restaurants. Before she left the young woman would know that this house was built before America was a country (in 1760) and that she'd slept in a room once used as a Catholic chapel (the closet was a confessional). At the Blackwater Wildlife Refuge, she'd see deer, eagles, Canada geese, and probably more species of birds in one day than she'd ever seen. Louise was a teacher before she became an innkeeper, and she knows that learning comes naturally, through suggestion and stimulation of awareness that form questions and curiosity.

You reach the inn, which is located along Cambridge's Choptank River, through a pretty residential section. It's about a mile to a waterfront seafood restaurant, where you can watch boats coming and going. For touring you're about an hour from Assateague and St. Michaels, one and a half hours from Chincoteague and Chestertown. Louise will plan a personalized journey for you with stops at shops, country restaurants, and villages. You might visit the lighthouses of the Chesapeake Bay from Cape Henry to Havre de Grace or make a tour of Georgian homes of the Eastern Shore.

You may want to ask about the inn's restoration—or then again, you may want to think it happened by magic. Louise and Martha have stripped, plastered, and scrubbed the place back to life, and now the three-story brick and clapboard home is on the National Register of Historic Places. "It's an easy, friendly home," says Louise. When you walk up the mahogany stairs, you find them spaced for comfortable foot-reach. There are seven fireplaces, and plenty of sunlight streams through the windows.

The rooms are filled mostly with Colonial reproductions. Some beds have handmade quilts; quilting is one of Louise and Martha's passions. The attic room has a painted floor and a dhurrie rug. The inn's white walls contrast with Colonial trim in soft colors like apothecary blue and muted green.

I came before Easter and found a tree hung with eggs and angels. (Angels are a theme in the dining room, too.) The tree has become a year-round custom. At Christmas it bears traditional ornaments; for Easter, eggs; in the summer, flowers; and in the fall, apples.

Louise is a good one for getting you to the historic churches in the area. She is adept at putting breakfast in the oven and then returning from Sunday service just in time for a 9:30 serving of Bishop's Eggs (the recipe comes from the bishop's wife), a heavenly tasting casserole. Everyone sits together for breakfast in the dining room, which encourages visiting and the comparison of temporal pleasures.

How to get there: From Route 50 drive into town on Choptank River bridge. Turn right at the first light (Burger King) onto Maryland Avenue and go 4 blocks. Cross the drawbridge and turn right immediately after bridge onto Court Lane. Continue on Court until it dead-ends at High Street. Turn right onto High and drive to the river and the inn.

Innkeepers: Louise Lee Roche and Martha Ann Rayne
Address/Telephone: 1500 Hambrooks Boulevard; (410) 228–0575 or for reservations
  (800) 373–7890, fax (410) 221–1831
Rooms: 10, including 3 suites and 3 cottages; all with air conditioning, 6 with private
  bath, 7 with fireplace, 5 with telephone, 3 with television. No smoking inn.
Rates: $75 to $150, double occupancy, EPB. Two-night minimum when Saturday stay included. Corporate discount.
Open: All year.
Facilities and activities: Croquet and horseshoes. Nearby: 5 minutes to nearest restaurant;
  Blackwater Wildlife Refuge. Day trips: Chesapeake Maritime Museum in St.
  Michaels, Assateague, Chincoteague, and Tangier Island. Tennis, golf, swimming.

Brampton Bed & Breakfast
CHESTERTOWN, MARYLAND 21620

Maryland's Eastern Shore topography surrounding Chestertown is one of alternating appearances. At times you pass the starkly flat cornfields, which attract the snow geese in the fall, and then you drive between rolling hills, where cattle graze on pasturelands. Upon a crest rises the historic home, Brampton.

"We're an architectural rarity among those on the historical register," Michael said when I described how the majestic height of the inn and surrounding trees had riveted my attention from the road. This three-story brick inn appears to emerge larger-than-life from the pages of a storybook.

Henry W. Carville built the home in 1860,

at the age of sixty, for his twenty-seven-year-old bride-to-be. The gentleman had adult children by a former marriage (his offspring totaled nine)—perhaps he wanted room for family gatherings. There is no other way to describe each room but as terribly comfortable, with high ceilings and great tall windows that let quantities of sunlight in and look out over the fields and farms.

Danielle, who's Swiss by birth, expresses her European heritage in the beauty of family heirlooms and the welcoming presence of down comforters and down pillows upon each bed. Several pieces were custom made to coordinate with the antiques and family pieces. Four of the queen-sized beds are canopied, and three have queen-sized beds with trundles beneath them.

In the parlor the well-stocked bookshelves rise to the ceiling, and handsome custom-made Sheraton-style sofas clad in a rich butter-yellow damask pair off before the fireplace. Along the wall is a family walnut secretary. In the winter it's a cozy place for visiting with other guests before going out to dinner.

Michael and Danielle are adept guides. You aren't far from the Eastern Neck National Wildlife Refuge for hiking or birding, and Remington Farms for a driving nature tour (February to October). The Hanscoms also help coordinate a reasonably priced customized bike tour with other inns of the Eastern Shore. Please call to request the brochure.

The spacious breakfast room is a collection of small, private tables where breakfasts arrive directly from the oven or skillet. It's hard not to gravitate into the kitchen where Danielle is working; she has friendly ways that make you feel as though you were visiting with a favorite neighbor. Restrain yourself and you'll be rewarded with the fruits of her large kitchen. It might be a stack of blueberry pancakes preceded by fresh, hot lemon-ginger muffins, or her Lob Scouse, a German dish composed of scrambled eggs, scallions, bacon or ham, and vegetables. Among the meats you might find a delicious sausage from the local Amish market. Hot sticky buns and orange-chocolate muffins are among the fresh pastries that have been known to appear from her oven.

How to get there: From Chestertown proceed 1 mile south on Route 20, following the signs toward Rock Hall, Maryland. The inn, surrounded by great trees, is located on the left side of the road.

Innkeepers: Michael and Danielle Hanscom

Address/Telephone: 25227 Chestertown Road; (410) 778–1860

Rooms: 10, including 2 suites and 2 cottages; all with private bath and air conditioning, 3 with television, 6 with desk, 2 with Jacuzzi, 8 with fireplace. Wheelchair access. No smoking inn.

Rates: $95 to $155, double occupancy, EPB, and afternoon tea. Two-night minimum most weekends. Corporate rates available.

Open: All year.

Facilities and activities: 35 acres, pond, sunroom. Nearby: restaurants, Chestertown Tea Party Festival (May), hiking, birding, sailing, golf, horseback riding, bicycling.

Recommended Country Inns® Travelers' Club Benefit: Stay two nights, get third night free, Monday–Thursday.

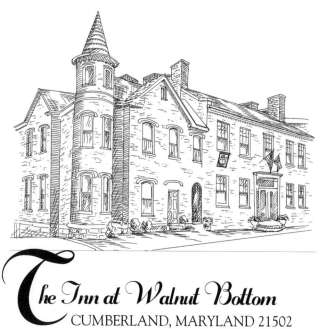

The Inn at Walnut Bottom
CUMBERLAND, MARYLAND 21502

We could easily see why artists trek to Cumberland. Church steeples rise from the town's hillsides, contrasting with the natural landscape. Those appreciative of nuances in color and light will find themselves wandering over the hills, dells, and dales of this rolling countryside. The artists are drawn by more than the lovely light, however. They know about Haystack Mountain Workshops and its staff of nationally recognized instructors, including Virginia Lee Williams, who teaches collage; Pat Deadman and Barbara Nechis, who teach watercolor; and Frank Webb, who spans the media. Weeklong art lessons, the camaraderie of colleagues, and a comfortable, friendly inn nearby will all inspire you.

When we entered the inn, we first heard soft, gurgling sounds that merged with a melody. In the parlor was a parakeet, Annabel. She sang along with a classical flute, forming a lulling, harmonic blend that couldn't be improved upon.

Named for the area once called Walnut Bottom, the inn is composed of two homes built by women, the 1820 Cowdon House and the 1890 Dent House. In the Cowdon parlor a large puzzle was spread across a card table. It was here that Kirsten directed us to her extensive collection of brochures and guided us on what to see and do. We mapped a walking tour that included stops at art galleries, antiques shops, and the Depot Museum, and made plans to take a steam train ride.

But first we went downstairs to lunch in the Oxford House Restaurant, where breakfast and dinner are also served. In the evenings four-course theme dinners are occasionally offered. The standard menu offers traditional inn fare—plump crab cakes and 2-inch-thick pork chops—as well as such nontraditional fare as salmon-filled schnitzel. For dessert chef Jaye Miller's princess torte, a Swedish layer cake covered with marzipan, and cocnut-cream pie with raspberries made us forget our pledge to watch the calories.

The inn's attractive bedrooms are cleanly furnished with antiques and reproductions and are warmly carpeted. For breakfast, depending on the chef's mood, you might have French toast, pancakes, chipped beef, or a hot casserole served buffet style.

Kirsten and Grant have a two-year-old, and they've made several changes since they purchased the inn in 1995 to make it more child-friendly. Cribs are available so that parents don't have to pack their own. Best of all, Kirsten stocks toys and games that are age-appropriate for each arriving family in the guest room.

Since Kirsten knew we were arriving from an eastern direction, she suggested we stop for the panoramic view at Sideling Hill, where a 380-foot vertical cut through the Appalachian mountainside recently opened the way for interstate travel. From a small visitors' center, we ascended for a compelling tower view of the surrounding mountains.

How to get there: Traveling east on I–68 (not on older maps), take exit 43A. Turn left at stop light and proceed to inn. Coming from west on I–68, take exit 43A, bear right, turn right at stop light. Turn into the alleyway and park behind the inn.

Innkeeper: Grant Irvin and Kirsten Hansen

Address/Telephone: 120 Greene Street; (301) 777–0003 or (800) 286–9718, fax (301) 777–8288

Rooms: 12, including 2 suites; 8 with private bath, all with air conditioning, telephone, and television. No smoking inn.

Rates: $69 to $160, double occupancy, EPB. Two-night minimum some weekends and holidays. Leisure package rates available.

Open: All year.

Facilities and activities: Lunch and dinner served Monday–Saturday; artist workshops. Mountain bikes available for rent for C&O Canal Towpath. Nearby: Cumberland Theatre, Western Maryland Scenic Railroad, Frank Lloyd Wright's "Fallingwater," Rocky Gap Lake Beach; Rocky Gap Country Music Festival in August; hiking, cross-country skiing, antiquing, golf.

Business travel: Telephone and desk in some rooms; fax and copy service available; free pickup from airport and train; corporate rates.

Spring Bank Farm
FREDERICK, MARYLAND 21701

Preservationists and others considering purchasing a historic home or who already own one should come here. Ray and Beverly Compton have been meticulously restoring their mansion, which has been on the National Register of Historic Places, for fifteen years.

Was it destiny that brought them here? One sunny afternoon they were riding their bicycles on the outskirts of Frederick near Route 15 when they came upon an immense, dilapidated home crowned by an Italianate belvedere tower. At first they speculated wildly, thinking they would love to restore it and open a bed-and-breakfast inn . . . now the most difficult tasks are completed. Some parts of the inn, like the 11-foot lower level (dug by a workman who misunderstood the dimensions), the third-floor servants' quarters, and some spaces so small it's difficult to comprehend their original purpose, may never be touched.

Ray, through patience and skill, is matching the original quality that distinguishes this home from modest dwellings. It's a preservation effort worthy of a lifetime. Ray pointed out the various locks and hinges used throughout the house—the more intricate being reserved for the formal rooms.

Each bedroom has an 11½-foot-high ceiling. The Sleigh-bed Room has a lovely bay window. The New Room has impressive antiques and adjoins a second-story porch. All have wooden shutters, several of which were grained by a friend whom the Comptons sent to an art course to learn the process. All have a historic feel.

Continental breakfast is, on occasion, brought to your room upon antique linens draped over four-legged antique trays and served on fine china. In each room there are table and chairs near a window, providing a view of the Maryland countryside. You might enjoy your breakfast here, or you can drink your coffee, eat freshly baked muffins, and munch your way through a fruit bowl in the back parlor.

Ray has his pilot's license and taught aerospace and marine science in one of the early "magnet" schools in the Washington area before becoming innkeeper. As master of the mansion, he's learned the intricacies of plumbing, wiring, and even stenciling. Beverly is employed in public health while Ray oversees and restores the inn. Both are present weekends and evenings.

Two parlors, one filled with books and a Victrola, are where you'll meet others in the evening. When I noticed an organ in the hallway, Ray said that he and Bev both play. "She more than I," he added, then sat down and launched forth. Playing an antique organ appears to be as much an aerobic exercise as a musical event and, therefore, is much appreciated by the audience.

How to get there: From Washington, D.C., take I–270 north to Frederick. In Frederick, continue straight on Route 15 north. Go 5 miles to mile marker 16. Turn right onto Route 355 (Worman's Mill Road), go ¼ mile, and turn left into the inn. From Baltimore take I–70 to exit 53, go north on U.S. 15, and follow directions above from marker 16.

Innkeepers: Beverly and Ray Compton
Address/Telephone: 7945 Worman's Mill Road; (301) 694–0440 or (800) 400–INNS, fax (301) 694–5926
Rooms: 5; 1 with private bath, all with air conditioning. No smoking inn.
Rates: $80, shared bath; $95, private bath; double occupancy; continental breakfast. Two-night minimum May, June, October, November, and holiday weekends.
Open: All year.
Facilities and activities: Nearby: restaurants, antiques shops of Frederick and New Market, Cunningham Falls State Park, Monocacy Battlefield, Appalachian National Scenic Trail, bicycling, historic touring.

Turning Point Inn
FREDERICK, MARYLAND 21701

The story of the Turning Point is all here, if you only look for it as you move through the inn. The heart-shaped WELCOME sign hangs on the front door, where it was hung after the flurry of late-night work that went on while the crumbling mansion was restored. Once Bernie (Charlie's stepfather) had finished the wiring, rebuilding, and painting of Dr. Perry's 1910 home, then Ellie (Charlie's mother) applied her art background. With her resourceful eye, she made each room warm and attractive. She placed a stone snail beside the fireplace, which must mean we are to take life at a snail's pace and relax here.

There's the family photo album on the living-room table of the trip to England—the trip that started all this, when the family stayed in bed and breakfasts. It whetted their appetite for their own inn and a challenge. After accomplishing their goals Ellie and Bernie were ready for a change, and naturally they turned first to Charlie, a stockbroker, who by now had helped out around the inn. The inn, aptly named, became a "turning point" in Charlie's life. Now it's Charlie who stops beside your dinner table in the Dr. Perry Dining Room to see that you're happy with every morsel.

Charlie's executive skills have created a new direction, a delicious one. He coordinates staff and expands the wine list, and he orders flowers and foods with the same savvy he once used to order up AT&T or IBM stock. Selections might include pan-seared Atlantic salmon with fresh basil sauce or, perhaps, lamb rib chops grilled with rosemary and roasted garlic. Desserts range from Kentucky Derby Pie to Strawberries Romanoff. In the summer, if you arrive when the enormous pear tree behind the inn is producing, you'll likely have a fresh dessert influenced by the seasonal backyard bounty.

The rooms are lovely. Named simply—the Victorian, the Room with a View, the Green, the Blue, and the Country—each has its own personality. If you'd like the whirlpool bath, go Country. In the Room with a View, Bentley the stuffed cat sits on the bed, and from the wedge-shaped windows, the countryside is your view. In the Blue Room you climb several stairs to get onto the high bed; the portrait in blue pastel on the wall is of Ellie's mother. The Victorian has white linens on the bed and fluffy white curtains; the Green has a comfortable pair of chairs and large double beds. Go prepared for a sound night's sleep in clean, quiet surroundings.

Two pretty cottages offer seclusion. The Carriage House is a two-story accommodation with a living room downstairs and a bedroom up. The Dairy House is decorated with country-style antiques.

Breakfasts are large. You can have what you like, which means that, if you can eat both pancakes and eggs, then you shall have them. On occasion, there's creamed chipped beef or home-fries along with ham and eggs, and always there are fresh fruits and breads. During the summer you might sit out on the deck and admire the rose garden and look upon the horse farm down the hill.

How to get there: From I–270 take exit 26 toward Urbana, turn east onto Route 80, and proceed to the stop sign; turn right on Route 355, go ²/₁₀ of a mile, and turn right into the inn's lane.

Innkeepers: Charlie Seymour; Irvin McQueen, manager
Address/Telephone: 3406 Urbana Pike; (301) 874–2421 or 831–8232, fax (301) 874–5773
Rooms: 7, including 2 cottages; all with private bath, air conditioning, telephone, and television, 2 with Jacuzzi; cottage wheelchair accessible. Pets allowed with prior permission; kennel available. Limited smoking inn.
Rates: $75 to $150 weekend, double occupancy, EPB.
Open: All year.
Facilities and activities: Dinner nightly except Monday ($14 to $22), lunch Tuesday–Friday, Sunday brunch, service bar. Nearby: Antietam Battlefield, Harper's Ferry, New Market (antiques capital), hiking at Sugarloaf Mountain, Gettysburg Battlefield.

Twin Gates Bed & Breakfast Inn
LUTHERVILLE, MARYLAND 21093

Leave your teddy bear home; one sits tucked into the corner of each stair step ascending to your room. The afternoon we arrived the bears wore paper rabbit ears that signified the coming of Easter. During the summer they wear sunglasses. At Christmas they are dressed for the season. But if I were to choose the real themes here, I'd select sunlight, inviting parlors, and attractive rooms. You find yourself looking for the merest of excuses to be here.

Lutherville was founded in 1852 by two Lutheran ministers. They bought several hundred acres along the railroad and sold lots to raise funds in order to build the first women's college south of the Mason-Dixon line. Today the town is an attractive National Historic District.

Twin Gates, an 1857 three-story mansion, was built by the college's first president. The builders, a couple named Sadtler, had the daring to build a secret trapdoor leading to a hidden area that Gwen and her husband, Bob, rediscovered while restoring the home. No one knows how many people were sequestered in this part of the Underground Railroad before being sent to freedom in the North.

I settled beside the gas fireplace in the "greeting room" with Gwen, who was giving directions and relating the best places to eat. The mantel had been adroitly marbelized. Two parlors, attractively furnished, offered inviting spaces.

Do you like antiques and fine dining? Nearby is York Road, lined with antiques shops as well as the renowned Milton Inn Restaurant, which serves lunch and dinner. Do you go in for wine tasting? The Boordy Vineyard gives daily tours year-round and wine-tasting dinners on Sunday nights during winter. The light rail station, 3 blocks away, is a twenty-minute ride from Baltimore. The renowned Ladew Topiary Gardens are in the vicinity. Is bicycling your thing? A 22-mile bike path through the country begins nearby. Arriving on business? Many business travelers find their way here. There's also a guest pantry with fridge, ironing board, and microwave.

At breakfast, you'll find savory, "heart-healthy" dishes that taste too good to be low cholesterol. But what you don't know will be good for you. Seasonal Maryland fruits like strawberries, apples, blueberries, and peaches are served with creamy sauces for your morning crepes. Homemade lemon bread might accompany light soufflés.

The rooms are decorated in pretty pastels and light wallpapers. One is named Sanibel for Sanibel Island, Florida, another the Maryland Hunt Room, a third the California Room. These names reflect treasured travel and vacation spots—good times and good places, like the inn itself.

How to get there: From the west and I–695, take exit 25 (Charles Street) and turn left at the light to cross over The Beltway. At the stop sign turn right onto Bellona Avenue and continue for 3 blocks. Turn left onto Morris Avenue and continue for 3 blocks to inn on corner, on right. From the east take I–695 west to exit 25 and turn right immediately onto Bellona Avenue. Follow directions above.

Innkeepers: Gwen and Bob Vaughn

Address/Telephone: 308 Morris Avenue; (410) 252–3131 or (800) 635–0370

Rooms: 6, including 2 suites; all with private bath and air conditioning, 1 with telephone and fax. No smoking inn.

Rates: $95 to $145, double occupancy, EPB. Two-night minimum if Saturday stay is included.

Open: All year.

Facilities and activities: Guest pantry, croquet. Nearby: train into Baltimore. Ladew Topiary Gardens, Boordy Vineyard, Hampton Mansion and Gardens, Evergreen House, Irvine Natural Science Center for bird-watching. Antiques shopping in Cockeysville, bicycling, golf at Pine Ridge Golf Course.

Business travel: Three blocks to train into Baltimore (20-minute ride). Telephone, desk, and fax available; corporate rates.

The Oak & Apple Bed & Breakfast
OAKLAND, MARYLAND 21550

We came in the fall when the Appalachian hillsides are a palette of crimsons, golds, and greens. We inhaled the beauty and stored memories of our drive: of valleys and farms, of Deep Creek Lake, of homes hidden in the trees. We were discussing the issues that people do when finally given a pocket of undisturbed time together in the car.

In the trunk were hiking boots so we might meander over some of the trails in Garret County's five state parks. We imagined the woods covered with snow and thought to ask after we arrived about the winter ski conditions.

"Excellent," said Jana. "Savage State Park is the roughest in winter for cross-country skiing

if you like the ungroomed feel. For groomed trails everyone goes to New Germany State Park."

Jana is part of a coterie of ex-urbanites who fled the city for a life that's closer to nature. She moved to Oakland because she once vacationed here and loved the area. When we arrived she had been open a year and was remodeling the fifth guest room. In the living room Jana pointed to the gleaming wooden floors and said she's still searching for the perfect Oriental rug to soften the step. She is sensitive to the sound of a footstep since she's also an audiologist. She is a considerate, resourceful young hostess.

The architectural style of the inn is Colonial Revival with Queen Anne elements; it has a charming, cohesive look, even if you can't quite place the style without asking. The feel is that of a fine home. A formal dining room is wallpapered in a soft rose. Upstairs a less formal parlor holds books and a table and chairs. The historic black and white photographs that hang on the wall are family portraits.

The inn is situated in an area that has more than 70,000 acres of public land and the waters of Deep Creek Lake, with its 65 miles of shoreline. Also nearby is Wisp Ski Resort, with downhill skiing in winter and tennis and golf during summer.

Continental breakfast at the inn includes homemade granola and breads served from a hand-

some, formal sideboard. A guest pantry provides teas and sodas and a fridge for storing beverages.

When you are ready to search out dinner, Jana is a well-informed source. She knows the best of the local restaurants (including seafood) and will recommend a casual or elegant spot to suit your taste.

How to get there: From I–68 take exit 14A and go south on Route 219 for approximately 25 miles to Oakland. In town turn right onto Crook Street (after first stop light) and proceed 1 block to Second Street. Inn is located at corner of Second & Crook.

Innkeeper: Jana Brown

Address/Telephone: 208 North Second Street; (301) 334–9265

Rooms: 5; 3 with private bath, 1 with Jacuzzi; telephone and television available. No smoking inn.

Rates: $55 to $80, double occupancy, continental breakfast. Two-night minimum holiday weekends.

Open: All year.

Facilities and activities: Nearby: Deep Creek Lake, golf club at Wisp, Wisp Ski Resort (downhill), Garrett State Forest, Potomac State Forest, Savage River State Forest, hiking, horseback riding, canoeing, fishing, tennis.

The Inn at Perry Cabin
ST. MICHAELS, MARYLAND 21663

Perry Cabin is an English country hotel, an elegant waterfront property where you can admire the beauty from the courtyard conservatory, read in the library (the one with the secret door), have coffee in the morning room and afternoon tea in the parlor. All public rooms and many bedrooms face the lovely Miles River. From these and other vantages, you see sailboats anchored in the harbor or looped along the dock of this park-like setting.

You have imagined right if you picture the rooms decorated in Laura Ashley fabrics. The inn has been decorated by a Washington, D.C., decorator using the Laura Ashley designer collection. You may request a room according to your favorite design, perhaps the Palace Garden, the Isabelle, or the Geranium (of which there are two colors). There is a book in the parlor with photographs of the rooms to give you an idea of the styles chosen. Among my favorites are Numbers 7 and 17 for their height and views.

Cocktails and dinner are ordered in the English-manor tradition. You may have an aperitif brought to you in the library or parlor and peruse the menu in comfort. Tea is served at 4:00 P.M. in the parlor. You select from scones, cakes, and tea sandwiches and take a seat in one of the public rooms while your tea is served.

Dinner emphasizes regional fare served with panache. You might find on the menu marinated

Atlantic salmon fillet with a sesame-shrimp roll, roasted asparagus, and a pickled-onion sauce, or shank of lamb glazed with tarragon vinegar and served with a sun-dried tomato sauce. Desserts have included chocolate noisette with hazelnut sabayon and sweet potato cheesecake with macerated Granny Smith apples. The waterview dining room, so bright and light with Summer Palace Laura Ashley wallpaper, is where you find yourself lingering into the night. Since you haven't far to go to your room, you'll want to take one last walk along the dock.

The next day you might select an English novel from the library and have a seat on the patio, where the sound of lines against the masts is a soft tinkling in the wind. Or in the winter sit in the Miles Room and work the puzzle, then go down the corridor for a game of snooker beside the fireplace. You'll find attention to detail—porcelain doorknobs, lights in the closets, heated towel racks—in most rooms. The beds are triple-sheeted. It's superb. If you sail over from Annapolis, there's complimentary boat docking for early arrivals and water-taxi service for anchored guests.

How to get there: From Chesapeake Bay Bridge take Route 50 east; before Easton, take 322/ Easton Bypass to Route 33 into St. Michaels. Pass through the village; the inn is on the right just beyond.

Innkeeper: Stephen Creese; Sir Bernard Ashley, proprietor
Address/Telephone: 308 Watkins Lane; (410) 745–2200 or (800) 722–2949, fax (410) 745–3348
Rooms: 41, including 6 suites; all with private bath, air conditioning, cable television, and telephone; 12 with Jacuzzi; wheelchair accessible. Pets allowed.
Rates: $195 to $575, double occupancy, EPB and afternoon tea.
Open: All year.
Facilities and activities: Lunch ($25), dinner ($57.50), cocktail service, docking privileges. Library, conservatory, garden room, snooker room with snooker table and fireplace. Swimming pool, sauna, and steam room. Bicycles and boats available. Nearby: St. Michaels Maritime Museum and village.
Business travel: Telephone, desk, and fax available; conference center with audiovisual equipment.

$\mathcal{V}$ictoriana Inn
ST. MICHAELS, MARYLAND 21663

While we sat in the white summer chairs along the canal, a robin trilled in flight and mute swans paddled up the creek. It's only fair to expect a waterfront inn to have a panorama, and Victoriana Inn looks out to the village harbor. From the porch a wide lawn stretches to the canal. Across the footbridge are the comings and goings of people, boats, and animals—enough to entertain you between sips of lemonade and a good read. In your lawn chair you're near the fish pond filled with koi carp and within chirping distance of the purple martin house. For privacy there's a white picket fence surrounding the spacious lawn. One block from here is the St. Michael's Maritime Museum, filled with boats and bay lore.

Janet sailed into St. Michaels several years ago and was smitten with the Chesapeake Bay village. She returned and found a house on the harbor in the very heart of town. Acting as her own contractor, she oversaw the renovation and stylish decorating of every detail. "This is it," she says. "This is where I'll stay." You'll be happy if you also decide to stay.

The inn is named for Janet's golden retriever, Victoriana, whose regal poses and mellow ways make her a charmer.

Arriving in the wintertime, you might have a seat in a windowed alcove of the living room. With the fire warmly crackling away, you can have a glass of sherry, play a game of dominoes, or plan your future. An exquisite antique grape-and-pear chandelier casts a soft light over the scene. Janet has fine taste, with comfort equaling style.

This is a good base for bicyclers, who can follow these flat Eastern Shore roads on a marked trail. Janet provides bicycle storage for those who bring their bikes. She will also set you in the right direction for sailing or boarding a wide range of boats.

The rooms are named for islands of the Chesapeake Bay. You sleep soundly, as if you are island-bound for the night. The antiques are of a fine quality, the towels are carefully folded and fill a basket, and the spreads are thick and comfy. These are beautiful lodgings with hardwood floors and handsome armoires.

In the morning flowers adorned the coffee cake. We visited with other guests. Everyone was seated throughout the parlor; we were before the fireplace, using small trays. Soon Janet brought in hot, delicious French toast and syrup. In the summer you can have breakfast on the veranda and watch the ducks swim along the canal or the boats depart for a day on the water.

The second week in December, Santa Claus comes to town. He rides down to the dock in a horse-drawn carriage, and all around him the boats are decorated with lights and holiday trim. There are special services at the churches, and the shops are filled with gifts and goodies. "The town," explains Janet with a contented smile, "looks like a Christmas card." Wintertime may be her favorite time in the village.

How to get there: From Main Street in St. Michaels, turn north on Cherry Street (toward the water), go to the Victorian fence, and turn right into the parking lot of the inn.

Innkeeper: Janet Bernstein

Address/Telephone: 205 Cherry Street (mailing address: P.O. Box 449); (410) 745–3368

Rooms: 5; 3 with lavatory, 2 with private bath, 2 with fireplace, and all with air conditioning. No smoking inn.

Rates: $102 to $148.50, double occupancy, EPB.

Open: All year, except 2 weeks in January.

Facilities and activities: Guest refrigerator. Nearby: restaurants, St. Michaels Maritime Museum, sailing, bicycling (storage provided at inn), annual Waterfowl Festival, Christmas walk second weekend of December.

Inn at Antietam
SHARPSBURG, MARYLAND 21782

As the sun rises over the Antietam Battle-field and the dew clings to the green rolling hills, you'll be sound asleep. At the appointed hour a knock is heard, and you step from the great antique sleigh bed to greet the innkeeper. He stands at the door with an antique wicker cart filled with a hot breakfast. If you prefer, you may join others in the dining room.

The allied forces in this inn, the Fairbourns (their pretty name sounds like a family from an English novel), make a strong team, whether it's getting you oriented to the area or preparing the superb breakfasts. They might present a light cheese quiche or coddled egg. Since this is fruit country, the morning desserts range from sour cream apple cake to luscious peach or blueberry cobbler. Betty excels with her English muffin bread and a wheat bread made with fresh-ground wheat from a nearby mill. In winter they offer hot cakes or pancakes served with Betty's blueberry or strawberry jams. Waffles are made with the "trusty old waffle maker," a 1930s model that works like a charm. Toast is browned to perfection in the 1920s toaster, which sits on the table.

On any spring, summer, or fall day when the flowers are in full bloom, you debate on where to carry a fresh cup of tea: out to the brick patio that overlooks South Mountain, toward the front-porch swing of the Victorian mansion, or to the wicker-filled sunporch. Wonderful places to relax abound at this inn. Families are encouraged to visit during the week, but the inn's facilities are not well suited to children under age ten.

The Fairbourns are experienced resources for restaurants (four excellent ones are each a ten-minute drive away) and for directing you to bike trails, walking trails, potters, tinsmiths, or antiques shops.

Each room is tastefully decorated and quiet because of the inn's location high on a hill back from the road. The Smoke House room is off the sunroom in the back. Its huge fireplace makes it the winter favorite. The bar sink was made by the local potter. In the bathroom, a "maid's tub," a short clawfoot tub, has bubble bath conveniently tucked next to the soap. This room also shows evidence of Cal's accomplished woodworking skills. The bed is located up a narrow stairway in the loft, overlooking the plaid chairs in front of the fireplace. Perfect writer's haven. The bookshelves hold volumes on the Civil War and Cal's gardening collection. If you want tips on planting, he's the man to ask.

I will not enter into matters of war and peace, but the story of the Battle of Antietam is chilling and fascinating. The Fairbourns say that the Canadians who visit study it more intensely than do Americans.

On the Persian carpet in the parlor rests an elegant porcelain-foot bathtub. You'll probably never see another like it.

How to get there: From Washington, D.C., take I–270 north to I–70 in Frederick. Follow I–70 to exit 49 (Braddock Heights). Turn left onto alternate 40 west. Proceed west through the village of Middletown and on to Boonsboro, to Route 34. Turn left onto Route 34 and drive 6 miles to Sharpsburg. Just past Antietam National Cemetery, which will be on the left, you will see the driveway to the inn.

Innkeepers: Betty N. and Cal Fairbourn
Address/Telephone: 220 East Main Street (mailing address: P.O. Box 119); (301) 432–6601, fax (301) 432–5981
Rooms: 4 suites; all with private bath and air conditioning, 1 with fireplace, 1 with television. One room wheelchair accessible. No smoking inn.
Rates: $95 to $105, double occupancy, EPB. Two-night minimum weekend and holidays. American Express only card accepted.
Open: Closed December 15–February 15.
Facilities and activities: Nearby: restaurants, Antietam Battlefield, Harper's Ferry, C & O Canal, antiques and craft shops, Heritage Crafts Festival.

Chanceford Hall Inn
SNOW HILL, MARYLAND 21863

A more incongruous name for a town whose elegant inn is the historic Chanceford Hall would be hard to find. Snow Hill is located in the southern flatlands of the Eastern Shore, surrounded by fields of corn, tomatoes, and melons. The highest spot in town is the courthouse, at 26 feet above sea level. The name traces back to the earliest settlers who arrived here in 1642 and named the town for a section of London. The county seat of Worcester, Snow Hill has a population of 3,000, twelve active churches, and the Pocomoke River, which lazes through town, attracting canoers and wildfowl lovers down its scenic waterways.

After a day of canoeing or bicycling through the pretty farmlands, you return to Chanceford Hall, a Georgian brick manor house whose exterior is stucco-on-brick (rarely seen today) and dates from 1759 to 1780. It's said to have been built by Robert Morris, a financier of the American Revolution. The inn is located in the village on an acre of land and is surrounded by several magnificent trees, including some 200-year-old walnuts.

The restoration is first-class. Michael and Thelma Driscoll have restored other homes before this one, so they were equal to the task. Michael, a cabinetmaker, has made several of the fine-quality pieces of furniture and has carefully upholstered some of the chairs and couches. If I were considering undertaking a serious renovation, these are two people I'd want to visit and see firsthand what they have accomplished.

Some of the details are visible in the woodwork and trim. You won't notice the air-cleaning system, the single-control faucets, the wool-fleece mattress covers on the beds, or the heavy-duty hot-water tanks. But you will sleep better for them.

Each room is a Colonial beauty. All bedrooms have canopied beds; most have fireplaces and Oriental rugs. For a casual setting, there's a sunroom that overlooks the lap pool in the backyard.

If you make advance arrangements for a romantic dinner, you will be seated beneath the crystal chandelier in the elegant dining room. On Thelma's menu are shrimp cocktail, lobster Newburg, and filet mignon. Her most requested dessert is chocolate-mousse crepes with English custard-cream sauce and strawberries on top. Everything must be selected in advance; dinner is served only to guests. There's also a restaurant in town.

Breakfasts are beyond your dreams. Thelma is quick with her fine-tasting ideas. What she comes up with is superior to what most guests can think of in the morning.

Depending on when you arrive, hors d'oeuvres may be served in the sunroom or before the fire in the parlor, outside, or in your room.

How to get there: From the intersection of Route 12 and Snow Hill Road in the village, go south 1 block on Route 12 and turn right onto Federal Street. The inn is 2 blocks on the left.

Innkeepers: Michael and Thelma Driscoll

Address/Telephone: 209 West Federal Street; (410) 632–2231

Rooms: 5, including 1 suite; all with private bath and air conditioning, 4 with fireplace. Limited smoking inn.

Rates: $115 to $135, double occupancy, EPB. No credit cards.

Open: All year.

Facilities and activities: Dinner served by advance reservation (from $50 per person). Lap pool, bicycles, yard games. Nearby: Pocomoke River, Chincoteague, historic villages, Chesapeake Bay, canoeing, antiquing, bird-watching.

River House Inn
SNOW HILL, MARYLAND 21863

It was one of those summer days of biting clarity, when the views across the open fields seem endless. A day when bicycling on the flat country roads and canoeing on the Pocomoke River seem a fortuitous privilege. A day when walking through a small riverside town is all that's needed to make you feel utterly alive and peaceful.

As I walked up the pathway to River House Inn, I was reminded of New Orleans, because black wrought-ironwork laces the front veranda. The image was confirmed when Larry showed me the way to the backyard lawn that stretches down to the river. I secretly imagined eating beignets and drinking chicory coffee; but iced tea within the shade of the screened veranda was certainly more cooling and appropriate.

When Larry and Susanne first walked into the building, she described the Pocomoke Parlor's wallpaper as "1890s"—and there beside the fireplace they found, scribbled beneath the wallpaper, "This room was papered by artistic paperers and paint slingers, Boehm and Russell, April 30, 1890." The Knudsens kept the scribble exposed for fun. Susanne's background is in restoration (this is their fourth).

There are two guest parlors, which Susanne has decorated perceptively with an eye for brightness and balance. In the red-painted twin parlors sit chairs covered with green-and-rust print fabric.

You might come here for dinner (if you've made advance arrangements). Susanne might serve crab au gratin for an appetizer, a rotisserie-cooked herb chicken, or grilled salmon steaks. For dessert there might be a birthday cake, if that is the occasion; or a summer yogurt with freshly baked homemade cookies may be served with your evening coffee. Or go across the street to a fine little restaurant.

The inn is furnished with a blend of reproductions and antiques. Susanne's decorating flair is subtle yet demands your attention. The foyer is a willow green. The Victorian inn dates from 1860, yet Susanne makes the old appealing in a contemporary way. Her collection of glassware and porcelain sits here and there; the oil paintings are water and boating scenes. Says the famous quotation that hangs in the parlor: "There is nothing—absolutely nothing—half so much worth doing as simply messing about in boats."

Outside your door in the morning you'll find the *Baltimore Sun*. Perhaps you'll have a cup of coffee on the veranda while you read the paper. Then guests are seated at small private tables, where tasty egg dishes, meats, and apple muffins are served. Breakfasts are lazy. Would you have it any other way when staying at a fine little inn?

How to get there: From the intersection of Route 12 and Market Street in Snow Hill, go east a few hundred yards on Market and turn left on Green Street, then right into the parking space.

Innkeepers: Larry and Susanne Knudsen

Address/Telephone: 201 East Market Street; (410) 632–2722, fax (410) 632–2866

Rooms: 11, including 2 suites and 1 cottage; all with private bath and air conditioning, 6 with fireplace, 2 with Jacuzzi. Suite suitable for families. Dogs permitted with prior permission. Two rooms wheelchair accessible. No smoking inn.

Rates: $92 to $150, double occupancy, EPB. $20 additional person, $10 additional child. Two-night minimum June–September.

Open: All year.

Facilities and activities: Dinner by advance arrangement ($30 per person for four courses, including wine). Located on Pocomoke River. Nearby: river tour aboard *The Otter;* canoeing, bicycling, golfing, boating; Chincoteague and Chesapeake Bay.

Recommended Country Inns® Travelers' Club Benefit: Stay two nights, get third night free, subject to availability.

Back Creek Inn
SOLOMONS, MARYLAND 20688

If I had a hot tub, I'd design and build it like the Back Creek's. It's framed in wood with side areas for sitting or placing a glass of champagne. Once submerged you're surrounded by gardens and cuddled by the sounds of the fountain trickling into the lily pond. The water view sweeps down to the sailor's haven, Back Creek, and out to the Chesapeake Bay. The hot tub is pleasant in the morning sun after an early jog, in the afternoon when you're lying about, or on a moonlit night when you want an experience to remember.

Lin and Carol's avocation is gardening. Besides the herb and vegetable gardens (whose bounty flavors breakfast), an abundance of flowers grows. The small white garden is modeled after Sissinghurst in England. Lin conceived the idea when touring English gardens with her mother. There's also a lovely rose garden.

The rooms are named for herbs. The "suite-rooms" are connected by a wooden deck to the inn, and one has a beautiful water view. My favorite is the six-windowed Chamomile, and my favorite suite is Lavender with the water view. Carol's mother and grandmother have contributed to the decor with their quilts.

The oil and watercolor paintings you see throughout the inn were done by Carol. She formerly taught art, and they reveal a talent she never mentions. She also designed the stained glass in the hallway and decorates shells. Lin fashions pretty floral wreaths, a natural outgrowth of her garden.

The varieties of boat trips available from Solomons run the gamut. You can board a large historic Chesapeake Bay bugeye from the Calvert Maritime Museum, join a tour boat to Hooper's Island, or take a small yacht cruise up the Patuxent River. Boat rentals include ski, speed, sail, and fishing boats. Landlubbers will find Carol and Lin know the best antiques shops. They recommend the historic Sotterley Plantation, which has a view of the Patuxent. You might ask them to prepare a picnic for either touring or bicycling.

In the spring, summer, or fall, seated under the shade of the paper mulberry, a Colonial tree, you are served a good breakfast. It begins with the inn's secret blend of delicious coffee. You might have egg casseroles with sausage and cheese, or eggs Benedict Back Garden style. Among the breads is a wonderfully moist carrot-date-nut muffin.

In the winter there's an inside view of the water in the common room where everyone enters the inn.

From spring to fall Wednesday tea is served on the patio, and everyone is invited by reservation. It's an opportunity to savor delicious sandwiches, scones, and cookies and chocolates after walking through the water-view gardens. Wouldn't that make a nice birthday gift for a friend?

How to get there: Take Route 4 to Solomon's Island (Routes 4 and 2 merge from the north). Before the bridge take Route 2 into Solomons; turn left onto Alexander Street. The inn is located at Alexander and Calvert.

Innkeepers: Carol Pennock and Lin Cochran
Address/Telephone: Calvert and Alexander Streets (mailing address: P.O. Box 520); (410) 326–2022, fax (410) 326–2946
Rooms: 7, including 2 suites and 1 cottage; all with private bath and air conditioning, 4 with telephone and television, 2 with fireplace and porch. One room wheelchair accessible. No smoking in rooms.
Rates: $85 to $140, double occupancy; $50 to $90, single; full or continental breakfast. Additional person $15. Package rates available. Two-night minimum holidays.
Open: Mid-February through mid-December.
Facilities and activities: Hot tub, dock. In season Wednesday tea served to public by reservation ($12). Nearby: tennis, pool, restaurants, day-sailing excursions, museum, Sotterley Plantation, antiquing, bicycling, jogging, fishing.
Recommended Country Inns® Travelers' Club Benefit: 15 percent discount, Monday–Thursday.

$\mathcal{A}$ntrim 1844
TANEYTOWN, MARYLAND 21787

The frosty light of the full moon emerged from the clouds and reflected off the snow as we drove; the farms and fields of rural Carroll County seemed to await passage to warmer days. We, however, found immediate warmth in the elegant Antrim 1844, named by its original builder for Antrim County, Ireland. Richard and Dort added the year it was built to its name.

Today the inn's twenty-three acres surrounding the brick plantation house have given the innkeepers the space to add an outdoor swimming pool, tennis court, croquet lawn, and chipping green. When they purchased the derelict property it lacked even electricity, and the neglected smokehouse, now a restaurant, was in marked disrepair.

The three-story building spans a hillside on the edge of a very small town. It's a large, sumptuous inn filled with antiques that knowledgeable collectors appreciate. After viewing the exquisite bedrooms, elegant mirrored parlor, cozy tavern, and the romantic dining areas, many a bride and groom choose this as their wedding site.

A wedding reception filled two of the parlors that night, but we felt we had the place to ourselves. At 7:30 P.M. Stuart, the maître d', seated us before a blazing fire in the smokehouse for dinner.

We began with a mushroom tartlet and then

had a fine salad of seasonal greens with Montrachet cheese, roasted peppers, and raspberry vinaigrette. I chose a salmon with an excellent barbecue sauce and a crème brûlée for dessert that came in a heart-shaped terrine with a crusty top, burnished as it should be.

For breakfast Richard might prepare Belgian waffles along with bacon and scrambled eggs. The sun blasts into the high-ceilinged dining rooms through great, lusciously curtained windows. On a winter's day the marble fireplace will be glowing.

In the evening, when you go up to your room, chocolates and cordials are served upon a butler's tray. Coffee, a muffin, and the newspaper arrive in the morning on the same tray, so you can emerge from your room slowly. You might have slept in a nineteenth-century rosewood half-tester from New Orleans or the 1790s canopied bed with its lace and ruffles, or the 1820 Honduras mahogany canopy with its 150-pound posts. The third-floor rooms have double Jacuzzis. Other choices include the remodeled barn overlooking the creek with its skylights and decks and the Ice House English cottage with a view of the pool and formal gardens.

Climb the ladder in the third-story hallway and take a look at the surrounding hills and town. During the Battle of Gettysburg, General George Meade climbed up here to see how events were progressing.

How to get there: From Baltimore Beltway 695, take exit 19 or 795 north. Exit Route 140 west to Taneytown. In town turn left onto Trevanian Road and go 150 feet to inn on right. From Frederick take 194 north to Taneytown. Turn right at light on Route 140, proceed ½ mile, turn right at fork onto Trevanian Road. Go 150 feet, inn on right. Signs indicate where to park.

Innkeepers: Richard and Dort Mollett

Address/Telephone: 30 Trevanian Road; (410) 756–6812 or (800) 858–1844, fax (410) 756–2744

Rooms: 14, including 5 suites and 4 cottages; all with private bath and air conditioning, 10 with Jacuzzi, 10 with fireplace, 2 with television. One room wheelchair accessible. No smoking, except in tavern.

Rates: $150 to $300, double occupancy, EPB plus afternoon and evening hors d'oeuvres. Special packages available on holidays. Two-night minimum if stay includes Saturday night.

Open: All year.

Facilities and activities: Tavern, 23 acres, swimming pool, tennis court, croquet lawn, golf-chipping green, volleyball, badminton, horseshoes, formal gardens. Dinner by reservation Wednesday–Sunday (fixed price $50, higher on holidays). Nearby: 12 miles to Gettysburg. Golf courses: Wakefield Valley, Carroll Valley, Bear Creek.

Business travel: Desk in 4 rooms; telephone, fax, and copy machine available; conference rooms; flip charts.

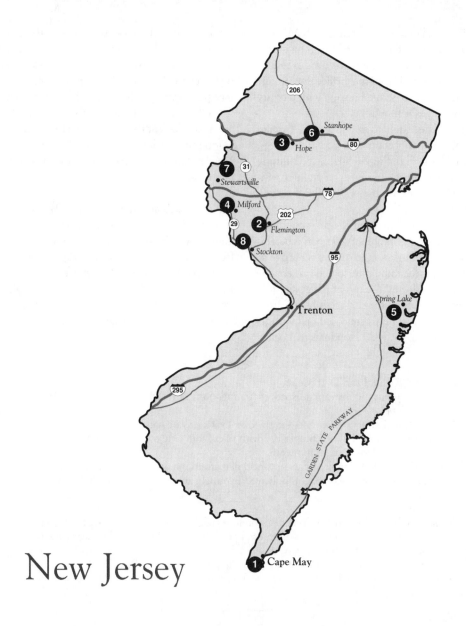

206

Stanhope

6

3

80

Hope

7

31

Stewartsville

78

4

Milford

202

29

2

Flemington

8

Stockton

95

Spring Lake

5

Trenton

295

GARDEN STATE PARKWAY

1

Cape May

New Jersey

New Jersey

Numbers on map refer to towns numbered below.

The Mainstay
CAPE MAY, NEW JERSEY 08204

The Mainstay is an inn with a story to tell. It is so famous that Tom and Sue Carroll give visitors an afternoon tour of their landmark lodging, followed by an elegant tea accompanied with sweet pleasures—delicious home-made cakes and cookies—stylishly served either on the summer veranda or in the winter parlor. Advance reservations are a necessity here. If you don't get a room this year, try next year. At the least come for the graciously delicious after-noon tea tour.

The Carrolls purchased The Mainstay in 1976, and it's their dream house. Built in 1872 as a "hotel casino," the former gentlemen's gam-bling house is a luxurious, high-style Victorian.

"We have decorated rather than restored," ex-plains Tom, "and much of the furniture was in place the day we arrived." The scale is grand and impressive, but you can also climb a ladder stair-way to the whimsical belvedere room for a view of the town through antique binoculars.

Using scaffolding and patience, the Carrolls created a showcase drawing room papered with wallpaper donated by Bradbury & Bradbury of California (who sought a stunning setting). Un-usual furniture—a "tête-à-tête" sofa for facing your companion and a rotating gaming table—furnish the room, along with ornate vases (Sue's taste) and clocks (Tom's taste). You'll probably spot the piece of music on the piano: "Sailing

Down the Chesapeake Bay." In the smaller parlor (furnished in equally commanding style), notice Tom's collection of bisque bathing beauties.

The rooms have handsome Victorian pieces; some have additional Bradbury & Bradbury wallpapers. You can select a room in the neighboring home that the Carrolls have restored. There are rooms with king- and queen-sized beds. In the newly restored Officer's Quarters, located across the street, every contemporary luxury, including fireplaces and whirlpool baths, have been provided.

Cape May has a bounty of excellent restaurants; most ask you to bring your own wines. Menus are available at the inn. You can walk from the inn to the restaurants.

Breakfast is served upon lace placemats with silver coffeepots and lovely china, and everyone begins comparing notes on Victorian manners and morals and basking in the luxurious grandeur. During the summer you might have tea on the veranda, where you can glance up Columbia Avenue and see a perfectly positioned series of front verandas—the Victorians wanted to see who was visiting whom. As you visit with other guests, you bite into Sue's buttermilk orange cupcakes or the memorable lemon bars that come with the iced tea. The ocean breezes blow gently, and you realize this moment will be with you forever.

How to get there: From the Garden State Parkway, merge onto Lafayette Street. Turn left onto Madison, right onto Columbia, to 635 on the right.

Innkeepers: Tom and Sue Carroll; Kathy Moore and Jill Turner, managers
Address/Telephone: 635 Columbia Avenue; (609) 884–8690
Rooms: 16, including 7 suites; all with private bath, 4 suites with fireplace, whirlpool, television, telephone, and VCR. One room wheelchair accessible. No smoking inn.
Rates: $95 to $245, double occupancy; $10 less for single; EPB, afternoon tea, and beach passes. Additional person, $20. Three-night minimum in season.
Open: All year; reduced number of rooms mid-December to mid-March.
Facilities and activities: Nearby: restaurants, beach, historic Cape May mansions, bicycling, bird-watching, sailing, trolley rides, State Park, lighthouse museum, carriage rides.
Recommended Country Inns® Travelers' Club Benefit: Stay one night, get second night free, Sunday–Thursday, November–April, excluding Thanksgiving and Christmas weeks, subject to availability.

$\mathcal{M}$anor $\mathcal{H}$ouse
CAPE MAY, NEW JERSEY 08204

For those of us who love Victorian architecture, few towns can match the turn-of-the-century ambience of Cape May. In the late 1800s this seacoast village on the tip of New Jersey, was the summer retreat of wealthy residents of Philadelphia and Baltimore, who embellished their mansions and cottages with the most elaborate gingerbread of the day, thereby creating a virtual catalog of Victorian architecture. A remarkable number of these homes can still be found along the tree-lined and gaslighted streets.

Nancy McDonald had been coming to Cape May since she was a child. When she and Tom married, they began visiting Cape May together, and their favorite place to stay was the Manor House. Eventually they decided to purchase their own inn and create one with all the ambience they loved so much at the Manor House. Just as their quest was beginning, they booked a room at the Manor House to participate in a cooking class. To their surprise, longtime owners Tom and Mary Snyder, who by this time knew the McDonalds well, said that they were ready to sell. The happy result is that the McDonalds purchased their dream inn, the Snyders sold it to a couple they knew would love and appreciate it, and we have the joy of being able to continue to stay in one of Cape May's finest inns.

On a quiet side street but in the heart of the historic village, the Manor House offers peace and tranquillity. We entered a foyer rich with burnished chestnut and oak. On the stair landing a polished oak window seat was surveyed by an ornate stained-glass window. Nancy invited us to the parlor, where, since it was winter, a fire crackled in the hearth. A selection of sweet and savory treats as well as port and sherry, were waiting. With the soft strains of classical music playing in the background, we soon relaxed from our drive and allowed ourselves to be pampered. In the warm weather guests sit in the beautiful and secluded English garden, which is alive in the spring with more than 150 different varieties of tulips.

Nancy and Tom have owned the Manor House since early 1995. Just as it did before, food plays an important role at the inn. Nancy is a gourmet cook and a connoisseur who knows the best places for lunch and dinner, and she fixes a superlative breakfast for her guests. The menu is prepared every afternoon so that guests can anticipate the morning meal. The hot entree might include a tomato tart, with tomatoes fresh from the garden in season, or a lemon-ricotta pancake,

or perhaps orange-custard French toast. Fresh fruit, hot-from-the-oven muffins or bread, and freshly squeezed juice accompany the meal. Rather than a buffet-style breakfast, Tom serves the courses. Guests are served in two seatings.

The guest rooms are tasteful and refined instead of fussy and Victorian. Number 9 has a turn-of-the-century French bed and green wallpaper, while Number 8 has red walls and a fantastic antique Victorian walnut dresser. Room 6 stretches across the front of the house and has a sleeping and a sitting area as well as a bath with a whirlpool tub. Some of the bathrooms are small, however, and two of the rooms share a bath.

How to get there: From the Garden State Parkway or the Lewes Ferry, take Route 109 south into Cape May. After crossing the bridge and passing the marina, you will be on Lafayette Street. Continue about 8 blocks to Franklin Street. Turn left onto Franklin, go 2 blocks, and turn right onto Hughes Street. The inn is in the second block on the left.

Innkeepers: Nancy and Tom McDonald
Address/Telephone: 612 Hughes Street; (609) 884–4710, fax (609) 898–0471
Rooms: 10, including 1 suite; 8 with private bath and air conditioning, 1 with television,
    1 with Jacuzzi. No smoking inn.
Rates: $85 to $185, double occupancy, EPB, beach tags and beach chairs. Two-night
    minimum weekends; 3-night minimum throughout July and August.
Open: All year except January.
Facilities and activities: Nearby: ocean beach 2 blocks away, Cape May house tours,
    Christmas festivities, walking street of shops and restaurants.

The Queen Victoria
CAPE MAY, NEW JERSEY 08204

An icy blast of Atlantic wind brushed our faces as we stepped out of the car. It shaped our quick movements—inside the gate, up the stairs, onto the porch, ring the bell, stamp the feet. Then Dane moved us quickly inside, where we inhaled the warmth and saw the parlor Christmas tree, strung with an edible assortment of nuts, fruits, pretzels, and even decorated eggs, beside the fireplace. Winter at the beach, with Christmas coming soon. At the Queen Victoria Christmas reigns, which means special festivities, including expert lectures and a party to decorate the inn's three trees, representing early-, mid-, and late-Victorian ornamentation.

Dane helps organize the annual Victorian Christmas Tour, which opens the inns of Cape May for lectures, music, plays, and other special events. (Request information in July to make your plans for November and December.)

We ascended to the third floor and selected a spacious room that boasted a white-wicker conversation area. It equaled all the others in comeliness and comfort, but we especially appreciated the views of the town's rooftops. You can base your choice on the amenities that you fancy, whether it's a whirlpool, a fridge for wine, or a gas fireplace. Queen-sized beds are taken for granted here. There's also a guest butler's pantry in each building adjacent to the parlor, so any time you feel like preparing a cup of tea or coffee, you may help yourself. This is one of the few inns that has family accommodations in an adjacent cottage.

The inn is composed of three neighboring Victorian buildings. Besides the dining room and parlors, there's a wraparound porch where you catch the summer sea breezes in your rocking chair; everything is immaculately kept.

In the parlor of the Queen Victoria is Joan's collection of Van Briggle pottery and impressive pieces of Arts and Crafts furniture. As former head of the Victorian Society, she has interesting insights into the era and has planted the inn's gardens to reflect the landscaping of the period.

Breakfast is served upon Roycroft china, buffet style, from the sideboard. There are generous portions of homemade granola, muffins, and hot egg-and-cheese casseroles. We also helped ourselves to thickly sliced ham. Guests have breakfast in either the Prince Albert or Queen Victoria dining rooms. Dane and Joan each oversee one, or they may separate and later compare conversations. Morning discussions revolved around the Arts and Crafts Movement, antiques, and local events. One guest commented on the high quality of the musical performance he'd seen the night before; we'd spent a happy evening in the inn parlor.

A kind touch at tea time: If you are spending an extra day at the beach, you are invited to return to the inn to use the beach showers and even for afternoon tea the day of your departure.

How to get there: From the southern end of the Garden State Parkway, continue straight into town (more than 1 mile) to merge with Lafayette Street. At second stoplight, turn left onto Ocean Street. Go 3 blocks, inn is on the right.

Innkeepers: Dane, Joan, and daughter Elizabeth Wells
Address/Telephone: 102 Ocean Street; (609) 884–8702
Rooms: 23, including 6 suites; all with private bath, air conditioning, refrigerator, and stereo, 14 with whirlpool tub, 8 with television, 4 with telephone, 2 with gas fireplace. Wheelchair access. No smoking inn.
Rates: $75 to $255, double occupancy, EPB, afternoon tea, parking, beach towels and passes. Additional adult or child, $20. Three and 4-night minimums during busy seasons and holidays. Two-night minimum weekends. Request special quiet-season packages and midweek and second-night rates, which begin at $75, from November to March. Payment by check preferred.
Open: All year.
Facilities and activities: Complimentary bicycles, use of butler's pantry. Nearby: beach 1 block, restaurants, historic tours of Cape May, bird-watching, fishing, Christmas tours, and Dickens Extravaganza.

The Cabbage Rose Inn
FLEMINGTON, NEW JERSEY 08822

The fire was going in our room—Lavender & Lace—and now, as we relaxed, we studied the photographs and prints—all of women—that accented the walls and dresser.

Later, as we visited with Pam and Al before the fire, we listened to stories about Al's childhood on the Maine seacoast, Pam's love of the theater, and how they met in the corporate world of AT&T. We were reminded of the effort that went into their renovation and how, after they finished, they were married in the inn parlor before they embarked on their new innkeeping career together.

We also received an update on the Fluck family, who built the home in the early 1900s and had returned for a family reunion. Pam and Al told them about the "will" found in the wall during their remodeling. It had been written long ago by an ancestor, the eleven-year-old Eleanor Fluck. The family revealed the young lady had a strong talent for ordering her life, but her will was written prematurely. She became a successful New York stockbroker and lived a long, rewarding life.

As we sat beside the fire, Al, with a sweep of his hand, referred to the town of Flemington, outside the front door. Sixty percent of the village is on the National Register of Historic Places. Many visitors overlook the historical sites because the surrounding area is so rich with biking, hiking, and touring opportunities. The neighboring towns of New Hope (Pennsylvania), Lambertville, and the wonderful Delaware riverside villages also beckon. Within a block of the inn are Flemington's village-style shopping outlets, including those that trace back to the glass-making industry that began at the turn of the century. You can also walk up the street and visit the courthouse where the famed Lindbergh kidnapping trial was held.

For dinner we ventured off to an old stone inn, where, adjacent to a fireplace in a most lovely setting, we respectively ate an excellent salmon and beef filet and visited with friends. (Dinner here is included in a package price provided, on request, by the Cabbage Rose.)

We were intrigued that there were midweek independent business travelers at breakfast, each enjoying the inn as much as any love-struck couple (well, almost!). The conversation at breakfast left people full and happy, as did the delicious oatmeal, fruit compote, appetizing muffins, fresh juices, and coffee. Al gave my companion directions to the nearest golf course; he occasionally escapes there himself on a sunny afternoon.

When Pam was a little girl, her Aunt Rose would gather her onto her lap and commence telling stories by pointing to a favorite charcoal drawing that hung on the parlor wall. It was Aunt Rose, too, who took her to auctions and antiquing and taught her to appreciate fine things. As you sign the guest book, you'll see the mysterious drawing, with its enticing woodland path that sparked many a happy afternoon.

Upon departure, we couldn't resist a box of handmade chocolates, which Pam sells at the inn. We departed with ornately designed milk chocolates—and memories that are as palpable as any quality antique or oil painting.

How to get there: From I–78 take exit 17 to 31 south to Flemington. From I–287 take exit 10 (on left) to 202 south to Flemington. Turn right at Flemington sign (opposite Grand Union), turn right again on Main Street, and continue to inn. Park in rear.

Innkeepers: Pam Venosa and Al Scott
Address/Telephone: 162 Main Street; (908) 788–0247
E-mail: cabbageros@aol.com
Rooms: 5; all with private bath, telephone, stereo, and air conditioning, 1 with fireplace. No smoking inn.
Rates: $80 to $125, double occupancy, EPB. Two-night minimum if Saturday included.
Open: All year.
Facilities and activities: Parking. Nearby: walking distance to outlet malls and downtown Lambertville, New Hope, hiking, biking, village touring, and golf course.
Recommended Country Inns® Travelers' Club Benefit: Stay two nights, get 50 percent discount on third night.

The Inn at Millrace Pond
HOPE, NEW JERSEY 07844

The Inn at Millrace Pond has a presence, a feeling of solidity and permanence. It's a lovely stone gristmill dating from 1769 that operated until the 1950s and then closed to lie fallow for thirty years. Restored in 1986, it's now a Colonial inn with contemporary American dining.

In the entry you're drawn to an overview of the millrace chamber, the canal where water flows from the millpond during spring and summer. The mill's great waterwheel stands in timeless beauty, and the austere stone walls form a richly textured background.

Downstairs is a large Colonial tavern with the original walk-in fireplace and brick flooring. Standing here with a drink in hand, you can hear the water rushing through from the pond's overflow. It travels along a hand-dug canal that is 15 feet deep in places and still runs. You can follow the canal or walk on a higher path back through the woods to the ten-acre pond.

Ascend to the dining room and order a grilled New York sirloin served over Madeira butter and garnished with wild mushrooms, or try a pan-seared salmon in sesame crust that's served with a sauce verte. Few leave without at least sharing a fresh pastry for counterpoint.

There's a clean warmth and beauty to the rooms and inn. Perhaps it reflects the Germans who emigrated from Moravia, fleeing religious persecution, and who settled Hope in 1769. The walls are a soft linen white, and the woodwork is painted in Colonial blues and greens or burgundy. In the main inn the rooms have original exposed post-and-beam construction and Colonial reproductions of quality. Every room has a desk. In the adjacent stone cottage, rooms share a small formal parlor.

This is an inn where your privacy is intact. It is one where the owners have received great reviews for food but modestly attend to their inn without pretensions. In the dining room, a pianist plays the grand piano to keep you attuned to the special occasions.

The village of Hope is a medley of charming buildings that are recognized as a National and State Historic Site. The Moravian settlers, who weren't as successful as they expected to be, left the town in 1807, but Hope is experiencing a renaissance. On the restaurant walls are photographs of early Hope. Can't you imagine these men sitting together beside the fire and selecting that name?

How to get there: From I–80 take exit 12, Route 521 south, 1 mile to blinking light in Hope. Go left on Route 519 and drive ²⁄₁₀ mile to inn on left. Parking beyond inn.

Innkeepers: Charlie and Cordie Puttkammer; John Lamagna, manager

Address/Telephone: Johnsonburg Road, (mailing address: P.O. Box 359); (908) 459–4884 or (800) 7INNHOPE, fax (908) 459–5276

Rooms: 17, in 3 historic buildings; all with private bath, air conditioning, and telephone, 9 with television, 5 with whirlpool tub. Three rooms wheelchair accessible. Designated no smoking rooms.

Rates: $85 to $165, double occupancy, continental breakfast. Two-night minimum if Saturday included.

Open: All year.

Facilities and activities: Dinner daily (entrees $19 to $23), tavern, 23 acres, 10-acre pond, hiking, tennis court. Nearby: shops, factory outlets, Waterloo Village (20 minutes), Poconos (30 minutes), golf, antiquing, canoeing, and fishing.

Business travel: Telephone and desk in room; fax and computer available; conference space.

Recommended Country Inns® Travelers' Club Benefit: 10 percent discount, Monday–Thursday.

Chestnut Hill on the Delaware
MILFORD, NEW JERSEY 08848

The Delaware River flows out front, the rare train travels down the single riverside track, and antique rockers line the front porch in anticipation of sunset on the river. Inside awaits a resplendent Victorian inn with innkeepers who keep life in good-humored perspective.

The inn is a Victorian gem. Ron and Linda painted it in shades of green ranging from seafoam to forest. I'll never forget the time I arrived to find Ron precariously hanging from a ladder as he painted the elaborate grapevine wrought iron that marches across the porch and down the columns. It creates a pretty frame for those of us who love to spend the afternoon rocking on the porch and watching the lazy river roll by.

You'll be greeted in the entrance hall by a mannequin dressed in nineteenth-century splendor graciously welcoming guests to her home. "May I show you to my parlor?" she seems to say. The tiny parlor to the right of the hall is intimate and charming with wonderful examples of antique Victorian furniture and silver.

In the Eastlake Parlor, on the opposite side of the hall, shelves of an old apothecary cabinet are filled with Linda's unique gift items (don't miss this!), and there's also an organ, a piano, a fancifully carved fireplace mantel, and another gentlelady mannequin. This one is dressed in the clothes worn by the actual lady of the house around the turn of the century. It's a setting that draws you in to peruse and appreciate, to enjoy and relax.

The rooms are decorated according to themes that arose naturally. The sheets are crisply pressed—some were designed by Linda. In the Rose Garden, the newest room, there's a window seat offering views of the river and a Jacuzzi in the bath. In Peaches and Cream, a 1908 marriage certificate hangs above the bed alongside the marriage proverb, "I will love you and honor you all the days of my life."

Bayberry Room has a lovely bay window that looks out to the river. And upstairs in Teddy's Place, which contains more than 150 teddy bears, sits a copy of a 1911 book that Linda found one day, *The Diary of My Honeymoon.* Many a marriage has gotten off to a good start here.

Breakfasts are served in formal style with fine china, silver, and linen in the ornately Vic-torian dining room. They include fresh seasonal fruit, delicious sausage and baked German apple pancake, and a variety of omelets and pastries, depending on the season. It's a chance to sit back and savor.

Linda's antique wooden rocker collection is cause for pause. Some came from Rice's Antique & Flea Market (open on Tuesdays), which is a bona fide bargain-hunter's dream located not far from the inn. Linda will direct you to special places. You could spend an entire quiet weekend here walking through the town, sitting on the front porch, walking along the river on Rob's new riverwalk, biking, dining at two fine restaurants in town, and easing up on life.

How to get there: Direct bus service from New York City. Request driving instructions. Located in village.

Innkeepers: Linda and Rob Castagna
Address/Telephone: 63 Church Street (mailing address: P.O. Box N); (908) 995–9761
E-mail: chhillinn@aol.com
Rooms: 6, including 1 suite and 1 cottage; 4 with private bath, all with air conditioning, 5 with telephone, 4 with television, 1 with Jacuzzi, cottage with fireplace. Wheelchair accessible. No smoking inn.
Rates: $85 to $140, double occupancy, EPB. Two-night minimum weekends. No credit cards.
Open: All year.
Facilities and activities: Walking and hiking along Delaware. Nearby: restaurants, tubing, canoeing, tennis, New Hope and Flemington (30-minute drive), Rice's Antique & Flea Market.

La Maison
SPRING LAKE, NEW JERSEY 07762

As we drove along Ocean Avenue, the tangy smell of salt air reminded us of childhood afternoons spent romping in the surf. Beaches are still my favorite destinations, and this white-sand beach stretches for 2 miles. Spring Lake's boardwalk was alive on this sunny day with bicyclists, joggers, in-line skaters, and walkers.

Spring Lake is a peaceful and charming seaside Victorian village unaffected by the fast-food emporiums and honky-tonk dives that characterize some other sections of the New Jersey shore. Stately mansions with broad lawns line the well-kept streets, and the village has an impressive collection of antiques shops, decorator showrooms, and cafes. Vitale & Vitale, specialists in

antique clocks, are located here, and their magnificent collection is as much a museum of horology as a salesroom.

La Maison, on a quiet side street, is perfectly suited to this fine-arts community. On entering the unassuming building, we found ourselves in a captivating French country home and art gallery. Colorful watercolors and oils fill the walls and climb the stairs, and all are for sale. Barbara described many of the local scenes in the paintings, and she knows the artists (one is Peter, her assistant innkeeper and partner). It's worth coming here to purchase the art even if you can't spend the night.

Barbara Furdyna is a gracious and engaging

innkeeper who adores France, so wherever you look you can imagine yourself in a little tucked-away corner of France. (Peter spends about six months a year at the inn and the rest in England, where he works for IBM.) Barbara was a French major in college and studied at the Sorbonne. The inn is romantic and seductive. We relaxed in the parlor with its gorgeous Persian rug and cozy fireplace, sipping sherry and munching hors d'oeuvres that had been laid out on the antique desk.

You'll find light and airy guest rooms with sleigh beds, carved armoires, iron beds, and ornate French iron chairs. The baths are luxurious and large. I especially like the King Juan Carlos Room, with its sexy bath that contains a two-person whirlpool and a skylight in the cathedral ceiling, through which we could view a full moon. A wonderful little cottage in back, with its own private garden, is open during the summer.

Breakfast is served *en famille* on a trestle table in the formal dining room. We started with mimosas, and then Barbara brought a tray of freshly baked muffins and breads, followed by Belgian waffles with whipped cream.

Barbara is an expert on activities in the local area, and we learned that Spring Lake is especially noted for its summer croquet tournaments. Barbara offers complimentary beach, pool, and tennis passes to her guests (chairs and umbrellas, too) as well as membership in the Atlantic Club, a full-service health club. She also has bicycles for her guests to use.

How to get there: From the Garden State Parkway, take exit 98 onto Route 34 south. Follow Route 34 to the traffic circle and then take Route 524 east to Spring Lake. After crossing the railroad tracks, take the second right onto Fourth Avenue. Proceed for 5 blocks and turn right onto Jersey Avenue. La Maison is the second house on the right.

Innkeepers: Barbara Furdyna and Peter Oliver

Address/Telephone: 404 Jersey Avenue; (908) 449–4860 or (800) 276–2088, fax (908) 449–4860

Rooms: 8, including 1 suite and 1 cottage; all with private bath, air conditioning, telephone, and television, 1 with Jacuzzi. Pets allowed in cottage only. Wheelchair accessible. No smoking inn.

Rates: $110 to $220, double occupancy, EPB and beach and tennis passes. Two-night minimum weekends; 3-night minimum weekends July–August.

Open: All year except January.

Facilities and activities: Bicycles available. Nearby: ocean beach 4 blocks, jogging, walking, croquet, health club membership.

Recommended Country Inns® Travelers' Club Benefit: Stay two nights, get third night free, Monday–Thursday, September 15–May 19 (1997 only), excluding holidays.

Normandy Inn

SPRING LAKE, NEW JERSEY 07762

Spring Lake is one of those discoveries you can't wait to share with best friends. Its uncluttered boardwalk, beautiful beach, and lovely residential tree-lined streets make favorable impressions.

The Normandy Inn is a Victorian lady, painted gold, olive, teal, and terra cotta, located one-half block from the Atlantic Ocean. The porch is a maze of wicker furniture; inside awaits a variety of rooms with antique furnishings, a rose-colored parlor, and a superb breakfast. It's an inn for vacationers, for those important idle hours, for those who want to take time enjoying a large, large breakfast, for making the brow furrows disappear, and for broadening the smile.

Breakfast is a grand event at the Normandy and absolutely delicious. The multicourse affair begins with a hot cup of coffee or one of a wide selection of teas served in the sunny breakfast room. Then hot or cold cereal—one of the best choices is porridge, a hot oatmeal—is served by waitresses. Next come more decisions: eggs however you'd like them, meats, pancakes, French toast, juices, and rolls or toast. You may not have to eat again until dinner.

The inn has period antiques, but it's very casual. The rooms are nicely furnished, and some have views of the ocean. The innkeepers have carpeted the rooms and furnished them appropriately to the setting and inn's origin. You can request a king- or queen-sized bed. You'll find the mattresses up-to-date and the antiques very beautiful.

The lobby is done in pinks and mauves. A marble bust of a woman looks on the scene approvingly, an étagère is filled with cut glass, palm fronds sit near the door.

The innkeepers have a collection of menus for making a dining choice. These include the big beachfront hotels, any new restaurants, local pubs, and a traditional seafood restaurant that's a ten-minute drive away.

It's a pretty town with a main street shopping area that leads to a lake surrounded by a jogging and walking path. Regardless of your beliefs, you may want to visit St. Catherine's, a church with ornate stained-glass windows. Michael and Susan thoughtfully provide bicycles for guests to see the town.

How to get there: From Garden State Parkway take exit 98 and follow Route 34 to first circle. Go ¾ of way around circle to Route 524 east; follow this to ocean. Turn right onto Ocean Avenue, go right onto Tuttle, and ½ block to the inn.

Innkeepers: Michael and Susan Ingino; Anne Marie Boyle, manager

Address/Telephone: 21 Tuttle Avenue; (908) 449–7172 or (800) 449–1888, fax (908) 449–1070

Rooms: 19, including 1 suite and 1 cottage; all with private bath, telephone, television, and stereo, 2 with fireplace, 2 with Jacuzzi. No smoking inn.

Rates: $120 to $290; children under 10, $10, over 10, $20; EPB. Three-night minimum July–August if includes Saturday, 2 nights weekends most other months. Twenty percent less off-season.

Open: All year.

Facilities and activities: Bicycles. Nearby: restaurants, ocean beach ½ block away, shopping, Garden State Art Center.

olive Metcalf

$\mathcal{S}$ea Crest by the Sea
SPRING LAKE, NEW JERSEY 07762

We love the turrets and gingerbread, bay windows, ornate fireplace mantels, and broad porches of fine Victorian homes. So naturally we love Sea Crest, a Victorian gem that has furnishings as Victorian as its architecture.

John and Carol Kirby fled corporate life for innkeeping in 1989, purchasing this 1885 home that has been welcoming guests for more than one hundred years. We walked across the wraparound porch to the ornate front door and were immediately immersed in the spell of the late 1800s. Tea and freshly baked cookies and cakes were waiting in the dining room when we arrived, and we relaxed as if among friends while John told us about the history of Spring Lake.

We learned about the Irish families who created this seaside resort, and we are glad that subsequent town fathers resisted the impulse seen in neighboring villages to line the beaches with recreation and amusement facilities.

It was a bright but cold winter day when we arrived, and the fire in the front parlor was a welcome respite from the chill. During the holiday season this room is festooned with boughs, and a massive tree occupies a corner. The "gift shop"— an overflowing cabinet by the front door—contains an assortment of gift items with the Sea Crest label as well as books and unusual jewelry, paintings, and craft items.

The guest rooms are fantasy retreats.

They're designed for adults who are seeking a romantic escape. Take the Casablanca room, for example. You will enter through a bead curtain, sleep on a rattan bed, and be surrounded by lamps and artifacts that John collected in Africa when he was an officer in the Merchant Marine. A trench coat hangs behind the door, and "the" movie is available in the video library to watch on the VCR in your room. The Mardi Gras room has feather fans, masks, hats, and a feather boa decorating the walls. Several of the baths are small, but they are nonetheless adequate. On our return from dinner, we were charmed by "James the Butler," who was standing in the stair landing holding a tray of melt-in-your-mouth homemade chocolates. I could easily have taken the entire tray to our room and eaten every one.

Breakfast is an elaborate affair that is served in the formal dining room and also in a cozy addition that boasts a woodstove. We started with breads and cereals served on a corner cupboard. This was followed by Mexican featherbed eggs and fresh fruit served on beautiful china.

Following breakfast John suggested a walk or bicycle ride (the inn has a fleet of English threee-speeds) along the 2-mile boardwalk, which he claims will use up "at least 400 calories." It sounded like just the thing to us.

How to get there: From the Garden State Parkway, take exit 98 onto Route 34 south. Follow Route 34 to the traffic circle and then take Route 524 east to Ocean Avenue. Turn right. Go 1 block, and turn right onto Tuttle Avenue. The inn will be on the left in 1 block.

Innkeepers: John and Carol Kirby

Address/Telephone: 19 Tuttle Avenue; (908) 449–9031 or (800) 803–9031, fax (908) 974–0403

Rooms: 12, including 2 suites; all with private bath, air conditioning, telephone, and television, 8 with fireplace, 1 with Jacuzzi. No smoking inn.

Rates: $115 to $250, double occupancy, EPB. Major credit cards accepted. Two-night minimum weekends September–June; 3-night minimum weekends July–August; 2-night minimum weeknights July–August; 3-night minimum holiday weekends.

Open: All year.

Facilities and activities: Nearby: ocean beach 1 block, bicycling, walking along boardwalk, band concerts on lawn by lake in summer, plays at Community House.

The Whistling Swan Inn
STANHOPE, NEW JERSEY 07874

LET ME WARM UP, PLAY ME SOFTLY reads a sign adjacent to an antique radio. We'd just shut the door to our room, called Waterloo Village (named for the nearby historic village, where we'd go the next morning). Earlier we'd entered the foyer and met Paula, a direct and accommodating innkeeper.

Two wingback chairs sit beside the radio opposite a crocheted canopy on our four-poster bed. We are content after our journey and want no more than to proceed to the parlor to meet guests.

I should like to make a study of the parlor; it casts an enticing web that catches everyone who tries to pass by. The ambience is born of a grandmother's hospitality, of Victorian lamps, and

chocolate-chip cookies in the cookie jar. Paula's grandmother taught her the ease of welcoming guests and always having something good to eat. The parlor works because it's subtle and right. The lighting from Victorian-style red-and-white lamps reflects off the deep red walls. The Victrola works, and the oak trim casts reflections.

Naturally, there are whistling swans on the piano, on the mantel, and elsewhere, but the name came serendipitously from an illustrated sign found in an antiques shop, which now hangs beside the inn's double front doors.

In the morning, after one bite of the three-cheese pie, we borrowed Paula's recipe. We also helped ourselves to plenty of juice, muffins, and toast while getting directions to the USGA Golf House Museum and a back-roads 3-mile route to Waterloo Village.

We were unprepared for the loveliness of Waterloo Village. Located on the banks of the Musconetcong River, its assorted trees and waterfowl are a romantic vision of the past. The village was once the thriving Andover Forge, where arms for George Washington's army were produced. You stroll along the streets, enter the stone gristmill, visit the canal—a major western channel in 1831—and explore the twenty-seven buildings. The New York Metropolitan Opera now makes Waterloo Village its summer home.

The inn guest rooms are named for the area—Walnut Valley, Cranberry Lake, High Point, and Lenape, for example. If I had a favorite, I'd name it, but I liked each as much as the next. On the third floor the room that forms

the peak of the inn has a high, pointed ceiling lined in wood. A small back room has the 7-foot-high stained-glass window that came from a church in Chicago. There's also the twin claw-foot bathtubs in a special bathroom that is reserved for guests. Terry-cloth robes hang in the closet, bubble bath sits on the shelf, and a needlepoint sign can be hung on the door: BATH IN USE. "It's our Victorian Jacuzzi," Paula smiled. She and Joe have saved the best of the past, including family heirlooms and handwork. Their inn expresses a secure sense of place.

How to get there: From I–80 take exit 25 (eastbound) or 27B (westbound), follow Route 206 until it becomes Route 183. At traffic circle go ⅔ way around toward Netcong. At Hess Gas Station (located on right) turn left onto Main Street. Follow Main Street to Number 110.

Innkeepers: Paula Williams and Joe Mulay
Address/Telephone: 110 Main Street; (201) 347–6369, fax (201) 347–3391
Rooms: 10, including 1 suite; all with private bath, telephone, stereo, and air conditioning. No smoking inn.
Rates: $85 to $135, double occupancy, EPB. Two-night minimum holidays.
Open: All year.
Facilities and activities: Nearby: Waterloo Village (open Tuesday through Sunday from mid-April through December, except for holidays), golf courses, USGA Golf House Museum, Mining Museum. Horseback riding, hiking, bicycling, cross-country skiing. Lake Hopatcong, Musconetcong River, Delaware Water Gap. Flea markets and antiquing.
Business travel: Phone, photocopy, television, fax, and secretarial services available; desk in 7 rooms; dataport in all rooms; corporate rates.

The Stewart Inn
STEWARTSVILLE, NEW JERSEY 08886

Lynne opened the door and, without fuss or ceremony, congenially led us to seats before a crackling fire. She poured hot cups of coffee, and we talked of boats and foods and Pitty Pat, the inn cat. Though Lynne was once a corporate president, she was born an innkeeper. She eased us immediately into a state of contented domesticity amidst a sixteen-acre bestiary.

The inn is a grand stone manor house a short drive from the Interstate. To one side of the front door is a handsomely placed Palladian window. In the foyer stands a silent grandfather's clock. It's still because the chimes might disturb guests. Everywhere you turn you find fine antiques and porcelain animals. Here's the

first clue that you should have brought your pet questions.

Lynne had a kennel for twenty years and is a keeper for distressed game in the area. She cares for raccoons, who live in large outdoor cages. They have no shortage of company. Other critters include sheep, eighteen geese, two peacocks, a parrot and parakeets, chickens (for fresh breakfast eggs), the goats, Alfalfa and Chloe, and so many barn cats that Lynne refuses to admit their exact number. With this menagerie to be fed, you're welcome to take a morning tour of the animal kingdom with Lynne.

Breakfasts at the inn are a feast. The breakfast room is filled with cozy tables for two, covered with fresh white linen. Order whatever you want, from pancakes, to fresh eggs, to an unforgettable granola served with fresh fruit and yogurt. Hot coffee sits in a thermos on your table. Now you have time to watch the birds that cluster around the outside feeders and to decide where your day's travels will take you.

The guest rooms are first-come, first-served and range in size from normal to large. My favorite is an expansive fireplace room with a sitting area and enormous bathroom. You can imagine Clark Gable sleeping here. In fact, he was a guest at one time. Lynne is a trusted restaurant connoisseur. One evening she directed us to one of her favorite pasta places, where we found the tortellini with carbonara sauce scrumptious. Makes you want to come back just to try "her places."

A shipment of sheep arrived while we were there—knee-high ones for Lynn's gift shop, which has grown with each visit. She is an accomplished knitter who appreciates and imports handmade goods for her foyer shop. You could count her sheep before you go off to bed but it's not necessary—you'll sleep well anyway.

How to get there: From the east on I–78, take exit 4 toward Stewartsville. Inn is ²/₁₀ mile on the left.

Innkeeper: Lynne McGarry

Address/Telephone: Stewartsville (mailing address: P.O. Box 6); (908) 479–6060, fax (908) 479–4211

Rooms: 8, including 2 suites; 6 with private bath, air conditioning, stereo, 3 with fireplace, 4 with refrigerator, all with television and telephone. One room wheelchair accessible. No smoking inn.

Rates: $95 to $135, double occupancy, EPB. Two-night minimum on weekends.

Open: All year.

Facilities and activities: Outdoor pool, 16 acres along creek, gardens, barn, farm animals, gift shop. Nearby: restaurants (15 minutes away), back-roads touring, antiquing; towns within 30 minutes: historic Clinton, Bethlehem, and Easton.

Business travel: Telephone in room; desk, fax, copy machine, and laundry facilities available; corporate rates.

Recommended Country Inns® Travelers' Club Benefit: Stay one night, get second night free, Sunday–Wednesday, November 15–April 15, excluding holidays.

olive Metcalf

The Stockton Inn
STOCKTON, NEW JERSEY 08559

The impulse is always there. I feel like bursting into a verse of "There's a Small Hotel with a Wishing Well" whenever I visit The Stockton Inn and see the little stone wishing well in the meandering courtyard garden. But then, this is the inn that the song was written about. Lorenz Hart often visited the inn and he wrote the song in 1936 for *On Your Toes*. It was later reprised for *Pal Joey*.

It was in the 1930s also that artist Kurt Wiese (who had illustrated the original *Bambi* book) began painting the colonial murals of Bucks and Hunterdon County sites that line the walls of three of the dining rooms. R. A. D. Miller later added more wall paintings in ex-

change for food and lodging. Our favorite has always been Toby's room, the original brick-floored tavern with its fireplace and romantic ambience.

The inn, built in 1710 from locally quarried stone, was originally a private residence. Through the years it has witnessed numerous historical events. George Washington used the nearby ferry to help move supplies and troops across the Delaware during the Revolution, and a tavern opened in the building in 1832, when the D & R Canal became a popular waterway. In the 1940s, 1950s, and 1960s, band leader Paul Whiteman closed his radio and television shows by announcing he was on his way to "Ma Colligan's" for dinner and for many years it was a retreat for famous writers and artists. (For some 60 years the inn was known as Colligan's Inn.)

Now the inn has regained its former luster. It includes guest rooms in the original stone structure as well as in three other historic buildings. The spacious guest rooms are especially well suited to business travelers. They feature period reproduction furniture, modern baths, stereos, coffeemakers, and televisions. Most have fireplaces, separate sitting areas, draped beds, and refrigerators.

Guests dining at the inn can opt for one of six romantic rooms, but the favorites are the mural rooms, especially on cold winter days, when a fire glows in the stone fireplaces and candles softly illuminate the paintings. During the summer, when the outside terraces are open, we love to sit beside one of the waterfalls or near the pond. The Garden Bar has a dance floor; a combo or pianist plays on weekend nights.

The food is excellent, reflecting the genius of chef Jeff Olimpo and the sensibilities of owner and former restaurateur Andy McDermott, who has operated the inn since 1982. You'll dine on potato-crusted sea bass served with a julienne of prosciutto and caviar-crème fraîche or, perhaps, roasted rack of lamb that's been crusted with mustards and herbed breadcrumbs and served with a rosemary-lamb reduction and minted-apricot chutney. An impressive wine list offers admirable accompaniments.

How to get there: From New York take the New Jersey Turnpike south to exit 14 and follow I–78 west to exit 29. Follow I–287 south to Route 202 south and take the second Lambertville exit onto Route 29, traveling north to Stockton. The inn is in the center of the village.

Innkeeper: Andy McDermott; Scott Serafin, Robin Hannan, and Jack Boehlert, managers

Address/Telephone: 1 Main Street (mailing address: P.O. Box C); (609) 397–1250, fax (609) 397–8948

Rooms: 10, including 8 suites; all with private bath, air conditioning, coffeemaker, television, 7 with fireplace, 5 with minirefrigerator.

Rates: $90 to $165, double occupancy, continental breakfast. Two-night minimum weekends April–December; 3-night minimum holiday weekends.

Open: All year.

Facilities and activities: Dining room open for lunch, dinner, and Sunday brunch; price $13.75 to $28. Nearby: Delaware Canal towpath ¼ mile, Mercer Museum, James Michener Art Center, art galleries, antiques shops.

Business travel: Desks in five rooms; fax and copier available; conference room.

olive Metcalf

The Woolverton Inn
STOCKTON, NEW JERSEY 08559

In the 1980s The Woolverton Inn was my special secret retreat. I would come on summer afternoons, to sit either on the upstairs porch or on the flagstone veranda, and write. In the evening after dinner, I would play the piano or complete a jigsaw puzzle into the wee hours of the morning. But then the innkeeper moved away and it just wasn't the same.

Therefore, it was with a keen sense of hope that I visited The Woolverton Inn again in late 1994, when I learned that it had been purchased by Elizabeth and Michael Palmer, an enthusiastic couple who had great plans for the majestic, 1792 stone manor house. By early 1996 the renovations were complete, and I found that this magnificent manor house once again met—and exceeded—my expectations. Private baths have been added to every guest room, and two rooms even have two-person Jacuzzis. There are canopy beds, lush fabrics, fireplaces in two rooms, and walls charmingly handpainted with flowers or pastoral scenes. The guest rooms are named for people who have had a connection to the house. My favorite is Amelia's Garden, which has a four-poster cherry bed with a fishnet canopy, a pretty sitting room, and an elegant bath with pink walls and a lovely walnut dresser outfitted with a sink.

Downstairs, in the living room, the piano remains in the corner, and the game table by the window is just waiting for a couple to put a jigsaw puzzle together. The antique furniture is elegantly upholstered, oil paintings embellish the walls, and a fire glows in the hearth in cool weather. On the wicker-filled side porch, guests relax with a book and enjoy the gardens, perhaps while enjoying tea, coffee, or lemonade with cookies, cheese, and fruit, which are offered every afternoon.

A full gourmet breakfast is served in the formal dining room. Elizabeth might prepare a baked apple or poached pear for the fruit course and perhaps an entree of blueberry johnnycakes or creamy scrambled eggs with asparagus and chives.

The inn is located on ten acres. Sheep graze in a meadow. There are a stone spring house, a picturesque barn that may one day be restored, and a carriage house with two guest rooms. Hiking trails meander about, and there's a croquet lawn and a horseshoes pit. For those of us who love country inns with a deep-felt passion, we can add another to our collection of favorites.

How to get there: From New York take the New Jersey Turnpike south to exit 14 and follow I–78 west to exit 29. Follow I–287 south to Route 202 south and take the second Lambertville exit onto Route 29, traveling north to Stockton. Travel through the village to the fork. Veer right onto Route 523 and go for ²⁄₁₀ mile. Turn left onto Woolverton Road. The inn is reached along the second driveway on the right.

Innkeepers: Elizabeth and Michael Palmer

Address/Telephone: 6 Woolverton Road; (609) 397–0802, fax (609) 397–4936

Rooms: 10, including 2 suites; all with private bath and air conditioning, 2 with fireplace, 2 with Jacuzzi. No smoking inn.

Rates: $95 to $180, double occupancy, EPB. Two-night minimum weekends; 3-night minimum holiday weekends.

Open: All year.

Facilities and activities: Located on 10 acres with croquet lawn, hiking trails, and horseshoes pit on property. Nearby: Delaware River towpath and park ½ mile, canoeing, rafting, historical sites, boutiques, antiques shops.

Recommended Country Inns® Travelers' Club Benefit: Stay 2 nights, get third night free, Monday–Thursday.

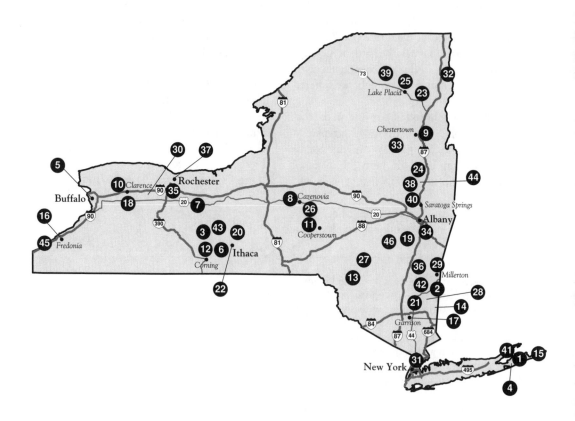

New York

New York

Numbers on map refer to towns numbered below.

Bluff Cottage

AMAGANSETT, NEW YORK 11930

We came on a blustery day. Locals referred to the windy, rainy weather as a "nor'easter" and referenced it as weak compared to the great storm that had swept through several years earlier, the barometer against which all such weather is measured here. When we opened the wooden gate and entered the high privet hedge that buffers the cottage, we had the sensation of being in an oasis. On the porch we shed our boots and went inside to warmth, security, and elegance.

Bluff Cottage is situated across the street from the Atlantic Ocean and 5 blocks from the heart of Amagansett, which has an important whaling history. The town marine museum is located directly opposite the cottage inn, but in midwinter it is closed. Atop the village Presbyterian Church rests a fish weather vane, a reminder of seafaring roots.

Whatever the season, there is no paucity of things to do. Amagansett proper boasts a cluster of quality shopping outlets, organized into a village square setting, and you can't appear here without paying a visit to the renowned Amagansett Farmers' Market with its fruits, vegetables, and flowers. The inn is a convenient departure point for bicycling and touring, but the Bluff Cottage's proximity to the Atlantic Ocean and beach is reason enough to come. For dinner you can stroll downtown to Gordon's Restaurant, which Clem maintains is one of the Hamptons area's finest.

Breakfast is continental style; either Clem or John dashes up the street to the market for croissants, sweet rolls, or scones. By the time he returns, the freshly ground coffee has finished brewing and the juice is properly squeezed.

Most guests select their rooms here according to their preference for an ocean or backyard view. The rooms have four-poster, queen-sized English rice beds, with stools for climbing up on them. There are period antiques throughout the house.

Clem taught psychology and was a dean at City College in New York before retiring to the innkeeping life. "I don't think they'll be much interested in that," he said modestly. "I paid the same as everyone else when I took the train to work." Now he and John take pleasure in providing directions and helping with suggestions of their favorite places and restaurants; their expertise results from owning Bluff Cottage for more than two decades.

We asked to see the kitchen, which is not where one normally finds guests who are busy amusing themselves in the Hamptons. On enter-ing the kitchen we were transfixed: The kitchen was in its original form and appeared much as it would have in the early 1920s. The striking ceiling-high wooden cabinets abutted high plate shelves, brimming with dramatic porcelains. The sink was the latest model—seventy-some years ago. I admired the seventeenth-century French marble baker's table and the collection of English ironstone. This lack of artifice captures one's attention perhaps better than the latest in kitchen design ever could.

Should you feel, after frolicking in the Hamptons for several days, in a confessional mood, there's a hand-carved seventeenth-century French confessional that dominates the corner of the living room. No one here would ever tell, since gentle souls reside within.

How to get there: From Route 27 or Main Street in Amagansett, turn south on Atlantic Avenue. Inn is located less than 1 mile on right at intersection of Atlantic Avenue and Bluff Road.

Innkeepers: Clement Thompson and John Pakulek

Address/Telephone: 266 Bluff Road (mailing address: P.O. Box 428); (516) 267–6172

Rooms: 4; all with private bath and air conditioning. No smoking inn.

Rates: $210 to $230, double occupancy, continental breakfast. Three-night minimum weekends; 4-night minimum major holiday weekends.

Open: Memorial Day through October.

Facilities and activities: Nearby: Atlantic Ocean beaches, Amagansett Farmers' Market, East Hampton Town Marine Museum, fishing, surfing, outlet shopping, bicycling, golfing, tennis.

Troutbeck
AMENIA, NEW YORK 12501

Remember the Mad Hatter's hat in *Alice in Wonderland*? It's here. It is made from burgundy leather and is trimmed with a wide black band. Appropriately, it sits atop a magnificent hall table at Troutbeck.

Innkeeper James Flaherty is an American and at the same time a British country gentleman. With a slight bow and a warm smile he welcomes you to the exquisite manor he oversees. Without hesitation James proffers you a drink from the Victorian bar in the red room and welcomes you to the harmonious surroundings. He adroitly choreographs your weekend or lets you indulge yourself in the silence of the surroundings. Whether it's for romance, the enjoyment of the great outdoors, or relaxation by the pair of pools—each one of luxurious proportions—everything is enhanced by fine dining.

The chef's talent tempts the guests to gourmandize themselves. He might prepare sautéed double lamb chops with a port-thyme sauce or a crisp paupiette of Norwegian salmon fillet with a saffron-lobster sauce. The extravagant desserts, called "evil" by some, range from outrageous soufflés to carrot cake with caramel sauce.

New Year's Eve, a black-tie event, is informally known as the "weekend of excess." But every weekend could be called that.

The rooms are distinguished. Jim has a talent for design and pattern. The parlors are enticing in their beauty. An unhappy thought isn't conceivable at Troutbeck. The inn's facilities are not well suited to children between ages one and twelve.

You walk across the stream to the Century Farmhouse. Depending on whether you turn right or left from the central lobby, you're in the 240-year-old farmhouse or the more contemporary addition that blends stylistically with the old. Every room has a writing desk and a good reading lamp. The manor has an excellent library of 12,000 books. Alarm clocks are to remind you of cocktail hour.

Outside are gently landscaped surroundings: the trout-filled Webatuck River, majestic sycamores planted brookside in 1835, and a seventy-year-old primrose garden. Sinclair Lewis once said of Troutbeck, "You live in a cathedral of trees." He might have added, "And a chapel of flowers."

How to get there: From New York take I–684 north from Brewster and then Route 22 north to Amenia. From Amenia, take Route 343 toward Connecticut; go 2⁴⁄₁₀ miles, turn right onto Route 2, cross bridge, and turn right into Troutbeck.

Innkeeper: James Flaherty; Garret Corcoran, manager

Address/Telephone: Leedsville Road; (914) 373–9681 or (800) 978–7688, fax (914) 373–7080

Rooms: 42, including 6 suites; 37 with private bath, all with air conditioning, telephone, and stereo, 9 with fireplace, 7 with whirlpool tub. Two rooms wheelchair accessible.

Rates: Friday–Sunday, $650 to $1,050, per couple; 1 night, $400 to $500 per couple; AP, includes all spirits. 7¼ percent tax. Two-night minimum holiday weekends.

Open: Midweek reserved for executive groups. Weekends open as a country inn.

Facilities and activities: Friday and Saturday dinner for outside diners $40 and up; Sunday brunch $26; Saturday lunch served. Tennis courts, walled gardens, outdoor and indoor swimming pools, fitness center, 422 acres, hiking, cross-country skiing, brook and creek. Nearby: Vanderbilt Mansion, Roosevelt Home, antiquing. Jim Flaherty maps out individualized tours.

Business travel: Desk and telephone in all rooms, fax, photocopy service, audiovisual equipment, extensive meeting and conference space available.

Gone with the Wind Bed and Breakfast
BRANCHPORT, NEW YORK 14418

The water is 104 degrees and swirling across our backs and over our bodies as the steam rises; through the misty window the moonlight glistens off the snow. Here in the hot tub we feel a certain clarity of mind as the remnants of tension in our muscles melt away in the sultry bliss. We are being pampered and we love it. We love the pleasant sensations experienced in this little inn on a hillside overlooking Keuka Lake.

On our first visit to this stone mansion inn with 21-inch-thick walls, we came in summer when the grapes still hung green on the vine and the weekly Amish market thronged with produce and crafts. This time we appeared in winter to savor the splendor and the cool serenity of the season. As we drove in we saw the dock where Robert keeps his boat and the pair of Canada geese that have made dockside home for the winter. In the gazebo Linda had placed a Christmas tree. At the foot of the hill two new stone pillars stood. In our absence Robert had been working, skillfully finishing each room. The only chore left for guests is deciding how to enjoy their comfort, with a lakeside or hillside view. We chose Rhett and Scarlett's suite, with its fireplace and lake-view porch. A heavy afghan lay beside the door so that we might venture out to the porch and sit and enjoy the stars. Each room, like the rest of the inn, has a sunny, festive mood. Antiques and reproductions are attractively and tastefully blended. There's a delightful vista from every window.

Robert and Linda are kindness personified. Those who come, return. He's the quiet, gentle-spoken craftsman, a native of the area, who looks at Keuka Lake with a familiar fondness. She adds the gourmet dimension to a visit through her cuisine and also reveals a decorator's panache: The Southwest room, with its head-board of natural bark, reminds her of her regional roots; she puts a crocheted canopy across a bed, a chocolate upon your pillow, and prepares the morning tastes that have you clamoring for her recipes.

Former guests have named everything edible: For breakfast it's Ashley's Stuffed French Toast, Aunt Pittypat's Pumpkin Pancakes, Melanie's Muffins, or Rhett's Rhubarb Rave, a coffee cake that's served moist and deliciously warm. In summer some guests develop a leisurely protocol: Visit the market, tour a winery, then go for dinner on the lake. Others like the nearby village of Hammondsport, where they stock up on wines. Others go for hikes, swim in the lake, and head for the hot tub.

Each visit takes on its own shape. You can easily come here and not venture out: on the third-floor foyer there's an area with books, games, and a large puzzle to work, and Linda keeps writing pads for guests. Outdoors you can hike over the property, sit on the porch, walk down the lane, or cross the road to the double-tiered dock and lie in the sun or borrow a boat and row out on the lake. We think the Finger Lakes match France and Italy for beauty but certainly exceed them for ease of travel and congeniality of innkeepers.

Linda once said of the inn, "It's our Tara, our dream." We all need a Tara. Even if it's for the weekend.

How to get there: From Branchport take Route 54A south 4½ miles to the inn on right. Enter between stone pillars at the sign.

Innkeepers: Linda and Robert Lewis
Address/Telephone: 453 West Lake Road; (607) 868–4603
Rooms: 6 rooms share 4 baths in stone Victorian house, 1 with fireplace and veranda; additional log house "Sequel" has 5 rooms, 3 with private bath and 2 that share, 3 with air conditioning. No smoking inn.
Rates: $70 to $125, double occupancy, plus 10 percent tax, EPB. Two-night minimum some holidays. No credit cards.
Open: All year.
Facilities and activities: Solarium with hot tub, 14 acres, 180-foot lakefront property for swimming. Nearby: Windmill Farm & Craft Market (seasonal, open Saturdays and holidays), wineries within short radius, Curtis Museum in Hammondsport.

Bridgehampton Inn
BRIDGEHAMPTON, NEW YORK 11932

What a joy it is to see a formerly derelict house refurbished and gleaming. The 1795 mansion that houses the Bridgehampton Inn sat forlornly on the edge of fashionable Bridgehampton for years until local caterer Anna Pump and her husband Detlef transformed it into their classy inn.

I remember what it looked like in 1993 when Anna and Detlef purchased it, and I remember the painstaking restoration that took place until the inn opened a year later. Today it is both a reflection of its historic past and of the Scandinavian heritage of its owners. Detlef is a builder, and Anna enjoys a terrific decorating sense. The inn is infused with their style.

When we arrived one dark evening, a welcoming fire glowed in the living-room fireplace, and wine and cheese were waiting in the bright breakfast room. The polished oak floors were covered with Oriental carpets, and a Victorian sofa was upholstered in a lovely forest-green velvet. A glass bowl of oranges sat on an antique table, while a pitcher of daffodils graced the mantel.

The guest rooms are unique, each furnished with a hand-carved four-poster bed and elegant antiques. Room Number 6 is furnished with a spectacular, eight-piece antique Biedermeier suite. All the rooms have wall-to-wall carpeting, burnished antique chests and tables, and a serene and restful atmosphere. This is an inn to relax and wind down in; its proximity to New York means that many guests come for that very reason. The gray marble baths have deep European sinks, wide countertops, and spacious showers with a center head, similar to those in Denmark.

Anna is known as the premier caterer in the Hamptons, and her breakfasts reflect her expertise. A continental breakfast featuring homemade blueberry muffins, scones and croissants, fresh juice and fruit can be supplemented, for an additional charge, with an egg dish accompanied by smoked salmon and ham.

On sunny summer days guests relax in the spacious gardens or on the covered porch or patio. The inn is merely five minutes from premier golf courses and three minutes from the glorious Hamptons beaches. Antiques shops, superior restaurants, and historic museums are all within walking distance of the inn. An old-fashioned soda fountain, cafe, and ice cream parlor, the Candy Kitchen, is just down the street. They still make their own ice cream and sell grilled-cheese sandwiches.

How to get there: From New York City take I–495 (Long Island Expressway) to exit 70 (Manorville) and follow Route 111 to Highway 27 (Sunrise Highway). Take Highway 27 (which becomes Montauk Highway) for 25 miles to Bridgehampton. Traveling east on Montauk Highway, the road becomes Main Street as it reaches Bridgehampton. The inn is on the left ½ mile beyond the traffic light at the entrance to Bridgehampton Common shopping center.

Innkeepers: Anna and Detlef Pump; Barbara Cavagnaro and Marie Yenick, managers
Address/Telephone: 2266 Main Street; (516) 537–3660, fax (516) 537–7130
Rooms: 8, including 2 suites; all with private bath, air conditioning, telephone, and television. No smoking inn.
Rates: $145 to $290, double occupancy, continental breakfast. Two-night minimum weekends; 3-night minimum holiday weekends.
Open: All year.
Facilities and activities: Gardens. Nearby: ocean beaches, Corwith Museum, Friday talks by celebrity authors at library in summer, restaurants, antiques shops, boutiques.

Beau Fleuve Bed & Breakfast Inn
BUFFALO, NEW YORK 14209

In Hawthorne's narrative "My Visit to Niagara," he approached the falls as if on a spiritual pilgrimage. We came in the winter, when these cataracts are a grand study in white, with their expanses of inert hoariness contrasting with the immense, noisy, thundering energy of water unleashed. The bankside trees where we walked were frozen, encased in clear crystal. The spring, summer, and fall are exquisite here as well, but on a sunny winter day, this place is magical.

But what better time to come indoors in Buffalo? What better time to reserve a seat for the Buffalo Philharmonic, visit the Albright-Knox, or snuggle together around a dinner at a great little restaurant that's not far from a great little inn?

Beau Fleuve ("beautiful river") was the name the French gave the Niagara River. Others, however, probably transformed the name to something easier and more familiar—Buffalo—even though these riverbanks never grazed the American beast.

Having chosen the area for its quality of life, Rik, a college professor in communications, and Ramona, an editor, searched for a historic home to restore. Built in the early 1880s, the inn blends an English half-timber style with the Queen Anne influence of the day. The interior has a gleaming oak staircase whose sunflower motif denotes the Aesthetic Movement (companion to Arts and Crafts). One room at a time, Rik and

Ramona have returned the residence to a historic showcase. It's located a block from Delaware Avenue, also known as Millionaire's Row. Buffalo is renowned for the industrialists who built large companies following the harnessing of Niagara's power in the 1890s. Drive on Delaware Avenue and see the grand mansions of the business magnates. Ramona offered a map indicating the location of Buffalo's five homes designed by Frank Lloyd Wright, three of which are still private residences. Wright also designed a downtown office building that has since been demolished.

The Whitakers named and decorated their rooms in recognition of the nationalities of those who helped build Buffalo: the French Room, the Irish Room, the German Room, the Italian Room, and the Polish Room. Each of the rooms is as tasteful and comfortable as the next and reveals a personal sense of style that combines the old and new.

You will find yourself marveling at the tapestries, prints, and porcelain that Rik and Ramona have collected from their global travels. Ramona has furnished the inn in a blend of antiques and colors in deep blue, burnished gold, burgundy, and muted green that are perhaps reminiscent of the Nile coursing through the desert at twilight.

As we visited at breakfast, while eating a delicious wedge of hot quiche served with fruits and muffins, Ramona commented, "I've always lived near water." Then she suggested a drive to Niagara Falls along the Niagara River.

How to get there: From I–90 eastbound exit at I–190, Downtown Buffalo. From I–190 take Elm Street exit and follow Elm Street to its end. Turn left, go past two lights, and follow Delaware Avenue sign. Turn right at Franklin (first street becomes Linwood), proceed to Bryant (about ¾ mile), turn left, then right into first driveway.

Innkeepers: Ramona and Rik Whitaker
Address/Telephone: 242 Linwood Avenue; (716) 882–6116
Rooms: 5; 1 with private bath, others share 2 baths, all with air conditioning and stereo. Television available. No smoking inn.
Rates: $67 to $80, double occupancy; $57 to $70, single; EPB.
Open: All year.
Facilities and activities: Nearby: Buffalo Philharmonic Orchestra, Albright-Knox Art Gallery, Buffalo Museum of Science, Elbert Hubbard Roycroft Museum, Herschell Carousel Factory Museum, *Maid of the Mist* Boat Tour, Old Fort Niagara, Antique Row, Frank Lloyd Wright homes, seasonal concerts.
Business travel: Located downtown. Desk in 4 rooms; corporate rates.

The Red House Country Inn

BURDETT, NEW YORK 14818

A gentle summer rain turned to mist as I drove on the hills of Schuyler Road through the Finger Lakes National Forest to the Red House. The inn sounded remote. In a sense it is. As the fog lifted the inn's five luxuriant acres of lawn and trees blended into the 16,000 acres of national forest. It's a minute's walk to the solitude of Mother Nature and 30 miles of summer hiking and winter cross-country skiing. There are thirty wildlife ponds.

In another sense the inn is closely linked to civilization. It's 12 miles from Watkins Glen and surrounded by thirty-six wineries in a 20-mile radius.

The Red House Country Inn, named for its barn-red exterior, is entered entertainingly through a hallway that doubles as a bountiful country gift shop.

During winter dinner is served on country-blue duck plates. You'll like the plates as much as the dinner. Besides having a sense of humor, Joan and Sandy are talented cooks. They often use local wines or imported liqueurs in dishes. The roast chicken is glazed with Grand Marnier and fresh oranges, and the roast duck is prepared with a raspberry-and-vodka sauce. You might taste a superb Red House chowder, and the fresh breads come with jam and jellies made with local wines that are also what you're drinking. Desserts include a shortbread pecan pastry, a cheese flan with gooseberry topping, and a cream puff served with ice cream and chocolate sauce. A sequel to cross-country skiing is an evening at The Red House. Afterward you might gather in the parlor around the piano, organ, or beautiful Spanish guitar, or just sit back and visit.

In the spring and summer, bring your galoshes. We trekked off into the woods toward the ponds, roused a pheasant, and identified trees. In summer you can cool off around the swimming pool. At night guests borrow blankets and lie across the lawn to watch for falling stars.

The decorating theme is red, white, and blue. Each room is a variation of these colors. The red room is small and cozy, but most guests prefer the private fireplace room. Each one is as neat, pretty, and clean as the next.

An Act of Congress hangs on the wall. The U.S. National Forest that surrounds the inn wouldn't exist if Joan and Sandy hadn't organized and held firm to prevent its dissolution. They also instigated the transformation of an empty church into a community center that's widely used by the area's elderly. Their contributions were symbolically stitched into a fine piece of artwork by a guest. Look for it in the dining room.

How to get there: From the north take I–90 exit 41 at Waterloo; go 36½ miles south on Route 414 to Hector. Go left on Schuyler County Road No. 2 for 3 ⁴/₁₀ miles to the inn. From the south go 8 ⁷/₁₀ miles north from Franklin and Fourth streets in Watkins Glen on Route 414 to Schuyler Road No. 2. Turn right and go 3 ⁴/₁₀ miles to the inn.

Innkeepers: Joan Martin and Sandy Schmanke
Address/Telephone: Finger Lakes National Forest, 4586 Picnic Area Road;
   (607) 546–8566, fax (607) 546–4105
E-mail: redhsinn@aol.com
Rooms: 5 share 4 baths; 1 with fireplace, 1 with air conditioning. No smoking inn.
Rates: $60 to $85, double occupancy, EPB. Two-night minimum weekends.
Open: All year.
Facilities and activities: Pool, gardens, hiking, cross-country skiing, animals. From November through April, 4-course dinner by reservation to guests (minimum four); $18 per person, BYOB. Nearby: restaurants (12-minute drive), Watkins Glen Gorge, Seneca Lake, Corning Glass Museum, winery touring.
Recommended Country Inns® Travelers' Club Benefit: 10 percent discount, Monday–Thursday, subject to availability.

Morgan-Samuels B & B Inn
CANANDAIGUA, NEW YORK 14424

Were I marking the changing of the seasons, this is where I'd come. In the first bloom of spring, I'd walk between the silver maples that line the lane; as the leaves hinted at harvest colors, I'd visit the fall wineries and select jams and grape pies from the roadside stands; following a snowfall I'd call for a winter's date on the horse-drawn sleigh; and when the first blush of summer heralds its becalming force, I'd canoe across the lake to out-of-the-way places. Whatever the season this refined setting with its placid rural surroundings offers elegant seclusion. A day spent luxuriating in this country house inn is a day complete in itself.

Julie's artistic background has gracefully in-fluenced each room; four have their own fire-places and one an antique French parlor stove. The suite is a dream. Its two-room bath has a shower, a tub, and a Jacuzzi lit by a window that overlooks the fields.

Julie recommends romantic pleasures. She gives thought to where you might go that would particularly suit your taste. She suggested a canoe ride for the two of us or a summer afternoon lunch in the Sonnenberg Gardens, with its sixty acres of plants, or maybe we just wanted to lounge beside the rose garden while listening to the fountain trickle and savoring our favorite tea.

John is the chef. Early every morning he and young son Jonathan depart together for the market to purchase the fresh fruits and oranges for juice. If an omelet has crossed his mind on the drive, he selects the six cheeses and green and red peppers that compose this delicious masterpiece. If a meat is called for, his own selection of savory garden herbs is admixed with the sausage that awaits frying.

Some mornings they call upon the nearby monastery for freshly baked whole-grain breads or flours for the fruit or nut pancakes. While all this is occurring, we are sleeping soundly.

The inn is named for Judson Morgan, an actor, and Howard Samuels, who invented the plastic bag. Each owned the mansion at one time. Yes, I should have asked more about the architecture and furnishings. I saw and marveled at the hand-hewn beam in the 1810 section and the stone- and brickwork and wondered who these early craftsmen were. The impressive array of antiques and oil paintings could have prompted innumerable questions as well. But one falls under a spell here and lingers on the patio under the trees or in the breakfast room beside the fire. One sits to breakfast, where the delicious pancakes or fabulous omelets emerge hot from the kitchen.

One steps out the mansion door not expecting to find a black Oriental chicken who busses the ground for seeds while a peacock turns his head sharply and then leisurely fans his massive tail feathers in a paced walk. One hears the rustle of leaves and sees cows peering from behind a stone fence. Or one returns to the library, hears the sound of the fire crackling, and smiles at the beauty of a moment shared with your spouse— whether you've been married for many decades or merely a day.

The location is rural, yet five minutes from Lake Canandaigua and the eponymous town— an ideal setting with articulate hosts.

How to get there: From I–90 East take exit 43 and turn right onto Route 21. Proceed to Route 488 and turn left. Turn right at the first stop sign onto Smith Road and proceed ¾ mile to inn on the right.

Innkeepers: John and Julie Sullivan
Address/Telephone: 2920 Smith Road; (716) 394–9232, fax (716) 394–8044
Rooms: 5; all with private bath and air conditioning, 4 with fireplace, 2 with Jacuzzi, 1 with parlor stove. No smoking inn.
Rates: $119 to $210, double occupancy, May through mid-September; $125 to $255 mid-September through mid-November; lower rates rest of year; EPB. Two-night minimum weekends May through mid-November.
Open: All year.
Facilities and activities: Dinner for 8 or more by reservation (approximately $50 each); BYOB. Forty-six acres, tennis court. Nearby: Horse-drawn sleigh rides during winter, Canandaigua Lake, Sonnenberg Gardens, Rose Hill Mansion, Bristol Playhouse, wineries.

$\mathcal{L}$incklaen $\mathcal{H}$ouse
CAZENOVIA, NEW YORK 13035

There are chic towns that get lots of press. And there are lesser-known towns, like Cazenovia, that never get the press they deserve. Motor in from the west along Route 20 and you rise and descend in a rhythmic movement of hill and valley until the car descends toward Cazenovia Lake, passes the Lorenzo Estate, and curves around toward the wide main street. There, on the corner, rises the three-story brick structure built as a stagecoach stop in 1835. The Lincklaen House still has a distinctly Colonial feel, with its brass chandeliers, antique white molding, and high ceilings in the two parlors.

Moments after arrival we were sitting before the fire and warming to the surroundings. We

asked to preview the dinner menu, which included a grilled duck breast glazed with cranberries and Niagara sauternes and seared tournedoes with roasted-garlic custard.

I could easily have spent the entire afternoon reading beside the fire in the parlor. On one table sat a guest book begun in 1873. A nearby antique photograph of a stagecoach showed at least fourteen people had boarded: Four tiers of passengers, three abreast, were seated on the outside. The photo revealed, as much as anything I had ever seen, the daring tenacity of the people who came here in years past. And despite what one might surmise on seeing the photograph in the parlor, the people who came to the Lincklaen in the nineteenth century were a genteel lot compared to some of the patrons of other inns (see Old Drover's Inn). In fact, Cazenovia became a summer resort for sophisticated New Yorkers and Philadelphians who built impressive summer homes along main street.

Upstairs the rooms are clean and practical, and I like their conservative, consistent nature. My favorites are on the third floor—Suite 304 overlooks the town, and 320, in the back, is small, but it certainly works for me.

Downstairs in the Seven Steps Tavern, jazz is performed every Friday night. In January through March banjo music fills the tavern on Saturday night. The woodwork has been initialed by local college students, and painted mu-

rals of local scenes line the wall.

You're likely to meet a wide mix of people here since the inn is conveniently located for visiting New York's only gaming casino (south of Syracuse) and a very large antiques show, held each August. It is also near cross-country and downhill skiing and, in summer, horseback riding along the forests and hillsides.

Have you noticed that pretty towns have historic inns?

How to get there: From I–81 take exit 15 (LaFayette) and proceed east on Route 20 for 17 miles into Cazenovia. Inn is in center of town on north side of street.

Innkeepers: Elizabeth Whiting and the Tobin Family
Address/Telephone: 79 Albany Street; (315) 655–3461, fax (315) 655–5443
Rooms: 18, including 5 suites; all with private bath, air conditioning, telephone, television. Pets allowed. No smoking inn.
Rates: $99 to $140, double occupancy, continental breakfast and afternoon tea. Request special winter packages.
Open: All year.
Facilities and activities: Dinner Wednesday–Sunday (entrees $17 to $24); lunch Wednesday–Saturday; Sunday brunch (entrees $15 to $18). Call in winter. Tavern. Nearby: Toggenburg ski area in Fabius, Chittenango Falls State Park, Labrador ski area in Truxton, horseback riding and cross-country skiing in Highland Forest, Turning Stone Gambling Casino. Seasonal: Winter Festival, Lorenzo Carriage Driving Competition, antiques fair in Madison, Antique Franklin Car Meet, and Stone Quarry Hill Art Park.
Business travel: Telephone in room; desk in 5 rooms; fax machine available; conference room.

The Friends Lake Inn
CHESTERTOWN, NEW YORK 12817

The counterpoint to a day of skiing at Gore Mountain is an evening at Friends Lake Inn. The firewood is stacked in a large wooden basket, parlor games lie upon the wooden benches that frame the sturdy brick fireplace, a VCR is ready for use. Afghans lie on the couch and chair, and a Scrabble board is spread across a small oak table. There's a tone of easy comfort. The long parlor is a cheery place to be with friends. The inn is warmly trimmed in the original chestnut woodwork with low ceilings. There's an outdoor patio that provides a pretty setting on a summer's evening.

To reach the lake you walk across the road and down a lane and into the shade of tall pine trees, where a canoe awaits your pleasure. There's a refreshing scent from the trees and the carpet of pine needles. You can read a book, strum a guitar, or bring a blanket, and the two of you can simply lie back and do nothing for a change.

During the winter you can cross-country ski into the mountainous woods behind the inn.

The rooms are carpeted, and larger rooms on the third floor have Jacuzzis. You'll find Waverly fabrics used in the curtains and spreads. In the hallways are modern pastels in soft, subtle shades, sketched by a friend of the innkeepers. The same artist did the painting in the bar, where the colors are deep and passionate.

Sharon was a civil engineer before she restored and opened the inn. She says there are similarities between running an inn and building a highway.

You can request special packages before you come. One includes lift tickets to Gore Mountain; other packages are for golfing, bicycling, and rafting; during the summer a mystery weekend might motivate the sleuth in you. The active crowd comes here: the hikers, the cross-country skiers, the outdoor enthusiasts who after a busy day seek a good meal in pretty surroundings.

The dinner menu tantalizes. You might have smoked chicken coated with maple horseradish sauce or the filet of beef coated with freshly ground peppercorns, flambéed tableside and smothered in a three-peppercorn demi-

glace. My dessert was a multilayered chocolate-raspberry torte, thick and rich.

Sharon has added a Cruvinet system (wine by the glass) to the tavern, and there's also a wine-cellar tasting room. It's a nice touch for her inn, which has won an "Ambience" award for dining as well as the coveted *Wine Spectator* Best of Excellence award.

Zach and Jake, blond Labs, often cajole guests into a friendly tug-of-war with a favorite sock.

How to get there: From I–87, take exit 25 and go west on Route 8 for 2 miles; turn left on Friends Lake Road and go 2 miles to the inn.

Innkeeper: Sharon Taylor

Address/Telephone: Friends Lake Road; (518) 494–4751, fax (518) 494–4616

Rooms: 14, including 8 suites; all with private bath, 5 with Jacuzzi.

Rates: $155 to $225, double occupancy, MAP; $120 to $190, EPB. Midweek promotions for rafting, Nordic skiing, and gourmet weekends. Request EPB and package rates. Eighteen percent meal gratuity added. Two-night minimum weekends.

Open: All year.

Facilities and activities: Dinner and breakfast daily, lunch sometimes served in winter. Lake-view bar, lake access across the road, Sunfish, canoe, 30 kilometers of groomed cross-country and hiking trails behind inn, outdoor hot tub. Nearby: Gore Mountain (18 miles), horseback riding, white-water rafting.

Recommended Country Inns® Travelers' Club Benefit: Stay 2 nights, get third night free, excluding saturday evenings.

$\mathscr{A}$sa Ransom House
CLARENCE, NEW YORK 14031

On Main Street in Clarence, you turn in at the red railing for some really fine food and a handsome inn named for Asa Ransom, the founder. You'll marvel at the size of Asa's original inn that warmed travelers around the hearth. The little taproom must have been very reassuring after a few days in the wilderness. It still is.

The library, with a cozy fireplace, is just the right size for reading or visiting. An unfinished jigsaw puzzle awaits your attention, or you may have a casual browse through the Sunshine Square gift shop off the library. Your frame of mind can't be other than relaxed and receptive in this warm inn.

Upstairs the rooms are furnished stylishly in

Early American. One has marvelous American bald eagles stenciled around the ceiling. Each room has good reading lamps and sparkles with cleanliness. King- and queen-sized beds are available. Judy, who has a degree in fine arts, is the tasteful force behind these American beauties. Most have fireplaces and private balconies.

The area is rich with activities, which begin for many travelers at Niagara Falls. Bob gives firsthand advice on cultural events and wineries. Fall through spring he holds occasional wine tastings presented by local wineries. He's an articulate source for back-roads routes to the local sites and a rail fan who knows the best train rides in the United States and Canada. A good time to visit with him is at breakfast, when he serves hot baked soufflés deliciously made with smoked corned beef and cheese.

On the menu the wines are rated from 0 to 7, for dryness to sweetness. Very helpful. But before dinner you might try one of the taproom's special drinks, like the rum and coconut or non-alcoholic sparkling cider.

Dinner is delicious. Take your time with the menu. Children read theirs from the apron of a Raggedy Ann doll or the sail of a boat. Judy came up with that innovation. She also designed the attractive water bottle at each table. The soup arrives in a hot bucket and is ladled out to suit your appetite. Then walnut-spice muffins and breads arrive with three flavors of butter, followed by salmon pie, a rich savory dish perfectly seasoned. There are vegetarian selections and a salmon steak baked in puff pastry served with hollandaise; or perhaps you'd like a thick, juicy cut of prime rib. After I had leisurely finished, the divinely rich walnut pie came with coffee in a silver pot.

In your room are radio cassette tapes. You can listen to "The Shadow," "Fibber Magee and Molly," and others.

I'd like to move this inn to my neighborhood.

How to get there: From I–290 take exit Route 5 to Clarence. The inn is on the right in the village limits, 1 block before the park. Fly-in: Buffalo International Airport. Amtrak: will pick up.

Innkeepers: Bob and Judy Lenz

Address/Telephone: 10529 Main Street; (716) 759–2315, fax (716) 759–2791

Rooms: 9, including 3 suites; all with private bath, air conditioning, telephone, and television, 7 with fireplace, 5 with balcony. Wheelchair accessible. No smoking inn.

Rates: $150 to $200, Sunday–Thursday, MAP; $90 to $150, Sunday–Thursday, EPB; Saturday MAP *only,* $200 to $270; all double occupancy; less for single occupancy.

Open: Closed January 2 through early February, Christmas, occasional holy days, and every Friday. Saturday dinner served only to houseguests.

Facilities and activities: Lunch on Wednesday; tea on Thursday afternoon; reservations appreciated. Taproom, gift shop. Nearby: Niagara Falls (28 miles), Artpark in Lewiston, opera in Lancaster, antiquing, golf, sports, winery tours.

Creekside Bed & Breakfast
COOPERSTOWN, NEW YORK 13326

"Let's do *Bohème*," Gwen said, "I have the costumes" (mostly in her size, eight). Ever since Gwen and Fred first met in a choral group twenty-five years ago, they've sung in key together. They have sung in more than 200 operatic performances and are founders of Glimmerglass Opera.

Walk up the stairs between photographs of their performances and friends. One (even a bishop wouldn't blush) is Gwen as a *Playboy* playmate of the month. Fred was a Catholic priest before they met; they shared much in common—they loved opera and people, and soon each other. Request the videotapes of

their performances to play on the VCR. Someone should write an opera of their lives. It's certainly been as dramatic as some of their performances.

Gwen is a nurturer. Five minutes after you've met, you're old friends. Gwen and Fred are activists, doers, accomplishers. Now they are turning their attentions toward other projects, but always their inn is the attention getter.

Although he just retired from the state university, where he was a dean, Fred continues to perform at Glimmerglass. He is the morning chef. While he mixes up scrambled eggs with herbs, makes waffles, or prepares low-cholesterol fare, everyone visits over fresh coffee. Fred and Gwen like nothing better than getting a good bunch together to roam over the world in conversation and laughter.

This isn't a formal or fussy inn. There's shag carpeting in the large common room—from here you see the tables and umbrellas on the patio in summer. The style varies from room to room, and you always feel at home. You can head down to the creek and float in the pool beneath the bridge, relax on the dock that swings out over the water in summer, just take a blanket and lie on the grass, or sit on the deck and catch up on being lazy for a change. In the music room are a piano and books on music if you feel a melody sweep over you. The bridal suite is dramatic in whites and laces as the sun streams in through the patio doors and across the 18x22-foot private living room with oak floor, crystal chandelier, Aubusson

rug, and hand-tufted leather sofa. The creekside cottage also has a private living room, deck, and canopied queen-sized bed.

It's said that the Indians wintered their horses in this valley. The lawn covered with snow and multiple trees is especially pretty at Christmas. If you come during summer, you might see a blue heron fishing along the creekside as you're dressing for the evening performances at Glimmerglass. Who knows, your hosts might even be performing.

How to get there: From Cooperstown go south (past Pepper Mill Restaurant) and turn right on County Route 26, continue to Fork Shop Road, and turn left to the inn on the left. From I–88, take 28 North (exit 17), pass Smith Ford, and take the first left on County Road 26; turn left on Fork Shop.

Innkeepers: Fred and Gwen Ermlich
Address/Telephone: Fork Shop Road (mailing address: R.D. 1, Box 206); (607) 547–8203
E-mail: fermlich@acl.com
Rooms: 2, plus 2 suites and 1 summer cottage for 2; all with private bath, cable television, HBO, and air conditioning. No smoking inn.
Rates: $70 to $125, double occupancy, EPB. Two-night minimum summer weekends.
Open: All year.
Facilities and activities: On 5 acres with a creek. Nearby: restaurants (5-minute drive), Glimmerglass Opera; Cooperstown with Baseball Hall of Fame, James Fenimore Cooper House, Farmers' Museum, Corvette Museum.

$\mathcal{R}$osewood Inn
CORNING, NEW YORK 14830

It was a serendipitous meeting among guests gathered about the blazing fire, with the scent of hot chocolate-chip cookies filling the air. We bounced ideas and experiences around like we were old chums. We touched on everything from the artists who have made Corning and its glass world famous to the national zeitgeist. The camaraderie we were experiencing made the Rosewood Inn seem like a modern-day salon.

Stewart encouraged us all toward the tea and reminded everyone that another batch of cookies was in the oven, while Suzanne alternately nudged the conversation or sat back and listened.

"What hippopotamus?" she once teased when a guest asked about the abundance of hip-

pos. We had seen purple, blue, pink, and a couple of slate gray ones around the inn. Eventually the hippo story came, as did so many others. The hippos were originally purchased by the Sanderses on their various travels. As the collection grew, their guests started sending interesting examples as well. Today there are more than 200 little hippos peeking out from shelves and bookcases and occupying prominent positions on tabletops.

This little glassmaking mecca has a population of only 13,000, yet Corning's international fame draws the finest artists, who either live here or come for lectures. The Corning Glass Museum is renowned not only for its depth but for its breadth—26,000 objects on display span the history of glass since 1500 B.C. Less known, say Stewart and Suzanne, is the Rockwell Museum, with its collection of American Western Art and 2,000 pieces of Steuben glass.

The shop-filled streets and easy drive to the nearby Finger Lakes vineyards also explain why this is the third most popular place to visit in New York State. It's the combination of small town, city museums, great restaurants, and an inn that you'd return to regardless of location. The Rosewood is located in a quiet neighborhood that's within walking distance of the heart of town.

Stewart is a chef by avocation; he prepares fresh fruits, lovely omelets, heavenly French toast, homemade breads, and fresh juices. Suzanne, meanwhile, sets an elaborate centerpiece for the breakfast meal, and everyone's place

has a nameplate for social ease.

While the inn's exterior is English Tudor, the interior is furnished with antiques and decorated with romantic Victorian collectibles. Choose from Eastlake or queen-sized canopy beds in rooms that are named for renowned personages, such as Mark Twain, Frederick Carder Steuben, and Lewis Carroll.

The mix of pleasures that compose Corning and the Rosewood is in your best interest. The inn is addictive, but this addiction is a happy, healthy one that your physician would recommend. You might even meet her here.

How to get there: From Route 17 take exit 46 into Corning and turn south on Chemung Street. Go 1 block, turn right onto East First Street, proceed to 134 on south side of street.

Innkeepers: Stewart and Suzanne Sanders
Address/Telephone: 134 East First Street; (607) 962–3253
Rooms: 7, including 2 suites; all with private bath and air conditioning, 2 with telephone and television. No pets but kennel nearby. No smoking inn.
Rates: $80 to $125, double occupancy, EPB plus afternoon tea. Two-night minimum holiday and special-event weekends.
Open: All year.
Facilities and activities: Nearby: Corning Glass Museum, Rockwell Museum of American Western Art, glass shops, National Soaring Museum, Watkins Glen International Race Track, Finger Lakes wineries, golf.

De Bruce Country Inn on the Willowemoc

DE BRUCE, NEW YORK 12758

"An inn along the banks of the Willowemoc" are words of magic to a trout fisherman. "The young men come," says Marilyn, "with a reverence in their eyes." They wish to see where fishing "firsts" occurred, to breathe in all that has happened here. No matter if you've never had a rod in hand. You'll enjoy the view, the hiking, swimming, and cross-country skiing of the Catskills. You'll enjoy reading William Burroughs, the Catskills' turn-of-the-century naturalist, and exploring the region about which he wrote. For contrast you'll enjoy the artwork.

The inn's dark-wood trim frames the cream-colored walls—background to changing art shows. Among them the works of SoHo artists.

Marilyn and Ron are also artists—both painters.

In the parlor is a large granite fireplace. Interesting magazines, neatly catalogued, line the wall. In the basement is a casual tavern where skiers and hikers gather.

Upstairs the rooms have brightly painted brass beds, hand-appliqued spreads, and cotton curtains. Select a room at the back and the sound of the Willowemoc will lull you to sleep.

Dinner might present opportunity for wonderful baked salmon. Or you might dine on a fish you caught yourself, which the chef is happy to prepare. Organic salads, hearty roasts, and homemade breads are served. And if you really did hike 8 miles, a piece of Black Forest cheesecake can be your delicious and memorable reward.

Over a full country breakfast, you can watch the sun rise over Bald Mountain. You can identify the New York birds. Marilyn keeps books readily available. You're likely to see scarlet tanagers, purple finches, red-winged blackbirds, cedar waxwings, and others. "The birds we knew as children are still here," comments Marilyn. Afterward take a walk down to the pond, out to the Willowemoc, or up a woodland trail.

How to get there: From Route 17, exit 96 (Livingston Manor); turn left and proceed east 4 miles on De Bruce Road to the inn on the right.

Innkeepers: Ron and Marilyn Lusker
Address/Telephone: De Bruce Road (mailing address: R.D. 1, Box 286A); (914) 439–3900
Rooms: 15; all with private bath. Pets allowed at innkeepers' discretion.
Rates: $150 to $175, double occupancy, MAP; single, $15 additional. Twenty-two percent tax and gratuity. No credit cards.
Open: All year. Mid-December to April: group lodging.
Facilities and activities: Dinner served by reservation, tavern, small outdoor swimming pool, pond, Willowemoc Creek, hiking, cross-country skiing, 50 acres. Nearby: state park 5 miles, with swimming, boating, fishing, hiking.

O ld Drovers Inn
DOVER PLAINS, NEW YORK 12522

Do you have plans for Valentine's Day? Perhaps, like Alice and Kemper, you'll purchase your favorite inn on the most romantic day of the year. Before this venerable place became theirs, they used to appear on the doorstep when the need for R&R (repose and romance) touched them. Now they make Old Drovers glow with nurturing.

If this building, which dates from 1750, could talk, it would heave a sigh of relief and say thank you for restoring my authentic old beauty, for decorating my windows with colorful chintz, for placing down-filled couches in my cozy parlors, for bringing people back to my hearth.

The Old Drovers is unique in the mid-Atlantic for its authentic character; you intuit a veritable sense of the past. The floors angle slightly and sometimes creak to the step as you descend to the romantic Old Tap Room. The "shell" cabinet in the second-floor library has its mate in the Metropolitan Museum of Art.

In the eighteenth century the drovers herding cattle into New York City would stop here with their herds for watering. "Only," explained Alice, pointing out the tavern sign that reads DROVERS AND ANKLEBEATERS, "the drovers were actually gentry. They came ahead of the anklebeaters, who performed the cattle-driving work."

This once-rowdy place has settled down. The toughest animals you'll find are Alice's three Yorkies, Gordon Bennett, Goodness Gracious, and Jedediah, who greet everyone as if they were born to hospitality.

Before dinner we visited in the library with a glass of wine (the inn won the *Wine Spectator* Award of Excellence), then descended the stairway to dinner. In the candlelight of the star-patterned hurricane lamps we perused the chalkboard menu. Even before a drink arrived, the deviled eggs came with fresh condiments. Some traditions have remained the same here since 1937, like the double drinks, the condiments and hickory salt, and the turkey hash (healthy, said Alice). I was intrigued, however, by a potato-crusted salmon with vinaigrette and cilantro that was simultaneously moist and crisp; it got superior marks. The chef knows his business. For dessert we ate the naughty but divine Key lime pie.

Our room that night had a double barrel-vaulted ceiling and a fireplace, where we nestled up in the cozy chintz chairs. There were robes in the closet, satin coverlets on the firm beds, and hooked rugs on the floors. And—need I say?—there's nothing historic about the modern bathrooms. Or the inn's membership in *Relais et Châteaux*.

On weekends the chef prepares a full breakfast; midweek there's a fine homemade granola and freshly squeezed juice. The coffee is served in great oversized cups; we filled ours and meandered into the parlor, where the finches were chirping. We admired the rolltop desk and the wall mural painted by Edward Paine.

Soon there will be more of Old Drovers to enjoy, as construction is scheduled to begin on five cottages.

How to get there: From New York City take I–684 to Brewster, then take Route 22 north. On Route 22 a sign for the inn is 3 miles south of Dover Plains. Turn east and drive ½ mile. Inn is on the right; guests park on south side and enter through the porch.

Innkeepers: Alice Pitcher and Kemper Peacock

Address/Telephone: Old Route 22; (914) 832–9311, fax (914) 832–6356

Rooms: 4; all with private bath and air conditioning, 3 with fireplace. Pets by prior approval.

Rates: $320 to $395, weekends per couple, MAP; $150 to $230, double occupancy, midweek, continental breakfast. Two-night minimum if Saturday included.

Open: All year, except two weeks in January.

Facilities and activities: On 12 acres. Dinner Thursday through Tuesday; Saturday, Sunday, and holidays served from noon (entrees: $17 to $35). Nearby: Hyde Park, golf courses, horseback riding, antiquing, country drives, fairs and festivals.

Centennial House
EAST HAMPTON, NEW YORK 11937

Let's confide a moment. Do you need pampering? Do you crave a gracious setting and a kind experience? And to amble down streets of privet hedges to the beach, catching the glint of the sun-struck leaves on a warm afternoon? Has the time come to step off life's carousel and return to tea in the parlor and a chat with kindly innkeepers?

David and Harry have completely restored the house in an irresistible manner. They saved the wide-plank pine flooring, added the appropriate amenities, then applied drapes of Scalamandre silks and selected antiques, which blend with furnishings of compatible ages and styles.

When we opened the door to our room, we found a queen-sized four-poster bed, a couch, and a coffee table upon which a tray containing sherry and scrumptious chocolate truffles was placed. In the bath was a lovely sesame-seed oil, which made oil-lovers out of us. Each room, you'll find, is unique. It's down-to-earth luxury.

If you could wrap the parlor up and take it home, you would. Two sitting areas create berths for conversing, for lounging, for reading. The innkeepers provide interesting reading materials—magazines, art, fiction, music, travel—that reveal a curiosity for the world and a love of beauty. A crystal carafe of sherry sits on a sideboard.

If you favor the small, discreet places in the world where plush comforts and good stories abound, then Centennial House will suit you.

Those who like to learn about the Hamptons can meet others and broaden their experience around the breakfast table. David specializes in buttermilk pancakes so rich you don't need to lace them with butter and in French toast that he learned to make from childhood family recipes. He's as quick to share his recipes as he is his ideas and insights on life in the Hamptons.

Were I at Centennial House at this moment, I'd be in either of two places: In summer I'd be stretched alongside the swimming pool, petting Louie and Edwinna (Lhasa apsos of a friendly disposition), admiring the clear skies and stark green of the trees and privet hedge; in win-

ter I'd be in the parlor near the gas fireplace, drinking hot tea and reading, occasionally looking up to see who comes and goes, falling into conversation and mostly savoring the moment.

"Fall," admits David, "is my favorite season. The lighting, the weather, the uncrowded beach, the Hamptons—everything has a beauty that touches the soul."

How to get there: Easily reached by jitney from New York City. Driving, take Route 27 into East Hampton. As you enter the village, the inn is on the right before the left turn, marked by a small sign.

Innkeepers: David Oxford and Harry Chancey; Bernadette Meade, manager
Address/Telephone: 13 Woods Lane; (516) 324–9414, fax (516) 324–0493
Rooms: 6, including 1 cottage (cottage available for seasonal rentals only); all with private bath, air conditioning, and telephone, 5 with television, 1 with fireplace and kitchen. No smoking inn.
Rates: $125 to $375, double occupancy, EPB. Two-night minimum, more on holidays. Request off-season rates.
Open: All year.
Facilities and activities: Swimming pool, exercise room, gardens, croquet. Nearby: restaurants, ocean beach, shopping, antiquing, village touring, maritime and local history museums.
Recommended Country Inns® Travelers' Club Benefit: Stay one night, get 50 percent discount on second night, November–March, excluding holidays.

The Huntting Inn
EAST HAMPTON, NEW YORK 11937

The warm woody tones of the oak wainscoting reflect the evening lights. Little Tiffany and unusual ornate lamps highlight small oak tables in front of plush green sofas. Oak mirrors, no two alike, hang on the wall opposite the oak bar. You might order wine that has been aged in oak barrels and settle into an oak booth to savor its flavor.

"There are twelve Palm Restaurants across the country," explains the raven-haired innkeeper, Linda Calder, "all interconnected through family. The first opened in 1920 in New York City." One family member decorated the tavern and dining room. Linda decorated the individual rooms, which she is constantly redecorating as if they weren't already fine. Several have bold cotton chintz on the walls, wicker, antiques, and fresh flowers in the hallways. They are soothing rooms. Linda adds her cheerfulness to these already bright surroundings. She also points to the safety features and sprinkler system throughout.

A white picket fence encircles the inn. Follow the path under the trees out to the English garden. In summertime the butterflies bounce between the flowers. There's a profusion of hollyhocks, baby's breath, daisies, and lilies. If you arrive in the cool of the early morning while the dew is on the grass, you can pull up a cushiony lawn chair and settle back with a cup of coffee and a newspaper. But the day hours are for the beach. Ask Linda for a beach pass.

Toward evening the candles are lit downstairs. Maybe you have plans to walk up the street for a movie after dinner. You're starved after a long walk on the beach and an invigorating day of sun and sand between the toes. You're glad you skipped lunch.

Say "The Palm," and it stimulates images of large thick cuts of steak, five veal dishes, and three- or five-pound lobsters along with handsome portions of fresh salads, potatoes, clams casino, shrimp cocktail, and fresh pastas. You can order a sixteen- or twenty-two-ounce prime rib that melts in your mouth. Gigi's Salad is unusual: It has no lettuce; instead, there's a panorama of string beans, onions, bacon bits, tomatoes, palmettos, and anchovies. Think hearty servings and you're in the right ball park.

The Hedges, a sister inn located 1 mile away on Main Street, is a handsome, historical home with a restaurant and grill room. You enter a summery foyer; to the right is a French-country breakfast room. In the evening you can sit on the stone patio and have dinner. In the winter you can cuddle beside the fire. The inn is within walking distance of the ocean.

We arrived for the annual December Christmas Inn and House tour, a charity event, and went inside The Hedges Inn for hot cider and doughnuts. Later a buffet lunch was served at the Palm Restaurant. Ask Linda for information about the tour. It's a wonderful time to visit the Hamptons.

How to get there: From New York City take I–495 east to exit 70. Take County Road 110 to Route 27. Follow Route 27 into East Hampton to where it merges with Main Street. The inn is at 94 Main, on the right side past the Presbyterian Church and Guild Hall Theater. Watch for the white picket fence. Fly-in: East Hampton Airport.

Innkeeper: Linda Calder

Address/Telephone: 94 Main Street; (516) 324–0410, fax (516) 324–8751

Rooms: 20, including 2 suites; all with private bath, air conditioning, telephone, and television, 1 with Jacuzzi.

Rates: $125 to $250, double occupancy, continental breakfast. Three-night minimum stay July 4 through Labor Day; two-night minimum rest of year. Request special package rates.

Open: All year.

Facilities and activities: Dinner nightly April–October; Thursday–Sunday November–March, but please confirm (entrees $20 to $35). Tavern. Nearby: beach, tennis privileges, golf, charter fishing, boating, swimming, sailboarding, bicycling, horseback riding, shopping, Guild Hall Theater, museums.

Business travel: Desk in 12 rooms; fax available; meeting room.

The Maidstone Arms
EAST HAMPTON, NEW YORK 11937

The ambience is that of a small European hotel with a kind staff trained in straightforward American good manners. They insisted we see as many rooms as possible since there have been so many changes since a major renovation. We saw delicate, floral wallpapers, and the once heavy antique pieces had been exchanged for more delicate ones. I've always preferred the rooms in the back that overlook the garden at The Maidstone and still recommend them. The more expensive rooms are my favorites. Nothing is overstated or fussy, and each is perfectly comfortable.

The pace here is just right, relaxed and unhurried. On a summer afternoon the inn might even be temporarily deserted, with everyone off to the beach or shopping downtown. In winter the dining room and its fireplace beckon, though sooner or later you'll be drawn to a seat in the Water Room, from which the town pond is visible through the snow. Make a point of visiting the original pondside graveyard where Lion Gardiner is buried. Gardiner traded with Indians for much of the land that shaped this part of Long Island.

The Water Room has new tartan seat coverings and window trims. This is where a continental breakfast of muffins, croissants, and freshly squeezed orange juice is served. For us visiting over breakfast while perusing the *Times* at The Maidstone has become a venerated tradition.

At dinnertime we discovered that the coat requirement that had once plagued my companion had been eliminated entirely, although many other guests still dressed quite formally. In the dining room crisply pressed white damask tablecloths were freshly laid. We'd come on a winter evening when a fixed-price, four-course menu was offered, as happens on occasion. Wine drinkers can choose from an extensive wine list including as many as sixteen Chardonnays. My companion began with the celery and fennel bisque. I ordered a Portobello mushroom tart with walnut mascarpone, which mingled amicably with a sapid Chardonnay. I then decided on the braised salmon with leeks and parsnip puree, while he chose a seared filet mignon with wild mushrooms and potato gratin. For dessert I soon dipped into a light, crisp crème brûlée.

While dining one often doesn't think about what the kitchen looks like, but that's where the inn's renovation began. The change is apparent when your dishes reach the table. Such a renovation draws the attention of a fine chef. If you build a proper working space, you attract someone with serious talents and experience.

East Hampton was originally named Maidstone by the settlers who arrived here in the early 1600s from Maidstone, England. The inn dates from 1740. It now serves three meals a day, like a traditional New England inn. But then, Long Island was originally part of Connecticut and New England, and in many ways it still does look northward to its regional roots in architecture and seafaring history. Why not also in innkeeping?

How to get there: From I-495 east take Route 27 east to East Hampton (where 27 intersects Main Street and turns left following first traffic light). The inn is a short distance on the left at 207 Main Street after left turn.

Innkeeper: Christophe Bergen; Coke Anne Saunders, proprietor
Address/Telephone: 207 Main Street; (516) 324–5006, fax (516) 324–5037
Rooms: 19, including 3 suites and 3 cottages; all with air conditioning, private bath, television, and telephone, suites with fireplace. No smoking except in Water Room.
Rates: $165 to $325, double occupancy, continental breakfast. Three-night minimum summer weekends and holidays; 2-night minimum weekends rest of year.
Open: All year.
Facilities and activities: Full breakfast, lunch, and dinner. Nearby: Atlantic Ocean (walking distance), village shops, museums, movie theater, bicycling, water sports, and boating.
Business travel: Desk in 7 rooms; fax and copy machines available; small conference room.

1770 House
EAST HAMPTON, NEW YORK 11937

Wendy (Perle) Van Deusen, her husband Burt, and her brother ans sister-in-law Adam and Joi Perle are carrying on the grand tradition started by their parents Mim and Sid Perle in the late 1970s. This picture-perfect, white-clapboard inn along a tree-shaded street in a lovely village is filled with the traditions, family mementos, and antiques that are cherished by their guests. Wendy has been the chef since the mid-1980s, and her menu continues to bring raves.

This is "a timely inn." Everywhere you look are visuals. Clocks, ornate French grandfathers', beautifully carved American timepieces, mantel clocks, and decorative clocks that merge into a soft tick-tocking in the dining room.

The original post office of East Hampton forms one part of the small inn office. There are lovely stained-glass windows that flash red and gold jewels across dining-room tables and a coat of arms over the dining-room fireplace mantel. The cozy library is paneled in fruitwood. Its fireplace casts a warm glow across the tiny bar and the shell corner cabinet filled with fine porcelain.

Each of the guest rooms is uniquely decorated with antiques; most have canopy beds. Number 2 is as spacious and as snug as a country hideaway can be. Pretty chairs are pulled up in front of a fireplace in a paneled wall—just the spot to sip a glass of port after dinner and strategize about the following day's activities, at least until the inviting canopy bed beckons. Number 3 has an antique highboy and canopy bed. The upstairs rooms are reached along a circuitous hallway that leads past a hall fireplace and a divided bench. The cottage in back offers privacy and seclusion.

At dinnertime you might select filet mignon with a perfectly blended sauce Diane, or gumbo filled with tender jumbo shrimp and boned breast of chicken. The fresh herbs are grown outside the kitchen door.

For dessert Wendy might serve a raspberry mousse sprinkled with fresh rosebuds, macadamia nut pie, or Chocolate Amaretto Rave that's been well named. The desserts are as expertly prepared as everything else. The evening's atmosphere is set by the rose medallion china, tall candles in etched hurricanes, cranberry glass, clocks, and classical music softly playing in the background.

How to get there: From I–495 East take exit 70. Take County Road 110 to Route 27. Follow Route 27 into East Hampton. The inn is past the Village Pond on the left at 143 Main Street. Fly-in: East Hampton Airport.

Innkeepers: Wendy and Burt Van Deusen; Adam and Joi Perle
Address/Telephone: 143 Main Street; (516) 324–1770, fax (516) 324–3504
Rooms: 8, including 1 cottage; all with private bath, telephone, and air conditioning, 3 with fireplace, 1 with television. No smoking inn.
Rates: $120 to $250, double occupancy, EPB. Lower rates in winter. Three-night minimum July–August and holiday weekends, 2-night minimum other weekends.
Open: All year.
Facilities and activities: Restaurant open Thursday–Sunday summertime, Friday–Saturday other seasons (fixed-price menu, $32 for 4 courses). Please call to confirm. Thanksgiving and New Year's dinners served. Nearby: beach, bicycling, boating, swimming, ice skating, museums, Guild Hall Theater and Art Gallery, antiques shops, boutiques, restaurants of East Hampton.

The White Inn

FREDONIA, NEW YORK 14063

Chautauqua County's Fredonia was the mythical town in the Marx brothers movie *Duck Soup*, and the Marx brothers played here during their touring days. It's an all-American village, site of the first Woman's Christian Temperance Union, the first Grange, and the first natural gas well in the country. Keeping within the classic American tradition, Duncan Hines visited here and gave The White Inn his seal of approval.

Since my first visit I've enjoyed watching the continuous improvements and artistic changes. The panache and diversity of rooms are impressive. In Number 265, the white-and-peach curtains have 30 yards of fabric at each window. You find rooms with elaborate antiques,

like the Eastlake in 314 and the rare queen-sized Victorian bed in the Lincoln Suite. The spacious Presidential Suite has a reading area and a whirlpool bath. One room has contemporary pine furniture and handsome tailored spreads, for a modern country look. Many have sitting areas, desks, and love seats. Kathleen's latest creation is the Lilac Room, so now you may select according to your mood. She's also coordinated the mural paintings of local scenes above the room doors by Fredonia artist Peggy Kurtz.

The area is beautiful, with vineyards and gently rolling farmlands. The inn is 3 miles from the shore of Lake Erie. You're thirty minutes from Chautauqua Institute for summer entertainment. The Lake Chautauqua ferry will carry you to a day of lectures or an evening concert. The wineries begin in Fredonia and pepper the countryside; you'll find antiquing, a fine country wool shop, villages, a rodeo, and Amish country. In the early evening you might take Kathleen's architectural map of Fredonia and take a walk along the tree-lined streets before dinner. You can stop in the inn's gift shop, located in the carriage house behind the inn.

The inn's chef prepares an excellent range of dishes. I was delighted with my poached Norwegian salmon topped with sautéed julienne vegetables and *beurre blanc* sauce. Everyone receives a salad and hot baked yeast rolls and breads. The chef has created equally interesting entrees with reduced cholesterol and calories. Desserts include the award-winning white-chocolate mousse and Tollhouse pie. When restaurateurs go out to dinner, this is where they come.

One lazy afternoon, as I lingered over a hot tea on the 100-foot veranda, I saw the members of the Shakespeare Society leaving the inn after their meeting. There was a smart spring in their steps, which I interpreted as inspiration derived from hearing Shakespeare in this elegant setting.

How to get there: Take Dunkirk-Fredonia exit (59) from I–90. Go left on Route 60 south. Turn right onto Route 20 west (Main Street). The inn is located on Route 20, Main Street, Fredonia.

Innkeepers: Robert Contiguglia and Kathleen Dennison

Address/Telephone: 52 East Main Street; (716) 672–2103, fax (716) 672–2107

Rooms: 23, including 11 suites; all with private bath, television, and telephone, 2 with fireplace, 2 with Jacuzzi. Designated no smoking rooms.

Rates: $59 to $179, double occupancy, EPB. Rollaway, $10. Two-night minimum college weekends.

Open: All year.

Facilities and activities: Lunch, dinner (dinner $10 to $20 with salad), tavern, gift shop. Nearby: Lake Erie, winery tours, antiquing, skiing, Chautauqua Institution, Amish country, music and cultural events of university.

Business travel: Telephone in rooms; desk in 17 rooms; copy machine and fax available; conference space.

Recommended Country Inns® Travelers' Club Benefit: 10 percent discount, Monday–Thursday.

The Bird & Bottle Inn
GARRISON, NEW YORK 10524

New York getting to you? Need out for the weekend?

The Bird & Bottle is where one satiates appetites, where New Yorkers retreat for privacy, where one ventures for Hudson River touring, and where one comes for two- and three-hour-long dinners beside the fire in a historic inn dating from 1761.

Sitting here dining, I imagined the Albany stagecoach driver galloping up to Warren's Tavern (as it was known back then) for fresh horses, the passengers tumbling out and into the inn for good hot food, the staff bustling to serve them in a ruckus while the horses are changed—then the driver shouts the call for New York, everyone re-

boards, and the creaking of wood and leather and the thudding of hooves against the ground are heard way on up the hill.

The pub, known as the Drinking Room, is framed in wood. A tall man bends down to enter and soon finds a seat near the fire and casts his eyes about the interesting setting.

The rooms are charming and romantic, with fireplaces where you may burn real wood—a rarity in inns today.

The Beverly Robinson Suite is decorated in a peach-and-beige damask that drapes across the canopy bed. Oriental rugs cover the pine floors, and there's a little balcony overlooking the entrance. For the ultimate in privacy, the Nelson

Cottage is tucked away amid the gardens. Its carved canopy bed is festooned in shades of pink and cream, and it has a fireplace.

There are six acres in which to walk, but those of is with a romantic streak will head for the little bridge that crosses the tumbling brook or strike out to explore the remnants of the old stone gristmill.

Every Thanksgiving Day guests arrive all dressed up ready to carve a beautifully roasted turkey at their private table without having lifted so much as a spoon in effort. This has become a traditional feast day at The Bird & Bottle, and an entire turkey is served to parties of six or more. Following dinner the leftovers are individually wrapped for you to carry home. This cozy setting is a delicious way to celebrate a holiday.

The breads here are magnificent; light, white yeast breads and a deeply flavored pumpkin bread (made with fresh pumpkin); you try not to eat too many of these to save your appetite. The pewter serviceware fits with the inn's era. One evening I selected the specials—a spicy dilled tomato soup followed by grilled vegetables served in puff pastry, which created a pleasurable tingling sensation in my mouth. Next a calming, light grapefruit sorbet. Then I sliced into thick scallops filled with slivers of smoked salmon.

The temperature dipped to below freezing that night. But my room was warm, the way I like it, and a fire was laid when I returned from dinner. A note on the bureau asked me to drip the water, and when that was finished, I felt I had done my part to help the inn through the chilly night. Settled into the Emily Warren room, I heard noises—the floor creaking from someone's footsteps, passing voices—then all fell asleep, soundly asleep.

How to get there: From Bear Mountain Bridge take Route 9D north 4½ miles; then take Route 403 to Route 9. Go 4 miles to the inn, which is on the right, well, well off the road.

Innkeeper: Ira Boyer

Address/Telephone: Old Albany Post Road, Route 9; (914) 424–3000 or (914) 424–3283

E-mail: birdbottle@aol.com

Rooms: 4, including 1 suite and 1 cottage; all with private bath, working fireplace, and air conditioning. Limited smoking inn.

Rates: $210 to $240, double occupancy, EPB and dinner credit of $75 per person, plus 12 percent service charge and tax. Two-night minimum weekends.

Open: All year.

Facilities and activities: Dinner Wednesday–Sunday (average $50 fixed price for 4-course dinner exclusive of wine), Sunday brunch, call regarding lunch; pub. Nearby: village of Cold Spring, Boscobel Mansion, historic Hudson River Museum, Kykuit (Rockefeller estate), wineries, nature center, sailing, biking, hiking, antiquing.

Recommended Country Inns® Travelers' Club Benefit: Stay 2 nights, get third night free, subject to availability.

$\mathcal{B}$elhurst Castle
GENEVA, NEW YORK 14456

Belhurst Castle offers privacy, interesting surroundings, and a view of beautiful Seneca Lake.

The inn was built in 1810 by an expansive millionaire. During the 1930s "Red" Dwyer, a local legend, transformed it into a gambling casino. Each of the rooms is named for Belhurst's past owners.

On the way to your room, you may want to see the wine spigot ensconced in marble in the hallway. It's self-serve for guests. You may even have a 2:00 A.M. glass of New York chablis.

The fireplaces throughout the inn, including those in the guest rooms, are masterpieces of craftsmanship. One is surrounded by mosaics.

Others are simply lavish marble. The woodwork gleams; it is polished to a permanent sheen. The rooms have views of the graceful grounds or lake.

One rainy evening we settled in within view of the fire for a fine repast. My companion let me sample his Chef's Trilogie—shrimp, veal, and chicken served with a smooth port wine and lobster sauce. I let him sample my fettuccine with lobster and vegetables, then we sent the dessert cart back minus two fruit tarts. The dinner menu ranges from roast duckling to filet mignon.

Several wineries are within driving distance. You can tour and taste by day and wine and dine by night.

How to get there: From I–90 take Route 14 south to Geneva. Continue south. The inn is on the left, the lake side, of Route 14 on the outskirts of Geneva.

Innkeeper: Duane R. Reeder; Marylin Palmer, manager

Address/Telephone: Route 14 (mailing address: P.O. Box 609); (315) 781–0201, fax same

Rooms: 13, including 2 suites and 2 cottages; all with private bath, air conditioning, telephone, and television, 4 with fireplace, 1 with Jacuzzi. Wheelchair access.

Rates: $95 to $295, May through October; $65 to $225, November through April; double occupancy; continental breakfast. Cot $30 extra.

Open: All year.

Facilities and activities: Lunch and dinner, Monday–Saturday; Sunday brunch; bar. Dock on Seneca Lake in front of inn. Nearby: boating, fishing, waterskiing, sailing, hiking, public golf course, winery tours.

$\mathcal{G}$reenville $\mathcal{A}$rms 1889 $\mathcal{I}$nn
GREENVILLE, NEW YORK 12083

Artists fill the inn on summer evenings. They discuss Cole and Church and the Hudson River painters known for capturing these farmlands and valleys. The artists, who range in ability from beginner to advanced, attend five-day sessions taught by nationally recognized instructors.

Eliot and Tish have seized the opportunity of hosting an impressive range of American artists. (For information on the workshops, request the brochure.) They have also decorated the rooms with well-chosen artwork. You need not be an artist to enjoy the inn.

For the athletically minded the innkeepers provide a cycling map and rental bikes. Or perhaps you'd like to visit a nearby flower market or

the antiques shops of the area. Letitia and Eliot are adept guides.

Eliot and Tish first came to the Greenville Arms, which was built by William Vanderbilt in 1899, on a weekend outing before their children were born. Eliot was a Hudson River boat captain, Letitia a graphic artist. After Anne Marie and Woody were born, they decided to become innkeepers. Eliot's knowledge of the Hudson and other eastern rivers is fascinating. Instead of negotiating barges and ships in hectic waters, he cheerfully serves Tish's apple-buttermilk pancakes in the sunny dining room and navigates the smooth traveling of guests.

Eliot and Tish's Victorian inn has a warm,

old-fashioned ambience. In the entryway delicately trellised woodwork frames the doorways. In the parlor Tish placed a down-stuffed love seat covered in a soft rose chintz. You might request the Bay Window Room or the Ivy Room, with its eighteenth-century French wall console, "grained" to match the wood trim.

On the second floor there's a sitting room, with television and a game table for relaxing.

Dinner in the elegant Vanderbilt Room presents a choice of three or four entrees. Perhaps you'll celebrate with a bottle of wine and the country chicken pâté; then have a baby-lettuce salad composed from the inn's garden (they even have a gardener) and a mixed grill of tournedos, veal medallions, and lamb cutlets served with a black pepper demi-glace or the swordfish with fresh herb butter. Tish's desserts might include her superb homemade ice creams or an irresistible apple tart served with a ginger-caramel sauce. Your waitress for the evening might be daughter Anne Marie, who is also the cordial guest greeter on occasion.

Keep in mind an early return from your explorations. You can cross the inn's small creek to the sparkling backyard swimming pool, which is often tended by Anne Marie's younger brother, Woody, also a hospitable innkeeper.

How to get there: Exit I–87 at 21B (Coxsackie–New Baltimore). Turn left on 9W south and go 2 miles to the traffic light. Turn right on 81 west, go 13 miles to Greenville, then turn left at light on 32S. Inn is on the right. Beware: There are three towns named Greenville in New York. This one is in Green County.

Innkeepers: Eliot and Letitia Dalton
Address/Telephone: Route 32, South Street (mailing address: P.O. Box 659); (518) 966–5219, fax (518) 966–8754
E-mail/URL: ny1889inn@aol.com / http://www.innbook.com
Rooms: 13, including 1 suite; all with private bath, 1 with air conditioning. Wheelchair accessible. No smoking inn.
Rates: $110 to $150, double occupancy; $85 to $110, single; EPB. Additional person, $35. Two-night minimum holiday weekends.
Open: All year except December.
Facilities and activities: Single-entree dinners served midweek, $20; a la carte, Friday, Saturday, and holiday Sundays, $25 to $30; wine and beer license. Swimming pool, conference room, games and play area. Nearby: Catskill State Park, Albany, Hudson River touring, biking, hiking, fishing, golf, nature preserve, Catskill Game Farm.
Business travel: Conference center and audiovisual equipment available.
Recommended Country Inns® Travelers' Club Benefit: 10 percent discount.

The Benn Conger Inn
GROTON, NEW YORK 13073

We slept—deeply—in the room in the house in the village where Dutch Schultz once hid away from the world. At 8:00 A.M. the church bells mutedly pealed a secular tune; gracefully we awoke, remembering the delicious night of gourmet excesses and camaraderie with friends.

We had become immersed in the gastronomic progression: eclairs filled with chèvre and skiitake and cremini mushrooms; then a savory creamy carrot soup followed by a light fresh salad with a scrumptious focaccia bread; moist slices of rack of lamb and a heavenly rich sauce; and, naturally, a crème brûlée at the end.

Dinner had been accompanied by an excel-

lent Vouvray and a Pomerol. The Benn Conger has won the *Wine Spectator* award nine consecutive years. I think you want to follow the chef of this chef-owned inn as you would a conductor: You want to taste his renditions of the beef, fowl, fish, and homemade pastas.

Were they born to it? I wondered. To innkeeping? To chefdom? Alison and Peter came here from New York City, where Peter produced ABC's "Nightline" and Alison worked with major publications.

Usually Peter's in the kitchen preparing for the evening. He adopted cooking responsibilities as a child and has loved cooking ever since. Interestingly, he finds an analogy between producing a television show and running a kitchen production.

Alison has an experienced understanding of comfort—like the triple pillows on our bed, the abundance of thick towels of all sizes, the bathrobes you don after stepping from the bath, and the Scalamandre silks or antique duvets.

With welcome on their minds, they've created several guest areas: the library, a second-floor common area with wicker, and a gazebo that's perfect for retreating outdoors for the afternoon with a book from their copious collection. Along the grand staircase is an original Japanese silk tapestry, and in the large foyer below there's an eighteenth-century French desk. Here Alison keeps material on the Finger Lakes; she hands you a guidebook and map and shares their appreciation of the area. There's also a portrait of Benn Conger, the Smith Corona corporate president, who lived here. In the town are a small park, tennis courts, swim-ming pool, and a nearby community golf course. You'll have time for it all, provided you don't sleep through the church bells, which you might. But you'll probably smell the coffee aroma and be downstairs in a jiffy for Alison's excellent frittata accompanied by another fine bread (this time it's her grandmother's recipe).

Walkers, joggers, mountain bikers, and cross-country skiers are in for a treat, and you can begin your treks directly from the inn. How often we seek a peaceful countryside in which to walk safely through farms, meadows, and valleys on the companionable horizon.

How to get there: From Ithaca take Route 13 north to Route 366 east through Freeville to Route 38. Turn left on Route 38; go north 4 miles to Groton. In town turn left at the Route 222 intersection and continue up the hill to inn on the right.

Innkeepers: Peter and Alison van der Meulen

Address/Telephone: 206 West Cortland Street; (607) 898–5817, fax (607) 898–5818

Rooms: 5, including 3 suites; all with private bath and television, 1 with fireplace. Smoking in library only.

Rates: $90 to $220, double occupancy, EPB. Two-night minimum most weekends.

Open: All year.

Facilities and activities: Dinner (entrees $17 to $24) Wednesday–Sunday, sometimes other nights (please call); exercise room; 18 acres; walking; bicycling; cross-country ski trail. Nearby: Finger Lakes wineries, villages, museums of Ithaca, golf, tennis.

Business travel: Desk in all rooms; fax available; conference facilities.

Bykenhulle House 1841 B & B

HOPEWELL JUNCTION, NEW YORK 12533

Bill and Florence Beausoleil raised six children in their seven-bath, seven-bedroom, and seven-fireplace home and when all were on their own, they decided to open the house to bed and breakfast guests. Bill—still working—is a lifer with IBM, and through the years the family lived in France and elsewhere in Europe. The fine antique furnishings and Persian rugs were acquired during their sojourns. Every piece is in pristine condition, as is the house. The silk fabric on the walls, for example, dates from the 1920s; the landscape wallpaper in the central hall is even older. There are a 1790s chest in the hall and a magnificent pier mirror. Florence collects Heisey glass, and it's displayed on shelves in the hallway.

A gold-encrusted set of Limoges china was acquired in France in the 1960s for $125.

We love this 1841 Georgian manor house, which sits behind a brick wall, for its relaxed pace and its fine furnishings. The house was built by Peter Adriance, a Dutch silversmith. To the left of the entrance, twin parlors have oak floors topped with Persian rugs and sparkling crystal chandeliers. The walls are painted a soft pink, and the woodwork is a bright white. Beyond is a wicker-filled sunroom overlooking the lovely flower garden, a gazebo, and a swimming pool. A glassed-in pavilion with French doors leading to a brick terrace was added in 1996 to accommodate wedding receptions, parties, and small meetings.

Upstairs the guest rooms contain additional fine antiques; several have four-poster or canopy beds. Valerie's Room is lovely, with a four-poster bed, wood-burning fireplace, and pretty bath. Two suites on the third floor, the Raspberry Room and the Almond Room, are extraordinarily spacious, with window seats beneath bay windows overlooking the grounds. Each has a two-person Jacuzzi in a private nook in the room as well as an impressive full bath.

Florence has attended the nearby Culinary Institute of America, and her breakfasts reflect the accomplishments of a gourmet cook. We had freshly baked muffins one morning, followed by French toast crusted with crushed corn flakes and then sautéed, accompanied by maple syrup and sausage. The entree might also include apple sugar babies (a combination of a pancake and a popover) or apple crepes laced with golden raisins and slivered almonds. Breakfast is served on fine china in the formal dining room, where the innkeepers liberally share information about the area.

The inn is perfectly positioned for touring the Hudson River Valley. There are several excellent restaurants nearby, and West Point is just across the river. Hyde Park is about 10 miles north, and Boscobel Restoration is just south, close to the antiques and craft shops of Cold Spring.

How to get there: From New York City take the Henry Hudson Parkway north to the Saw Mill River Parkway. Follow the Saw Mill River Parkway north to the Taconic Parkway. Traveling north on the Taconic, go 3 miles past I–84 and turn right onto Carpenter Road (at the Muscoot Restaurant). Take the first left, which is Bykenhulle Road. The inn is on the left, ½ mile.

Innkeepers: Bill and Florence Beausoleil
Address/Telephone: 21 Bykenhulle Road; (914) 221–4182, fax (914) 227–6805
Rooms: 6, including 1 cottage; all with private bath, air conditioning, telephone, and television, 2 with fireplace, 2 with Jacuzzi. No smoking inn.
Rates: $125 to $145, double occupancy, EPB. Two-night minimum in October.
Open: All year.
Facilities and activities: Swimming pool. Nearby: golf, skiing, West Point Academy, Mills and Vanderbilt Mansions, antiques shops and boutiques in Millbrook and Cold Spring.

Buttermilk Falls Bed & Breakfast
ITHACA, NEW YORK 14850

On summer afternoons you can walk across the lawn to Buttermilk Falls and go for a swim in the cool waters. From the back-float position, the water glistens and splashes down the rocks. There's a path you can take up to the top for a lovely view of the surrounding hills. Seven hundred and fifty-one acres compose the park, and a circular trail leads back to the inn. If you go in winter, a silence envelops the place when the falls freeze. October can be a spectacular time, when the area seems momentarily forgotten by others yet the trails are still inviting with the changing of the leaves.

Wake up first thing in the morning and Margie hands you a cup of coffee while she pre-

pares a hot, hearty, and healthful breakfast. It's an opportunity to visit and learn about Ithaca and the Cayuga Lake area. When everyone is seated in Windsor chairs around the breakfast table, classical music plays softly in the background. You might have a hot fruit compote in the winter or a delicious mix of fresh fruits in summer. Hot grain breads are served along with the cereals she's created. Margie encourages companionship round the breakfast table with the adeptness of a captain at the helm.

The guest rooms are comfortably furnished with country furniture and antiques. The upstairs rooms have quilts and down comforters in mauve and eggshell colors. They overlook the piney woods or the tumbling falls. A Hansel and Gretel cottage is entered through a romantic trellis covered with grapevines. But wherever you are the tantalizing hush of the falls will lull you to a sound sleep.

Margie travels to a new part of the world annually. The living room is informally and comfortably decorated. You'll find wooden games and treasures that Margie has found on Indian and Asian travels.

Discovering that Margie occasionally has lunch at the Moosewood Restaurant (known for its vegetarian cookbooks), we stopped there for lunch. It's located in a former school building, which is now filled with shops and restaurants. For dinner there are fine restaurants about 2 miles from the inn, including a first-rate seafood place that specializes in freshness.

Margie is a well-informed source. She imparts her experiences in positive exchanges—an idea here, a special fruit-drink recipe, a word there, a piece of music you've not heard, a book you've not read, a place you must see.

How to get there: South of Ithaca where Routes 34, 13, and 96 merge, follow Route 13 to the entrance to Buttermilk Falls State Park. Inn is second house on left at the foot of the falls.

Innkeeper: Margie Rumsey; Kristen and Heather Rumsey, assistants

Address/Telephone: 110 East Buttermilk Falls Road; (607) 272–6767

Rooms: 5, including 2 suites and 1 cottage; all with private bath and air conditioning, 2 with television, 1 suite with double Jacuzzi, fireplace, and VCR. One room wheelchair accessible. No smoking inn.

Rates: $74 to $250, double occupancy, continental breakfast. Two-night minimum special event weekends. No credit cards.

Open: All year.

Facilities and activities: Buttermilk Falls State Park across lawn, swimming, cross-country skiing. Nearby: Ithaca restaurants (short drive), Finger Lakes wineries, sailing, hiking gorges, museums, antiquing. Cornell University and Ithaca College.

Hanshaw House Bed & Breakfast
ITHACA, NEW YORK 14850

Located on a quiet road 1 mile from Sapsucker Woods is a fetching little country cottage of an inn surrounded by a white picket fence. From the inn's living room there's a backyard view of Helen Scoones's private bird sanctuary. The apple tree, pond, and woods form an intimately and eminently watchable succession. Birds, a muskrat, and peeping frogs are among the wildlife who call this home.

The sun feels warm and the dhurrie carpet soft beneath our feet the day we arrive. I am pleased to find one of the pretty upstairs bedrooms ours for the night. Helen's emphasis is on lightness and brightness. In winter down comforters and pillows keep you warm. In summer white and print coverlets grace the beds. Two of the rooms have private sitting areas. Fine touches include paintings and books.

For the afternoon Helen sends us to Sapsucker Woods—Cornell's ornithological lab, open to the public. You can step out the inn's door (wear galoshes in the spring and bring binoculars), walk 1 mile to the lab, and then delve into the 4 miles of trails at will. Helen has alerted us to see the Agassiz watercolors in the lab's hallway. I browse my way through the art and pass the Library of Natural Sounds, which holds the world's largest collection of bird songs. It is momentarily silent. Then I position myself before a telescope trained on the ten-acre pond.

A sign reads: QUIET PLEASE. EXCESSIVE NOISE OR SUDDEN MOVEMENT DISTURBS THE BIRDS. Outside the geese make a commotion, flapping their wings against their bodies and noisily drowning out the other birds with their strident calls. Apparently there's no sign reminding them we are listening to all the birds, not just the biggest and loudest. The lab's namesake is the yellow-bellied sapsucker, who won't return until summer.

The inn is about ten minutes from Ithaca, the Johnson Art Museum, and craft shops, and it's a launching point for wineries and gorges. There's also a gamut of restaurants available. For more walking Cornell has gardens and paths located not far from the inn.

The next morning a blue jay wakes me from a sound night's sleep, and I stretch beneath the warmth of the goose-down cover. After a shower and dressing, I'm downstairs drinking fresh-roasted and -ground hazelnut coffee from Finlandia cups. We all visit with Helen, who manages to entertain us while she prepares delicious individual soufflés that we cover with crème fraîche; she also fries Empire apples from a nearby Cornell University hilltop. Even the delicious apple juice she serves comes from the Cornell orchards. Helen's artist-made teapot stimulates a discussion of fine crafts, and she makes suggestions as we make mental notes on special shops and exhibitions. No one hurries; it's a morning we'll long remember.

How to get there: Take Route 13 east from Ithaca toward the airport, turn right onto Warren Road. Go 1 mile and turn left onto Hanshaw Road. Go 7/10 mile and turn left onto Sapsucker Woods Road (sign says PRIVATE ROAD but ignore that). Inn is second house on the right.

Innkeeper: Helen Scoones
Address/Telephone: 15 Sapsucker Woods Road; (607) 257–1437, (800) 257–1437
Rooms: 4, including 2 suites; all with private bath and air conditioning. No smoking inn.
Rates: $68 to $120, double occupancy, EPB. Special weekends slightly higher. Additional person, $35 to $40. Single and educational rates available. Extended-stay discount. Packages available. Higher rates peak season. Two-night minimum if Saturday stay included.
Open: All year.
Facilities and activities: Nearby: Ithaca restaurants (5 miles), Sapsucker Woods, Cornell University, shopping, gardens, cultural events, winery touring, hiking, sailing, downhill and cross-country skiing.

$\mathcal{R}$ose Inn
ITHACA, NEW YORK 14851

What makes an inn linger in your memory like fine wine? What brings a smile to your lips every time the Rose Inn is mentioned? You could, of course, say it was the sunken whirlpool bath and the beautiful evening with the spring peepers calling away. Or the superb meal of artichoke heart strudel and honey-almond duck enhanced by a Finger Lakes wine. Perhaps it was the myriad adventures you'd enjoyed throughout the day, thanks to Charles and Sherry's recommendations of wineries to visit and the Mackenzie-Childs' pottery shop down the road. But of course, a European-style inn is the culmination of all of the above and that's why you went to Rose Inn.

Sherry, who has earned advanced degrees in microbiology and social planning, has an expert's eye for interior design. Charles trained in Europe and managed seven major hotels before he joined Cornell's School of Hotel Administration. Turning their full-time attention to the Rose Inn, they've created a small, elegant European-style hotel, where your hosts speak eight languages fluently.

The Rose Inn has a mystique in the area. It was known as "the home with the circular stairway" because a museum-quality stairway was crafted from Honduran mahogany by a master craftsman who disappeared without a trace.

The luxury is overt and detailed. Never too much, never too little. Our room, Number 11, was contemporary in design with light and privacy as well as a romantic touch—a sunken whirlpool bath beneath triple Palladian windows and a white brocade love seat near the fireplace.

Dinner at the Rose Inn is served in small dining rooms. You make your selections in advance. Among the choices are smoked oysters in *beurre blanc* on puff pastry, châteaubriand with sauce béarnaise served with a bouquetière of vegetables, and scampi Mediterranean flambéed with brandy and a touch of tomato, curry, and cream. I chose the Chef's Surprise, a tender almond duck (and carried away the recipe). Dessert was a rich multiflavored chocolate-raspberry-hazelnut torte.

Behind the inn is the apple orchard, which is the source of Charles's delicious, long-baked

German apple pancakes. His recipe derives from his native Black Forest youth. His breakfasts begin with a tasty freshly squeezed blend of juice from imported oranges.

You enter unpretentiously through the kitchen, but be not deceived—romance lies beyond this unusual entrance. Later you'll say, "Do you remember that evening at the Rose?"

How to get there: From Rochester take I–90, exit 40; follow Route 34S 36⁶⁄₁₀ miles; the inn is on the left. From Ithaca Airport turn right on Warren Road and go 1³⁄₁₀ miles; turn left on Hillcrest Road for 1½ miles to the end. Make a right onto Triphammer Road (joins Route 34) and go north 4⁴⁄₁₀ miles. The inn is 10 miles from Ithaca.

Innkeepers: Charles and Sherry Rosemann; Patricia Cain, manager
Address/Telephone: Route 34N (mailing address: P.O. Box 65766); (607) 533-7905, fax (607) 533-7908
E-mail: roseinn@clarityconnect.com
Rooms: 10, plus 5 suites; all with private bath, air conditioning, and telephone; 4 suites with whirlpool bath, 2 with fireplace. No smoking inn.
Rates: $100 to $150, rooms; $175 to $250, suites, double occupancy; EPB; weekends Easter–Thanksgiving: $125–$175, rooms, $200–$275, suites. Two-night minimum April–November if stay includes Saturday.
Open: All year.
Facilities and activities: Dinner Tuesday–Saturday (prix fixe $50, 4-course). Wine served. Twenty acres with fishing pond, apple orchard, rose garden. Nearby: winery tours, ski Greek Peak, lake mailboat tours, bicycling, cultural events, Cornell University.
Business travel: Desk in all rooms; conference center; secretarial services; fax; e-mail.
Recommended Country Inns® Travelers' Club Benefit: Stay one night, get second night free (tax and service charge excluded), Monday–Thursday, May 1–November 30; Sunday–Friday, December 1–April 30; excluding holidays.

The Bark Eater Inn
KEENE, NEW YORK 12942

A fire burned in the hearth; occasionally someone got up and stimulated the coals amid the discussions of gray squirrel, acid rain, sugar maples, sheep farming, and cross-country skiing. People from Canada, Vermont, Virginia, New York, and Maryland chatted. They had met an hour before. A once quiet fellow, encouraged by Joe-Pete, revealed a rich sense of humor. Gradually, everyone's day was discussed and along with it the special places—mountains and forests and meadows and boulder fields—to which Joe-Pete Wilson had sent everyone according to his or her individual tastes. Ages ranged from twenties through sixties.

Joe-Pete, a former biathlon coach and Olympic skiier and coach, grew up in the moun-

tains and on the land he loves and shapes as he sees fit. He hosts a nightly dinner party and morning tableside chats. He thrives on people and this geographical place on the earth where he grew up and has returned to live.

"Where else can you find a meadow," he asks, "with a mountain view like this?" Sentinel Mountain, a holy Indian mountain, rises to the south. Horses graze on the hillside, a dog runs in play, and cats sleep on the porch. His 750-foot-deep well provides all the fresh water. He's moved two house-size boulders to frame an entry to the pond located down the hill.

A wooden boardwalk leads up to the inn, a former stagecoach stop dating from 150 years ago, where Joe-Pete's parents opened their inn when he was a youngster. It's warmly heated with two fireplaces and all the people who gather here. The living room isn't large but always seems to accommodate everyone.

The stables accommodate fifty horses. You can ride into the woods and emerge at the meadow pond and gallop home. In the winter the trails are snow covered, and cross-country skiing from the inn couldn't be more convenient.

At night you fall quickly asleep from all the exercise. Many of the beds were handmade by Joe-Pete. It's common for guests to ask him to make one for them. All have a country look. The carriage-house rooms are steps from the inn and decorated in country contemporary. The main inn is older but nice, and the log-cabin lodgings are the most private (a short drive or walk away).

Evening meals are served around community tables. You might begin with a warm multigrain bread and a carrot-orange soup served with strawberry-spinach salad with poppy-seed dressing. Perhaps you'll have grilled swordfish with sauce verte or a beef tenderloin wrapped in phyllo. Over coffee and a dessert of blueberry-crumb pie or white-chocolate mousse, you solve the problems of the universe.

You say goodnight and look forward to meeting everyone at breakfast.

How to get there: Take I–87 to exit 34 from the north or exit 30 from the south and proceed to Route 73 West (toward Lake Placid). One mile past Keene bear right onto Alstead Hill Road at the inn sign. The inn is ½ mile on the right.

Innkeeper: Joe-Pete Wilson and Brandy Wilson; Roberta Brame, manager

Address/Telephone: Alstead Hill Road; (518) 576–2221, fax (518) 576–2071

Rooms: 15, including 2 suites in inn, carriage house, and log cabin; 12 with private bath, 1 with telephone. No smoking inn.

Rates: $98 to $136, double occupancy, EPB. Plus 7 percent tax. Two-night minimum weekends; 3-night minimum holiday weekends. Packages: hiking, skiing, climbing, and horseback riding.

Open: All year.

Facilities and activities: Dinner served every night but Sunday (5 to 6 courses, around $21). BYOB. Outside diners by reservation. Trail lunch: $6. Stables, horseback riding, hiking, mountain biking, skating, snowshoeing, swimming, and cross-country trails on 300 acres, pond. Nearby: skiing, Lake Placid.

The Lamplight Inn Bed and Breakfast
LAKE LUZERNE, NEW YORK 12846

We came on a clear winter afternoon and soon scurried up the street to the frozen lake, where we cross-country skied until sundown. Then we returned to relax by the fire and visit over cups of tea in the great room. It was a magic time of serenity. Gene and Linda are naturals at making people happy.

Their inn story began when they followed their intuition. They were on vacation in Lake Luzerne and saw a derelict mansion on a hill that would make a great inn. Impulsively, they acted on their romantic streaks and bought it. Two years later their dream became a beautiful reality. They also had vital talents to back that challenging decision. Gene knows construction,

Linda is a textile designer, and together they make a dynamic team.

The inn looks like a dream inn should. The great room is 20 by 44 feet, trimmed warmly in chestnut and arranged with several seating areas, a waiting chess game, and the crackling fireplace. In an oak chest is Linda's collection of Madame Alexander dolls and her small turtle collection. It's a place you want to linger. Notice the Christmas cards she designed; she's a talented artist. The furniture vies for your attention; each piece suggests it's more comfortable than the next.

The Lamplight has a terrific location. Gene and Linda's inn is near the oldest rodeo in the United States, Lake George, Saratoga Springs and its sights, horseracing, white-water rafting, snowmobiling, and bicycling, and it's within walking distance of the town lake. Scenic touring is a breeze. You'll never need to search for activities. The inn is a short drive away from two fine restaurants. Request the inn newsletter for special events.

Each bedroom has its own personality. Ten are located up the keyhole staircase in the mansion, and five more are in the new Brookside Guest House. The sheets and towels are color coordinated, and during winter flannel sheets cover new mattresses. You tuck yourself in beneath thick, fluffy comforters. Ten of the rooms have gas fireplaces; each has an individual heat thermostat, and one has a large skylight. The teddy bears across the pillow are the final word on a good night.

Gourmet breakfasts are served in the sunroom. There are hot fruit compotes, homemade granola (deliciously made by Linda), huge chocolate-chip muffins or sour-cream coffee cake, stacks of hot French toast or waffles, or even a four-egg omelet (expertly made by Gene). Your taste buds memorize a meal this fine in this sun-filled setting.

How to get there: From the south on I–87 north, take exit 24 (Albany); then proceed on the Northway (I–87) to Exit 21 (Lake George/Lake Luzerne). Follow Route 9N south for 11 miles to Lake Luzerne. Inn is on the right.

Innkeepers: Gene and Linda Merlino
Address/Telephone: 2129 Lake Avenue (mailing address: P.O. Box 70); (518) 696–5294 or (800) 262–4668
URL: http://adirondack.net/tour/lampinn
Rooms: 15; all with private bath, telephone, stereo, and air conditioning, 10 with gas fireplace, 5 with television, 4 with whirlpool tub. One room wheelchair accessible.
Rates: $85 to $150, double occupancy, EPB. Two-night weekends; 3-night minimum holiday weekends. Weekend packages available.
Open: All year.
Facilities and activities: Service bar; 10 acres with trails, brook, garden. Nearby: restaurants, Lake Luzerne, white-water rafting, cycling, horseback riding, cross-country skiing, snowmobiling, professional rodeo summer Friday nights, Lake George (10 miles), Saratoga Springs (18 miles).
Business travel: Fax and copy machine available; conference room.

The Interlaken Inn and Restaurant
LAKE PLACID, NEW YORK 12946

The Olympics forever changed Lake Placid. At times it looks European, other times American, but what distinguishes it are three things: the endless sporting competitions; the people who converge here and their love of skiing, hiking, and sports; and the ski-jump complex on its eastern horizon.

At the end of an athletic day, however, one likes to retreat to a romantic little village inn. The Interlaken Inn is located outside the fray, 2 blocks from Mirror Lake and the village center, on a residential street. Carol and Roy Johnson and clan were scattered about the inn preparing dinner with their guests in mind.

I'd arrived just in time for afternoon tea.

One of the Johnsons takes the opportunity to visit. It was while munching on Key lime tarts and lovely petits fours that I discovered that Carol (the master chef) and Roy (an architect) had come east from California to establish their Adirondacks inn. "You need an architectural background," Roy explained, "to restore and repair a 1906 country inn." Combining their talents—Carol's art degree and Roy's building experience—they also build and paint birdhouses, jelly cabinets, Christmas decorations, and other craft works for their inn gift shop.

Dinner happened like this: Around 6:00 P.M. guests began arriving in the parlor for a drink. My traveling companion headed for the pub, where he immediately found Roy and Carol's golf ball collection and discovered that they shared his love of golf.

Soon we were seated in the posh dining room and reading the dinner menu: "Mushroom strudel, salad with Caesar dressing, scallops in puff pastry, filet mignon with mustard-cognac cream sauce, poached salmon with fresh dill sauce, chicken Normandy with a sauce of Granny Smith apples and calvados." Happily, decisions were concluded and gastronomic directions taken. Finally the evening tapered; coffee came with individual chocolate pots and Chantilly cream; couples moved to the living room or small bar; some lingered; some went for an evening walk down to the lake.

Upstairs the pretty rooms are softly furnished, some with lace curtains and thick car-peting; you'll find several antiques from the Johnsons' California home.

On each bedroom door hangs a straw hat garlanded with flowers. There's also one on the front door near the doll carriage filled with antique dolls. The hats are Carol's touch. She's reminding us we're on holiday, and that's, indeed, the mood that Interlaken induces.

How to get there: From the intersection of Main Street and Saranac Avenue, continue north (a left turn from Saranac, a right-hand turn from Main) on Main Street along the lake. The second street on the left is Interlaken. Climb the steep hill and you'll see the inn on the left. (*Note:* There might be no street sign for Interlaken Avenue.)

Innkeepers: Roy and Carol Johnson; Kathy and Jim Gonzales, Kevin Johnson, managers
Address/Telephone: 15 Interlaken Avenue; (518) 523–3180 or (800) 428–4369
Rooms: 11, including 1 suite; all with private bath. Smoking permitted in common areas.
Rates: $120 to $180, double occupancy, MAP and afternoon tea. Plus 22 percent gratuity and state tax. EPB rate available Tuesday and Wednesday, $60 to $120. Two-night minimum on weekends.
Open: All year.
Facilities and activities: Dinner Thursday–Monday. Public invited by reservation ($30). Pub, parlor with television, gift shop. Nearby: lake and shops of Lake Placid, hiking, downhill and cross-country skiing, horseback riding, Olympic sites, year-round sporting events, golf.
Recommended Country Inns® Travelers' Club Benefit: Stay two nights, get third night free.

$\mathcal{L}$ake $\mathcal{P}$lacid $\mathcal{L}$odge
LAKE PLACID, NEW YORK 12940

It was a sunny October afternoon when we arrived. We immediately fetched a glass of wine from the cozy bar and retired to Hawkeye, our generous two-level retreat to watch the sunset from our upper deck. As the sun slid behind Whiteface Mountain, it cast its dark reflection in the waters, as we watched the streaking sky change from orange and fuschia to the palest pink. It was then that I realized I could happily stay right here and write for the rest of my life.

This former 1882 Adirondack camp was renovated and opened to guests in 1994. True to its origins, it has a log exterior, and its decks are framed by arching unpeeled birch branches. The guest rooms have beds made of twisted birch trees,

and walls made of logs, bark, and bead-board panels. There are twig furniture and sofas and chairs dressed in bright patterns. Most rooms have stone fireplaces with log mantels, and several, including Hawkeye, have two fireplaces. There are six buildings scattered about the grounds, each containing several rooms or suites. Even the smallest rooms on the ground floor of the main lodge seem spacious, and they have their own private patios, with terrific views of the lake.

After watching the evening spectacle, Managing Director Kathryn Kincannon, full of energy and enthusiasm, escorted me through the inn's common rooms, where some guests were playing billiards and others were completing a jigsaw puzzle, and then down to the marina to see the fleet of restored boats. She pointed out a nature trail that leads past trees labeled with identifying tags. We walked to the boat dock, where several couples were just returning from the sunset cocktail cruise on the inn's open-deck sightseeing barge.

It was warm enough at night to eat on the restaurant deck, romantically lighted by flickering candles. Following a dinner of confit of duck leg with sautéed potatoes and foie gras, deliciously ending with a summer pudding with raspberries, we returned to our room to contemplate the difficult decision before us: Should we take a relaxing soak in the two-person Jacuzzi; wrap ourselves against the evening chill and sit on the deck awhile longer, listening to the night sounds; or light the fire in one of the massive stone fireplaces? Reluctant to spoil the mood of this amorous place, we chose the latter and lingered

with a port before snuggling into the luxurious featherbed, knowing we would be warm enough to leave the windows open all night as we listened to the loons call across the water.

Bright and early in the morning, as the sun was rising, and with the heavy scent of pine permeating the room, I arose to join Kathryn on the boat deck for tai chi, and my companion did his morning jog around the golf course. We left feeling relaxed, rested, and renewed.

How to get there: From I–87 take exit 30. Travel northwest on Route 73 for 30 miles to Lake Placid. In the village take Route 86 for 1½ miles toward Saranac Lake. At the top of the hill, turn right onto Whiteface Inn Road. Follow it for 1½ miles and turn right at the LAKE PLACID LODGE sign. Travel through the golf course to the lodge.

Innkeepers: Christie and David Garrett; Kathryn Kincannon, managing director

Address/Telephone: Whiteface Inn Road; (518) 523–2700, fax (518) 523–1124

Rooms: 22; all with private bath, Jacuzzi, telephone, television, and VCR, 18 with fireplace. Children welcome. Pets permitted in 2 rooms at $50 per day. Wheelchair access. No smoking inn.

Rates: $175 to $425, double occupancy, meals extra. Two-night minimum weekends; 3-night minimum holidays.

Open: Year-round.

Facilities and activities: Championship 18-hole golf course, 4 tennis courts, hiking trails, sandy lakeside beach, canoes, fishing boats, paddleboats, Sunfish, open-deck sightseeing barge, mountain bikes, cross-country ski touring center in winter. Nearby: downhill skiing, ice skating, hunting.

Business travel: Desk in room; dataport; fax and secretarial services available, meeting rooms; audiovisual equipment; photocopy services.

Stagecoach Inn
LAKE PLACID, NEW YORK 12946

Have you ever seen a yellow birch-bark stairway gleaming in the afternoon sun? Or a fire blazing within the beauty of a birch-bark fireplace mantel? Who was the workman who left this legacy? Who conceived it? Who composed these masterpieces back in 1830? "No one knows," says Peter, "but the part of the inn containing this artistic rustic work predates the 'great camps' by twenty years and is therefore a precursor." It's a mysterious beauty left for us to enjoy in a fine little inn.

During the 1860s the historic Stagecoach Inn served as tavern, general store, post office, vacation lodge, and stagecoach stop of the Elizabethtown–Lake Saranac run. Adirondack pho-tographer Seneca Ray Stoddard said of his 1873 stay, ". . . the North Elba Hotel, a very pretty little two-story house, with wings extending out from the main part, accommodating about 25 guests . . . [has a] proprietor [who] is considered to have a sort of fatherly interest in everything going on in the neighborhood."

Innkeepers Peter and Andrea continue the tradition by joining their guests in morning discussions and directing them to the events and vacation activities of the area. The inn is a long, two-story structure with a balcony, parlor, and dining room where one may relax; both rooms have beautiful fireplace mantels. The parlor is a cozy setting filled with chairs and couches, and from the overhead landing one can appreciate the sign that reads SWEET REST HAVEN. Woven wool rugs cover the floor, and a tablewide puzzle spreads out in a state of near completion.

There's a delightful selection of rooms. Two have fireplaces, and several have the original woodwork, which is as solid as the day it was installed. My room was a reverie of woods. When I stepped barefoot on the floor, it was cool to the step, and on a summer night, I left my window open to receive a fresh breeze.

Andrea and Peter serve breakfast around a long table. You might have a good helping of scrambled eggs and sausage, savory French toast, or a piping hot soufflé. There are always juice

and seasonal fruit and homemade bread and conversation around the wood-burning stove.

Learning about the Adirondacks, discovering the trails winter or summer, skiing, exploring the past and present, visiting the nearby craft center, attending special events, and staying in the Stagecoach Inn—these are the pleasures of Lake Placid.

How to get there: From I–87 north take Route 73 west. Take a left after the Olympic ski jump on Old Military Road and proceed 1 mile. The inn is on the left. From the west take Route 86 toward Lake Placid, turn right on Old Military Road, and proceed 2 miles to the inn on the right.

Innkeepers: Andrea and Peter Moreau
Address/Telephone: 370 Old Military Road; (518) 523–9474
Rooms: 9, including 4 suites; all with private bath, 4 with balcony, 2 with fireplace. Pets allowed with prior permission. Limited smoking permitted.
Rates: $60 to $90, double occupancy, EPB. Prefer 2-night minimum weekends.
Open: All year.
Facilities and activities: Nearby: restaurants (½ to 5 miles), Lake Placid Olympic sites, Whiteface Mountain Ski Area, cross-country skiing, ice skating, horseback riding, golf, tennis, hiking.

The Horned Dorset Inn
LEONARDSVILLE, NEW YORK 13364

The Horned Dorset is named for the beautiful Dorset sheep. This elegant inn is an aesthete's retreat and never advertised. Inside awaits gourmet dining, classical music, sophisticated surroundings, and a lovely time. Opposite the inn is the startling contrast of untended buildings. It's an outstanding inn in the middle of an unlikely setting in the hamlet of Leonardsville.

You enter under an ornate church chandelier, three impressive Palladian windows give southern exposure, and a marble fireplace and travertine staircase are to the left. You ascend to a small library, which is the cocktail lounge. The three dining rooms are elegant. One has a wall lined with walnut bookshelves and enticing ti-

tles. A beautiful spray of flowers scents the air.

The rooms are next door, in the white Federal house with the high picket fence. In its parlor are a piano and a glass-covered coffee table filled with curling medals and magazines. My companion loved the old *Life* magazines. The innkeeper says he gave so many away as gifts that he finally decided to keep these for the guests.

Upstairs two angels sit in the hallway. Down comforters are on the beds, and the antiques are well-chosen, quality pieces. Each room has a table. Fresh fruit and a crystal pitcher filled with ice water sit on a silver tray. The next morning your continental breakfast is placed here. Again on a silver tray, the coffee in a silver pot, the croissants flaky and hot, the raspberry jam home-made. One room and one suite have pretty, working fireplaces. What a romantic place.

The chef prepares classic French cuisine. The tournedos with châteaubriand sauce melt in your mouth. The rice is flavored with pine nuts. You might have the Veal Horned Dorset, a loin of veal sautéed and served with mushrooms, blue cheese, and avocado with a glaze over the top. The choco-late bombe is delectable. We celebrated late into the night. Bruce directed us toward the hilltop to watch the setting sun from the apple orchard.

How to get there: From I–90 take Utica exit. Go south on Route 8 for 22 miles to Leonardsville. The inn is on the east side of the road. Fly-in: Utica Airport.

Innkeeper: Bruce Wratten

Address/Telephone: Route 8 (mailing address: P.O. Box 142); (315) 855–7898, fax (315) 855–7820

Rooms: 4, including 2 suites; all with private bath and air conditioning, 2 with fireplace.

Rates: $90 to $110, double occupancy, continental breakfast.

Open: All year except Mondays and Christmas Day.

Facilities and activities: Dinner Tuesday–Sunday ($17 to $28). Hiking or cross-country skiing through 100-acre apple orchard at hilltop. Nearby: Cooperstown, with Baseball Hall of Fame; James Fenimore Cooper House; Farmers' Museum (30 minutes).

Beaverkill Valley Inn
LEW BEACH, NEW YORK 12753

Rich in the lore and the history of trout fishing in America, Beaverkill Stream is a premier experience for devotees of fly-fishing. The inn, owned by Laurance Rockefeller, is located in the Catskills wilderness along a mile of the renowned stream. During April, May, and June, Joan Wulff teaches fly-casting, and students of all ages lodge at Beaverkill. But you need never have cast a rod to appreciate discreet charms and natural beauty.

Cross the bridge over the Beaverkill and the American flag sways gently in the breeze above the inn's country porch. Like a tiled oasis shimmering in the sunlight, the blissful, enclosed swimming pool can be just glimpsed. What you can't see next to the pool: the self-serve ice cream parlor, where you may delve at will into the cool, creamy goodness. Around the corner a locker room for pool changing resembles a posh health club.

There's plenty of room for everyone, inside and out. A shady porch filled with wicker winds around the inn; a sun deck off the Victorian bar looks out to the meadow and the stream. There's a country parlor and a card room (each with fireplace), a billiard room, and a Ping-Pong room.

The cozy bedrooms have handmade quilts on the beds and are prettily wallpapered and simply furnished. You can choose a queen-sized bed or twin beds. Number Ten is a favorite because it has a creek view.

Every evening guests gather around square oak tables in the dining room. Innkeeper and chef Graham Watson (whose oak kitchen is as lovely as the dining room) creates delicious country foods, serving one or two entrees from what is fresh and available. When I arrived one Friday night, a wonderful buffet awaited. The seafood and veal stew were divine, served alongside fresh whole-grain breads and salads. You might begin with an endive-and-grapefruit salad and end with tangy orange-custard tart or strawberry shortcake for dessert. Breakfast is buffet style; an array of hot and cold dishes composes the selections.

Near the inn are conference rooms. Every electronic piece of equipment you might request is available. One family staged a family reunion with films and slides they'd collected through the years and happily added to their repertoire with a vacation along the secluded Beaverkill.

This is a very child-friendly inn. A playroom is stocked with amusing games, there are organzied activites on holidays, and child care can be arranged.

How to get there: Directions sent with reservations.

Innkeeper: Graham Watson; Laurance Rockefeller, proprietor

Address/Telephone: 136 Beaverkill Road; (914) 439–4844, fax (914) 439–3884

Rooms: 21; 13 with private bath; window fan on request, wheelchair access in 1 guest room and public areas. No smoking in rooms.

Rates: $260 to $330, double occupancy, AP; $160 to $195, single, AP. Children under 2 free; special rates, 3 to 12. Bed and breakfast plan available, Sunday–Thursday, $170 to $240, double occupancy, EPB. Two-night minimum weekends; 3-night minimum holiday weekends.

Open: All year, with some exceptions.

Facilities and activities: Air-conditioned dining room open to public by reservation. Victorian bar, enclosed swimming pool, billiards, Ping-Pong, card room, ice-cream parlor, hiking and cross-country ski trails, 2 tennis courts, pond, 60 acres, 1 mile of Beaverkill Stream.

Business travel: Desks in 6 rooms; telephone, fax, copier, typewriter, and audiovisual equipment available; conference room.

The Mill at Bloomvale Falls
MILLBROOK, NEW YORK 12545

To be perfectly honest, this eclectic and unusual inn is not to everyone's taste. For those who require a private bathroom, for example, this inn will not do at all. For travelers looking for an unparalleled setting, however, amid a wide array of original art, few inns in America can match it.

Don Salvato, an artist with a impressive talent, has owned the picturesque stone cider mill for some thirty years. It's said that applejack was produced here during Prohibition, and today it's listed on the National Register of Historic Places. Don raised his daughter here, beside the tumultous waterfall on Wappingers Creek that crashes from a rocky ledge. Another rushing torrent, the remains of the original mill raceway, continues to

cut a swath that seems to course directly beneath the building. Ghostly stone walls from a much earlier mill enclose a pretty courtyard and fountain. A pathway leads across a suspended bridge to the opposite banks, where a gazebo made from locust branches awaits you. Just below guests can splash in the pool at the base of the falls. Another path leads even higher along the cliff to Don's new multilevel studio.

To reach the entrance we climbed a series of stairs to a midlevel point, where a covered rock patio leads to a doorway. Except for the cars parked below, the mill appears to be deserted. Inside, however, the old mill is alive. Stone walls glow with art that ranges from Picasso-like abstracts, to large, bold florals, to realistic contemporary pieces. A grand piano waits for players, a multitude of books fills shelves, and comfortable sofas and chairs are oriented toward the stone fireplace and a view of the falls. There are corner cupboards and hutches holding brightly colored pottery, wicker rockers, and an abundance of collectibles. Healthy plants abound.

The guest rooms are located up a steep stairway. Don is also an architect, and the rooms are cozy and snug. Several have impressive views of the falls, and the soft hiss is sure to ensure a night's deep sleep. The Garden Room, in a private setting just off an upstairs terrace, has an iron bed and its own woodstove. My favorite, however, is the Red Room, so named because of the brilliant acrylic featuring a stand of poppies that graces one stone wall. It has a view of the falls, warm oak floors that are covered with hooked rugs, and an 1850s rope bed. There's one bath off the hallway, another full bath in the master bedroom, and a half bath downstairs.

Frieda, an ex-banker, prepares a full breakfast daily. A typical menu includes juice and fresh fruit, freshly baked breads, quiche, and poached pears with raisin sauce, or perhaps the entree will be thickly sliced French toast or blueberry pancakes served with bacon or country sausage.

Don told me that the stream is noted for its exceptional trout fishing; guests frequently bring their fishing rods. Millbrook has some fine restaurants, and it's noted for its exceptional antiques shops. There are wineries nearby to tour and numerous equestrian events to enjoy.

How to get there: From New York City take the Henry Hudson Parkway north to the Saw Mill River Parkway and then go north to the Taconic Parkway. Follow the Taconic Parkway north to the Route 44/Millbrook/Poughkeepsie exit. Travel east on Route 44 for 1 mile. Turn left onto Route 82 north and go for 1⅓ miles. You will see the inn sign on the right.

Innkeepers: Don Salvato and Frieda Gattine
Address/Telephone: Route 82; (914) 266–4234, fax (914) 266–4061
Rooms: 4 share 2½ baths; 1 with woodstove. Pets by prior permission only. No smoking inn.
Rates: $85 to $115, double occupancy, EPB. Two-night minimum May–November.
Open: All year.
Facilities and activities: Swimming and fishing. Nearby: equestrian events, wineries, Ecosystem's Botanical Gardens, Innisfree Gardens, Culinary Institute of America, skiing, and golf.

$\mathcal{S}$immons' Way Village Inn & Restaurant

MILLERTON, NEW YORK 12546

Welcome a change of seasons with a change of scenery. Drive out from the city, put on your baggy tweeds or soft cottons, walk around the village, go to a concert, sit by the parlor fire with a book of poems, and have a leisurely dinner. Return to the rural landscape of hills, farms, lakes, and villages. Over scones and piping-hot tea, you acquire the village pace that prevails ninety minutes from New York. It feels like that of another century.

Upstairs you can retreat to your own room. The rooms are large, and the style is country contemporary; light pine furnishings are accented with antiques. Nancy had some of the curtains made by Laura Ashley in London. Each room is sunny and warmly attractive, and all the quilts and linens are 100 percent cotton. There are magazines, desks, and good reading lights.

Dinner begins with a discriminating wine list that offers tastes from Dom Perignon to reasonably priced New York wines and champagnes. On the evening of my visit, entree selections ranged from yellowfin tuna served with a green-peppercorn-and-cream sauce to baked trout stuffed with crabmeat, which was tender and fresh. Diverse appetizers included a tasty Brie and sun-dried tomato soup. The breads were hot and came with a complimentary salad. The desserts were heavenly. My favorites were the strawberries with a sublime chocolate-anisette sauce and the light white-chocolate mousse cake. The chef, I discovered, is a fellow chocolate lover.

You might meet Baden, the large black-and-white Bernese mountain dog, named for a village, according to Swiss custom. The Carters lived in Baden, Austria (near the Swiss border), and visited Baden, Germany. If Baden tiptoes by while you're in the parlor visiting or reading by the fire, you'll be impressed with his lightness of foot. Also in residence are Max, the African gray parrot, and Shatzi, the cat.

For breakfast you might have homemade granola, fruit, fresh goat's-milk yogurt, and freshly baked muffins, hard-boiled eggs, cheese, and hot croissants, or perhaps a delicious sausage. These are healthful, filling meals to consume while admiring the African masks, sculptures, and works of art.

When Dick (Dr. Carter) worked for the United Nations, they called home various places in Thailand, Austria, and Africa. Nancy has worked in the international corporate field. But while they traveled they knew their destiny was innkeeping, which requires a world of experience. In the center of town, Simmons' Way has a solid Victorian presence, but its warm, welcoming innkeepers are refreshingly international in outlook and a pleasure to visit with.

How to get there: From New York City take Henry Hudson Parkway to Saw Mill River Parkway, then I–684 to end and start of Route 22 north to Millerton. Turn right onto Main Street (which is Route 44). Proceed up the hill for 3 blocks; inn is on the left.

Innkeepers: Richard, Nancy and Erich Carter
Address/Telephone: 33 Main Street; (518) 789–6235, fax (518) 789–6236
E-mail: swvi@taconic.net
Rooms: 10; all with private bath and air conditioning, 1 with fireplace and porch.
Rates: $145 to $175, double occupancy, continental-plus breakfast. Additional person, $30. Two-night minimum weekends May–October, 3-night minimum holidays. Packages: skiing, Lime Rock Auto Racing School, New Year's Eve.
Open: All year.
Facilities and activities: Dinner Wednesday–Sunday ($11.95 to $26), Sunday brunch, afternoon tea on Saturday and by reservation, full beverage license. Nearby: antiquing, lakes, vineyards; New England Chamber Music Festival, Lime Rock Park, Tanglewood, and Berkshire Theater within 1-hour drive.
Recommended Country Inns® Travelers' Club Benefit: 10 percent discount, Sunday–Thursday, excluding major holiday weekends. Must mention club when making reservation.

Genesee Country Inn
MUMFORD, NEW YORK 14511

A country inn born a classic, but with all the fascination of Rochester merely 11 miles away.

At the convergence of Allen and Spring creeks, Oatka Creek emerges from beneath the 150-year-old stone inn (formerly a mill) and transforms the backyard into a hidden paradise. Ducks float along the tree-draped stream, birds sing from the willows, and a trout named Pearl swims in the shadowy depths. On a sunny day you can settle back on the deck and let the tranquillity pervade your sense of being.

The walls of the completely restored inn, which dates from 1833, are 2½ feet thick, and the interior is painted a fresh white; these be-

came a canvas for Glenda and two artist friends who spent nearly three months stenciling their way through the inn. Although stenciling was popular at the time of the mill's origin, the result is more than historical accuracy: It's a folk art form that makes each room distinctive. They are furnished with reproductions and are clean as a new whistle. Select a room at the back and the sound of the gurgling stream will effortlessly carry you off to slumberland. From selected bedrooms you can step out your private entry onto a deck and into a misty twilight garden.

One of the finest restaurants, a five-minute drive away, is one of the most romantic. It serves thick lamb chops, veal Oscar, frog legs, and excellent New York steaks in a candlelight-and-white-linen setting. Glenda will coordinate a romantic evening for two.

The inn is well located—near a nature center for hiking or cross-country skiing and 1 mile from the Genesee Museum, a community of thirty-eight buildings that span the history of New York town-and-country life. You can visit the home of George Eastman, tour the only Gallery of Sporting Art in America, and speak with knowledgeable costumed interpreters. This is a relatively undiscovered museum and ranks with the best. A half hour away are the Rochester museums and the Strong Museum and Photography Museum.

Before returning to your habitual world, retreat back to the deck and the sounds of the stream and fountain. Take a copy from Glenda's current *New York Times* best-seller bookshelf and linger in a setting of quiet beauty. Inside you might take time to pet the cats: Katie and Sylvester.

Breakfasts at Genesee (an Indian word meaning "pleasant valley") are served overlooking the water. Hot coffee and fresh-squeezed juice precede a rich egg-and-cheese casserole or perhaps Glenda's superb French toast, plump with cream cheese.

How to get there: From I–90 take exit 47 and follow Route 19 south to Le Roy. In Le Roy take Route 5 east to Caledonia. Then take Route 36 north to Mumford, turning left onto George Street. The inn is 1½ blocks on the right.

Innkeeper: Kim Rasmussen; Glenda Barcklow, proprietor
Address/Telephone: 948 George Street; (716) 538–2500, fax (716) 538–4565
Rooms: 9; all with private bath, air conditioning, television, telephone, 3 with fireplace.
   No smoking inn.
Rates: $85 to $135, double occupancy, EPB. Two-night minimum some weekends
   May–October.
Open: All year.
Facilities and activities: On 8 acres along stream; gift shop. Nearby: 7 restaurants within 5-mile radius, Genesee Country Village and Museum, Eastman Philharmonic, biking and walking tours of historical landmarks, trout fishing.
Business travel: Telephone in room; desk and fax available; conference room.

ed and Breakfast on the Park
NEW YORK (BROOKLYN), NEW YORK 11215

"You *can* see the Statue of Liberty!" I exclaimed happily to my companion as he climbed the stairs to join me. We had just been escorted to the Lady Liberty Room by Liana Paolella, and we walked through the double French doors to our private deck and then up another level to the roof, where the Empire State Building, the World Trade Center, and Lady Liberty herself spread before us.

The Lady Liberty Room, where we would be spending the night, was a Victorian gem. An elaborately swagged canopy bed was fluffed with plush pillows, several Victorian dressers with marble tops held fanciful Victorian lamps, and a plate of freshly baked cookies waited on the

nightstand. Liana also proudly showed us the Park Suite, which overlooks Prospect Park. It has a lacy crown canopy bed, a stunning stained-glass window, and a dressing room that's fully paneled with bird's-eye maple, including the mirrored closet doors and a built-in vanity.

Liana was an antiques dealer when she purchased this grand old house in 1985. It needed a tremendous amount of work, but she knew what to do. Stripping the paneled walls, doors, stair railings, detailed fretwork, and window frames, she converted this Victorian derelict into a rare ruby. She then filled it with antiques that might have been used when it was first built. There are fringed sofas and chairs in one parlor, along with a floor lamp with beaded fringe. Ask to see the powder room hidden behind carved paneling in the vestibule. A marvelous collection of oil paintings intrigued us. Liana said that several were painted by her stepfather.

This is a lovely section of Brooklyn, known as Park Slope. Tree-lined streets are faced with elegant townhouses and brownstones. This wide, gray mansion, built in 1892, still has its original stoop and outside trim. Directly across the street is Brooklyn's crown jewel, the 526-acre Prospect Park, created by Frederick Law Olmsted and Calvert Vaux, designers of Manhattan's Central Park. We walked through the park later in the day to take a ride on the restored carousel and to visit the magnificent Brooklyn Museum, one of New York's secret treasures. We were fascinated by the re-created rooms from New York houses.

It was a warm, balmy night, and Liana had suggested a charming restaurant nearby, which we walked to. The streets were filled with neighbors who were walking and greeting one another. Had we decided to go into Manhattan, it would have been just a fifteen-minute subway ride away.

The next morning, as we sat around the dining-room table comparing notes with the other guests, Liana's daughter, Jonna, who has assumed many of the innkeeping duties, brought out a delicious sweet-potato frittata, along with an array of fresh fruit and home-baked breads. We ate on antique Victorian china and were served from pretty silver serving pieces while the parakeet, Nonni-Nonni, strutted across the table picking up crumbs.

Next time I want to come in the spring when the daffodils are in bloom at the Brooklyn Botanic Garden.

How to get there: From Manhattan take the Brooklyn Bridge to Brooklyn. After crossing the bridge continue to Atlantic Avenue. At the intersection with Fourth Avenue, turn right. Continue on Fourth Avenue for 1 mile to Fifth Street. Turn left onto Fifth and continue to the end. Turn right onto Prospect Park West. The inn is 2 blocks farther on the right.

Innkeepers: Liana and Jonna Paolella

Address/Telephone: 113 Prospect Park West; (718) 499–6115

Rooms: 7; 5 with private bath, all with air conditioning and television, 2 with garden. No smoking inn.

Rates: $100 to $250, double occupancy, EPB. Two-night minimum weekends; 3-night holiday weekends.

Open: Year-round.

Facilities and activities: Nearby: Brooklyn Museum, Brooklyn Botanic Garden, Brooklyn Library, Brooklyn Academy of Music, Prospect Park, bicycling, antiques shops.

The Inn at Irving Place
NEW YORK (MANHATTAN), NEW YORK 10003

As I sat in my room overlooking Gramercy Park's Irving Place late one night, I felt myself transported in time to an earlier New York. Like a page from *Time and Again*, I could imagine Washington Irving emerging from his home across the street to walk briskly to a friend's home for dinner or O. Henry scurrying along in the chilly air to reach the warm, convivial atmosphere of Pete's Tavern to finish writing *Gift of the Magi*. The street has changed little over the years, and these two townhouses, recently converted to a sumptuous bed and breakfast inn, retain their original stoops, wrought-iron balustrades, and elegant entrances. The inn is so discreet that there's not even a sign announcing it.

John Simoudis, the innkeeper, warmly greeted me in the gracious parlor, as cozy as a friend's home with its fire burning in the hearth. I was just in time for afternoon tea in Lady Mendl's Tearoom, and John joined me as he told me about the restoration. "The buildings were in need of tremendous work," he explained, and the owner wasn't sure what to do with them. "She loved the tall ceilings and grand windows, and decided that an elegant turn-of-the-century-style inn would be a nice addition to the city and a perfect use for the buildings." And they are. The side-by-side townhouses contain elegant moldings, polished floors, burnished banisters (one newel has a bronze Fleur de Mai statue), and elegant furnishings. Every room contains fine antiques, but it's all done with a restrained dignity that would have been foreign in most fussy Victorian homes.

My room, quiet and urbane, is named for Stanford White, who certainly trod this street. It has a carved bed, elaborate ceiling moldings, a magnificent armoire, and an inlaid floor. The sophisticated bath has a tile floor. Another of my favorites is the one named for Washington Irving. It has a matching bed and armoire inlaid with a musical-instrument motif. The room named for O. Henry has a brass bed, a carved armoire, and a huge bath with a pedestal sink.

Rather than leave this rarefied and genteel ambience, I met a friend in the charming restaurant on the ground floor. Verbena is leased to an outstanding chef, and we were fortunate to have chosen a night warm enough to allow us to sit in the pretty outdoor garden, although two fire-places create a cozy inside atmosphere in winter. I had a sturgeon steak with semolina gnocchi, melted sorrel greens, and roasted carrots. For dessert I had a bittersweet-chocolate soufflé baked in a rum-soaked savarin cake and served with chocolate-chip ice cream, truly an outstanding and unusual dish.

The next morning a gentle knock announced my breakfast tray of freshly baked pastries, fruit, and coffee. Although I had opted for breakfast in my room, some guests prefer to eat in the tearoom or the parlor. I wonder which option Edith Wharton would have chosen? Since she generally spent her mornings writing in bed, I imagine she would have done just as I.

How to get there: Irving Place is an extension of Lexington Avenue, separated from it by Gramercy Park. The inn is between East 17th and East 18th streets.

Innkeeper: John Simoudis; Naomi Blumenthal, proprietor
Address/Telephone: 54 Irving Place; (212) 533–4600, fax (212) 533–4611
Rooms: 12; all with private bath, air conditioning, telephone, and television.
Rates: $250 to $350, double occupancy, continental breakfast.
Open: All year.
Facilities and activities: Nearby: access to Equinox Health Club; Greenwich Village, Soho, restaurants.
Business travel: Desks in room, fax, pager, cellular telephones, laptop computer with Internet access available.

Inn New York City
NEW YORK (MANHATTAN), NEW YORK 10003

I should explain that I absolutely love New York. I never tire of it. Therefore, it was a marvelous pleasure to have found this charming "country" inn tucked away on a side street near Lincoln Center and Riverside Park. Inn New York City has long been my own secret treasure (although I admit I share the secret with several others). When Ruth Mensch and her daughter Elyn converted this townhouse to a four-suite bed and breakfast in 1989, they had no idea how popular their inn would become.

I remember my enchantment as they showed me around that first time. In the front parlor the elaborate moldings, inlaid hardwood floors, and crystal chandeliers evoked a nine-

teenth century nostalgia. "This is where guests often meet friends before walking to one of the nearby restaurants," Ruth told me.

Although all of the guest rooms are decorated with unusual flair, I was especially enchanted with my own. Ruth has a knack for taking architectural ornaments and turning them into furniture, or room dividers, or interior decor. My room, The Spa Suite, is on the top floor. It has a king-sized bed with a headboard set into an antique chestnut armoire. The sybaritic bath, however, is the pièce de résistance. It has a double Jacuzzi on a platform, a fireplace with a carved mantel, an old barber chair, a cast-iron foot bath, a Victorian dresser with a sink set into its marble top, a sauna for two, and a glassed-in shower.

I also love The Parlor Suite, which has an 18-foot living room with 12-foot-high ceilings. The vestibule has a stained-glass ceiling, and there's a Baldwin grand piano in the living room. The bedroom has a balcony, a fireplace, and a queen-sized bed with a headboard containing cabinets with stained-glass doors. Every room has personal touches such as private libraries, fresh flowers, and fluffy robes.

It was a warm, balmy afternoon the day we arrived, so we walked over to Central Park and rented a canoe for a ride on the lake. Afterward we sipped a glass of wine on the deck of the Boathouse restaurant while we watched the ducks bob for bread tossed into the water. Later we had dinner at a nearby restaurant.

On returning to the inn, we used several of the bath's pleasures and then snuggled into our room for a peaceful and quiet night's sleep. There's a little kitchen in each suite, and Ruth or Elyn fill the refrigerator with fresh goodies at night before retiring. When we rose in the morning, we popped several delicate fresh muffins into the microwave and read the *New York Times* while nibbling on fresh fruit and sipping freshly brewed coffee.

Shhhh. Don't tell anyone.

How to get there: The inn is located on the south side of West 71st Street, between Broadway and West End Avenue.

Innkeepers: Ruth and Elyn Mensch

Address/Telephone: 266 West 71st Street; (212) 580–1900, fax (212) 580–4437

Rooms: 4 suites; all with private bath, telephone, television, and air conditioning. No smoking inn.

Rates: $195 to $295, double occupancy, continental breakfast. Two-night minimum.

Open: All year.

Facilities and activities: Nearby: Lincoln Center, Riverside Park, Central Park, Museum of Natural History, New York Historical Society.

$\mathcal{L}e$ $\mathcal{R}efuge$
NEW YORK (CITY ISLAND, BRONX), NEW YORK 10464

You imagine Pierre as a child, blond haired and with a twinkle in his eye. Perhaps he's standing in the kitchen of his parents' hotel in Normandy. His mother hands him a large wooden spoon that has stirred the evening's pot of chocolate mousse, or a cup of vegetable soup. The flavors and scents of those happy days evidently made such an impression that he never wants to be too far away from a busy, fragrant kitchen. That's how a fine chef is born and in turn creates a French restaurant in New York City known as Le Refuge.

Two decades ago Pierre opened his French restaurant near the Metropolitan Museum of Art. The reviewers continue to say the food's superlative. Now he's opened a bed and breakfast of the

same name in the City Island house where he and his family once lived. Here he's at your culinary command (by advance reservation) and will prepare whatever you wish for a private dinner. It's a gastronomic opportunity waiting to happen.

The urban landscape slips away at the bridge as you cross over Eastchester Bay to Pelham Bay Park then take a smaller bridge to City Island. On the island's center street, among seafood restaurants, shipyards, chandlers, and marine antiques shops, you'll find a three-story Victorian building behind a high wooden fence.

You open the door to a spacious parlor, where oak beams stand exposed in their rustic beauty. Here, on Sundays, Pierre hosts Baroque concerts that begin around noon.

During the day you're likely to play in Pelham Bay Park, New York City's largest, with more than 2,000 acres, two eighteen-hole golf courses, wooded trails for horseback riding, and a sandy beach. Mayor Fiorello La Guardia customarily retreated to Pelham Bay Park's Bartow-Pell Mansion, now a public museum, operated by the International Garden Club, which conducts tours and tends the gardens.

"What kinds of foods do you like? Fish, fowl . . .?" Pierre obviously enjoys making people happy at the table: Your dinner menu emerges from a discussion that elicits your tastes in foods and seasonings. Say you like ravioli; then it becomes ravioli with lobster for an appetizer. Mention beef and he suggests a filet of beef with green peppercorns. You prefer to begin with something hot? Then a soupe d'amour you shall have, and he will smile engagingly.

A man of taste prepares his rooms as he prepares his foods. These are simple and clean, with the best-quality mattresses. I prefer the suite and its neighbor room overlooking the backyard.

In the inn parlor stands a handcrafted French grandfather clock that was in Pierre's family. It stood in the Normandy hotel where he grew up. You probably won't notice the time slip by. During warm weather guests pass through the kitchen, where they're asked if they'd like cappuccino and croissants, and walk out back to the deck overlooking the backyard. You feel like you've gone hundreds of miles from the city, but it's only an island away.

How to get there: From I–95 take exit 8B toward City Island. Cross bridge and turn right before first light. Continue to City Island (around traffic circle), cross 2-lane City Island bridge, and turn right on City Island Road. Inn is 200 yards on left.

Innkeeper: Pierre Saint-Denis

Address/Telephone: 620 City Island Avenue; (718) 885–2478 or (212) 737–9279, fax (718) 885–1519

Rooms: 8, including 2 suites; 2 with private bath, all with air conditioning and television. Pay phone in kitchen. No smoking inn.

Rates: $75, double occupancy; $65, single; $125, suite; continental breakfast. American Express only card accepted.

Open: All year.

Facilities and activities: Dinner with advance reservation ($40 fixed price for 4 courses). Nearby: Seafood restaurants. Pelham Bay Park: horseback riding, hiking, tennis courts, Colgate Sailing School, bicycling, Pelham Bay Golf Course, Split Rock Golf Course, Bartow-Pell Mansion and Museum.

Recommended Country Inns® Travelers' Club Benefit: Stay five nights, get two nights free, subject to availability.

Elk Lake Lodge
NORTH HUDSON, NEW YORK 12855

Elk Lake is a wilderness lake to behold. From the shore you can see the peaks of Boreas, Colvin, Nippletop, Dix, and Macomb. You can climb the high peaks and follow woodland trails to pristine (100-foot-deep, two-acre-wide) Clear Pond. You can canoe to tree-filled islands and beaver ponds. And walk along the shore in the moonlit silence, recognizing stars in familiar formations. Each time I return the beauty of this 12,000-acre preserve overwhelms me.

The lodge is covered with weathered shingles and is the only dwelling group on the lake. You enter the great camp–style common room, where the log beams glisten and the fire burns in the great stone fireplace. Animal skins hang on the walls near a fishing basket. The Stickley furniture is covered in dark-brown leather. In the corner are two "aesthetic rustic" cupboards. They are unusual and were once borrowed for display by the Adirondack Museum.

In addition to the lake, there are 600 acres of inlets, islands, bays, and open waters to explore by canoe or rowboat and 40 miles of trails. Fishermen and -women might catch brook and lake trout and landlocked salmon.

The meals at Elk Lake are all-American. You find thick pork chops, tender pot roasts, beef Stroganoff, and chicken in every style deliciously imaginable. On Saturday evenings fresh fish is served. Desserts range from homemade berry pies to cheesecakes and ice cream. Often guests request a picnic lunch and bring a small pack so that they can lengthen their day in the woods.

The rooms in the inn are small, pine paneled, and have linoleum floors with small rugs. The cottages are similar but larger, and several have fireplaces and wonderful lake views. Everything is clean.

One family began coming to Elk Lake Lodge long ago. First it was the two of them. Next they brought the baby. Then the toddler and the new baby. Now it's a family tradition, and all seven of them look forward to their wilderness outing. One day, perhaps, these children will favor their children with an experience in nature.

How to get there: From I–87 North, take exit 29, or U.S. Route 9 at North Hudson. Go west toward Newcomb for 4 miles, turn right at the sign, and proceed 5 miles to the inn on the private road.

Innkeepers: Percy and Janet Fleming, managers

Address/Telephone: Blue Ridge Road (mailing address: P.O. Box 59); (518) 532–7616, fax (518) 532–9262

Rooms: 6, plus 7 cottages; all with private bath, some cottages with fireplace and lakeview deck.

Rates: $100 to $115, May–June; $120 to $135, July–October; per person; AP. Plus 15 percent gratuity. Two-night minimum. Children ages 2 to 6, 50 percent discount; 7 to 12, 25 percent discount. No credit cards.

Open: May through October.

Facilities and activities: Breakfast, lunch, dinner for guests only, BYOB; 12,000-acre private forest preserve located directly on Elk Lake and Clear Pond; canoes, rowboats, swimming, fishing, hiking, mountain climbing, bird- and animal watching.

Garnet Hill Lodge
NORTH RIVER, NEW YORK 12856

It's a sunny Adirondack winter afternoon, and we've come to cross-country ski. We open the wooden door to the 1936 lodge and find people playing Ping-Pong, and billiards and chatting before the fire. Today we hurry. It's still daylight. After changing we walk down to the ski hut where the merry-eyed, avuncular George Heim oversees 50 miles of cross-country ski trails and 600 acres that include the extensive forest paths of Garnet Hill, which stretch to Thirteenth Lake. When George is not guiding others into the woods, he's skiing and maintaining the trails.

The trails are wide, quiet beauties that lace into the woods and down the hills, giving you an effortless gliding ride. When you reach the hill's base, a waiting van picks you up and takes you back to the mountaintop. That's my style. You can also ski from the top of Gore Mountain all the way to Garnet Hill—a distance of 10 miles. On one of my visits, George was headed out for a moonlit cross-country expedition to ski across Thirteenth Lake under the stars. Afterward everyone returned to the lodge for hot mulled wine and cocoa around the fire.

During April and May there's wet-suit white-water rafting on the Hudson River at the bottom of the hill. During summer there's swimming along the inn's beach, boating in the lake, and hiking to the garnet mine. This inn is named for the garnets that once came from this mine.

They sparkle from the stones of the exquisite fireplace in the Log Cabin lodge; minuscule garnets even gleam from the driveway gravel.

The rooms are diverse. Several in the Log House have small balconies, pine paneling, and queen-sized beds. A short distance away is the modern Birches, and in The Manor House are seven country-contemporary rooms.

The Log House, where we returned for a drink before the fire after skiing, has a beautiful lake view and a bounty of areas to settle into. In the central room are picnic tables where everyone comes in the evening for a large four-course dinner. Saturday-night smorgasbords are served during skiing and rafting seasons. You find plenty of vegetables and homemade breads and classic entree choices like juicy roast beef or boneless whole trout sautéed in butter and sprinkled with fresh lemon and almonds. Desserts might include fresh fruit pies and cakes and seasonal cobblers or cheesecakes. At breakfast you're given choices like pancakes or French toast and eggs. Hot fresh breads are delivered with a large pot of coffee. You savor the moment; it's a gem of a place.

How to get there: From I–87 take exit 22 onto Route 9 north. After Warrensburg take Route 28 west through Weverton to North River. From Weverton it's 11½ miles to the left turn onto Thirteenth Lake Road and the inn's sign. Follow this road (mostly paved) 5 miles to the inn.

Innkeepers: George and Mary Heim

Address/Telephone: Thirteenth Lake Road; (518) 251–2821, fax (518) 251–3089

Rooms: 30, in 4 buildings; all with private bath, some with balcony, 2 with Jacuzzi. Wheelchair accessible.

Rates: $75 to $110, per person, MAP. Children 10 and under, $30 (in room with parents; babies negotiable). Two-night minimum weekends, 3-night minimum holidays. Nordic, white-water rafting, and other seasonal packages.

Open: All year.

Facilities and activities: Breakfast, lunch, and dinner, service bar, sauna, hot tub, and exercise room. Cross-country skis and mountain bikes to rent. Hiking, swimming, canoeing, fishing, tennis courts, garnet mine. Nearby: downhill skiing at Gore Mountain, Adirondack Museum (summer), boat cruises, spelunking, bird-watching, dogsled rides, white-water rafting.

Recommended Country Inns® Travelers' Club Benefit: 10 percent discount, Monday–Thursday.

Highwinds Inn
NORTH RIVER, NEW YORK 12856

The road to Highwinds rises and turns beautifully through the trees to an elevation of 2,700 feet, where, amid the mountain wilderness, you pass a garnet mine. The Barton family, who supply 90 percent of the world's garnets, began mining here during the 1880s. You can tour the mine in the peaceful mountain air (the operating mine is located several miles away) and visit a small museum to learn how garnets are mined and used for industry (garnets are nearly as hard as diamonds) and jewelry.

Guests should plan trips around cross-country skiing during the winter. The inn's 30 kilometers of private trails link with Garnet Hill Inn and another 50 kilometers of trail to form superb cross-country skiing. There are also miles of ungroomed wilderness trails for the adventurers.

The home, with a spectacular wilderness view, was built in 1933 by C. R. Barton to accommodate family and friends. The living room is softly decorated with shades of pastels and lovely curtain swags. An elaborate garnet-stone fireplace framed by two iron elves held a massive log that was burning the night we arrived. In the corner stands the firmly stuffed family bear. "The furry creature," explained Holly with a twinkle, "has been known to appear unexpectedly outdoors at places where various Bartons or friends have demonstrated strong uphill skiing techniques."

Every room has a view of the mountains. I'd request the rooms on either end of the inn; they are a little larger and have more windows. The furniture includes family pieces and contemporary couches and chairs, all of a fine quality.

On a brisk winter evening, we lounged in the beautiful living room after a day of cross-country skiing. Soon we were led to a candlelit table for two, where we began an odyssey of tastes. A scrumptious anisette bread preceded a thick, juicy, stuffed smoked pork chop. Before my traveling companion appeared scallops, deliciously sauced and served in a pastry shell. For dessert a fresh berry compote of raspberry, strawberry, and rhubarb came out with a pecan-chocolate-chip tart served warm.

When we arrived at sunset, the Siamese Ponds Wilderness area of tree-covered mountains met a sky brilliant with blue and washes of pink. The combination of fine food, wine, and wilderness is my idea of "roughing it."

How to get there: From the south exit I–87 at Warrensburg, proceed 32 miles on Route 9. From junction of Routes 28 and 9, proceed north on Route 28. Turn left at Barton Mines Road and go uphill 5 miles on paved road to the mine entrance. Follow the signs and keep going to the top.

Innkeepers: Holly Currier; the Barton Family, proprietors
Address/Telephone: Barton Mines Road; (518) 251–3760 or (800) 241–1923, fax (518) 251–3655
Rooms: 4, all with private bath; 2 log cabins, each accommodating 6. Limited smoking.
Rates: Winter: $150, Friday or Saturday night; $120, other nights; double occupancy; MAP. Midweek specials.
Open: All year.
Facilities and activities: Dinner served nightly to guests; to public, by advance reservation only; BYOB. No smoking in dining room. Thirty kilometers of cross-country trails, hiking trails on 1,600 private acres contiguous with 108,000-acre Siamese Ponds Wilderness, tennis court, stocked fishing ponds. Nearby: downhill skiing at Gore Mountain, spring white-water rafting and canoeing on the Hudson River, horseback riding.

olive Metcalf

Old Chatham Sheepherding Company Inn
OLD CHATHAM, NEW YORK 12136

Is this heaven or am I merely dreaming? We are sitting in a wicker rocker on our private porch looking beyond the sunken garden with its fountain to the lush green pastures brimming with sheep. The quiet is punctuated occasionally by a baby lamb bleating for its mother, but otherwise the air is still. This will always be my first memory of the Old Chatham Sheepherding Company Inn—this and the extraordinary cuisine, that is.

"I'm just a farmer at heart," owner Tom Clark laughed one night in the relaxed but sophisticated living room of the inn, as he tried to describe how he and his wife created their unique inn and its unusual by-products. "From the time I raised and exhibited three sheep at the local

Dutchess County Fair," he went on to say, "I've had an interest in sheep."

This interest in sheep has led the couple to create an entirely new American business. Not only does the inn offer overnight lodging and a fine-dining restaurant, but on their 500-acre farm, the Clarks also raise sheep that are producing milk used for cheese, yogurt, ice cream, and other products. Although the dairy is in its infancy, there are great plans for the future. One morning my companion and I rose early to walk down to the Shaker-style sheep barn to watch the 6:30 A.M. milking and to pet the baby lambs. The operation is as modern and as interesting as a large-scale dairy operation.

The inn is gracious and charming—but that's not surprising, since Nancy is an interior designer and also an artist. Her luminous watercolors decorate several guest rooms. Fine antiques are liberally combined with unusual new furnishings, and elegant fabrics cover chairs, love seats, and beds. There are carved four-poster beds padded with fluffy lamb's-wool cushions. A nearby cottage contains two suites that are perfect in every detail. The masculine Cotswold Suite has a high four-poster bed, a brick fireplace, and a private deck, while the Hampshire Suite is charmingly done in shades of pink and yellow. Two more units are being created in the Carriage House.

As elegant as the inn appears, however, innkeeper George Shattuck best described the casual atmosphere when he said, "We want guests to feel comfortable. We know we've achieved our goal when they come to breakfast in their terry robes," and he swears it's actually happened.

The dining room is presided over by Executive Chef Melissa Kelly, a graduate of the Culinary Institute of America and the protégée of such acclaimed chefs as Larry Forgione and Alice Waters. Her rack of lamb was exquisite, as was the grilled ahi tuna. A kitchen garden was being created when we visited, but she is already creating a distinctive new cuisine using sheep's milk instead of cow's or goat's. A separate bakery where the talented pastry chef will have his own ovens and a temperature- and climate-controlled wine cellar will also be completed soon.

The manor house was originally the home of John S. Williams, Sr., whose interest in Shaker life was piqued by his home's proximity to several major Shaker communities. He began collecting examples of Shaker artifacts and eventually opened a museum across the street from his home. The museum contains one of the finest collections of Shaker-made articles in the world.

How to get there: From New York City take the Taconic Parkway to Route 295 east to East Chatham. Turn left at the sign for Old Chatham and follow this road for 3 miles. Turn left after the country store onto County Road 13. Follow this road for 1 mile and bear right onto Shaker Museum Road. The inn is ½ mile farther on the left.

Innkeepers: George Shattuck III and Melissa Kelly; Nancy and Tom Clark, proprietors
Address/Telephone: 99 Shaker Museum Road; (518) 794-9774, fax (518) 794-9779
Rooms: 8, including 2 suites; all with private bath and air conditioning, 2 with fireplace, 1 with whirlpool. Wheelchair accessible. No smoking inn.
Rates: $150 to $325, double occupancy, EPB. Two-night minimum June–October; 3-night minimum selected holiday weekends.
Open: All year except January.
Facilities and activities: Walking and hiking on 500 acres; seminars and events throughout the year, ranging from sheep-shearing demonstrations to cooking classes and wine dinners; tennis court is being installed. Nearby: Shaker Museum is across the street.

Oliver Loud's Inn
PITTSFORD, NEW YORK 14534

On such a night we sought refuge. We came before dark, and I imagined, through the falling snow, raising a camera lens toward the white-drizzled scene along the Erie Canal. The buttercup yellow canal house came slowly into view as we circled round and landed the car canal-side at the Oliver Loud's Inn. Vivienne invited us into the parlor/office for hot coffee and cookies. While we sat warming ourselves beside the fire, we watched a skier moving purposefully along the canal's towpath. Vivienne poured hazelnut coffee from an ornate, early nineteenth-century tea set into an exquisitely patterned floral cup while I noticed the Nanking porcelain hung above the fireplace. This was so civilized, so re-

fined, so comfortable a setting, that I could scarcely imagine the "canal rats" she described that frequented the tavern and lodging establishment during the mid-1800s. Later I discovered some of these Erie Canal characters depicted in the paintings and other folk art that she's collected for Oliver Loud's Inn, once a bawdy, rollicking drinking-and-eating establishment.

The canal house evolved from an 1812 farmhouse located in Bushnell's Basin on the eastern edge of Rochester. The basin provided turn-around space for the canal boats and became a hub of activity, transforming the farmhouse into a rambling, authentic inn. After buying the canal house, Vivienne purchased Oliver Loud's, a former stagecoach inn located 4 miles away. She thereupon had the inn sliced in half and transported up the road; it now stands, reassembled, just a few hundred feet from the canal house!

The inn's rooms have contemporary baths, thick carpeting, king-sized beds, and reproduction Stickley furniture as well as carefully chosen paintings and prints that might have been displayed in a fine home during Oliver Loud's life. The doors are grained in the faux mahogany popular in Loud's day, and each room is trimmed in wallpapers reflecting the period. Every detail throughout the inn was carefully researched.

Even on a snowy night, the dining rooms were festive, with people eating savory venison or beef stews, Mahi Mahi encrusted in nuts and butter, traditional roast duckling, salads dressed with an outstanding vinaigrette. The ham and asparagus appetizer had been adapted from a George Eastman dinner menu, dated 1905. The desserts included a strawberry dacquoise and a light, heavenly white-chocolate mousse. The menu is available in five different languages—Vivienne plans ahead for her international crowd.

Following a knock on the front door the next morning, we found a large picnic basket filled with a thermos of hot coffee, warm croissants, fruit, and a delicious jam. On such a morning, filled with sun and blue sky, we felt nourished, relaxed, and ready to travel. We did so with a cache of pleasant memories.

How to get there: From New York State Thruway, at exit 45, take I–490 west to Bushnell's Basin exit (#27); descend ramp, turn right, drive 400 yards to Oliver Loud's Inn. It's in Bushnell's Basin on Route 96, or 1474 Marsh Road.

Innkeeper: Vivienne Tellier

Address/Telephone: 1474 Marsh Road; (716) 248–5200 bed & breakfast, (716) 248–5000 restaurant, fax (716) 248–9970

Rooms: 8; all with private bath, air conditioning, television, and telephone. Designated no smoking rooms. Wheelchair accessible.

Rates: $125 to $155, seasonal, double or single occupancy, continental breakfast.

Open: All year.

Facilities and activities: Dinner Monday–Saturday (fixed price $35 for 3 courses), lighter menu Monday–Friday in pub; located on Erie Canal. Nearby: International Museum of Photography, Strong Museum, Rochester Museum and Science Center, Susan B. Anthony House, Genesee Country Village and Museum, Ellwanger Garden.

ℬeekman Arms
RHINEBECK, NEW YORK 12572

The Beekman Arms is a busy in-town inn that's grown from a stagecoach stop to almost a village within a village. The lodgings are in several buildings. The main inn has several wing-back chairs gathered around a stone fireplace in the lobby, and it's here or in the large Colonial living room that people meet before they go in to lunch or dinner. You might be seated in the old wooden tavern section, in the carpeted room that's part common area, or in the Main Street glass-enclosed garden room.

I do have favorites here, but unfortunately, you can't reserve a special guest room. The oldest rooms in the original inn were transformed in 1995 from old-fashioned and spare to quite ele-

gant with stylish period-reproduction furnishings, including some canopy beds. Rooms in the Delamater House, a gothic cottage on Main Street that was built in 1844, were remodeled a few years ago. Some of those in the Carriage House have skylights and gray-stained wood. Several modern rooms form a courtyard that's off Main Street. The motel rooms aren't for inngoers.

The inn restaurant is under the guiding hand of Larry Forgione, the well-known New York restaurateur, who also owns An American Place in Manhattan. He has created a distinctive cuisine that balances traditional Colonial recipes with new American preparations, and it lures pilgrims from far and near. For dinner in the fall, you might have traditional cedar-planked Atlantic salmon served with julienned local squash and toasted pumpkin-seed vinaigrette; or country-style meat loaf with mashed potatoes, grilled onion rings, and roasted ketchup gravy; or hand-cut Hudson Valley venison chili with black beans and warm cornbread.

The inn's sign says it dates from 1766. It has changed and grown a great deal since its Colonial inception. You can request a room where George Washington reputedly slept. Until its occupants arrive, it's often left open for other guests to see.

How to get there: From I–87 north exit onto Route 209 east and travel across the Kingston Rhinecliffe Bridge. Continue to 9G, turn right, go 1 mile, turn right on 9 to Rhinebeck. The inn is in the center of town.

Innkeeper: Charles LaForge; Eve Diaz, manager

Address/Telephone: Route 9 and Mill Street; (914) 876-7077, fax same

Rooms: 59, including 2 suites in 10 buildings; all with private bath, air conditioning, telephone, and television, 23 with fireplace. Wheelchair accessible. Pets allowed in some rooms. Designated no smoking rooms.

Rates: $85 to $125, double occupancy, EPB. Children under 12 free. Two-night minimum weekends.

Open: All year.

Facilities and activities: Breakfast, lunch, dinner, Sunday brunch; tavern; 3½ acres, garden, courtyard. Nearby: Rhinebeck Aerodrome, county fair, Antique Auto Show in May, Antiques Fair in October, Roosevelt and Vanderbilt estates in Hyde Park, golfing, boating, horseback riding.

Business travel: Desk in all rooms; fax available; complete conference center with all facilities; midweek corporate rates.

Belvedere Mansion
RHINEBECK, NEW YORK 12580

One day, on a visit to the Culinary Institute of America in Hyde Park, as I was driving along Route 9, I discovered an elegant mansion, obviously in the throes of a major renovation. My curiosity was piqued. It seemed too large for a private home, and I was right. This majestic Greek Revival–style house, with its fluted Corinthian columns, was destined to become a stylish new inn. For several years I watched its transformation until it was ready to receive guests.

Patricia Rebraca, the innkeeper, with her husband, Nick, welcomed us warmly as we walked into the charming foyer of the mansion. On one previous visit I had watched a local artist as he painted a colorful mural on an upstairs wall,

and now his artistry was also evident on lustrous panels beside the fireplaces in the first-floor dining rooms.

The guest rooms, located on the second floor, and reached by a magnificent carved-cherry staircase, are French jewel boxes, filled with exquisite antique French beds, tables, and armoires and embellished with lush damasks and brocades. (The Rebracas also own an antiques store, Cartouche, in Rhinebeck, which specializes in French antiques.) We stayed in Astor, a large room with garnet walls and a garnet-colored damask duvet on the bed.

Belvedere means "beautiful view," and the view down sloping lawns to Route 9 and then beyond to the Hudson River were, in fact, beautiful. We enjoyed a glass of sherry from the decanter in our room as we watched the sun set. Lafayette, just across the hall, has a similar view and is done is sunny yellows. The baths have smart black-and-white marble tiles, pedestal sinks, and, in some cases, claw-footed tubs.

In addition to the five guest rooms in the mansion, there are ten rooms in an adjacent carriage house. These all have private baths and range in size from The River Queen, which has a sitting area and a king-sized canopy bed, to tiny little rooms (Patricia calls these "cozies") with an alcove just big enough for a double bed.

The dining area is located in three main-floor rooms with wood-burning fireplaces, and tables are also placed in the foyer and in the tiny bar. A covered side deck has tables for summer dining. For dinner my pan-seared Atlantic salmon was accompanied by a parsnip pancake and wilted red Swiss chard in a balsamic reduction. My companion sampled the spinach-stuffed

roulade of chicken with tarragon au jus and garlic mashed potatoes. We finished by sharing a crepe filled with chestnut mousse and sauced with passion-fruit purée.

In the morning we enjoyed a full breakfast that started with juice and delectable fresh muffins and scones. This was followed by a fruit plate of pineapple, kiwi, blood orange, and banana. We had a choice of eggs Benedict, an omelet, or crepes filled with apples.

The inn is located on ten acres that include a pond overseen by a gazebo—the perfect place to finish the latest romance novel.

How to get there: From New York City take Henry Hudson Parkway north to the Saw Mill River Parkway, following that north to the Taconic Parkway. Continue north to Route 55 and travel west to Poughkeepsie. In Poughkeepsie take Route 9 north. The inn is 5 miles north of Hyde Park and 3½ miles south of Rhinebeck.

Innkeepers: Nikola and Patricia Rebraca
Address/Telephone: 10 Old Route 9 (mailing address: P.O. Box 785); (914) 889–8000, fax (914) 889–8811
Rooms: 15; all with private bath, 6 with air conditioning, 3 with fireplace. Smoking in bar only.
Rates: $85 to $195, double occupancy, EPB. Two-night minimum weekends; 3-night holiday weekends.
Open: All year.
Facilities and activities: Swimming pool, pond, walking trails, exercise room. Nearby: the Southlands Foundation, an equestrian center and internationally recognized riding school, which offers horse shows, hunter trials, and lessons; Franklin Roosevelt's Hyde Park home and library; Wilderstein; the Vanderbilt Mansion; the Mills Mansion.
Business travel: Three rooms wuth desk; fax available; meeting facilities.

Stanford White's Carriage House

RHINEBECK, NEW YORK 12572

In a secluded glen far from even a hint of traffic noise, this brick carriage house with its peaked dormers offers a classic retreat. Yes, Stanford White did design the carriage house. It was part of an 1892 estate called The Grove that he designed for Philip Schuyler. The grand proportions of the building are typical of his work. Restored in 1995 by innkeeper Chuck Atkins, the inn is surrounded by six acres of manicured lawns and formal gardens. An extravagant floral display ranges from daffodils and tulips in spring to lilies, clematis, and potted geraniums in the summer. The rear garden is ablaze in white flowers.

The impressive 1,000-square-foot living room is smartly furnished with sink-into sofas and chairs, all in pristine white. It's ultrasophisticated. A fireplace warms one end, oak floors gleam with polish, and a wall of windows and French doors bathe the room in light. Beyond, a terrace and garden lead to the pool, which is surrounded by a brick wall.

The guest rooms are equally svelte. They are all white from the walls to the painted floors and the white duvets covering the beds. Even the luxe baths are done in white marble. Rooms A and B share a hall bath; the bath for room C is also across the hall. But it's the studio that's the pièce de résistance. This grand suite (also in pristine white) has a cathedral ceiling and contains a palatial living room, a full kitchen, and a luxurious bedroom overseen by a giant fan window offering views of the gardens and pool. This is the ultimate romantic retreat, and Chuck tells me that it has become especially popular with honeymooners. It's no wonder. One evening at dusk we saw deer grazing on the lawn.

Breakfast is served in a pretty kitchen that's embellished with colorful tiles or in the summer, outside on the terrace. It might include blueberry pancakes or scrambled eggs with Canadian bacon, fresh muffins, and seasonal fruit.

A concert grand piano in the living room entices amateur and professional performers alike, but soothing classical music plays throughout the day. There are board games and books for your enjoyment as well.

How to get there: From New York City take the Hudson River Parkway north to the Saw Mill River Parkway north and then the Taconic Parkway north. Take the exit marked Red Hook/Pine Plains/Route 199. Take Route 199 west. At the traffic light continue straight ahead onto Route 308 west. Continue on Route 308 for approximately 4 miles to the sign on the left. The inn is about ¼ mile down the driveway.

Innkeeper: Charles (Chuck) Atkins
Address/Telephone: 252 Route 308; (914) 876–7257, fax the same
Rooms: 4, including 1 suite; 2 with private bath, all with air conditioning, 1 with television and kitchen. No smoking inn.
Rates: $100 to $200, double occupancy, EPB. Two-night minimum weekends in late spring, summer, and fall; 3-night minimum holiday weekends. No credit cards.
Open: All year.
Facilities and activities: Pool, gardens. Nearby: skiing, 30 miles away; hiking trails; numerous historic houses, including Montgomery Place, Wilderstein, Clermont, and Franklin Roosevelt's Hyde Park.

$\mathcal{W}$histlewood Farm

RHINEBECK, NEW YORK 12572

New York cowgirl Maggie Myer named her contemporary ranch-inn for the winds that whistle through the trees. Inside, you feel as though you've stepped into the West. The wood-burning stove casts a warmth in winter; there are photos, sculptures, and books referring to horses. The *Horseman's Journal* lies on the table.

When you arrive the harvest table in the kitchen will be loaded with treats. On a recent visit we found a blueberry cobbler, lemon poppy seed cake, cookies, muffins, and fruit. You then sit in the front sunroom, which overlooks the corrals, a winding lane, and the distant soft hillsides. A row of rockers was to my left. This casual country place is ten minutes or less from downtown Rhinebeck. Some guests rise early in the morning to help feed the horses.

In the handsome skylit barn, Maggie showed us the stalls lined with soft rubbery cushions for equine comfort, the foal-viewing room, and the feed room. Down the hill is her new horse pond. On these 13½ acres she cares for horses and a dog. The Lab, Cherokee, she purchased while on vacation in California. He came along home on the plane in kennel class, not knowing that he was a very lucky dog.

Breakfasts are served buffet style in the large kitchen/dining room. Her coal- or wood-burning Gold Coin stove dates from 1904 and is used occasionally. From the hutch you fill your bowl with fresh fruits, spread hot muffins with home-made jams, and find your niche either in the sun-room or out back on the patio. You might want to sit in the kitchen's dining room beneath the horse mural. Before long Maggie brings out the morning's special, which might be French-bread toast, scrambled eggs, or a hot cheese strata. She also serves homemade granola. No one leaves so much as a crumb when it tastes this good. As you enter the inn, you get a view of her garden, framed in a picket fence.

The four guest rooms are simply furnished with country antiques and twentieth-century pieces; the beds are queen-sized. There are no pretensions. One room has a private backyard and Southwest flair. Maggie made the bed in the master suite. An Old Town canoe, made in wood as they originally were, hangs from the ceiling; and wide patio windows look out to the lane.

Maggie's touring recommendations might take you to a winery that serves gourmet lunches under the trees, to a nearby park that leads you down to the Hudson River for a walk, or out for an afternoon of sailing on the Hudson River with a captain who holds a U.S. Coast Guard cap-tain's license. She's also a country antiques lover and knows the shops in the area.

Maggie's an outdoor gal, so when you call, she might be out feeding the horses. She'll call you back.

How to get there: From Rhinebeck, drive 3 miles east on Route 308. Turn left at Pells Road and turn right at the fifth driveway on the right.

Innkeeper: Maggie Myer

Address/Telephone: 11 Pells Road (mailing address: R.D. 1, Box 109); (914) 876–6838, fax (914) 876–5513

Rooms: 4, including 1 suite, plus 1 cottage; all with private bath and air conditioning, 1 with fireplace, 1 with Jacuzzi. Pets allowed, $15 per day. No smoking inn.

Rates: Double occupancy: $115 to $165, weekends; $95 to $125, midweek; single: $55 to $85, Monday through Thursday; EPB. Cot $15. Two-night minimum weekends May–October. American Express only card.

Open: All year.

Facilities and activities: 13½ acres, farm animals, horses, hiking. Nearby: restaurants (3-mile drive), Rhinebeck and seasonal flying circus, Hudson River wineries, Roo-sevelt and Vanderbilt mansions.

428 *Mt. Vernon*

ROCHESTER, NEW YORK 14620

Up through century-aged trees—pines, beeches, and maples—we drove to the hilltop Irish manor house, whose solid brick presence and countrylike setting give quiet sanctuary in the city; 428 Mt. Vernon was once a nunnery for the Sisters of Mercy. The inn's two acres are contiguous with the renowned "tree park," Highland Park, the oldest in Rochester, whose 150 acres were laid out in the 1880s by Frederick Law Olmsted. You can walk on the paths that meander gracefully through 150 acres of flowers, shrubs, and rare species of trees—identical to some of comparable age that surround the inn.

For eighteen years Claire and Phil Lanzatella lived 3 blocks away, where they raised their chil-

dren. Phil is a professional restorer of historical properties. To tackle a building of this magnitude, one would need previous experience.

We entered the foyer and Claire led us up to our lovely room, which overlooked the backyard. Soon we were served iced tea and found homemade cookies waiting for us on an antique plate. Refreshed, we descended to the spacious living room where Max, the mixed Lab, perched on a long window seat and gazed into the trees. There were lovely antiques, a piano, an original maple fireplace, and bookcases—a haven of traditional comforts. From the former chapel you can watch the backyard birds through a powerful telescope. Claire and Phil, who are birders, are knowledgeable about their feathered guests and the trees that host them.

We fetched a Highland Park Guide from a basket and mapped our walk. Down the hill we headed and then back up again into the hills of spruces, near the larches, past the hornbeams, around the magnolias, lilacs, azaleas, and Japanese maples, then over to the hickories, birches, ashes, chestnuts, and oaks. Among the rare trees were a Caucasian wingnut, a Japanese Stewartia, and a Hokkaido magnolia. Many of them were labeled, and when we returned to the inn, Claire pointed to her equally rare trees, among them a tricolor beech.

For dinner we went off with a good recommendation and were pleased to find that fine dining at reasonable prices was only three minutes away.

Very conveniently, we had checked our breakfast preferences from a menu the night before, and now we were treated to hot apple-buttermilk pancakes, scones, homemade jams, fruits, and hot coffee. We could have chosen any array of combinations, and we like being given the choice in this manner. Crisp white linens underlined the dogwood-pattern plates.

Before we left we took one last brief walk in the park to admire the trees planted more than one hundred years ago. We were fascinated by the size and variety of the species. These legacies, like inn restorations, are important for the future.

How to get there: From New York State Thruway, take exit 46 (390 North), to Route 15A (exit 16). Go 2 blocks and turn right on South Avenue; go 3 blocks and turn right on Alpine Street, turn left onto Mt. Vernon. Go 1 block to intersection with Doctor's Road, make a left, then turn immediately to right and up through inn's gates (on left).

Innkeepers: Claire and Phil Lanzatella
Address/Telephone: 428 Mt. Vernon Avenue; (716) 271–0792 or (800) 836–3159, fax (716) 271–0946
Rooms: 7; all with private bath, ceiling fan, air conditioning, telephone, and television, 3 with fireplace. Wheelchair accessible. Restricted smoking.
Rates: $110, double occupancy; $90, single; EPB.
Open: All year.
Facilities and activities: Nearby: restaurants (within 5-minute drive), Ellwanger Garden, Museum of Photography, Strong Museum, Rochester Museum of Science and Planetarium. University of Rochester and Medical School.
Business travel: Telephone in room, 4 rooms with desk; small conference room; corporate rates.
Recommended Country Inns® Travelers' Club Benefit: 10 percent discount, Monday–Thursday.

The Mansion
ROCK CITY FALLS, NEW YORK 12863

Once I came in spring, and another time in winter: Each time I was touched by the lyrical beauty of the place—by the paintings, the books, the music that seemed to penetrate in all the right ways, the balm of the flowers that fill the inn. In winter orchids, potted daffodils, mums, and bromeliads were in exquisite bloom. In summer one hundred rose bushes framed the lawn; and fuchsias, beloved by hummingbirds, marked the entry; clematis and foxglove hugged the side porch, where wicker seats invited a "sit." Inside are bouquets of every description. I listened to Mozart, reassuringly touched the hand-carved statue of St. Francis, and found this quiet haven as inviting as remembered.

Alan Churchill can make a flower grow with a glance. He's a genuinely kind soul who nurtures his guests and then discreetly disappears to tend to his matters, which include raising sheep and preparing five-course gourmet feasts for breakfast.

The inn was built as a summer home in 1866 in the style of a Venetian villa by George West, successful inventor of the folded paper bag. Six different woods compose the building and parquet floorings. Among the historical details are Grecian themes: ladies, warriors, and chariots. Begin with a lovely background, add kindly innkeepers and fine taste—an Eastlake parlor, Tiffany chandeliers, Waterford globes, Empire furnishings—and you have an inn about which sonnets are written. Some guests have written poems to their hosts—some while they were here, others after they had gone away.

Up the thickly carpeted stairs are antique beds and armoires in the sun-filled rooms. Even here a fresh bouquet of flowers sits on the bureau. Something beautiful distinguishes each room from all the others.

Breakfasts are served at private tables in the elegant dining room. Alan prepares the day's dawning feast with the same experience with which he recommends the best restaurants. He begins with vanilla-almond or Irish cream coffee. An ornate dish of fruits follows with fresh hot homemade breads. Then come his omelet of ham, cheese, and mushrooms, or his orange French toast with warm Vermont maple syrup. Outside the window the birds are busy around the bird feeder, and inside the music is playing softly.

As if this weren't pleasure enough, you might come for a performance by Yo-Yo Ma or Midori, or perhaps for a ballet, a concert, or to see the museums of the cultural haven of Saratoga.

Why must it always come, that bittersweet moment of departure?

How to get there: From I–87 (from south), take exit 13 north (Route 9). Proceed on Route 9, which becomes Broadway in town; turn left onto Route 29 west (Washington Street) and go 7 miles to the inn on the right.

Innkeepers: Tom Clark and Alan Churchill
Address/Telephone: 801 Route 29 (mailing address P.O. Box 77); (518) 885–1607, fax the same
Rooms: 7, including 2 suites plus 2 rooms in cottage; all with private bath and air conditioning. No smoking inn.
Rates: $95 to $185, double occupancy; 1 suite and extra person, $25 additional; EPB. Two-night minimum weekends May–October. No credit cards.
Open: All year.
Facilities and activities: 4 acres with pool, gardens, croquet. Nearby: restaurants (7 miles away in Saratoga), horse races, National Museum of Racing, National Museum of Dance, concerts, opera, jazz, ballet, cultural events, 2,000-acre park.
Business travel: Telephone, desk, fax, message service, and business supplies available.

The Point

Our biggest decision one cool fall afternoon was whether to take a canoe out on the lake or to play a round of tennis. The canoe won out this day because we decided we wanted to see if we could spot some of the other Adirondack camps that line the shores of Saranac Lake.

It's always seemed to me as if the barons of industry who built these rustic log retreats in the early 1900s must have craved the casual ambience they provided as a total antithesis to their luxurious abodes in the cities. Here they could wear old clothes and tramp through the woods, hundreds of miles in distance and spirit from their fast-paced city lives. The Point was the retreat of William Avery Rockefeller, a great-nephew of John D., and its stone fireplaces, spacious porches, and adjacent cottages are considered among the finest of this type of architecture.

When David and Christie Garrett purchased The Point in 1986, it had already been converted to an inn to accommodate travelers to the 1980 Olympics at nearby Lake Placid. They retained its rustic simplicity but added a wealth of antique furnishings, moose and deer heads on the walls, and Oriental rugs on the hardwood floors. They upholstered the furniture in spritely checked wool fabrics. Today it offers the ultimate in sophisticated but casual accommodations and has earned just about every award bestowed on inns.

The inn is secluded on ten acres that occupy a point of land thrusting into the lake. From the main inn as well as most of the cottages, there are romantic, misty views of the lake in the morning, and, the sun glistening over the mountains in the afternoon. There's a beach by the lake for swimming, and the inn also offers hiking trails, sunset cruises, volleyball, badminton, bicycling, cross-country skiing, and ice skating.

Meals are a highlight of a stay at The Point. Chef Sam Mahoney worked and trained in Europe. One night I had a bouillabaisse that was thick with lobster, scallops, shrimp, clams, mussels, and fish, while my companion had a roasted poussin served with sweet corn fritters, wild mushrooms, and roasted potatoes. For dessert the individual soufflés are luscious, but so is the tarte bordalou (a pear tart with almond cream) and the roule marquis (a dark-chocolate sponge cake rolled with sweet cream and served with fresh raspberries and strawberries).

There are some things that you can never have enough of. Among them are love, chocolate, and The Point.

How to get there: From New York City take the New York State Thruway to exit 30. Follow Route 73 north for 34 miles to Upper Saranac Lake. Detailed directions to the inn are given when reservations are confirmed.

Innkeepers: David and Christie Garrett; Pamela and Jacques Berry-Brouchier, managers
Address/Telephone: HCR #1 Box 65; (518) 891–5674 or (800) 255–3530,
   fax (518) 891–1152
Rooms: 11, including 1 suite; all with private bath, fireplace, and balcony or patio. Pets
   allowed with prior permission.
Rates: $825 to $1,175, double occupancy, AP, all recreational facilities. Two-night minimum weekends; 3-night minimum holiday weekends. American Express only card
   accepted.
Open: All year except 3 weeks in early spring.
Facilities and activities: Rowboats, waterskiing, hiking, tennis, sunset cruises, swimming,
   volleyball, badminton, bicycling, croquet, horseshoes, fishing, cross-country skiing,
   ice fishing, snowshoeing, and ice skating. Nearby: downhill skiing, golf.

Six Sisters Bed & Breakfast

SARATOGA SPRINGS, NEW YORK 12866

The Six Sisters is named for Kate Benton and her five sisters. "My six brothers are still waiting," admits Kate. From the porch of this small inn, you can easily see the gates to the racing track and stroll down to the Racing Museum on Union Avenue. It's a familiar sight to native Saratogian Kate, whose background is well suited to being an innkeeper. Being raised with eleven siblings gave her an accommodating approach and tolerance for others; she also grew up in the hospitality business. Her family owns the Grand Union Motel on Broadway Avenue and recently built the Crystal Spa, with facilities for massage, mineral baths, and facials.

"My dad served as mayor of Saratoga Springs when we were children, and he gave us all a respect and appreciation for the history of the town where we grew up," Kate said. The strength of her ties to Saratoga drew Kate and Steve back from Hawaii, where they'd met and resided for over a decade following college.

The influence of those years are felt throughout the inn. The first furnishing they bought as newlyweds in Hawaii was the dining-room table, where guests now enjoy a full breakfast. Steve rises early to prepare the French toast or custard quiche that are among his wide-ranging specialties.

During racing months, when almost everyone has the track in mind, Steve and Kate often prepare a buffet-style hot breakfast casserole.

Those who want to be off and running can enjoy a full breakfast yet still catch the first race. Occasionally he proffers the Kona chocolate-macadamia nut coffee, and sometimes he cooks a vegetable-and-cheese omelet seasoned with jalapeño pepper. In that case he might serve soda biscuits or freshly baked poppy seed muffins on the side, along with juices and coffee.

The rooms exhibit a Victorian influence, with their wallpapers and flowered spreads. The suite has a king-sized bed, some rooms have plants, and three have private porches.

Steve was president of the New York Bed and Breakfast Association and has had an opportunity to meet with innkeepers from around the state.

You might meet the newest family member, young son Jared. His companions in play include two well-behaved wire-haired terriers, Kela and Asta.

The inn is an 1890s Queen Anne, whose scalloped roofline gives it a festive look. The innkeepers opened the inn in 1989, when Kate preceded Steve back from Hawaii to initiate the project. When the snow banks rise, they occasionally smell the fragrance of Kona coffee brewing and remember the Hawaiian beach wistfully. But they remind themselves there's cross-country skiing in the park, a new ice skating rink, and plenty of winter sports and local events. And they can always go down to the spa for a soak in 100-degree water and a blissful massage.

How to get there: From I–87 take exit 14. Continue into town on Union Avenue, at third light take a right onto Nelson Avenue, and immediate right onto Morton Place. Inn is on right.

Innkeepers: Steve Ramirez and Kate Benton

Address/Telephone: 149 Union Avenue; (518) 583–1173, fax (518) 587–2470

Rooms: 4, including 1 suite; all with private bath, air conditioning, and television, 3 with porch, suite with fridge and king-sized bed. No smoking inn.

Rates: $75 to $105, November–March; $95 to $115, April–October; $225 to $260 during racing season (July–August) and holiday weekends; EPB. Special packages include theater, dinner, and spa combinations. Three- to 6-night minimum some weekends.

Open: All year.

Facilities and activities: Off-street parking. Nearby: outlet center (70 stores) in Lake George, Saratoga Springs State Spa and Park, Spa Theater, golf course, horseback riding, Yaddo garden.

Business travel: Computer, modem, and fax available.

Recommended Country Inns® Travelers' Club Benefit: 50 percent discount, Sunday–Thursday, November 15–May 15. Receive free passes to Racing Museum and Harness Track.

Union Gables Bed & Breakfast
SARATOGA SPRINGS, NEW YORK 12866

Jody learned about Tom's plans for Union Gables at a party. A colleague of Tom's accidentally mentioned how amazing it was that she, a mother of four children, could also find time to restore and run a twelve-room bed and breakfast. Jody thought it interesting that Tom had forgotten to mention to its pivotal manager—her—that he wanted to buy and restore a dilapidated mansion.

"We had a rather long discussion that night when we returned home," she now laughs. The result of that discussion is an inn with spacious, interesting, and comfortable rooms. Each is named for one of their brothers or sisters, and each was designer decorated when it became a decorator showhouse.

"We didn't get to see the rooms until they were done," admits Jody. Brother Bruce especially likes his namesake, decorated with a masculine Adirondack theme and white woodwork. Edward's Room is pink and feminine; he's still trying to switch with the green plaids of Kate's Room. Regardless of names, you'll sleep peacefully in every one of these luscious rooms, with their dramatic contemporary designs and trendsetting decor. The 14-foot-high ceilings and large windows allow the morning sunlight to pour in (if you forget to pull your shades).

This distinguished Queen Anne Victorian, designed by the architect R. Newton Breeze, is on the National Register of Historic Places, and the inn registers with everyone who passes by. When you drive by the inn on Union Avenue, its color scheme, grandiose size, wide wraparound porch, and gables strike a chord of balanced beauty.

In the morning you'll fetch your continental breakfast and find yourself a place on this porch with its slender columns. You might read the day's racing forms, peruse the upcoming events at the Saratoga Performing Arts Center, or consider a visit to a spa. You might contemplate borrowing a bicycle and riding out to the park or walking down to the Horse Racing Museum.

When you arrive you'll see Jody and her assistant in the office—an elegant, circular room whose walls are painted to suggest a gazebo. The woodwork is exquisite. Raised, carved bird's-eye maple shaped like bamboo rises from the window frames.

The inn has a temperature-controlled exercise room with all the essential equipment in the neighboring carriage house. A hot tub is filled and ready for use just outside the door.

From the inn you can easily walk to a number of restaurants located along Broadway.

Jody and Tom are both native Saratogians. Tom's real estate office is located in another Union Avenue mansion, located directly across the street from the inn. He got the idea for a bed and breakfast while showing a client through the dilapidated building. Tom didn't want to tell Jody about the notion until he had all his information together. Luckily for Tom, Jody has an easy disposition, and she had been looking for a project, since all the children are now in school.

How to get there: From the Northway (I–87) take exit 14 and turn right onto Route 9P (Union Avenue) into town. Inn is located on the right, 2 blocks past the National Museum of Racing. Park in the rear by turning right on Court Street.

Innkeepers: Jody and Tom Roohan
Address/Telephone: 55 Union Avenue; (518) 584–1558 or (800) 398–1558, fax (518) 583–0649
Rooms: 12, including 2 suites and 2 cottages; all with private bath, air conditioning, television, telephone, and fridge. Dogs allowed. No smoking in guest rooms.
Rates: $205 to $250, racing season (July and August); $85 to $120, rest of the year; double occupancy, continental breakfast.
Open: All year.
Facilities and activities: Exercise room, tennis court, basketball hoop, hot tub, bicycles. Nearby: National Museum of Racing and Hall of Fame, Saratoga Harness Hall of Fame, Saratoga Spa State Park, Congress Park, Union Avenue Racetrack, Skidmore College, National Museum of Dance, boat rentals on Saratoga Lake, music and ballet at Saratoga Performing Arts Center.

The Westchester House
SARATOGA SPRINGS, NEW YORK 12866

The annual July–August racing season in America's historic spa town, according to Bob and Stephanie Melvin, brings a crowd that is as interesting to watch as the horses. At Fasig-Tipton, the annual horse auction held in July, the auctioneer and his spotters wear tuxedos, the men present wear elegant suits, and the women who attend are dressed in evening gowns and jewels. Oblivious to damaging their finery and fancy footwear, many of the attendees migrate through the muck and dirt of the arena, carefully examining the horses. Bob also told us about a guest who sojourned at the inn last summer. It seems this guest was planning to bid on a horse worth a cool million dollars.

At the breakfast table, where there are lively discussions, we discovered that the innkeepers are cultured music lovers. In fact, Stephanie is an accomplished vocalist. In the hallway upstairs a bulletin board of musical events, art exhibits, lectures, shows, and spa events is kept up to date. The list of artistic events here is awe-inspiring: opera, ballet, orchestral and chamber music as well as jazz and popular music. There are also art exhibits, theatricals, lectures, and more. Depending on when you come, you might meet a ballet dancer, the publisher of a prestigious horsey publication, or a writer.

Bob and Stephanie know this town from the inside out, including its restaurants.

For dinner we went off to a little place called Eartha's, where the food was marvelous—the aïoli by itself merited a return; the grilled shrimp and tuna were done to perfection.

The inn's rooms have a Victorian ambience; they possess some wonderful antiques as well as lace curtains, elegant shades with swag pulls, and carefully selected wallpapers. Every room has an attractive bathroom, and most have king- or queen-sized beds. Good reading lights, too.

Throughout the inn are works from Bob and Stephanie's art collection—a variety of prints, sculpture, and glassware. Also scattered about are books about Saratoga, gardening, and the arts.

The inn was built by Almeron King, a wood craftsman, as his private home; he used chestnut throughout. You will appreciate the handsome dining-room cabinets, the fireplace mantels, and the inn's Eastlake detail in the woodwork. Speaking of detail, Stephanie sees to it that fresh

flowers and Westchester House chocolates are strategically placed in your room.

Breakfast included cereals, fresh fruit, and a delicious assortment of freshly baked breads.

We drove down Broadway Avenue to see the mansions, Skidmore College, and Saratoga Springs Park, where the original baths are found. They still give you the full treatment of these luxurious, carbonated waters, and massage. We saw people skiing in the park beneath a colonnade of magnificent towering pines. We also scouted the shops downtown and took time to recharge at the Westchester House.

How to get there: From I–87 (Northway) take exit 13N to Saratoga Springs. Go 3⁹⁄₁₀ miles on Route 9, turn right on Lincoln Avenue, and go ³⁄₁₀ mile to the inn, on the right. Turn right into a parking area.

Innkeepers: Stephanie and Bob Melvin

Address/Telephone: 102 Lincoln Avenue; (518) 587–7613 or (800) 581–7613

Rooms: 7; all with private bath and air conditioning; telephone and television available on request. No smoking inn.

Rates: $70 to $150, double occupancy, continental breakfast; higher rates in racing season (July–August), $195 to $250. Credit cards accepted, prefer cash and checks. Two-night minimum weekends.

Open: All year except January.

Facilities and activities: Parking. Nearby: Saratoga Race Track, restaurants, downtown, Saratoga Springs Spa State Park, Congress Park, Horse Racing Museum, National Museum of Dance. Cultural events: ballet, opera, music.

Business travel: Desk in 3 rooms; telephone, fax, dataport, television, and answering machine available.

The Ram's Head Inn
SHELTER ISLAND, NEW YORK 11965

The inn is located on the clear waters of Coecles Harbor.

You'll go home with tales of sailing on a summer's afternoon, biking on the island roads and seeing osprey nests atop the telephone poles, and dining on fine foods by candlelight. You'll whisper the words "perfect little waterfront inn." You want to keep it a secret. But a wonderful summer holiday can't be kept a silent memory; it must be shared.

Two 13-foot O'Day sloops, two Sunfish, a kayak, and a paddleboat sit dockside. In seconds you're off to explore the shores of the island sanctuary of unspoiled beauty. Literally one-third of the island is a nature conservancy.

The inn is a large, weathered-shingle, center-hall Colonial, built as an inn in 1929. It is light and airy. The rooms are simple and have carpeted floors, white curtains, and maple furniture. The favorite "end" waterside rooms are reserved one year in advance. A favorite "offwater" room is Number 16. At night the inn is so quiet that guests open their louvered summer doors (each room has a double door—one louvered and one solid) to let in the cool evening breezes.

There's a slate patio with flowers abloom in heavy clay flowerpots. Everything is conducive to "settle-back summer" fun. There are a hammock and two swings. A child's play set is mounted at the edge of the expansive lawn. Two paths to the water wind around either side of the tennis court.

Dinner at the inn is a saucy event, with sophisticated fare that might include tuna steak in parchment with ginger butter and julienne vegetables, rack of lamb with honey-and-pine-nut glaze and a port wine sauce, or smoked-salmon-and-scallop mousse with domestic caviar and dill crème fraîche. The desserts have a touch of panache, like the dinners. You might try frozen hazelnut terrine with chocolate truffle in the center or a pear tartlet topped with apricot and rum glaze. When you spoon it to your mouth, it's delicate and delicious.

How to get there: Take Route 114 through Sag Harbor to the ferry (there is a moderate ferry charge for cars). On Shelter Island take Route 114 north to the traffic circle and continue straight on Cartright Road to the stop sign. Turn right on Ram Island Drive and go right over the causeway to the inn.

Innkeepers: Linda and James Eklund

Address/Telephone: 108 Ram Island Drive; (516) 749–0811, fax (516) 749–0059

Rooms: 17, including 4 suites; 5 with private bath, all with telephone and ceiling fan. No smoking in rooms.

Rates: November through March, $65 to $80; April through October, $110 to $150; double occupancy; $140 to $230, suite for 4 people; continental buffet breakfast. 10 percent discount Sunday through Thursday; additional person, $15. Two-night minimum on weekends.

Open: All year.

Facilities and activities: Dinner ($35–$40), bar, sunroom, sailing, 800 feet of beachfront, exercise room, sauna, tennis, 13 moorings. Nearby: bicycling, golfing, swimming, boating, fishing, hiking.

*L*akehouse Inn

STANFORDVILLE, NEW YORK 12581

Judy and Richard Kohler owned a Victorian gingerbread house that they called the Village Victorian Inn in Rhinebeck for many years, but when they built this contemporary home overlooking tiny Golden Pond in 1991, they created a thoroughly sophisticated and elegant retreat, as different from the fussy Victorian as Jekyll is from Hyde.

At first sight the cedar-sided house appears modest and unremarkable; even when we walked along the flying-bridge entrance to the house, we were unprepared for the gracious and urbane interior. The house envelops its guests in country charm but also offers luxurious and spacious private retreats. For a total getaway from the fast-paced city, I can't imagine a more relaxing sanctuary.

The living room is decorated with flair in gentle earth tones. The vaulted, rough-sawn pine ceiling and the wall of view windows toward the lake give the room a warm, inviting glow. It's furnished with antiques, Oriental rugs on oak floors, twig furniture, comfortable sofas, piles of magazines and books, and an ornately carved oak English bar on which Victorian flow blue china is displayed. It's surrounded by a wraparound deck overlooking the lake.

Lakehouse Inn is the ultimate romantic retreat. The Casablanca Suite, for example, has its own fireplace, laid with logs and ready to be lighted, and a private deck. There's a pink damask sofa on which to watch the flames with a loved one while sipping a glass of wine chilled in the refrigerator. The canopy bed is swathed in lace. A TV, VCR, and CD player hide in a pine armoire. In the bath, a Jacuzzi for two has a serene view and is surrounded by a lip holding an array of fat candles.

The equally spacious Master Suite, located downstairs, has a private deck offering a view of the lake. Oriental rugs cover oak floors, another lace canopy decorates the bed, fat shutters shield the windows, and the pink-tile bath has another Jacuzzi. Each of the rooms is so large and so well equipped that it's possible to spend an entire weekend in the room and never feel claustrophobic.

Every possible amenity is provided. As Judy explained, "We just want our guests to be comfortable. We're too far from a town for them to run out for a soft drink, so we provide all of that in the room. We have soft drinks, wine, cookies, appetizers such as smoked salmon, truffles, and even Baby Watson cheesecakes in the refrigera-tor in case someone has a late-night sweet-tooth craving."

In the morning our breakfast was delivered to our room in a covered basket. One day it included an individual quiche with fresh fruit and breads. Another day we had cheese blintzes and chicken Chardonnay.

If guests do venture forth, they will find rowboats and paddleboats for use on the lake, hammocks, trails through the twenty-two-acre property, and a VCR library that includes almost 150 selections. Historic mansions, local wineries, and superb restaurants are located nearby.

How to get there: From New York City take the Hudson River Parkway north to the Saw Mill River Parkway, and then travel north on the Taconic Parkway to the Rhinebeck/Route 199 exit. Turn right onto Route 199 and go ½ mile. Take the first right onto Route 53 (South Road). Go 3 ½ miles. Turn right onto Shelly Hill Road and go exactly ⁹⁄₁₀ mile. Turn into paved driveway. The Lakehouse Inn is the second house.

Innkeepers: Judy and Richard Kohler
Address/Telephone: Shelly Hill Road; (914) 266–8093
Rooms: 5; all with private bath, air conditioning, telephone, television, stereo, CD
    player, minirefrigerator, wet bar, coffeemaker, balcony or deck, fireplace, and
    Jacuzzi. No smoking inn.
Rates: $295 to $495, double occupancy, EPB. Two-night minimum weekends.
Open: All year.
Facilities and activities: Rowboats, paddleboats, hiking. Nearby: historic Hyde Park home
    of Franklin Roosevelt, Wilderstein, Montgomery Place.
Business travel: Fax, computer, and copy machine available.

Taughannock Farms Inn
TRUMANSBURG, NEW YORK 14886

Taughannock Farms Inn sits astride a high promontory directly overlooking Cayuga Lake. It's a beauty, crowned with a widow's watch. Taughannock Falls State Park lies directly below.

Take a seat in the elegant dining room—it's light and sunny, and the lake view spreads out before you. Dinner begins as it has for nearly half a century in this classic inn. You can order from an excellent variety of dishes that are preceded by relish, appetizers, soups, rich orange-date bread (you can take the recipe home). You feel special; you're treating yourself to a grand evening with all the trimmings. I chose an excellent fish that arrived still sizzling on the plate, accompanied by plump, fresh vegetables. You might consider the roast Long Island duckling served with a fruited sauce. It's assumed that a fine meal deserves a fine sweet. After a long recitation I chose a Southern pecan pie, but I was also tempted by the numerous ice cream concoctions.

I was up early the next morning. The sun was streaming in my window; the lovely furnishings and lakeside view gave me a composed feeling. Each room is attractive and clean. Antiques are everywhere. You'll find elegant highboys and original bentwoods, nice pieces. Several of the antiques were brought from Europe when the mansion was built in 1873. Nancy le Grand's grandparents began the tradition of innkeeping more than forty years ago.

Nancy summered here as a child. She's probably the only little girl her age who played with an authentic Victorian music box, which now sits in the inn. "Listen to the Mocking Bird Sing" was her favorite song.

The inn has a longtime staff with close ties to the innkeepers. The pastry chef has been here for more than forty years and her husband, the chef, for more than thirty. You can expect the same good foods each time you return.

From the inn you can walk to Taughannock Falls and up into the 783 acres of woods and hiking trails. Opposite the inn Cayuga Lake offers swimming and fishing. Drive 9 miles to Ithaca and you can board Keith's boat, the MV *Manhattan*, for a dinner cruise or arrive dockside for a moonlight cruise.

Breakfast next morning might be served on the outdoor patio where the kittens (ten at last count) play at your feet. It's fresh fruits, granola, and delicious breads served to the sound of birds chirping in the trees.

A fine inn is adopted by travelers and the community. If you hear the locals comment that a highboy has been moved, it's because they regard the inn as their own. Everyone takes it personally.

How to get there: The inn is located on Route 89, 9 miles north of Ithaca. The state park signs are your cue you've reached the inn. Look up the hill and climb up to the entrance. Fly-in: Ithaca Airport.

Innkeepers: C. Keith and Nancy le Grand

Address/Telephone: 2030 Gorge Road; (607) 387–9509

Rooms: 7, including 2 guest houses; all with private bath, guest houses with air conditioning and fireplace. No smoking inn. Guest houses wheelchair accessible.

Rates: $95 to $135, double occupancy; single, $10 less; continental breakfast. $175 for guest house for 4. Two-night minimum fall weekends.

Open: Easter to Thanksgiving.

Facilities and activities: Dinner (entrees $17 to $23), service bar; on 10 acres on Cayuga Lake in Taughannock Falls State Park, with boating, swimming, hiking, cross-country skiing. Nearby: skating pond, bicycling, vineyard tours, lake cruise, golfing, tennis.

The Merrill Magee House
WARRENSBURG, NEW YORK 12885

Ken and Florence Carrington have purposely kept the Merrill Magee legacy; photographs of the woman as a child and late in life hang framed upon the wall of her nineteenth-century home. They've added the inn to the National Register of Historic Places. I think Merrill Magee would like what's become of her summertime home. The place has a nice feeling and the food is good.

The stone walk, just wide enough for two walking abreast, is lined with lanterns. Under the maple tree two friends sat chatting while their wives went off antiquing. Through a picket fence we saw a couple swimming in that divine Olympic-sized pool. Later I heard music carried over on the wind from the town bandstand. The

entire inn is surrounded by a white picket fence. The location is in town; the setting is parklike.

If you come during the winter, you'll be enticed into the tavern, lit by a warm fire, by Ken, the white-haired innkeeper whose accent denotes English birth. After a good chat you'll be led into the dining room, where you can debate over the menu. He'll also give you directions to the village cross-country ski trails, which are free to everyone.

For dinner I ordered the Sole Vanessi, which was freshly prepared with crabmeat, mushrooms, and cheese filling and topped with a light wine sauce. We had such a good time with our friends that we belatedly noticed that everyone else had gone to bed or home. Kindly innkeepers like these wouldn't think of rushing their guests.

The furniture has been kept simple, in Merrill's honor. The original wallpapers have been saved for the most part and still hang on the walls and hallways. Antiques furnish the upstairs suite. Walk down the path, pass through the wicker gate, and you come to the Peletiah Richards Guest House, where ten contemporary rooms bear herb titles. Several look out to a field, and all have a private fireplace. It's a short distance from the rooms to a small exercise room, where the whirlpool steams warmly. It's especially inviting after a day of cross-country skiing.

The Schroon and Hudson rivers converge in the town of Warrensburg, and if you head to the town's outskirts, you're soon in the country alongside beautiful rivers. Each October the "world's largest garage sale" is hosted by Warrensburg. You may want to arrive when the town is less crowded, or perhaps you thrive on the bustle and the coming of another brilliant autumn. In the morning you wake up to a "North Country breakfast" and know the day will go in your favor after a beginning like that.

How to get there: From I–87 exit Route 9 into Warrensburg. Continue on 9 or Main Street to First Street; turn left. In 1 block turn left onto Hudson. The inn is on the right; turn down the alley before the picket fence and park behind the inn.

Innkeepers: Ken and Florence Carrington

Address/Telephone: 2 Hudson Street; (518) 623–2449

Rooms: 10; all with private bath, air conditioning, and fireplace. One room wheelchair accessible. Limited smoking permitted.

Rates: $105 to $125, double occupancy; EPB. Two-night minimum July–August and special-event weekends. Special getaway package.

Open: All year.

Facilities and activities: Dinner and lunch; tavern. 5 acres, exercise room, outdoor swimming pool, indoor whirlpool. Nearby: antiquing, shops within walking distance, canoeing, white-water rafting, hiking, Gore Mountain 16 miles, cross-country skiing, snowmobile trails, horseback riding, Echo Lake ½ mile, Lake George 5 miles.

Recommended Country Inns® Travelers' Club Benefit: Stay two nights, get third night free, Monday–Thursday.

The William Seward Inn
WESTFIELD, NEW YORK 14787

You come to do what you've always wanted to do—but never found the time for: surprise your love with chocolates and champagne; take your mother, daughter, or friend to a women's bonding weekend; or come for a program at the Chautauqua Institute. Choose a season—spring, winter, summer, or fall—and decide among the inn's leisurely pursuits, which include "don't call me until breakfast (tea or dinner) because I'd prefer not to move out of the rocking chair in the sun."

The busiest time of all is summer, when the Chautauqua Institute offers drama, music, classes, sports, and lectures on everything from international relations to philosophy. In the fall the vintners of this area of southwestern New York are harvesting their grapes and offering tastings. In winter skiing (downhill and cross-country) is available, and the inn is well located for antiquing in nearby Westfield. At other times Jim and Debbie organize special events, such as a wine-tasting seminar or a hike to Chautauqua Gorge with a gourmet picnic lunch waiting at your destination. Every November a women's retreat focuses on women's health and growth. For Thanksgiving, New Year's Eve, and Valentine's Day, special gourmet events are planned. You can request the Chocolate Lover's Tea anytime, served either in the library or in your room; it includes a sumptuous tray of confections. After years of banking for Jim and organizational work for Debbie, they have turned to the pleasures of country innkeeping—cooking and conversing. The inn was owned at one time by Secretary of State William H. Seward. Four rooms of the inn date from about 1770, and six adjacent rooms date from 1821 to 1827. Each one has an interesting chair or sofa, and Debbie has added Waverly wall coverings and fabrics in most of them. A four-room carriage house is newly furnished with English country reproductions and queen- or king-sized beds. Jacuzzis are available.

Dinner is served at the inn year-round from Thursday through Sunday, and your selections are decided when you make your room reservations. (The dinner is optional.) The choices may include rack of lamb with caramelized shallots and thyme or breast of duck with pistachios and Amaretto. Desserts tend toward the outrageously indulgent; a chocolate-raspberry cheesecake or chocolate-macadamia nut torte might be served along with your coffee, which comes piping hot.

"Do not overmix," says Jim about baking muffins, "and learn to experiment once you've achieved perfection. Make it an art." Despite his advice to experiment, I played it safe and took copies of his muffin recipes: peanut butter-chocolate chip, butterscotch, blueberry, and strawberry-rhubarb. Each one has turned out as perfect as the previous. Breakfast is a multicourse event that includes muffins accompanied by a fruit course; then everyone selects an entree. You might want a triple-cheese omelet with fresh herbs, French toast that's soaked overnight in Amaretto, or mixed berry pancakes. You may also want to stay another night so you can eat another breakfast.

How to get there: From I–90 take exit 60 to Route 394 and drive east to intersection with Route 20 in Westfield. Continue another 3½ miles on Route 394 to the inn, on the right.

Innkeepers: Jim and Debbie Dahlberg
Address/Telephone: 6645 South Portage Road (Route 394); (716) 326–4151 or (800) 338–4151, fax (716) 326–4163
Rooms: 14; all with private bath and air conditioning, 4 in carriage house with Jacuzzi, 1 with fireplace; telephones available. Wheelchair accessible. No smoking inn.
Rates: $85 to $170, double occupancy, EPB. Corporate rates available. Request special package brochure. Two-night minimum if Saturday included and holiday weekends.
Open: All year.
Facilities and activities: On 1½ acres, dinner for guests Thursday–Sunday by reservation ($36). Nearby: Chautauqua Institute (3 miles), sailing, Cockaigne Ski Area in Cherry Creek, cross-country skiing in county parks, Panama Rocks trail, wineries, antiquing, country drives.

Albergo Allegria Bed & Breakfast

WINDHAM, NEW YORK 12496

What a bold name envelops this inn: Albergo Allegria is Italian for "inn of happiness." The name is precedence, image, and purpose; it expresses the proper feeling from the moment you open the front door.

In the dining room sunlight reflects from the polished oak tables and nurses the plants. Breakfasts are prepared with the experienced hands of Chef Vito, whose smiling eyes and soft Italian accent influence the cuisine. From Vito's large kitchen might arrive pancakes made with polenta, or whole-grain pancakes, and perhaps a vegetable frittata. Homemade granolas and fresh fruits cover the oak sideboard. You can have Belgian waffles, eggs however you like them, or special nonfat German sausages and hams. You can expect breakfast to be a plentiful experience. It comes with more than twenty-five years of experience.

Lenore told me the first Johnny Weissmuller Tarzan movie was filmed here on Batavia Kill. We walked beyond the inn to the kill, where a single tree now hangs over the stream. You can descend the bank to a pool of water, but you won't find any vines to hang on, and the vegetation that must have been here has disappeared.

You are likely to find other golfers, bicyclers, hikers, skiers, and food lovers lodging here. La Griglia Ristorante, just across the street, was made renowned by Vito and Lenore. They have turned over the tradition to a fine young chef, and most guests dine there at least once during a visit. Their son-in-law and daughter, Leslie and Marianna Leman, now assist with the innkeeping duties.

From the inn it's less than a mile to the golf course and Windham ski slopes and a brief drive to Windham village. After a busy day, you might dip into your private whirlpool bath.

The inn is composed of two buildings dating from 1876, formerly called Osborn House, a boardinghouse complex that has received guests for the past one hundred years. The rooms were carved out anew; therefore, the bathrooms are modern. Lenore decorated with mauve carpeting, print wallpapers, antiques, and modern queen-sized beds. The two common areas have several sitting areas. A chest filled with games sits in one.

Windham is a growing village with a fine little European inn surrounded by nearby hills and scenic drives.

How to get there: From the intersection of Route 23 and Route 296 in Windham, turn south on Route 296. The inn is visible past the bridge on the left side, opposite La Griglia.

Innkeepers: Lenore and Vito Radelich, Leslie and Marianna Leman, managers
Address/Telephone: Route 296 (mailing address: Box 267); (518) 734–5560 or (800) 6–ALBERGO, fax (518) 734–5570
Rooms: 21, including 4 suites and 5 cottages; all with private bath, telephone, and television, 1 with whirlpool bath. Wheelchair accessible.
Rates: $75 to $175, double occupancy, EPB. Additional person, $15. Two-night minimum weekends; 3-night minimum holiday weekends. Special midweek rates.
Open: All year.
Facilities and activities: On 4 acres overlooking Batavia Kill Creek, with fishing. Nearby: restaurant, 18-hole public golf course, tennis courts, swimming hole, Ski Windham, Catskill hiking, biking, ethnic festivals.
Recommended Country Inns® Travelers' Club Benefit: 10 percent discount each night; or stay 2 nights, get third night free; Monday–Thursday, holidays excluded.
Business travel: Desk in 3 rooms; fax, copy machine, dataport available; laundry facilities.
Recommended Country Inns® Travelers' Club Benefit: Stay two nights, get third night free, Monday–Thursday, excluding holidays.

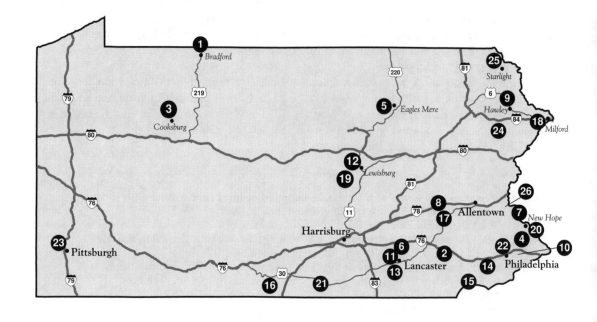

Pennsylvania

Pennsylvania

Numbers on map refer to towns numbered below.

Glendorn

BRADFORD, PENNSYLVANIA 16701

Imagine yourself on the private porch of a secluded stone cabin tucked away among stands of hemlock and maple. In the hush of this misty morning, you've already watched several deer graze on the lawn, and you scarcely breathed when you saw a red fox dart from the woods to race across the clearing. A family of rabbits is still nibbling on the flowers in the beds. Just beyond a stone bridge crosses a gentle stream, and you believe you saw several trout hugging the shady waters under the overhanging bank. It's this seamless communication with nature that we experienced on our visit to Glendorn.

Once the family retreat of the Dorn family, founders of Forest Oil Corporation, the family converted their 1,280-acre estate into a country inn in 1995. Clayton Glenville Dorn began building the complex in 1930 with the construction of the Big House, a remarkable all-redwood structure that contains a 27-by-45-foot great room with a 20-foot-high cathedral ceiling and a massive two-story sandstone fireplace. The dining room is now located at the end opposite the fireplace. Additional cabins with fireplaces (one even has three fireplaces) were added for family members over the years. These, and the Big House, now contain guest rooms.

The guest rooms at Glendorn are far from ordinary. Reminiscent of the style that the Dorns enjoyed in the 1930s and 1940s, they are spacious and elegant. They feature butternut- or chestnut-paneled walls, oil paintings, and beds, chairs, and sofas covered in floral prints and checks. The rich, warm woods give the rooms a soft glow, and even in the Big House, most have stone fireplaces. We loved the Dorn Suite in the Big House, which has a fireplace in both the living room and the bedroom as well as a private sunroom. We had both a tub and a shower in the bath.

All meals are included in the room price, as is the use of all the recreational facilities, which are extensive. Indeed, it would take weeks to sample them all. There are fishing streams, three stocked lakes for fishing, 20 miles of marked trails for hiking and cross-country skiing with promontories offering romantic picnic sites with views (the inn will pack a lunch), three tennis courts, skeet and trap shooting (guns, clay pigeons, and instruction provided), an archery range, canoes, and bicycles;

a gymnasium with a NordicTrack, vertical ascent climber, weights, and a half-basketball court; a 60-foot outdoor swimming pool, snowshoeing, and a game room with billiards and pool.

Few places in America offer an escape from the workaday pressures in such a serene setting. The Dorns have long known that their retreat offered a unique, environmentally sensitive sanctuary that had an ability to restore the spirit and renew the psyche. Now we are able to share it.

How to get there: From I–80 exit onto Route 219 at DuBois. Go north on Route 219 to Bradford. In Bradford take the Elm Street exit. Follow Elm Street to Corydon Street. Travel for 5 miles to the Glendorn gate, which is just after a bright red barn. The complex is 1½ miles farther on a private paved road.

Proprietors: The Dorn Family; Linda and Gene Spinner, managers
Address/Telephone: 1032 West Corydon Street; (814) 362–6511 or (800) 843–8568, fax (814) 368–9923
Rooms: 11, including 4 suites and 5 cabins; all with private bath and telephone, 9 with television, minirefrigerator, and fireplace (several with multiple fireplaces). Wheelchair accessible.
Rates: $295 to $895, double occupancy, AP, including all recreational facilities. Two-night minimum for some cabins and weekends July–October as well as holiday weekends. No credit cards.
Open: All year except March.
Facilities and activities: Tennis, skeet and trap shooting, archery, canoes, fishing, bicycling, swimming, hiking, cross-country skiing, snowshoeing, billiards and pool. Nearby: golf, downhill skiing, horseback riding, licensed guides for deer and bird hunting, the Allegheny National Forest.
Business travel: Desk in room; fax, copier, audiovisual equipment available; conference center.

The Inn at Twin Linden
CHURCHTOWN, PENNSYLVANIA 17555

Our physical state of arrival—hot and exhausted—improved so swiftly that we wondered: Did the outside world exist any longer? If it did, we'd forgotten, having stepped into the small world of the stone mansion inn. Bob had smiled in his direct, relaxed manner and led us up the stairs to our quarters. Along the way we admired his photographs of Italy, Ireland, Maine, and the farmlands surrounding Twin Linden. Sweet indulgence—the tenor of our visit—focused on the palate and the garden and tea on the patio. We could have been on a ship in the sea, contentedly marooned with a chef and photographer at the helm.

The inn is in Philadelphia's bread basket, Lancaster County, where the rich farmland produces strawberries the size of a fist; vegetables are consumed within hours of picking; and choice meat, fowl, and fish can be had from a number of local purveyors. It's also convenient to Temple University, where Bob teaches photography.

Our suite was a study in light and grace with a comfortable sitting area; the Palladian window overlooked fields, a distant farm, and a low mountain range beyond. I concluded that winter here must be as cheering as the warm months. I envisioned myself perusing a book of photography, Chardonnay in hand and woolen lap afghan in place, while toasting in front of our room's wood-burning stove and occasionally gazing outside at Mother Nature's frosty finery.

Many of the rooms have handmade four-poster beds, which were delivered upon a horse-drawn sleigh. The walls are ivory with Colonial-green woodwork. Donna has added Laura Ashley quilts and handmade afghans, warm touches that beckon.

After a soak in the Jacuzzi in our room, we went to tea, which was served in the large foyer, where a three-tiered tray held luscious cookies and sweets. Some couples settled in the parlor, others at nearby tables or on the patio, which overlooks the linden trees and garden—a small, spectacular affair of benches and bushes, flowers, and orna-mentals. Nearby are more benches for observing the fields beyond. We would come here after din-ner with our cordials to watch the soft summer breeze sway the corn and wish for a falling star.

Dinner was served in the Hunt Country Restaurant, where travelers in search of innova-tive, vibrant tastes savor Donna's creations. (The menu changes weekly.) It was elaborate. We began with summer-asparagus tips with lemon and herbs in pastry, followed by Belgian endive with tortellini, pesto, and red peppers. For an en-tree I was presented with the scrumptious grilled jumbo shrimp, served with fresh-roasted red-pepper coulis. My companion chose the jumbo sea scallops with a heavenly champagne and tar-ragon sauce, baked under a flaky, light pastry lid. For dessert the freshest of strawberries arrived with rich whipped cream.

Breakfast began with fruits, fresh-squeezed juice, and pastries; then came an elaborate cheese omelet. We learned that Donna was invited to cook at the prestigious James Beard House in New York City, an engagement offered only to outstanding American chefs.

Two souls have put together their talents, and the outcome is a place done right.

How to get there: From the Pennsylvania Turn-pike take exit 22 (Morgantown) to Route 23 (less than 1/10 mile) and proceed west 4 miles into Churchtown. Inn is on the left, in the center of village.

Innkeepers: Bob and Donna Leahy

Address/Telephone: 2092 Main Street; (717) 445–7619, fax (717) 445–4656

Rooms: 7, including 1 suite; all with private bath, air conditioning, and television, 3 with fireplace, 2 with Jacuzzi. No smoking inn.

Rates: $100 to $210, double occupancy, EPB and afternoon tea. Two-night minimum if Saturday included and holidays.

Open: All year except January.

Facilities and activities: Dinner served Friday and Saturday ($16 to $24 Friday, $37 fixed price Saturday) by reservation. BYOB; garden and gift shop. Nearby: The People's Place and Old Country Store in Intercourse, Railroad Museum in Strasbourg, coun-try quilt shops, factory outlets, Artworks Complex, farmer's markets.

Gateway Lodge Country Inn and Restaurant
COOKSBURG, PENNSYLVANIA 16217

The place captures you, instilling a sense of safety and comfort, and leaves you with recurring fantasies of being back in the lodge living room before the fire.

The Lodge sits like an immense hillside sentinel near the gateway to 6,422-acre Cook Forest State Park, where hemlocks and white pines have grown steadily taller for the past two or three centuries. Reflecting the surrounding forest, massive logs shape the lodge's walls. The ceilings are of pine and hemlock, the walls of wormy chestnut; the flooring is oak. The mood is one of inherent warmth.

Anne Marie, a young woman on the staff with a pleasant demeanor, showed us the inn on the way to our room. She paused before the smallest tavern with cozy dark woods and petite tables. Then we advanced to the game room, where afternoon tea would be served.

Next we entered the living room; a fire crackled in the stone fireplace while guests reposed in the warmth. A mother and daughter were letting their hair dry naturally after a swim in the inviting indoor pool. (Both the pool and sauna are heated with a wood-burning stove, which Joe built.)

Linda and Joe happened upon the lodge nearly twenty years ago and were so smitten that they drove up and knocked on the front door. Built for vacation travelers in the 1930s, it was then a private home. The owners sold them the lodge several years later. Lucky us.

At tea time Linda pauses to visit and introduce everyone before the wood-burning stove, just as she did more than ten years ago, when I first ventured here. Then you help yourself to tea and delectable sweet bars and cookies. The place (or is it Linda?) seems to dissolve tension. The staff deserves special mention—each member is as soft spoken, personable, and helpful as the next.

When we went to dinner in the dining room, the lanterns around the wooden tables were lit. We spent the evening catching up on Linda and Joe's projects and learned that they are booked for New Year's Eve through the year 2002. "But we do nothing for New Year's; it's like every other night here—quiet, the fire blazing, dinner and wine by soft light in the woods," commented Joe. "That's why they love it," my companion responded, "because it's a time for peace and renewal. But you don't really need an official holiday to come for that."

We began with a large, fresh salad laced with a delicious dressing. I chose a baked flounder amply stuffed with a spinach, crabmeat, and feta-cheese filling. For dessert the Chocolate Lover's Delight was enormous and sinfully delicious. Freshly baked pies and lighter desserts are also available.

At bedtime you climb the stairs (a slight creak here or there), insert the key, open the plain wooden door, and there it is: tiny, cozy, as snug as the handmade quilt on the bed and the print curtains on the latched windows. You undress and crawl into bed thinking, "Wake me in a year."

How to get there: From I–80, take exit 13 to Route 36 north for approximately 16 miles. The inn is on the right just before the park. Fly-in: Clarion County Airport.

Innkeepers: Linda and Joseph Burney

Address/Telephone: Route 36 Cook Forest (mailing address: P.O. Box 125); (814) 744–8017; Pennsylvania and Maryland only (800) 843–6862

Rooms: 16, including 8 cottages; 11 with private bath, 8 with fireplace, 1 with Jacuzzi; 2 cottages wheelchair accessible. No smoking inn.

Rates: $105 to $120, EP; $130 to $167, EPB; $190 to $228, MAP; double occupancy. Two-night minimum September–May; 3-night minimum June–August.

Open: All year except Thanksgiving and Christmas.

Facilities and activities: Dinner daily except Monday, reservations required; tea served daily. Tavern, indoor swimming pool and sauna for lodge guests (not cabin residents), gift shop. Nearby: theater, cross-country skiing, fishing, hunting, golfing, bicycling, canoeing and tubing on Clarion River, horseback riding, carriage and sleigh rides, 6,422-acre Cook State Park.

The Inn at Fordhook Farm
DOYLESTOWN, PENNSYLVANIA 18901

Fordhook Farm, a fieldstone manor house located on sixty acres of woodlands, meadows, and gardens in Doylestown, is where W. Atlee Burpee began the Burpee Seed Company.

Enter the gate, park near the barn, and ring the doorbell. You're greeted by one of the Burpees or by Janice Webb. You're invited into a country home that's a living legacy of photographs, china, furniture, grandfather's clocks, and stories. The oldest part of the house, the kitchen, dates from the 1700s, and the central structure dates from the late eighteenth and early nineteenth centuries.

The living room is a great room with high ceiling and long windows. Adjacent is the masculine-looking office where W. Atlee and later David ran the company. There are dark mahogany beams, a double desk, and an outside door that opens to the lawn; this entrance was probably used by the growers to avoid stepping through the house in their boots.

A stairway leads directly up to the spacious master bedroom. Often requested by honeymooners and anniversary celebrants, it has two window seats and a private balcony. Each bedroom is named after a family member and has an individual appeal. From the Palladian window of the carriage house (built with chestnut wood), the American seed-trial beds are visible.

You can walk over the estate with a map

that Carole gives you and, after the stroll, come into the butler's pantry where guests may brew their own tea or coffee. Afterwards perhaps you retreat to the study or living room or take a seat on the tiled terrace under 200-year-old linden trees with lawn and trees for a view. During winter guests are invited to bring skis and cross-country on the property. Or you might borrow a seed catalog, as I did, and begin planning additions to your own spring garden.

On this recent visit Carole told me of an early 1900s diary by one of the Burpee women that recently surfaced. The Burpee collection of papers are in the Smithsonian's Horticulture Branch, but several books about the family sit in the bookcase. Carole and Janice are also working with the current Burpee company to develop the ongoing seed beds on the property.

After touring the nearby Mercer Mansion and tile works, you acquire a greater appreciation for Fordhook's dining room. It's a lovely setting;

the tiles surround the fireplace, the ceiling is richly beamed, and the morning sun filters through leaded stained-glass windows. "It's here around the breakfast table that many new friendships are made, while guests eat a leisurely breakfast," says Carole. "To those of us who run the inn, it's the heart of Fordhook. It's my favorite room, as it was when my husband's family shared meals here."

It was here that I tasted the Burpee recipe for lemon tea bread, and Carole graciously sent a copy along with me. I now often serve this lovely bread at my own table with friends.

How to get there: From Doylestown follow Route 202 south (State Street) past the hospital and over the 611 bypass; watch carefully and turn left onto New Britain Road (next to gate for Delaware Valley College). Inn entrance is ¼ mile on left through two stone pillars. Follow drive over little bridge to stone house on right.

Innkeepers: Carole L. Burpee and Janice Webb
Address/Telephone: 105 New Britain Road; (215) 345–1766; fax (215) 345–1791
Rooms: 7, including carriage house; 4 with private bath, all with air conditioning, 2 with fireplace; telephone available. No smoking inn.
Rates: $100 to $200, double occupancy, EPB and afternoon tea. Two-night minimum weekends.
Open: All year.
Facilities and activities: 60 acres, library with television and VCR, gardens, hiking, boccie, badminton, sledding, cross-country skiing. Nearby: restaurants, Mercer Museum, Fonthill, Moravian Pottery and Tile Works, Pearl S. Buck's home; Bucks County: antiquing, historic sites, and covered bridges.
Business travel: Office space and telephone available; conference room.

Pine Tree Farm
DOYLESTOWN, PENNSYLVANIA 18901

I'll never forget my first visit to Pine Tree Farm, the stunning fieldstone manor house with slate roof that Joy and Ron Feigles have made into an inn. When we arrived the deer grazing under the apple trees barely looked up and a bunny scampered out from under a fern. The inn has sixteen and a half acres of rolling fields and woodlands where humans and wildlife live contentedly side by side.

Joy and Ron have been welcoming guests to their 1730s home for nearly a decade, and it's hard to imagine more gracious hosts. Joy has a degree in hotel administration and is a talented decorator; in addition, she loves to cook. Guests are treated as treasured friends at Pine Tree Farm rather than as overnight travelers. While we became acquainted we had a glass of wine and nibbled on the cheese that had been set out for the guests.

The living room, with its abundance of plants, is gracious and charming and overlooks the pool and gardens. The dining room has a fireplace in the corner. The tiny library, which has another fireplace and stacks of interesting books, is the cozy retreat that I like best. A patchwork cloth in rich velvet covers a round table, and puffy love seats face each other in front of the fireplace. There's a French door that leads to the gardens and to the pond in the distance.

I love the enchanting guest rooms that Joy

and Ron have created. My favorite is the Pink Room with its romantic white twig canopy bed draped in floral chintz. Upstairs a two-room suite has a white iron bed, and a pretty yellow room contains a window seat overlooking the pond and a pine pineapple post bed. The bathroom is stenciled. Each of the rooms has its own personality, but they are all crisp and bright, with an abundance of pretty fabrics.

Joy's breakfasts are bountiful and convivial. We started with fresh fruit and homemade granola, a cranberry scone, and coffee cake made from a recipe that Joy's mother had used for years. It's a rich, buttery confection topped with brown sugar and nuts. Joy next served Grand Marnier French toast with maple syrup and German sausage. Other favorite offerings include puffed-apple pancakes, eggs Benedict, and omelets.

Although we felt removed from all hint of civilization on this low-key estate, we especially appreciate it because it's so close to the attractions of Bucks County. The Mercer Museum, Moravian Tile Works, and James Michener Art Museum are just up the road, and there are excellent restaurants in Doylestown and the surrounding villages.

How to get there: From Philadelphia travel north on I–95 to the Street Road exit (Route 132). Turn left onto Street Road and travel 18 miles to the dead end at Lower State Road. Turn right onto Lower State Road and travel 4 miles to Pine Tree Farm, which will be on the right. From New York City, take Route 202 (*not* Route 202 bypass) directly through Doylestown. Bear left at the second traffic light onto Court Street, which becomes Lower State Road. The inn will be on the left in 1¼ miles.

Innkeepers: Ron and Joy Feigles
Address/Telephone: 2155 Lower State Road; (215) 348–0632
Rooms: 4; 3 with private bath, all with air conditioning and telephone. No smoking inn.
Rates: $140 to $160, double occupancy, EPB. Two-night minimum weekends.
Open: All year.
Facilities and activities: Pool, pond, garden, bicycling. Nearby: cross-country skiing across road, downhill skiing, golf, antiquing, Mercer Museum, James Michener Art Museum, Moravian Tile Works.

Eagles Mere Inn
EAGLES MERE, PENNSYLVANIA 17731

Thrilling winter toboggan rides across a star-lit lake, summer swims in the cool waters, and the sublime food of a small inn are the obvious attractions. One also comes here for subtler reasons.

The remote mountain village of Eagles Mere and its few great "cottages" surround a small, deep lake. You drive up through acres of forest, catching sight of eagles riding a mountain current in this sparsely populated county in Pennsylvania, where Peter and Susan have restored life to a late-1800s inn. But the story of this winter-sports oriented village begins with an ice slide.

In 1904 E. S. Chase watched his grandchildren at play and decided to enhance their winter sledding. He conceived and built an ice slide

that's become a village tradition. Every year, usually in January, when the 90-foot-deep lake is assuredly frozen, the Eagles Mere Slide Association, using block ice–building tools and a conveyer belt, creates the annual hillside toboggan track. Riders can reach speeds of 60 miles per hour when they zip their toboggan down the hill and across the frozen lake. To decrease speed the ice across the other end of the lake is sufficiently roughed up. "Or we'd never stop," said Susan. All ages participate, and between four and six people share a sled. Night rides are the best, according to the local aficionados.

In the summer the closely wooded mountain lake has laurels so high they tower over one's head. When we walked, the fallen pine needles covering the trail emitted a fragrant, dusky scent.

Despite the out-of-the-way location, the fare at Eagles Mere can hardly be described as rustic. The small but extremely discriminating wine list, for example, includes a 1961 bottle of Chateau d'Yquem and more reasonably priced California, German, Italian, and French wines. My companion described the menu to friends. "Imagine this remote village setting. We had no idea what we'd find to eat. Seated at a white linen–covered table, we began the feast with an applewood-smoked poussin. Also on the plate was this divine pheasant sausage with a wild-rice crepe that defied anything I've yet or since tasted." Susan's desserts include cheesecake and chocolate cake, both rich yet light. Their cooking skills form a good marriage.

The rooms are simple and spotless; care has been taken to place the best-quality mattresses on the beds.

In the basement there's a room for youngsters with a game table and juke box. In the next room, the tavern, a couch sits before the stone fireplace. The artist who painted the surrounding wall mural married the stone mason who built the fireplace—they met while working their respective talents and married before the fireplace.

In passing, Susan noticed a guest laboring at balancing his tea and a book. She quietly reappeared with a tea table and, smiling, went on her way. The caring details at this inn come not from professional degrees and experience but from Susan and Peter's aptitude for innkeeping and obvious pleasure in nurturing their guests.

Before you take the ice slide, read the tag that will hang from your winter coat: "The Eagles Mere Toboggan Slide is a vigorous downhill ride at high speed ending in a slide across a frozen lake, over which there is little or no control." Then push off and "let 'er rip."

How to get there: Drive into town on Route 42. Two blocks south of the town clock (and shops), turn south onto Mary Avenue. Inn is 1 block farther, at corner of Mary and Sullivan avenues. Coming from the north, turn left onto Mary.

Innkeepers: Susan and Peter Glaubitz

Address/Telephone: Mary and Sullivan Avenues (mailing address: Box 356); (717) 525–3273 or (800) 426–3273

Rooms: 17, including 2 suites; all with private bath and ceiling fan, 8 with air conditioning, 1 with Jacuzzi. One room wheelchair accessible. No smoking inn.

Rates: $135 to $195, double occupancy, MAP. Two-night minimum weekends. Add 15 percent service charge and tax.

Facilities and activities: Nearby: Tobogganing, hiking, cross-country skiing, horseback riding, country club golf, and lake swimming; Wyoming and Tiadaghton State forests surround Eagles Mere.

The Inns at Doneckers
EPHRATA, PENNSYLVANIA 17522

In 1961 Bill Donecker opened a fashion store. It's inconspicuously located in a residential neighborhood, yet 300,000 people arrive annually in Ephrata, a town of 12,000. Many of them dine at his fine French restaurant and sleep beneath the downy comfort found in the four inns. More recently Mr. Donecker transformed a former shoe factory into studios and immediately drew a select community of artists to fill Artworks. You'll find Pennsylvania Dutch Redware, kaleidoscopes, bronze and wooden sculptures, paintings, handmade quilts, stained glass, handcrafted furniture, and photographs. It's closed Wednesdays. (Request to be on the Artworks mailing list for exhibitions.)

The 55,000-square-foot contemporary shopping area includes women's, men's, and children's clothing, designer collections, and household items that are used throughout the inn. On Thursday, Friday, and Saturday, in season, a farmer's market is held.

The inns are composed of four former homes and have a small common area with a television. Each room is decorated with antiques, stenciling, and items from the home shop. One room has a nineteenth-century, English black-lacquered bed that once belonged to Liberace (it's a lounging daybed). Our comfortable room had an antique double bed and a wonderful whirlpool bath.

Six blocks away is the 1777 House, which has ten more rooms, and there are two luxury suites in the Carriage House. The home was built by clock maker Jacob Gorgas; one of his clocks stands in the hallway. On the floor are the original tiles, and throughout there are antique hand-painted chests and armoires imported from Europe. One block away is the lovely Gerhart House. You might also lodge in the Homestead, a former home with pretty rooms, located up the street.

We had a wonderful meal. I chose the special of red snapper served with a savory rosemary sauce and an appetizer of asparagus with a light lemon sauce. Both were fresh and seasoned to perfection. Our sommelier selected a dry white wine, so fine that it enhanced everything and still lingers in my memory. Later I nodded at the shapely cream puffs on the dessert tray; they were the right accent with cappuccino.

Complimentary breakfast is served indoors every morning, or you can carry it outside on the porch during summer. You help yourself to cereals, juices, muffins, coffee, and hot cinnamon-apple casserole, which is delicious in any season.

Doneckers is a destination in itself, but on a first visit, plan to include the nearby Ephrata Cloisters, then Artworks, the farmer's market, and an easy walk back to the inn for fine dining.

"Sunday is antiquing day in the area," says Jan. She'll get you moving in the right direction.

How to get there: From Route 222 exit 322 west into Ephrata, turn right onto North State Street, and proceed 4 blocks to the inn.

Innkeeper: Jan Grobengieser; Bill Donecker, proprietor
Address/Telephone: 318-324 North State Street; (717) 738–9502, fax (717) 738–9554
Rooms: 40, including 14 suites and 2 cottages. Guesthouse in 1777 House, Carriage House, Homestead, and Gerhart House; all with private bath, air conditioning, and telephone; some with whirlpool bath, television, and fireplace. One room wheelchair accessible.
Rates: $59 to $185, double occupancy, continental buffet breakfast. $10 for rollaway; $8 for crib. Two-night minimum on holiday weekends.
Open: All year.
Facilities and activities: Lunch daily and dinner nightly except Wednesday (dinner entrees $17 to $28) and Sunday; full beverage license. Shopping, Artworks Complex. Nearby: Ephrata Cloister, Amish country, farmer's market, antiquing.
Business travel: Telephone, fax, and desk available; conference room.

Historic Smithton Country Inn
EPHRATA, PENNSYLVANIA 17522

While visiting this inn, you should think of a fine painting where the details are revealed slowly.

Almost everything in the Historic Smithton was made by hand. Each bed and desk was designed, handmade, and then oxidized to form a rich hue. You'll find the beauty of the craftsman's work in the tiles surrounding the whirlpools, in the hand-woven bed canopies and drapes, and in the hand-stitched quilts on the beds. When you place your suitcase on the painted chests, you admire the colorful hand painting. Even the floorboards were hand hewn.

Carefully selected books are in the rooms. Featherbeds are available on request. The details in every room reflect a composition of comfort.

Once I came downstairs early to find a fire burning off a slight morning chill. In the dining room hung a colorful collection of quilts beautifully hand sewn by local women. Atop the windowsill were pieces of folk art made by local artists. Around wooden tables, everyone gathers each morning for breakfast. You eat blueberry waffles and fresh fruits and drink coffee while visiting.

For those who plan ahead, you can call the inn regarding the Adamstown antiques markets, where as many as 6,000 dealers appear on special weekends. Dorothy's suggestions reveal her experience and insight. She was born in Lancaster County.

"You cannot live in this area and not be influenced by the Amish and Mennonites," she says softly. I don't think you could visit this historic inn and not be favorably influenced.

In the living room Dorothy's baskets of knitting and a small wool spinner sit near the fire. She's a member of a spinning guild. Through a door is a small library-office. An abundance of magazines and books is available for guests. An encyclopedia sits open for use. A fire burns in winter. It's small and inviting.

Whenever I return to Lancaster County, I first consult my guide, *Smithton's Suggestions*. It covers restaurants, touring, shopping, and area history. It's beautifully written.

Lancaster County still represents the rural beginnings of America. The contemporary Amish live as the majority of Americans did only a century ago. The Smithton is within walking distance of Ephrata Cloister, an early American Protestant monastic society, where the German medieval style architecture dates from 1732.

Beside the inn is a garden with a pond and fountain for sitting in the afternoon or evening. Several lop-eared pet rabbits live here in the summer shade of trees. Relaxed in a chair, you might hear the clop-clop of a horse-pulled buggy traveling down the road. You rest contentedly.

How to get there: From north or south take Highway 222 to Ephrata exit. Turn west on 322 for 2½ miles to the inn on your left.

Innkeeper: Dorothy Graybill

Address/Telephone: 900 West Main Street; (717) 733–6094

Rooms: 8, including 1 suite; all with private bath, air conditioning, and fireplace, 6 with small refrigerator, 3 with whirlpool bath. One room wheelchair accessible. Pets by prior arrangement. No smoking inn.

Rates: $75 to $170, double occupancy, EPB. Children, no charge up to 18 months, $20 up to 12. $35 additional person. Two-night minimum if Saturday included and holidays.

Open: All year.

Facilities and activities: Nearby: restaurants, Ephrata Cloister, Artworks Complex, museums, Adamstown antiques market, farmer's markets, factory outlets.

Isaac Stover House
ERWINNA, PENNSYLVANIA 18920

When Sally Jessy Raphaël and her husband and manager, Karl Soderlund, purchased the brick Bucks County manor house with a mansard roof known as the Isaac Stover House in 1987, it was on a whim. But Sally dived in with her characteristic enthusiasm and put together a hodge-podge of rooms that were filled to the brim with old furniture and campy paraphernalia acquired at flea markets and antiques shops.

But that was then, and this is now. In 1995 Sally decided to start over, and this time, acknowledging the stately old house's Federal style, she chose a refined and elegant decor, combining period antiques with personal mementos collected on trips around the world. The transfor-

mation included a bright coat of white paint on the exterior trim, a sparkling new kitchen, and guest rooms that are dignified and charming. Located across the street from the Delaware River, many of the rooms have lovely views of the lazy river.

The common rooms, which earlier had seemed dark, are now painted a white-on-white scheme so that the marble fireplaces are featured. The random-width pine floors gleam, uncovered by rugs. Pretty French chairs and love seats in the double parlors are lighted by a crystal chandelier and backed by palms. In the Victorian tap room, the pecan wall panels cast a soft glow. There's a piano along the wall, and a bar, where wine and cheese are served every afternoon, is in the corner.

The guest rooms contain a combination of antiques and period pieces, all accented with rich fabrics and wallpapers. The Bird Room, for example, has an iron bed and fanciful bird wallpaper. The Blue and Cream Room combines moire fabric with French toile wallpaper and has a dark-wood bedroom suite with flowers painted across the drawers and headboard. Sally hand-painted several of the drawers herself. In the Yellow Room an iron canopy bed is covered with a rich tapestry and Pierre Deux paper covers the walls.

Vinny Howe, the innkeeper, is a great cook and justifiably proud of his new kitchen. Guests are invited into the kitchen while he prepares breakfast. In fact, they're invited into the kitchen at any hour of the day. It's just that kind of place. For breakfast he will have muffins and breads, fresh fruit and juice, and perhaps an omelet with home fries or eggs Benedict. Sometimes (although not often) Sally herself shows up to make her favorite French toast.

The inn is located on ten acres and is directly across from the Delaware River, where the old towpath makes a great walking trail. For an afternoon of pure relaxation, however, I love to take a book out to the hammock under the evergreen trees and lose myself in a well-told story.

How to get there: From New York City, take the New Jersey Turnpike south to exit 14 and then take I–78 west to exit 15 (Clinton/Pittstown). Make a left at the end of the ramp onto Route 513 south and go for 11 miles to the New Jersey town of Frenchtown. Cross the Delaware River on the Frenchtown Bridge and turn left onto Route 32 south. Follow Route 32 for 2 miles. The inn is on the right.

Innkeeper: Vincent Howe; Sally Jessy Raphaël and Karl Soderlund, proprietors
Address/Telephone: 845 River Road (Route 32); (610) 294–8044, fax (610) 294–8132
Rooms: 7; 4 with private bath, 3 with semiprivate bath, all with air conditioning. Small pets permitted with prior permission. Smoking in common areas only.
Rates: $150 to $175, double occupancy, EPB.
Open: All year.
Facilities and activities: Nearby: walking on the Delaware River towpath, canoeing, rafting, fishing, boating, hot-air ballooning, bicycling, antiquing, golf.
Business travel: Meeting room, telephone, fax.

*G*lasbern

FOGELSVILLE, PENNSYLVANIA 18051-9743

Had I passed by chance, I'd have stopped and driven down the cobblestone lane, intent on discovering what purpose this visually compelling structure held.

Beth Granger gave the inn its name, Glasbern, meaning "glass barn." It's a Pennsylvania German barn architecturally transformed in 1985 by the Grangers to create a unique contemporary inn amidst the serenity of a stream, a pond, and the green hills of the countryside.

You enter the Great Room, the heart of the inn. Intact are the original haymow ladders. The beams in the vaulted ceiling are exposed, and the stone walls were cut open with a diamond-edged saw to let in the sunlight. The lighting reminded me of a cathedral designed by Le Corbusier I once visited in France. The Great Room is an elegant setting within a former hand-hewn "bank" barn.

The inn is a good place to commune with nature. On a clear fall day, you can board a hot-air balloon that departs from the inn. Walk along the inn's country paths. Travel to the nearby antiques markets or the sights of Historic Bethlehem. Then return, this time perhaps on a winter's eve after a day of skiing, and ease into the whirlpool with the warmth of the nearby fireplace for total bliss. You may never leave the place.

The carriage-house suites have fireplaces framed either in stone or barn-wood siding. In the corner suites two-person whirlpools are surrounded by windows opening out to the countryside. The rooms are a blend of today's comforts, good lighting, and quality-built furnishings tastefully selected by Beth.

By evening guests gather in the Great Room, where you must reserve in advance, since the chef has a following. First you have a drink around the great stone fireplace. Once you're seated hot fresh breads are served with crisp salads. You might have ordered a New York strip steak brushed with olive oil and rosemary, then broiled; perhaps you selected a range chicken or Dover sole sautéed with country-style vegetables, tomatoes, herbs, in a reduced sweet cream sauce and served with lemon angel-hair pasta. Later comes a light cheesecake soufflé coated with raspberry sauce. Some guests enjoy a liqueur upon returning to the stone fireplace or go for a walk around the pond.

Breakfast is served, in leisurely style, in the sunroom. That morning we ate whole-wheat pecan pancakes coated with maple syrup and thick slices of bacon. We felt recharged. And we noticed others looked that way too. Was it the fresh air, the country walks, the fine meal, the whirlpool and the fireplace? Or had someone anointed us with newfound energy during the night?

How to get there: From I–78 take Route 100 north short distance to Tilghman Street and turn left. Go ⅓ mile and turn right on North Church Street; go ⁷⁄₁₀ mile and turn right on Pack House Road. The inn is ⁸⁄₁₀ mile on the right.

Innkeepers: Al and Beth Granger; Erik Sheetz, manager

Address/Telephone: 2141 Pack House Road (mailing address: R.D. 1); (610) 285–4723, fax (610) 285–2862

E-mail: innkeeper@glasbern.com

Rooms: 24, including 13 suites; all with private bath, air conditioning, television, VCR, and telephone, 11 with fireplace, 17 with whirlpool bath. Two wheelchair accessible rooms. Designated nonsmoking rooms.

Rates: $105 to $315, double occupancy; $95 to $160, single; EPB. Additional person, $20. Two-night minimum on certain weekends.

Open: All year.

Facilities and activities: Dinner nightly (entrees $19 to $38), service bar. Outdoor swimming pool, pond, hot-air balloon rides, 16 acres farmland. Nearby: Hawk Mountain Sanctuary, antiquing in Kutztown and Adamstown, ski Blue and Doe mountains, wineries, Historic Bethlehem.

Business travel: Telephone and desk in all rooms; fax, photocopies, dataport available; conference rooms.

The Settlers Inn
HAWLEY, PENNSYLVANIA 18428

I passed the clear, blue lake on this brisk spring day and drove through the town to the village inn opposite Bingham Park. It was around lunchtime and already there were people gathered before the fire, doubtless noticing the delicious aromas.

A chef-owned inn is a sign of unusually tasty dishes. Grant and Jeanne are committed to regional cuisine. Grant continually explores and encourages local sources. He serves an Amish cheese, locally raised veal, a young poussin chicken accented by apple chutney, seasonal produce from an organic farmer, smoked meats and fish, and birds from a nearby pheasantry in the form of a boneless pheasant breast with herb-

sausage stuffing. You can also select from several Pennsylvania beers, wines, and a local apple cider.

Lunch and dinner begin with home-baked breads, perhaps a pumpkin or a moist, nutty cranberry, or maybe a light yeasty roll so good that the innkeepers have written a bread cookbook. Then, discreetly, they parade in veal Oscar topped with asparagus spears and crabmeat coated with a creamy hollandaise sauce, sautéed filet mignon wrapped in bacon with a sauce béarnaise, and pork chops with apple stuffing and a savory cider sauce.

The portions are large. Let that not prevent dessert. The rich maple walnut cake is a match for goodness. This is where the locals eat, too.

Before the massive fireplace there's a social gathering place near the inn's English-look tavern. It's here that guests enjoy a complimentary cheese spread and later return to a goodnight chat by the fire.

Lake Wallenpaupack's 53-mile shoreline is five minutes by car from the inn, or you can take the inn's trail to a creek for trout fishing. In summer you can hike, swim, visit museums, and attend concerts in the park. In winter guests go ice skating and skiing. Before striking out, expect to enjoy a large country breakfast.

The rooms have rose-flowered wallpapers, quilted bedspreads, and white-wicker or antique furnishings.

Each time I journey here, Jeannie and Grant have made thoughtful changes. They display art-work and occasionally host special events—like the storyteller who came to share stories about the lake and mountain district of Pennsylvania. On one visit I found newly hung photographs. "Louis Hensel," explained Grant, "was a local photographer whose work has been rediscovered." Hensel photographed Hawley residents at work and leisure; Jeannie pointed to lover's lane, a Fourth of July boating party, and the ancestors of families they know. The innkeepers' interconnections and love for the people and places of the area permeate this classic country inn.

How to get there: From I–84 exit onto Route 6 into Hawley. Pass through town; the inn is on the left opposite the park.

Innkeepers: Grant and Jeanne Genzlinger
Address/Telephone: Four Main Avenue; (717) 226–2993 or (800) 833–8527, fax (717) 226–1874
E-mail: settler@prolog.net
Rooms: 18, including 4 suites; all with private bath, air conditioning, and telephone, 9 with television. No smoking inn.
Rates: $75 to $120, double occupancy, EPB. Two-night minimum weekends July–October.
Open: All year.
Facilities and activities: Lunch, dinner ($12 to $20), Sunday brunch, tavern; private guest parlor; on 5 acres; fishing in river on property; opposite park with tennis courts. Nearby: Lake Wallenpaupack for fishing, boating, beach swimming; Satellite Station Tour, Zane Grey Museum, steam train rides, skiing at Tanglewood and Mast Hope, cross-country skiing, Promised Land State Park, hiking, antiquing.
Business travel: Thirty-five miles to Scranton. Telephone and dataport in all rooms; desk in 3 rooms; copy machine, computer, fax, audiovisual equipment available; conference room.
Recommended Country Inns® Travelers' Club Benefit: Stay two nights, get third night free.

Barley Sheaf Farm
HOLICONG, PENNSYLVANIA 18928

This was the first bed-and-breakfast inn to open in Bucks County back in 1976, and it was once the home of George S. Kaufman. Its solid reputation is still deserved. It's bucolic and unfussy. In residence are Prelzel and Rutton, the cats, George and Timothy, the dogs, a bevy of sheep in the meadow, and a hive of safely distant bees who annually produce 300 pounds of honey.

Much is revealed about an inn by the common areas and outdoor spaces where people may gather together or, if desired, sequester themselves away during restful moments. This inn has several idyll-time settings: a spacious living room with natural conversation niches formed around a fireplace; a dining room with a view of birds,

flowers, and trees; a small television room; and the swimming pool, which is nicely shaded by trees.

We love what Veronika and Peter Suess, a friendly Swiss/German couple who purchased the inn in 1994, have done to the guest rooms. The baths are thoroughly upgraded with sparkling tile, and some retain claw-footed tubs and pedestal sinks. The rooms have all been painted in light, soothing colors, and spritely floral fabrics are used liberally. There are iron beds, sleigh beds, brass beds, and four-posters. I've always loved the cozy little cottage rooms—with beamed ceilings, a brick floor, a window seat overlooking the meadow, a fireplace, and reached along a stone path between waist-high tiger lillies—but now there are also two spacious suites in the barn, one with a woodstove.

Adjacent to the barn, a multilevel conference center, complete with private interview offices, overlooks the grazing sheep. It seems to me that only congenial decisions could be made in such a relaxed setting.

A large breakfast is served at the tables that fill the dining room. It usually begins with freshly squeezed orange juice; a fruit precedes fresh farm eggs in one form or another or waffles, and a sweet roll or muffins, as well as country sausage. If fresh honey is served, it's been combed right here on the farm. Everyone enjoys a chat around the long tables in this setting filled with plants. In the winter a wood-burning stove is well stoked for the final touch.

Barley Sheaf is appropriate whether you're newly married, a high-powered pair of professional talents, or celebrating your fortieth anniversary. Next time I'd like to be there for Peter and Veronika's bread-making or wine-tasting events.

How to get there: Directions sent when reservations made. Barley Sheaf is 6 miles south of Delaware Toll Bridge on Route 202, on the south side of the road.

Innkeepers: Peter and Veronika Suess
Address/Telephone: 15928 York Road, Route 202 (mailing address: Box 10); (215) 794–5104, fax (215) 794–5332
Rooms: 12, including 4 suites; all with private bath and air conditioning; 9 with telephone, 3 with fireplace. One room wheelchair accessible. No smoking inn.
Rates: $105 to $255, double occupancy, EPB. Two-night minimum, 3-night minimum holidays. Rates vary according to season.
Open: All year.
Facilities and activities: Outdoor swimming pool, pond, fishing, sheep in pasture, 30 acres. Nearby: restaurants, antiquing, bicycling, barge rides, mansions along the Delaware, Mercer Mile in Doylestown, Peddler's Village.
Business travel: Dataport in 9 rooms; desk in 5 rooms; meeting rooms for small conferences with full audiovisual capabilities and telephone hookups.

The King's Cottage
LANCASTER, PENNSYLVANIA 17602

The sun was well up. I had slept soundly, but the aroma of a magnificent sausage compelled me to rise from the canopy bed and look from comforting quilt to windows veiled in curtain.

We had gone the night before to a little neighborhood restaurant, where the food was good, the atmosphere unassuming but pretty, and the conversation companionable. Karen and Jim have a knack for getting their guests to the right local restaurant.

Afternoon tea and cookies, served daily from 4:00 to 7:00 P.M., provided an opportunity to acquire a richer feeling for the area from your hosts Karen and Jim, and their assistants. Between bits of lemon squares and cottage cookies, Karen pro-

duced a thick packet of bike tours, which range from 11 to 72 miles and carry you through the countryside from various beginnings. The quilt people are sent to the Amish quilt-maker's house, the art lovers to the Artworks, and shoppers to the factory outlets. If you plan ahead you could have dinner with a "plain sect" family. Advance reservations are necessary.

I do have a favorite guest room, but each of them has its own charms. The cozy Baron on the top floor, under the eaves, has a window seat for reading; the Contessa, on the first floor, a private porch and a grand antique cherry secretary and bookcase. I have luxuriated in the antique cherry four-poster in Princess, and I love to stand on the balcony and watch the koi in the pond. But my favorite is the utterly private and thoroughly romantic Carriage House, with its canopy bed, fireplace, and Jacuzzi.

Three spacious areas, the library, the formal parlor, and the Florida sunroom, are entirely for guests. In the fall and winter, a fire is going; in the summer you can read and sip tea in the sunroom, which is fan-cooled. The neighborhood around the inn is pleasant for walking.

Breakfast begins with freshly squeezed orange juice and coffee and is served in the formal dining room. Take a bite of the heavenly peaches-and-cream French toast while you discover why King's Cottage is on the National Register of Historic Places.

"It's not for one particular style," said Karen. "It's because the house is the culmination of several styles that existed at the time." There's a

Georgian fireplace, an Art Deco fireplace and stained-glass windows, Spanish Mission stucco and red tile on the exterior, and heavy oak beams and a carved stairway. The inn has earned historic-preservation awards, and the days of neglect have been replaced with a sparkling and tasteful decor, teas in the parlor, and breakfasts on white linens and fine china. The innkeepers offer kindness and common sense, which reminds you that the way back to the inn is never far.

How to get there: From Route 30 take Greenfield Road exit; at the end of the ramp, turn left onto Greenfield Road. Go under the one-lane bridge and turn right at first light onto Route 340 west. Go through 2 lights (first one bears you right onto Route 462, or East King Street); after second light go $^4\!/_{10}$ mile and turn right onto Cottage Avenue. Turn left into the inn parking area.

Innkeepers: Karen and Jim Owens

Address/Telephone: 1049 East King Street; (717) 397–1017 or (800) 747–8717, fax (717) 397–3447

Rooms: 9, including 1 cottage; all with private bath, telephone, and air conditioning, 1 with fireplace, 1 with whirlpool, 1 with television. One room wheelchair accessible. No smoking inn.

Rates: $69 to $160, double occupancy, EPB and afternoon tea. Two-night minimum weekends; 3-night minimum holidays.

Open: All year.

Facilities and activities: Television in parlor. Nearby: restaurants, Lancaster sites, Visitor's Center, antiquing, Landis Farm Museum, biking, golfing, tennis, factory outlets.

Recommended Country Inns® Travelers' Club Benefit: 10 percent discount Sunday–Thursday except holidays and special events. Cannot be used with other offers or discounts.

Business travel: Desk in 7 rooms; telephone and fax available; meeting room.

Recommended Country Inns® Travelers' Club Benefit: Stay two nights, get third night free, Monday–Thursday, November–August, subject to availability.

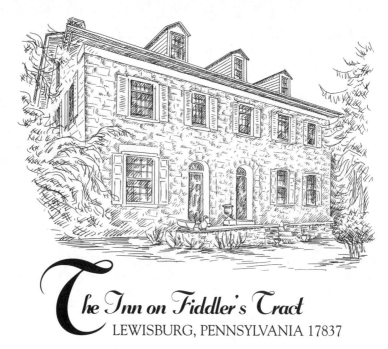

The Inn on Fiddler's Tract
LEWISBURG, PENNSYLVANIA 17837

I arrived about four in the afternoon, when the sun cut a bright swath over the soft gray limestone inn; on the hillside a hot tub overlooked the Amish fields of newly sown grain; up behind the inn stretched the thirty-three acres of country inn property.

During the 1780s a traveling fiddler gave a concert attended by John Penn, son of William Penn. So moved was Penn by the musical evening that he deeded the performer 1,600 acres of property. The fiddler eventually abandoned his landed cottage and returned to his native England. Today his cottage has been subsumed into the inn, which is named for him.

The inn furnishings reveal Natalie's tradi-

tional tastes (her father was a maker of pine furniture) and Tony's contemporary preference. In the living room are a black-lacquer-and-glass table and modern couches and chairs; Natalie's wizard sits on the coffee table, reminding us to appreciate the magic in life. The bookshelves are filled with medical books left by former owners, two of whom were physicians. Year-round a Christmas tree adorns the room.

I appreciate the emphasis on comfort in these attractive bedrooms—the superb mattresses, down comforters, and 100-percent-cotton sheets. Each room has a color-coordinated teddy bear and silk flowers and lace curtains.

Breakfast is served in the formal dining room,

with the fire blazing in the winter time. It's buffet style and more than the typical continental breakfast. Natalie serves fruit and fresh bread—croissants, muffins, or a warm coffee cake—and everyone helps themselves to cereals and a bowl of hard-boiled eggs. In this convivial setting everyone falls easily into conversation.

Natalie also accommodates guests who've made dinner reservations well in advance. You can dine on prime rib with Yorkshire pudding or crabmeat served in puff pastry. Name a favorite dish and it's likely she can prepare it for you. Her five-course meals often include birthday and anniversary cakes.

The inn is located in the country 3 miles from Bucknell University and a historic river town, Lewisburg. During the summer a riverboat ride on the Susquehanna is popular, and during the winter Bald Eagle State Park (15 miles from the inn) provides cross-country skiing.

When I rang the front doorbell, Mikki and Maude, the small inn dogs, greeted me alongside Natalie. It was the beginning of a happy interlude.

How to get there: From I–80 take exit 30 south to Route 15 south. Go 5½ miles to 192 west, turn right, and go 2½ miles to the inn on the right.

Innkeeper: Paula Boiadi; Natalie and Tony Boldurian, proprietors
Address/Telephone: Buffalo Road, Route 192 West (mailing address: R. D. 2, Box 573A); (717) 523–7197 or (800) 326–9659
Rooms: 5 suites; all with private bath, air conditioning, and ceiling fan, 1 with fireplace. No smoking in rooms.
Rates: $75 to $95, double occupancy, continental breakfast. Corporate rates available Sunday–Thursday. Two-night minimum for university weekends.
Open: All year.
Facilities and activities: Dinner served to guests and public by advance reservation ($30 and up), BYOB; hot tub and sauna, television room, 33 acres. Nearby: Bucknell University, riverboat ride, historic mansions, railroad excursion, Mifflinburg Buggy Museum, Amish country, cross-country skiing.

Swiss Woods Bed & Breakfast
LITITZ, PENNSYLVANIA 17543

Why is it that when I turned in the lane the sweet scent of a freshly baked strudel came my way? Was it the memory of my previous journey, evoked anew at the sight of the heart cutouts that surround the balconies?

On my first journey I had found Werner and Debrah's dad finishing the Anker Stube (great room), which now gleams with warmth. Werner's hand-cut stones form the impressive fireplace; the light pine furnishings, attractive couches, and handmade Swiss chairs fill the room. You'll study the tapestry of a Swiss cowherd, the collection of cow bells, the farm tools on the wall, then step out onto the patio. Trees, sun, and the lake below form a pleasurable composition.

Debrah's comment, "We are committed to being here for a long time," pleased me. After living for several years near Werner's family in Switzerland, where he finished a degree in tropical agronomy, they've returned to the area where Debrah grew up. Her family goes back five generations, though she's of Swiss heritage. They built the Swiss-style inn they both love.

Debrah's mother's family owned a bakery, and certainly this influenced her exceptional baking skills. Using family recipes, she creates very fine quiches, apple strudels, and cinnamon-raisin French toast. Her father's family owned a well-known meat company, and her selections of local sausages and bacons are knowledgeable.

The rooms look European and have magnificent hand-carved, four-poster pine beds. They have appropriately romantic names; the Appenzell room has a balcony facing the woods, and the Lake of Geneva, where I slept so soundly, has a lake view. They are spotless, as you'd expect. Mine also had a skylit whirlpool bath.

If you plan ahead, Debrah and Werner will arrange for you to have dinner with a plain family. This is an opportunity to experience a way of life that is remarkably different yet in some ways similar to our own.

Swiss Woods is quiet, hidden, yet easy to find and near the important sites of Lancaster County, including the nearby Moravian town of Lititz and the town of Hershey. Return after a day's touring and you can walk down the country road to a small lake, where the Mosimanns keep a canoe for guests. As the day comes to an end, you can go for a paddle, then return and sit before the fire sipping tea and visiting.

How to get there: From Lititz go 3 miles north on Route 501; turn left on Brubaker Valley Road, go 1 mile, and turn right onto Blantz Road and left into the inn's lane. From Ephrata take Route 322 west to Brickerville, turn left (south) onto Route 50, go 1 mile to Brubaker Valley Road, turn right, and follow as above.

Innkeepers: Werner and Debrah Mosimann

Address/Telephone: 500 Blantz Road; (717) 627–3358 or (800) 594–8018, fax (717) 627–3483

Rooms: 7, including 1 suite; all with private bath, telephone, balcony or patio, and air conditioning, 2 with whirlpool bath, 1 with television. One room wheelchair accessible. No smoking inn.

Rates: $90 to $140, double occupancy, EPB. $15 for each additional person or child. Two-night minimum on weekends, April–December; 3-night minimum holidays. Corporate rates available.

Open: All year.

Facilities and activities: Guest kitchenette, 30 acres, extensive gardens, hiking trails, lake, canoe. Nearby: restaurants, Landis Farm Museum, chocolate and pretzel factories, Ephrata Cloister, antiques markets, farmer's markets, country roads, Lancaster sites, Hershey.

Historic General Warren Inne
MALVERN, PENNSYLVANIA 19355

Snuggled into a king-sized brass bed in the Presidential Suite of the General Warren, you have thoughts like, "Why not spend the entire day in bed?" For a few moments the notion is a real possibility. Then you remember you've a busy day ahead and will return for a fine dinner at this professionally run inn.

For starters you're about to see the Wharton Esherick Museum, a little-known gem located in Paoli, which may be on your list of important things to do. The studio and home is a masterpiece of woodwork by an imaginative artist, who was both a painter and a sculptor. We enjoyed our tour immensely. Next there are Longwood Gardens, the Wyeth paintings, and back roads to explore. Perhaps you've come for the Devon Horse Show and the day will be spent pursuing a favorite hobby. Regardless of the pastimes, a delicious meal at the inn is the final touch. Over an excellent lunch of salmon and pasta, my companion and I mapped our travels.

The General Warren has two moods. By daylight the Colonial-blue trim and quality reproductions give it a classy appearance. By evening the lights are low, the candles are flickering at the individual tables, and the oil paintings on the wall provide the final touch on the romantic scene.

Entrees include selections of tableside preparations that bring your waiter with a cart and elaborate final cooking procedures.

Curiously, I ordered the Beef Wellington, which was a tender cut of beef served within a flaky pastry and accompanied by a classic wild mushroom sauce. It's curious because over dinner I discovered the inn was a popular Tory stronghold and Loyalists had met in this very room, plotting against the Colonial aggressionists. To make amends after the Revolution, the Admiral Warren Inne was renamed the General Warren for an American hero in the Battle of Bunker Hill. I must have intuited the English presence.

The rooms are chosen according to a variety of preferences. If spaciousness is a priority both in bed and out, then the Presidential Suite will suit. If you'd like a red whirlpool bath with space to sip your champagne, then the Franklin Suite is the one you want. Perhaps a fireplace? Take the Warren Suite. Window? The William Penn Room has a cathedral window original to the inn.

How to get there: From Route 30 west of Paoli, turn left onto Old Lincoln Road, go ⅛ mile up the hill, and turn right onto West Old Lancaster Highway. The inn is a short distance on the right.

Innkeeper: Karlie Davies; Jutta Derry and Patrick Byrne, managers

Address/Telephone: West Old Lancaster Highway; (610) 296–3637, fax (610) 296–8084

Rooms: 8 suites; all with private bath, air conditioning, cable television, and telephone, 3 with fireplace, 1 with Jacuzzi.

Rates: $90 to $140, double occupancy, continental breakfast. Weekend packages available.

Open: All year except Christmas Eve, Christmas Day, and New Year's Day.

Facilities and activities: Lunch Monday–Friday, dinner Monday–Saturday. Tavern (dinner entrees $17.50 to $25). Nearby: Valley Forge Park, Brandywine Battlefield, 30 minutes to Longwood Gardens and Brandywine River Museum, Devon Horse Show; Wharton Esherick Museum, open weekends March–December.

Fairville Inn
MENDENHALL, PENNSYLVANIA 19357

Have you ever arrived at a moment so precisely "right" that you knew no amount of coordination could have achieved this fortunate happenstance? We came at 4:30 P.M., during the middle of tea. Kind words and a scrumptious diversity of Swedish butter cookies (made from traditional recipes) served beside a warm fire in civilized surroundings have a way of composing you after a day's travel. Of course, we had these disputes, if you will, about whether the vanilla crescents were tastier than the Brussels or the chocolate-chip cookies more eminently flavored than the macaroons, but those were tongue in cheek because every bite was bliss.

Ole (pronounced Ola), who is Swedish, and Patricia had two different inns in Vermont but are happiest in the heart of the Brandywine, the region where Patricia was born. Their story is romantic. Both were ski instructors and both also skippered boats. They agreed to roam the world together during their first five years of marriage. Then, almost to the day, their first of two daughters was born, and they were ready to settle down to inn life.

The inn is well run. When we arrived Ole greeted us and directed us to a room at the back with a view of the pond and soft hills. I like these back rooms and their view. Barn rafters accent several rooms. Each is spotless. In our bathroom was a spacious European Victorian bathtub that was put to good use on several occasions.

On another visit, I stayed in the carriage house, where I had a secluded deck with pots of geraniums and a huge red hibiscus. The gardens and pond were just beyond.

Patricia chose tasteful flower prints for the wallpapers. Everything has clean, uncluttered lines. Patricia's dad helped with the restoration and building of the inn.

Fairville Inn is the central location for Brandywine's renowned triumvirate: Winterthur Museum and Gardens, 3 miles away; Longwood Gardens, 3 miles away; and the Wyeth collection in the Brandywine River Museum (ask for the backroads route), 5 miles away.

By chance an outdoor European light-and-sound show—fountains and lights choreographed to music—was held that evening in the Longwood Gardens. With Ole's assistance we coordinated dinner with this colorful seasonal event.

I asked Ole about the handsome copper coffee table in the parlor. There are also copper sinks in four of the rooms. He explained that the work was done by skilled roofers who are experienced coppersmiths. It's a crafted touch that shows that great thought and design sense went into the building of this inn.

Continental breakfast the next morning was served in the tea room. We found choices like oat-bran muffins, homemade jams, fruit, and exquisite homemade Danish made by the inn's baker.

Ole has created an inn guide that suggests drives in this area. Be sure to allow time for back roads wandering.

How to get there: From Route 1 west of Chadds Ford, take Route 52 south to Mendenhall. The Fairville Inn is ½ mile past Mendenhall on the left side.

Innkeepers: Ole and Patricia Retlev

Address/Telephone: 506 Kennett Pike/Route 52 (mailing address: P.O. Box 219); (610) 388–5900, fax (610) 388–5902

Rooms: 15, including 2 suites; all with private bath, air conditioning, telephone, and television, 7 with fireplace, some with private deck. One room wheelchair accessible. No smoking inn.

Rates: $125 to $190, double occupancy, continental breakfast and afternoon tea. Two-night minimum weekends; 3-night some holiday weekends.

Open: All year.

Facilities and activities: On 3½ acres. Nearby: restaurants (5-minute drive), Winterthur, Longwood Gardens, Chadds Ford and Brandywine River Museum, antiquing, golf; Wilmington, Delaware.

Business travel: Thirty miles to Philadelphia and 8 miles to Wilmington. Telephone in room; desk in 12 rooms; fax available; corporate rates.

The Mercersburg Inn
MERCERSBURG, PENNSYLVANIA 17236

Once you've seen the inn's view of the Tuscarora Range of the Blue Ridge Mountains and the town's clock steeple rising in the near distance, it stays with you forever. To reach this viewpoint you've stepped inside a prominent 20,000-square-foot mansion, which some historians believe is the largest private residence ever built in the state of Pennsylvania.

The mansion was built to impress in 1909 by successful Harry Byron. Downstairs were a full-scale bowling alley and walk-in safe for the family valuables. The safe is now the wine cellar, the bowling alley a carpeted television/billiard room. Upstairs the former billiard room is a mission-style parlor with Craftsman chandelier and a wall of windows. Wicker furniture gives it a casual warmth.

In the foyer massive scagliola columns and a pair of ornate iron staircases lead to second- and third-story bedrooms. The beds were handmade by local craftsmen and have been equipped with new mattresses. You might find designer sheets by Laura Ashley or Ralph Lauren and down comforters on your bed. Pastel colors accent dark woodwork and light oak floors. To give you an idea of the scale on which the family lived, Mrs. Byron's dressing room makes a spacious bedroom (among my favorites), and the baths in "his" and "her" bedrooms are the largest I've seen.

From the third floor Chuck showed me his favorite views of the Tuscarora Range. It's as if you've stepped into the shoes of a Byron and are on top of the world dreaming of faraway places that you know one day you'll see, as soon as the trunks are brought down and packed.

The six-course dinner at The Mercersburg Inn is designed and prepared by an innovative chef. He prepares entrees best described as scrumptiously memorable. You might have a classic filet mignon flamed with cognac or free-range chicken sautéed with cashews, goat cheese, and wild mushrooms preceded by an appetizer of perfectly grilled shrimp accompanied by mango-kiwi chut-ney. This might culminate with the heavenly tasting dark-chocolate mousse torte, which I chose, or a poached pear with a Cointreau zabaglione.

You'll dress up for a meal of this magnitude. I appreciate Chuck's attitude, however. No tie is required for the men. It's a matter of personal comfort.

How to get there: From Washington, D.C., take Routes 270 and 70 west, Route 81 north, exit Route 16 west, and proceed 10 miles to Mercersburg. The inn is on the immediate left as you enter town.

Innkeepers: John Mohr and Sally Brick; Charles Guy, proprietor
Address/Telephone: 405 South Main Street; (717) 328–5231, fax (717) 328–3403
Rooms: 15; all with private bath, air conditioning, and telephone, 2 with fireplace, some with balcony. No smoking inn.
Rates: $115 to $200, double occupancy, continental breakfast. Two-night minimum weekends October and during ski season.
Open: All year.
Facilities and activities: Dinner Wednesday–Saturday. Television/billiard room. Nearby: Mercersburg Academy's famed Gothic cathedral, Whitetail Ski Resort (6 miles), Gettysburg, Antietam Battlefield, Harper's Ferry, golf.

Longswamp Bed and Breakfast
MERTZTOWN, PENNSYLVANIA 19539

Early in the morning as the summer sun is rising, Elsa often takes off for a bike ride along the country roads. She then returns to begin breakfast preparations for her guests in her large kitchen. Joining her for a New Orleans brew of coffee, you'll see the beginnings of a delicious frittata made with garden herbs, or cheese blintzes, or fresh peach cobblers. She also serves two kinds of granolas, or muesli, and occasionally a homemade sausage. Wander over to the summer kitchen, where breakfast is served, and sharpen your appetite perusing the cookbook collection. Elsa has an innovative approach to cooking and likes trying new dishes and preparing whatever strikes her fancy. She's a seasonal cook, and fresh fruits that

she uses, like peaches, apples, pears, and blueberries, are grown at the inn.

You enter the inn through a long, screened summer porch and walk down the foyer to reach the heart of the inn, the living room–library. A large selection of music ranging from classical to jazz fills the shelf. Pull up a sunny seat at the round table or sit back on the couch and sip some cider, fall into a conversation, browse through the book collection, or simply listen to a favorite Bach.

There's a handsome barn that was recently hand-hewn to replace a historic barn destroyed in an ice- and windstorm in 1994. It has a wet bar, and dance classes often take place here. Bicycles for guest use are also parked here. Outside a badminton net and a regulation-size boccie court might tempt you into some old-fashioned games. Ask Dean to show you the young espalier orchard. He will arrange for a tour of Rodale gardens if you like.

The inn rooms are bright and lovely with sunlight and cooled in summer with large ceiling fans. I like their flavor of cheerful country-home style. Cottage rooms are more private and were part of the Underground Railroad through Pennsylvania. A fireplace is in the cottage.

The area is an antiques lover's dream. Elsa and Dean will get you going in the right direction. Three times a year Renninger's holds antiques "extravaganzas"—call for details and dates. The first Sunday in October, the Dimicks host a 10-kilometer race that begins at the inn and culminates with a large breakfast. Eighty or more participate in the country-inn jog. There is an entry fee and besides getting in shape, you receive a Longswamp T-shirt.

Dean is a physician, and Elsa was a psychiatric counselor before they opened an inn. You are in healing hands.

How to get there: From Allentown take Route 222 south to Route 100 south. Go left onto Route 100 for 1 mile, then right onto Spring Creek Road for 1⁷⁄₁₀ miles. Turn right after the railroad tracks (before Iron Horse Inn) for 2⁶⁄₁₀ miles. Bear left at the Y; go ³⁄₁₀ mile to the inn on the left.

Innkeepers: Elsa and Dean Dimick

Address/Telephone: 1605 State Street; (610) 682–6197, fax (610) 682–4854

Rooms: 10, including 2 suites, in inn and cottage; 6 with private bath, all with air conditioning, 2 with fireplace, 2 with television. No smoking inn.

Rates: $78 to $83, double occupancy; $68 to $73, single; EPB.

Open: All year.

Facilities and activities: Bicycles, television in summer kitchen. Nearby: restaurants (15-minute drive), ski area, Kutztown antiques markets, Renninger's Saturday antiques market, Reading factory outlets (30 minutes away), velodrome, Rodale gardens.

Business travel: Ten miles to Allentown; telephone and fax available; desk in 3 rooms.

$\mathscr{P}$ine $\mathscr{H}$ill $\mathscr{F}$arm

MILFORD, PENNSYLVANIA 18337

Cross the open meadow in the fall and you might catch a deer, turkey, or quail fleeing at your unfamiliar presence. Walk to the moss-bottomed creek in the spring or summer and follow it to the small cascade that trickles down the rocks. Or put on your cross-country skis in winter and enter the snowy woodlands. The inn is located on a mountaintop with a diversity of terrain that affects you; I suspect it reorganizes a few molecules and sets the priorities straight. What's remarkable is Pine Hill's easy accessibility—it's only ninety minutes from Manhattan, yet, like the mythical Shangri-la, it's a billion mental miles away.

You'll step through the porch and into the washed-pine living room that serves as the heart of the inn; here, American antiques and collectibles form a pleasurable composite. We absorbed the contentment; all thought of another existence faded away while we visited with Bob and Lynn by the fire.

"How did you find this unusual place?" I asked. "Kismet," said Lynn. "But first let's show you the inn."

The inn has received a great deal of attention; they've remodeled the kitchen with a general-store counter and created total privacy in the lovely hillside cottage suites. There's occasion to meet others around the breakfast table before the fireplace—over a perfectly delicious array of hot fruit compote and Eggs McLynn, an egg-bacon-and-cheese dish baked in muffin tins—or on the summer patio overlooking the distant Delaware River and mountains.

Often the choice to stay in an inn so seemingly far away requires a drive to dinner, but Pine Hill is only minutes from the restaurants and antiques shops of Milford.

Lynn and Bob are lovers of and dealers in American country antiques. Their permanent collection fills the inn; and each treasure, it seems, comes with a story. They have whimsical things with personal meaning, like Bob's Patton paint signs (since Bob is in advertising) or their antique egg containers (since this was once a chicken farm). But perhaps the most unusual story of all is how they came to acquire the inn.

"Invariably, when our family gathered for the holidays," explained Lynn, "someone mentioned the farm my great-aunt and great-uncle had once owned. It was on a mountaintop, and on a summer afternoon you could lie on the patio and smell the white pine. It became a family myth, that one day we'd rediscover the place."

One day they were handed a 1930s brochure that had been hidden in a chest they sold. It described a farm overlooking the Delaware River. The following weekend the Pattons came up this mountain road outside Milford. Urged inside by the friendly resident caretaker, Lynn recognized the family furniture that had stayed with the residence.

The property was for sale. "We never intended to move," said Bob. But how many of us are presented with the opportunity to create an inn in Shangri-la?

How to get there: Directions sent with reservation.

Innkeepers: Lynn and Bob Patton
Address/Telephone: Milford (mailing address: P.O. Box 1001); (717) 296-7395
Rooms: 5, including 2 suites; all with private bath and air conditioning, 3 with television (2 include VCR). No smoking inn.
Rates: $95 to $120; double occupancy; $85 to $110, single; EPB. Additional person, $25. Two-night minimum weekends July, October, and holidays.
Open: All year.
Facilities and activities: On 268 private acres with 5 miles of trails for hiking, cross-country skiing, birding, and snowshoeing; antiques shop. Nearby: Delaware Water Gap National Recreation Area with canoeing, rafting, waterfalls, and Milford Beach; Grey Towers estate, Pinchot Falls, Peter's Valley anqtiues center, Pinchot Mansion, antiquing.
Recommended Country Inns® Travelers' Club Benefit: 10 percent discount, Monday–Thursday.

The Inn at Olde New Berlin
NEW BERLIN, PENNSYLVANIA 17855

When we arrived I stood in the foyer and watched Nancy, who was in the dining room. I guessed it was she because she had a pleasant smile and was leaning toward a guest, visiting; there was a softness in her expression, enhanced by candlelight and the glow of lamps. I felt comfortable in this welcoming space, where the oak stairway gleamed. In the parlor I could see a piano and an organ; it was reminiscent of early American Victorian parlors, of traditional ways, of quality, and of good character.

When John, who grew up here, was in grade school, he initiated Berlin's first turtle race behind his parents' grocery store. Every Fourth of July about 200 people still come to watch their children and grandchildren nudge their reptiles along the track.

A third of Union County is farmland, and half is forest. Tourism will grow because Amish and Mennonites have relocated here, many from Lancaster County. To get a feel for these communities, visit the Carriage Museum in Mifflinburg. At John and Nancy's recommendation, we also visited Walnut Acres on Penn's Creek, a 500-acre organic farm and food store that serves light lunches. Walking trails weave through the fields and around the barns.

In our travels through the county, we were reminded of the Lancaster area before the advent of tourism; we also found, among the locals, a measurable appreciation for the inn and its restaurant, called Gabriel's.

We thought Gabriel's reputation was well earned. Dinner was impeccably served and featured gingered duckling, a half duck accented with cinnamon and gingered pears. The dessert pie was a heavenly pecan. From the window we could see the church's weather vane across the street—Gabriel blowing his horn. As we dined we visited with the innkeepers and learned about their growing family and how content they are.

The bedrooms are romantically furnished with antiques, and each has a handmade quilt on the bed and lace curtains across the windows. Nancy and John have made each gracious and inviting; while the two front rooms are the largest, I'd also recommend one of the smaller, secluded rooms in the back.

We breakfasted on expertly prepared waffles, freshly squeezed orange juice, and a fruit com-

pote. Over coffee we browsed through a history of New Berlin we'd found in the parlor and read the description of John's career and his parents' store. He reddened slightly when we pointed to his full-page picture. "That was a surprise," he admitted.

It's easy to predict the inn's success and longevity because John and Nancy have created a sterling, hospitable atmosphere.

After breakfast we didn't see any turtles down along the green at Penn's Creek. Perhaps they were swimming or mud bathing, thinking the Fourth of July was a way off and fondly remembering the schoolboy who'd come back to town.

How to get there: From the intersection of Routes 204 and 304, turn west on 304 for 200 yards. The inn is on north side of road, opposite the church. Berlin is 9 miles west of Lewisburg and U.S. 15.

Innkeepers: John and Nancy Showers
Address/Telephone: 321 Market Street; (717) 966–0321, fax (717) 966–9557
Rooms: 5; all with private bath and air conditioning. Television and telephone available on request. A country cabin is occasionally available for rent. No smoking inn.
Rates: 80 to $95, double occupancy, EPB. Two-night minimum some weekends.
Open: All year except first 2 weeks of January.
Facilities and activities: Dinner Wednesday–Sunday (dinner entrees $11 to $16); Sunday brunch, extensive gift shop. Nearby: Amish country, Mifflinburg Buggy Museum, Walnut Acres Organic Farm (closed Sundays and holidays), Woolrich Outlet, Slifer House Museum, Penn's Creek Pottery, gristmill, railway excursion to Lewisburg; quilt, craft, and antiques shopping.
Business travel: Telephone, fax, and desk available; corporate rates available midweek.

Mansion Inn
NEW HOPE, PENNSYLVANIA 18938

For years we would walk along the streets of New Hope, browsing in the bookstore, in Katy Kane's antique-clothing and -linen store, and in the lovely antiques and craft shops, wishing that someone would restore the unique Victorian mansion with its mansard roof that sits in the heart of the village. It had all the Victorian excesses we love—a porch embellished with gingerbread, a fanciful cupola, and a grapeleaf wrought-iron fence. At last it's happened, and best of all, it's a bed and breakfast that we can all enjoy.

When Dr. Kenneth Leiby decided to sell the house that had long been his home and office, the entire town was concerned about its possible fate. Although it was on the National Register of Historic Places, there was concern that it might be gutted for shops or offices. Not to worry. When Keith David and Dr. Elio Bracco toured the house and talked to Dr. Leiby, they knew what they had to do. And they did it right.

Today the house fairly gleams. They painted it a buttercup yellow with white trim so that it's possible to enjoy the carved brackets, arched windows, and wooden cutwork. Inside Dr. Leiby had carefully preserved doorways and hardware within the walls whenever he made changes, and the new partners, with Dr. Leiby's help, were able to return the house to its original configuration.

The central hall with its magnificent mahogany staircase and darkly burnished wood floors, topped with Oriental rugs, has a drawing room on one side and a double-length living room on the other. Arched mantels echo the arched entryways. A decanter of sherry with stemmed glasses sits on a silver tray on an antique side table.

We were escorted to the Ashby Suite by innkeeper Susan Tettemer. The pretty blue-and-white room has a carved canopy bed hung with a blue-and-white French fabric that is repeated in the drapes and wallpaper. A Victorian loveseat and chair are covered in the same fabric, and a beautiful silk Persian rug is on the floor.

We slept like contented babies. The baths offer all the modern amenities we enjoy today. The floors are tile, as are the tub surrounds, mirrors are liberally placed across the walls, and there are such extras as bath salts and oils sitting on a glass shelf. The featherbeds are dressed with starched white Porthault sheets and matelassé spreads. Upstairs the Windsor Suite contains a magnificent four-poster bed and a pretty sitting area. A fireplace lends romance, as does the two-person whirlpool tub. This is a favorite retreat.

The house is surrounded with flowers that bloom throughout the spring and summer, and there's a pretty private garden with a gazebo in back. A full-sized heated pool is located behind a picket fence.

For breakfast we feasted on a variety of sweet breads, muffins, and fresh fruit attractively displayed on an antique Dutch chest, and Susan offered a choice of raspberry-croissant French toast or an omelet with tomato chunks. Both were delicious. We decided that a *long* walk through the village streets and across the bridge to Lambertville, New Jersey, was in order to walk off our breakfast.

How to get there: From New York City take the New Jersey Turnpike to exit 14 and take I–78 west to Route 202 south. After crossing the Delaware River, exit onto Route 32 south to New Hope. At the traffic light (Bridge Street), turn right. Turn left into the first alley on the left to reach the parking area.

Innkeeper: Susan Tettemer; Kimberly Woehr, manager; Keith David and Elio Filippo Bracco, proprietors

Address/Telephone: 9 South Main Street; (215) 862–1231, fax (215) 862–0277

Rooms: 9, including 3 suites; all with private bath, air conditioning, and telephone, 7 with television, 5 with fireplace, 3 with Jacuzzi. No smoking inn.

Rates: $150 to $250, double occupancy, EPB. Two-night minimum weekends, 3-night minimum holiday weekends.

Open: All year.

Facilities and activities: Pool, gardens, parking area. Nearby: Parry Mansion, Washington's Crossing Park, Bowman's Hill Wildflower Preserve, golf, bicycling, river rafting, antiquing, walking.

Business travel: Desk in 2 rooms, fax, copy machine, corporate rates.

The Wedgwood Inns
NEW HOPE, PENNSYLVANIA 18938

Whenever I long for a village inn, I come here. I like hearing Carl's voice on the phone. From the first time I ever called, he was friendly. And he was modest (his inn is renowned); I liked that too. That time long ago, when I was still a stranger, he mentioned that he and Dinie had a dog and that there were two gazebos in the yard and that it was a good place for walking (only five minutes' walk to the Delaware). I could practically smell the chocolate-chip cookies baking in the background. And then the tea kettle went off, and I said I'd be there that weekend and to save a room, any room, but that I'd be there.

And naturally, it was charming and such an easy place to be. Since I had arrived before the other guests, Dinie showed me her rooms, which she's transformed into an intimate reverie of old-fashionedness—lace curtains, paintings, unusual pieces like an antique brush-and-comb set that sits on the desk in one of my favorite rooms (near the antique queen-sized sleigh bed). Dinie is an experienced auction-goer, and one of her prizes is that bed. If you plan ahead she'll inform you about the best midweek auctions and farmer's markets and will give you directions and tips. One of the markets is 150 years old.

It was Carl and Dinie, these savvy innkeepers, who first piqued my curiosity about the village. Now I return—to walk beside the river and the canal, to roam through neighboring

Lambertville, to visit the galleries, and perhaps to see a play before a late dinner or to go to a club for music. Always they have discovered some new place I must see (this time it was a nursery with outrageously beautiful Dutch bulbs), or an artist's studio, or the latest exhibit.

Carl and Dinie opened their inn in 1982, so it's with experience that Carl has coauthored a book on running an inn. He also teaches an introductory class on innkeeping, and I've heard him speak informatively on the topic. The inn consists of the 1870 Victorian, the neighboring 1833 Stone House, and, a short walk up the street, the Aaron Burr House. Several of the inn suites have handsome wood-burning stoves, and always there's a glass of Carl's homemade almond liqueur at bedside.

Breakfast is served in the sunroom or on the outside deck, with a pretty view of the yard.

You'll have great huge muffins, like Dinie's carrot recipe, and fruits along with a delicious blend of coffee. Plenty to keep you charged until lunchtime. If you wish to visit with others, that's easy, since the tables for two are near one another; or if you're romancing you may seclude yourself away. The innkeepers are understanding. Then use the inn map to chart a private journey to everything important that you must see. These are village innkeepers in the best sense of the word in this heart-of-New Hope location, location, location.

How to get there: From New York, take I–78 west to I–287 south. Then take Route 202 south across Delaware River. Go south on Route 32 to traffic light in New Hope. Turn right onto Route 179. Inn is on the left in 2 blocks.

Innkeepers: Nadine Silnutzer and Carl Glassman

Address/Telephone: 111 West Bridge Street; (215) 862–2520, fax (215) 862–2570

Rooms: 19, including 6 suites and 1 cottage; all with private bath and air conditioning, ceiling fan, 14 with telephone, 7 with fireplace or wood-burning stove, 3 with television, 1 with whirlpool. One room wheelchair accessible. Pets allowed with prior permission. No smoking inn.

Rates: $100 to $195, double occupancy, continental breakfast and afternoon tea. Two-night minimum if Saturday included.

Open: All year.

Facilities and activities: Extensive gardens, croquet, badminton. Nearby: pool and tennis privileges, ⅛ mile, restaurants, barge rides, bicycling, Bucks County Theater, walking tour, art galleries, Delaware River, Lambertville, carriage rides, Washington Crossing State Park, steam-train rides, Flemington factory outlets, Mercer Mile.

Business travel: Telephone and desk available; conference room.

The Whitehall Inn
NEW HOPE, PENNSYLVANIA 18938

Chocolate, you say, is your not-so-secret addiction?

Suella does for chocolate what Beethoven and others have done for music. Every April she and Mike host the chamber group from the Philadelphia Orchestra, who perform during Chocolate Lover's Getaway. She teases the appreciative nuances and lifts the spirits of gourmandizers through the palate. Every delicious morsel (even the tea) is chocolate. While those scents and sounds linger in your recent memory, the following morning consists of an entire chocolate breakfast.

"We are told by musicians," said Mike, "that the acoustics of our living room are like the small European chamber halls." I imagined the sounds: the harpist who plays on New Year's Eve and the Rondeau Players with their baroque music rippling through the inn in May.

While some come for the gala events of Candlelight Champagne New Year's Evening Concert, the Baroque Tea Concert, or Picnic Weekends, others prefer the quiet times. They enjoy the inviting waters of the swimming pool, have a look at the thoroughbred horses, and are seen heading out the lane toward the country roads. You can also follow "inn-side" tips to mansions, art galleries, covered bridges, and antiques shops. You might get hooked by the puzzle that covers the table on the front porch. Or linger beside the fire in the great room, which is lined with bookshelves, family antiques, and Suella's needlework.

Rarely, I feel, should one arrive precisely on time—but never, ever arrive late at Whitehall. Tea is served at 4:00 P.M., and a relaxed 3:30 P.M. arrival is suitable. Later you'll congratulate yourself.

Breakfast is served at 9:00 A.M. It begins with a secret blend of coffee and freshly squeezed orange juice. Two baskets soon appear: In the first is an artistic, prize-winning cinnamon bread; another bears a feather-light sourdough biscuit. Now taste the baked pear stuffed with golden raisins, walnuts, and lemon rind and coated with caramel sauce. You think you'll never eat another bite, but at the appearance of a gravity-defying soufflé with aromatic Bucks County sausage, your appetite sharpens anew. Handmade Whitehall chocolates are the vivacious finale. You feel like applauding.

The sunny rooms are attractively furnished with antiques and are expertly wallpapered. All contain canopy or four-poster beds. Everywhere you turn are thoughtful details. Reading lights, robes, and other amenities contribute to the quality of the experience.

King Ferdinand of Spain so coveted chocolate when it first came to Europe that he kept it a secret by ordering to death anyone who let its existence become public knowledge. The king would rejoice here. Mike and Suella would treat him as they do everyone every day of the week— as gastronomic royalty.

How to get there: From New York City take New Jersey Turnpike south to exit 10, Route 287 north for 15 miles to U.S. 22 west and U.S. 202 south. Take U.S. 202 south to Delaware River Bridge. Continue on U.S. 202 south toward Doylestown for 4⁹⁄₁₀ miles to Lahaska. Turn left on Street Road (past Jenny's Restaurant). Go to the third intersection and turn right on Stoney Hill. Turn left on Pineville Road. The inn is on the right, 500 yards.

Innkeepers: Mike and Suella Wass
Address/Telephone: 1370 Pineville Road; (215) 598–7945 or (888) 37–WHITE
Rooms: 6, including 1 suite; 4 with private bath, all with air conditioning, most with fireplace. No smoking inn.
Rates: $140 to $190, double occupancy, EPB and afternoon tea. Two-night minimum weekends, 3-night minimum holiday weekends.
Open: All year.
Facilities and activities: On 13 acres, swimming pool, rose garden, horse barn. Nearby: restaurants, walking or biking country roads, James A. Michener Arts Center, art galleries of New Hope, Mercer Mansion in Doylestown, antiquing, historic sites.

Hickory Bridge Farm
ORRTANNA, PENNSYLVANIA 17353

I've seen the seasonal mantle that swaths Hickory Bridge in all of its appearances. Once we came in the spring and drove through orchards white with apple blossoms; there was the summer that peaches scented the air; I remember that autumn when the tree branches were laden with ripening red apples; this time we came after Christmas and, before turning south to the inn, saw the festive night lights of the downhill slopes at Ski Liberty.

The small office of the farm is found in the kitchen, which dates from 1750. Here a pot once simmered the whole day. Mary Lynn has prepared entire meals using the old cooking methods.

On weekends the barn, now transformed into an inviting country restaurant, is where she prepares Pennsylvania Dutch meals. Everyone begins with cheese and crackers and hot apple cider stylishly served upon an open sleigh. There are three entrees from which to choose; you might select the crab imperial, which is everyone's favorite, or pork tenderloin with amaretto sauce, or crunchy fried chicken accompanied by freshly steamed vegetables. Afterward there's often a choice of blueberry cobbler, walnut pie, or coconut custard pie—the kinds of desserts that sport purple ribbons at state fairs. Granite pots and pans collected by Mary Lynn's mother, Nancy Hammett, decorate a high shelf. The restaurant is entered through an interesting gift shop.

We stayed in a cottage room on this recent trip, and from the front porch, we could hear the trout brook running and the occasional car passing on the wooden bridge. When we returned from dinner, we lit a fire in the Franklin stove in our room—how relaxing it was.

The rooms in the farmhouse inn are snug and homey. In one is a Pennsylvania Dutch chest that represents the family's heritage. Downstairs in the living room are other family antiques and china.

At breakfast, while we chatted with other guests and munched on delicious, freshly baked biscuits and cinnamon-sugar–coated baked grapefruit, Mary Lynn prepared scrambled eggs and sausage. The small dining room is a cozy place. Blue tiles surround the fireplace, and an unusual Delft tile hangs nearby—the blue with the white walls is agelessly pleasing, and the innkeepers are cordial caretakers.

Dr. Hammett serves everyone coffee before he goes off to work at his country clinic. He practices with his son, who is the third generation of Hammetts to practice in the area. "Between us," Dr. Hammett said, "we have 115 years of doctoring." Guests can sleep peacefully knowing there's Dr. Hammett's clinic nearby.

Adams county is famous for its fruit orchards. One afternoon we visited a nearby winery where fruit wines are a specialty. You can borrow bicycles and travel a mile to the nearest winery. Request the Hickory Bridge map, which will ease the way to favorite shops and local sights.

How to get there: From I–81, take Route 16 east, which merges with Route 116 before Fairfield. Continue into the town and turn left at the gas station toward Orrtanna. Go 4 miles and at the sign turn left, then a short right, and a short left again. Go over the tracks and down into the farmstead. Signs lead the way.

Innkeepers: Robert and Mary Lynn Martin
Address/Telephone: 96 Hickory Bridge Road; (717) 642–5261
Rooms: 9, including 4 cottages; all with private bath and air conditioning, 4 with wood-burning stove. One room wheelchair accessible. No smoking inn.
Rates: $79 to $89, double occupancy, EPB. Two-night minimum weekends.
Open: All year.
Facilities and activities: Dinner Friday, Saturday, and Sunday ($17), BYOB. Fifty acres, country museum, collection of antique farm implements, trout fishing, hunting, bird-watching, and walking. Nearby: Gettysburg Battlefield (10 minutes), antiquing, Ski Liberty (8 miles), 3 golf courses.

olive Metcalf

Thomas Bond House
PHILADELPHIA, PENNSYLVANIA 19106

In the eighteenth century Second Street in Philadelphia was home to the city's leading citizens, and it is still part of the Independence National Historic Park. At the height of its popularity, Thomas Bond, a well-known physician and surgeon, occupied a stately brick home on Second Street, separated from the home of William Penn by just a garden. When his son got married in 1769, Dr. Bond used his garden to construct a classic Georgian Revival–style home for his son. Today both the elder Bond's home (it's now a parking garage) and that of Penn (it's now a courtyard and park) are gone, but Thomas Bond Jr.'s home remains. Over the years it has served as a leather tannery, manufacturing plant,

customs brokerage, and a retail shop. The house is on the National Register of Historic Places and is owned by the National Park Service. It's been a bed and breakfast since 1988.

The parlor appears much as it did in Thomas Jr.'s day. There are oil paintings on the wall, a fire in the hearth, and shelves lined with books. An Oriental rug covers the polished floor. At a desk by the window, a family was playing a board game on my last visit. Wine and cheese are laid out every afternoon, and a plate of fresh cookies waits in the evening for guests to return from dinner or a cultural event.

Across the central hall the gracious dining room is located on several levels and is appointed with pewter plates and candles. A continental breakfast is served here during the week, and a bountiful full breakfast is offered on weekends. Popular entrees include peach French toast, a baked dish similar to bread pudding, and baked eggs with three cheeses.

The guest rooms are furnished with Federal reproductions, mostly Chippendale style. The Dr. Thomas Bond, Jr., room is one of the nicest. It has a canopy rice bed, a working fireplace, and a whirlpool tub. Just above, the Dr. Thomas Bond, Sr., room has a high-poster rice bed, a working fireplace, and another whirlpool tub. In the top-floor Robert Fulton room, there's a pine cannonball bed and a dormer window with a view of the Delaware River. All the baths are modern, although a few are small and some have the sink in the bedroom. Half the beds are queen-sized, and the rest are double.

The inn is within walking distance of the historic sites of Philadelphia, including Indepen-dence Hall and the Liberty Bell. Philadelphia is a great walking town—and a not-so-great bicy-cling one, due to the numerous cobblestone streets in this section of town. There are excel-lent restaurants and shops nearby.

How to get there: From I–95 southbound take exit 17 (I–676/Central Philadelphia). Stay in the right lane until you go down the hill to Cal-lowhill Street, then move to the left lane. Con-tinue straight onto Second Street at the traffic light. The inn is on the left ½ block beyond Chestnut Street. From I–95 northbound take exit 16 (Washington Avenue/Delaware Ave-nue). At the end of the ramp, turn left onto Delaware Avenue. Continue north through 5 lights to Dock Street. Turn left onto Dock Street and go 1 block to Front Street. In 1½ blocks enter Philadelphia Parking Authority Garage and park. Walk out the Welcome Park entrance and turn right. The inn is on the right.

Innkeeper: Joe Killingsworth; Thomas Lantry, manager

Address/Telephone: 129 South Second Street; (215) 923–8523 or (800) 845–BOND, fax (215) 923–8504

Rooms: 12, including 2 suites; all with private bath, air conditioning, telephone, and television, 2 with fireplace, 3 with whirlpool.

Rates: $90 to $160, double occupancy, continental breakfast, weekdays; full breakfast, weekends. Two-night minimum weekends.

Open: All year.

Facilities and activities: Nearby: Philadelphia's historic attractions, fitness club.

Business travel: Located in central Philadelphia. Desk in every room; fax available; meeting room.

The Priory
PITTSBURGH, PENNSYLVANIA 15212

Has someone written a book on the semiotics of urban architecture? The steeples and steel monoliths of Pittsburgh convey authority, power, and prestige. But at the end of a business day, you'd prefer to forget the signs and symbols and simply retreat to a sanctuary. Located in the North End is a former priory where the Benedictine monks of St. Vincent prayed, ate, and sang. Mary Ann Graf purchased the building and with the help of a sensitive architect and $1 million, created a place for you to sleep in sound comfort— the structure was built five bricks thick to facilitate quiet contemplation in the city.

The Priory is located in a redeveloping neighborhood known as Deutschtown, where there are still German taverns serving delicious spicy sausages and sauerkraut. It's opposite a high-rise retirement building close to urban thoroughfares. Thanks to the care and privacy, pretty rooms, and intimate parlor that can be enjoyed at the inn, it is preferable to other local accommodations. Here you are in your own cloistered world, with an inviting courtyard and a kind staff solicitous of your needs.

In the evening business travelers might ask one of the staff to help select a favorite restaurant. In Pittsburgh there's no shortage of restaurants to please any palate.

The rooms are attractively furnished with antiques and quality pieces. The rooms overlooking the courtyard are my favorites; they afford views of the stained-glass window of the neighboring church, which is backlit at night. If you descend early, a continental breakfast of cereals, fruits, and muffins is served buffet style on an enormous, carved antique sideboard in a formal dining room. The dining room also serves well for small corporate meetings. During summer you might carry a tray to the adjacent patio, where you'll find peaceful respite from the hustle and bustle of the city.

When she purchased the building, Mary Ann didn't know that her husband's grandparents had attended the neighboring church, which she now also owns. In fact, they were married in the Priory's parlor, where guests now relax before the fire. She showed us the parlor, then continued into a smaller room that held the walk-in safe, where church documents once included the grandparents' marriage certificate.

Today you step inside to borrow books about Pittsburgh.

The framed architectural diagrams that hang in a hallway show precisely where the monks lived and worked in this setting. When several monks returned to see what she'd accomplished with their once-deteriorated priory, they brought a gift of flour from their stone mill and gave their blessings to the inn.

Business travelers are offered a ride downtown in the comfort of a black, 1983 Cadillac, provided by Mary Ann.

How to get there: From Route 80 take I–79 south to I–279 south to exit 15, East Street, which is one way. At third light turn right onto East Ohio Street. At first light turn left onto Cedar Avenue, go 3 blocks, and turn left on Pressley Street. Continue to end of street; inn is on the left and parking lot (gravel) is across the street.

Innkeeper: Mary Ann Graf; Joanie Weldon, manager
Address/Telephone: 614 Pressley Street; (412) 231–3338, fax (412) 231–4838
Rooms: 24, including 3 suites; all with private bath, telephone, and television, 1 with fireplace. One room wheelchair accessible.
Rates: $65 to $150, double occupancy, continental breakfast.
Open: All year.
Facilities and activities: Honor bar in the parlor. Nearby: Carnegie Science Center, The National Aviary, Andy Warhol Museum, Mattress Factory Art Gallery, Pittsburgh Public Theater, Children's Museum, and Three Rivers Stadium.
Business travel: Located in North End, ½ mile from downtown; parking. Complimentary limo downtown. Telephone in room; desk in 10 rooms; conference room. Corporate rates available for multiple visits.

The Sterling Inn
SOUTH STERLING, PENNSYLVANIA 18460

Nature's "walking sticks" fill the ski racks on the front porch. They are found in the woods by guests, and gradually they are becoming seasoned from use, since they are borrowed and returned with silent understanding.

It's spring, and The Sterling Inn is surrounded with rhododendrons, white mountain laurel, tulips, daffodils, hyacinths, and flowering apple trees that blaze your path around the grounds.

In winter cross-country skis are available. Mary Kay or Ron will direct you to the 6 miles of ski trails that weave through the inn's 103 acres. Ice skating and sledding are nearby. In the fall you can hike through the crimson woods. What-

ever the season you can swim in the enclosed pool.

The Sterling Inn makes special events out of holidays. At Easter the Easter Bunny is an invited guest; on July Fourth there are barbecues and dancing; and at Christmas stockings hang on your door.

The guest lounges are large, with television and comfortable furnishings. They have stone fireplaces. The newly remodeled suites have a fresh country look. Yours might have a four-poster rice bed, a matching armoire, and a pair of Oriental tables beside the sofa. The suites are perfect for those romantic occasions and for sharing a glass of champagne before the wood-burning stove. Request the streamside Nearbrook or Wayside suite.

Dinner at the inn is informal (though men usually wear jackets) and served upon Royal Doulton china. Entrees might begin with my favorite, fresh salmon baked in a light puff pastry; thick, beautiful tournedos of beef; soft-shell crab in season; or grilled mahi mahi with herbs and citrus. You may request low-cholesterol or other diet-conscious dishes. Expect homemade breads and fresh seasonal vegetables. Desserts include the exotic, rich chocolate-bourbon cake. Fortunately, amidst this gourmet feasting, the inn hasn't lost its perspective. The inn's honest-to-goodness local-fruit-and-berry pies continue to be served. We're never too sophisticated to appreciate a large slice of blueberry or blackberry pie adorned with a dollop of vanilla ice cream.

This is an inn for all generations, with plenty of room to spread out. Whether you're coming for a honeymoon or a golden anniversary or somewhere in between, there are the mountains to roam over, the seasons to enjoy, and the mix and match of all the ages.

The inn has added a new property, The French Manor, which addresses the desire for a romantic weekend in a secluded setting. From the stone veranda you can dine on French cuisine and enjoy the elegant mountain views from this mansion.

How to get there: From I–84 take Route 507 south through Greentown. In Newfoundland, take Route 191 south. It's 4 miles to the inn.

Innkeepers: Ron and Mary Kay Logan

Address/Telephone: Route 191; (717) 676–3311 or (800) 523–8200, fax (717) 676–9786

Rooms: 55, including 12 suites, in the inn and cottages; all with private bath and telephone, 18 with television, 12 with fireplace or woodstove, 3 with whirlpool. Five rooms wheelchair accessible. Designated no smoking rooms.

Rates: $130 to $220 per couple, MAP. Special rates for children under 16. Two-night minimum most weekends, 3-night minimum most holidays. Add 15 percent gratuity. Weekly rates amd packages available.

Open: All year.

Facilities and activities: Indoor swimming pool and whirlpool; 106 acres, with hiking, mountain biking, and cross-country trails, 9-hole putting course, tennis court, pond, ice skating, tobogganing, ski rentals, sleigh rides. Nearby: Pocono Playhouse. Wildflower Music Festival, Lacawac Sanctuary.

Business travel: Telephone with dataport in all; desk in 25 rooms; fax available; complimentary newspaper; airport transportation; conference room.

Recommended Country Inns® Travelers' Club Benefit: 10 percent discount, Monday–Thursday.

The Inn at Starlight Lake
STARLIGHT, PENNSYLVANIA 18461

This is a quaint lakeside inn in the northeastern lake district of Pennsylvania. It's on a quiet little road that fronts Starlight Lake, where boats float gently along the docks. You enter into a busy and friendly lobby. In cold weather two wood-burning stoves crackle and burn. Through the glass doors is a busy game room with pool, Ping-Pong, and plenty of children's toys to keep the young ones occupied.

During the winter there's a professional ski instructor on the staff, and a ski shop forms part of the inn. In the taproom hangs a cross-country ski map and your day on snow begins on the frozen lake. In the summertime you might take a sail on the lake, swim, or go for a hike or bicycle along country roads. Adirondack furniture sits along the porch and on the lake dock.

The rooms are country-simple, pleasant, and clean. My preference is for the lakeside rooms. Keep in mind that the inn dates from 1909. The sounds of the inn blend in with the frogs and the silence outdoors. It's the way you might imagine "ye olde" little country inn.

Jack and Judy and their four children came from New York City to the inn back in 1977. Jack left the recording business, and Judy brought theatrical talents that she had honed at the Yale Drama School. Their love of music permeates the inn. A collection of albums is easily accessible, as is the grand piano stacked high with song sheets.

On top sits *The Best Hits of the 1920s and 1930s*.

It's nothing short of wonderful to have a fine meal with Starlight Lake for a view. The lusty steak au poivre is sautéed in crushed peppercorns with brandy and cream. For a light mood try the fresh fish of the day, either steamed, baked, or sautéed. I do like it when you can order freshly brewed coffee with dessert. The chocolate desserts satisfy the appetite perfectly. Afterward you can take a lakeshore stroll in the fresh evening air, with the stars lighting the way.

I think I shall never forget that first moment of opening the door to this inn. My traveling companion and I entered from a snowy night into a Currier & Ives scene: comings and goings before the fire, skis hanging on the wall, people reading, others chatting in the next room, one small group playing a game together. An image like that stays with you and returns with each visit regardless of the season.

How to get there: From Route 17 in New York, take exit 87 and go into Hancock, New York. Take Route 191 across the Delaware to Route 370 and turn right. Follow the signs to the inn. From I–81 take exit 62, Route 107 E to 247 NE to 171 N to 370 E. Follow the signs to the inn.

Innkeepers: Jack and Judy McMahon and family

Address/Telephone: Starlight (mailing address: P.O. Box 27); (717) 798–2519 or (800) 248–2519, fax (717) 798–2672

Rooms: 26, including 1 suite and cottages; 20 with private bath, suite with double whirlpool bath, 1 with fireplace. Limited smoking.

Rates: $115 to $200, double occupancy, MAP. Single rate available. Suggested gratuity 12 percent. Weekly rates available. Children under 2 free; ages 2 to 12, $37 to $40; MAP. Two-night minimum stay high season, 3-night minimum holidays.

Open: All year.

Facilities and activities: Lunch, bar. Spring-fed lake, 10 miles of cross-country ski trails, ski shop, canoeing, small sailboats, rowboats, tennis court, bicycles, swimming, hiking, shuffleboard, volleyball, and Ping-Pong. Nearby: 140 lakes, golf, Upper Delaware trophy trout fishery, riding stables, downhill skiing at Mt. Tone and Elk Mountain.

Recommended Country Inns® Travelers' Club Benefit: 10 percent discount, subject to availability.

Bridgeton House
UPPER BLACK EDDY, PENNSYLVANIA 18972

Give me a country inn room with a water view and I turn cocoon. Enticing me out requires lengthy descriptions of invigorating walks along the Delaware Canal, details of the excellent restaurant choices that lie minutes beyond the inn's threshold.

First you must choose the nature of your water view. Bridgeton House has rooms that offer different sizes and moods for a diversity of tastes. For the old-fashioned cozy warmth of homemade quilts and antiques, there are the small balcony rooms. For those who imagine being whisked off to London or Paris for the night, it's a posh garret room. And for those who like to go to the top, it's the Penthouse.

If you go to the top (we did), the Penthouse has 800 square feet of space and is spanned by windows overlooking the Delaware River. There's a raised marble fireplace, and double doors open to a mahogany-and-marble bath. Think nouvelle luxury, with a king-sized bed, black-leather lounging chairs, and a handcrafted bar with stained-glass doors, stocked with sherry. A desk for writing your memoirs is strategically placed to capture reflections of the midnight lights of the river bridge.

The Federal inn is riverfront and roadside in a wisp of a village. Charlie, a talented builder, has transformed the inn, remodeling with originality, skill, and a palette of ideas. We first met one spring when he was busily installing handsome designer windows and a new fireplace. On a recent trip Bea's decorating had finalized the inn's transformation.

You enter on the water side through a small, eclectic living room. Bea and Charlie's shell collections are displayed near stacks of magazines. Next is the dining room with its Colonial ambience. White walls are border-stenciled; dried bouquets are in the windows; the gas fireplace glows warmly.

Up the stairs and down the hallway, you pass a Bloomsbury-influenced design that was painted by Cheryl Raywood, Bea's artist-cousin. One suite is painted with stars and moon on the ceiling. The wood trim is pickled white; as you climb to the Penthouse, you admire the contemporary hallway window that pours in light.

Bea selects her breakfast menu carefully; it reveals someone who keeps in touch with new food trends. Everyone is served at private tables. We began with a baked pear covered with a cream-and-butter sauce followed by orange-walnut waffles. Another morning you might awake to an asparagus–cheddar cheese omelet with pear-and-apple bread. The combinations are deliciously creative. We visited against a background of guitar music. We lazily browsed over the covered-bridge map and decided to amble down the river, following our whims, stopping to walk through villages and explore antiques shops. Oh, precious, unbridled time along the Delaware.

How to get there: From New York City take Holland Tunnel to New Jersey Turnpike south to exit 14. Follow signs to Route 78 west. Take Route 78 west to exit 15 (Clinton/Pittstown). Go to the light and turn left. The road becomes Route 513 south. Go 4 miles. After Hoff Mill Inn turn right. Stay on 513 to Frenchtown. Cross the bridge to Pennsylvania, turn right onto Route 32 north, and go 3½ miles to the inn on the right.

Innkeepers: Bea and Charlie Briggs
Address/Telephone: 1525 River Road (Route 32) (mailing address: P.O. Box 167); (610) 982–5856
Rooms: 12, including 4 suites and 1 cottage; all with private bath and air conditioning, 8 with private porch, 5 with fireplace, 4 with television, 2 with whirlpool. No smoking inn.
Rates: $69 to $250, double occupancy, EPB and afternoon tea. Two-night minimum weekends, in summer all rooms; only fireplace rooms in winter.
Open: All year.
Facilities and activities: Located on Delaware River, swimming and fishing from private dock. Nearby: restaurants, covered bridges, New Hope, Washington Crossing State Park, art galleries, theater, shopping, antiquing, tennis, river rafting.

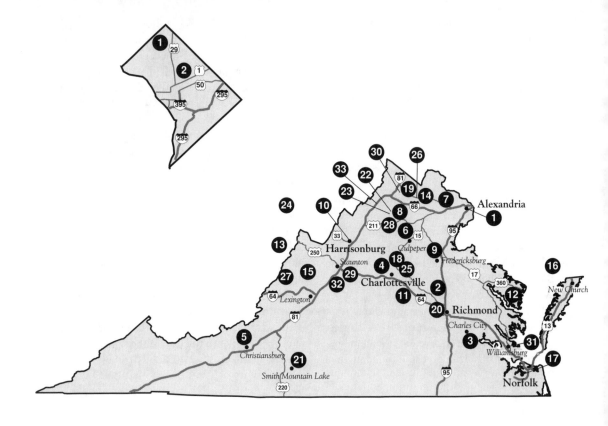

Virginia &
Washington D.C.

Virginia and Washington, D.C.

Numbers on map refer to towns numbered below.

Morrison House

ALEXANDRIA, VIRGINIA 22314

In Old Town Alexandria, tucked along a side street, is an inn with a European flavor. The Morrison House was built in 1985 as a 1790s Federal mansion. Behind the front door lies the Italianate marble reception area perennially graced by an ornate bouquet of flowers. You will be led to your room by an English butler or someone politely trained in those traditions.

Every afternoon tea is available in the parlor. Working with Harney and Sons of Connecticut, the tea master has created a special blend, which is offered along with the traditional favorites and herbal infusions as well as tea cakes, finger sandwiches, and scones with jams and crème fraîche. The tea menu gives a brief history of afternoon tea; the custom was begun by Anne, seventh duchess of Bedford, in the late 1700s. At the tea's conclusion the duchess would offer champagne or sherry. In her memory this is the custom at Morrison House.

The crystal chandeliers are Baccarat; a peach-colored damask covers the couches and chairs; you'll admire the fine paintings and antique artifacts as your tea is poured. Neighboring the parlor is a mahogany-paneled library with horsehair-upholstered mahogany furniture, damask draperies, and Oriental rug.

Dinner at the Morrison House occurs in the Grill, composed of an English-style clublike room with mahogany tables. Among the appetizers might be a country-style pâté with corni-chons, pearl onions, Pomméry mustard, and a lingonberry sauce. Then you might have a Chesapeake Bay seafood chowder followed by grilled yellowtail tuna on caramelized onions or a mixed grill of sausage, liver, lamb chop, and chicken with Madeira sauce. The desserts are sinfully delicious. You might go light with a sorbet or a white-chocolate cheesecake. Following a brandy, in a rarefied state of satiation, you can take a walk down through the old town and along the waterfront.

An elevator lifts you to your room. Note the artwork that graces the ceiling. Each guest room is individually decorated with authentic-period, lush Axminster carpeting; extra-high, oversized beds, including four-posters and canopies in sev-eral rooms; and custom-made armoires. The rooms are painted in pastels; wooden blinds typical of the late eighteenth century hang at the windows. In the Italian-marble bathrooms are thick Scottish terry-cloth towels and the room's second telephone. Most corner rooms have the advantage of three windows for plenty of sunlight. Nothing is harsh in color or fabric; soft, muted tones bathe the senses.

How to get there: Ten-minute walk from Alexandria Metro Station. Ten-minute limo ride from National Airport. From 495 south of Alexandria, exit Route 1 North and proceed to Prince Street, turn right, go 1 block, and turn left again on South Alfred.

Innkeepers: Peter Greenberg; Wanda McKeon, general manager
Address/Telephone: 116 South Alfred Street; (703) 838–8000; in Virginia (800) 533–1808, outside Virginia (800) 367–0800, fax (703) 684–6283
Rooms: 45, including 3 suites; all with private bath, air conditioning, telephone, and television. Wheelchair access. Designated no smoking rooms.
Rates: $150 to $295, double occupancy, EP. Children no charge. Seasonal specials. Parking $5 a day.
Open: All year.
Facilities and activities: Breakfast, lunch, afternoon tea ($13.50), dinner (entrees S13 to $27); full beverage license; 24-hour room service; elevator. Nearby: walking and carriage tours of Old Town Alexandria, Potomac River cruise.
Business travel: Located 15 minutes from Washington, D.C. Telephone and desk in all rooms; fax and audiovisual equipment available; conference room; corporate rates.

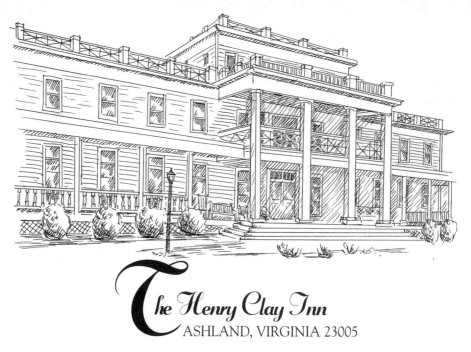

The Henry Clay Inn
ASHLAND, VIRGINIA 23005

"Ashland, the center of the universe," say the locals about their little railroad town. Then they redden slightly and chuckle at their audacity. Born as a railroad town in the mid-1800s, Ashland, only 15 miles north of Richmond, became a commuter's suburb. By the early 1900s the expansive Henry Clay Inn, named for Hanover County's famous resident, was built. It burned in 1946, however. Today's Henry Clay Inn was built in 1992. It's an exact replica of the original, except that it surpasses its grandfather in worldly comforts.

The Georgian Revival is the color of a newly blossomed yellow tulip. Massive Doric columns front the long porch, lined with rocking chairs. Seated here you can imagine the trains that once passed by, bearing names like *Sun Queen*, the *Robert E. Lee*, and the *Havana Special*. Some guests still arrive by train from New York, Philadelphia, or Washington, D.C. Special stops are occasionally made on request; others are scheduled.

In the wide foyer, with hearth and fireplace, people sat visiting. Others were enjoying a late lunch in the dining room. We walked through the art gallery, browsed through an expansive gift shop, and in the front parlor found Carol.

Upstairs the bedroom furniture is a collection of oak, pine, and cherry reproductions. Carol selected the vibrant paints and matching spreads and linens. The armoires were handmade by a local craftsman. When we crossed the threshold of the first bedroom, we listened attentively as the first train passed and realized how well insulated the structure is. We knew we'd get a sound night's sleep.

The dining room is a popular spot for lunch, dinner, and Sunday brunch. For dinner we sampled a lacquered salmon fillet, which had been marinated in Asian spices, and a loin lamb steak with goat-cheese sauce. Both were excellent. Our waitress said that the Chesapeake bay crab cakes, which are served with a red-chili mayonnaise, are the most popular item. A wine suggestion is paired with each entree, appetizer, and salad; we were amazed to see the range of choices offered.

A good way to get acquainted with the area is to stop at the visitor's center opposite the inn. The second Saturday of May, the Camptown Races are held at Graymont Farm, 5 miles north of Ashland on Route 1. Organized as a charity fund-raising event in the early fififties, it continues to grow and now includes a mule race. The first Saturday in June, thousands arrive for the Strawberry Faire. When planning an agenda consider including the historic Barksdale Theater, located 5 miles away in Hanover, Virginia.

Whether or not you're a train lover, there's something exciting about the trains and original depot that houses the visitor's center. You look across to Randolph Macon College or up the small main street, where the houses face the railroad, and then return to your lemonade and rocking chair and bond with the center of the universe.

How to get there: From I–95 take Route 54 west and proceed 1½ miles to railroad track. Turn right onto Railroad Avenue and parallel track, cross over to the inn 300 yards on left.

Innkeepers: Carol C. Martin, Ann-Carol Houston, and Judith Kosten-Bauder

Address/Telephone: 114 North Railroad Avenue; (804) 798–3100 or (800) 343–4565, fax (804) 752–7555

Rooms: 15, including 1 suite; all with private bath, air conditioning, cable television, and telephone, 2 with Jacuzzi. One room is wheelchair accessible. No smoking in guest rooms.

Rates: $80 to $145, double occupancy, continental breakfast.

Open: All year.

Facilities and activities: Lunch Tuesday–Saturday, dinner Tuesday–Saturday (entrees $12 to $19); Sunday brunch. Nearby: Randolph Macon College, Scotchtown (Patrick Henry's home), Barksdale Theater in nearby Hanover Tavern, King's Dominion, Richmond National Battlefield Park, Richmond.

Business travel: Fifteen miles from Richmond. Telephone with dataport and desk in all rooms; fax and copier available; conference room; corporate rates.

$\mathcal{E}$dgewood Plantation
CHARLES CITY, VIRGINIA 23030

Edgewood Plantation is not for everyone. Some will find the vast collection of Victoriana overwhelming and think it overly cluttered. Others, however, will revel in the immersion in the Victorian era.

The house itself is an 1849 Carpenter Gothic, once part of Berkeley Plantation, across the street. It has a restrained collection of Victorian wicker on the front porch. Inside, though, every single table, mantel, chair, sideboard, dresser, windowsill, and even the floor space not absolutely needed to get from one room to the next are covered with collections of Victoriana. Even the kitchen is filled with kitchen queens, tables, chairs, baskets, and stoves covered with

Victorian artifacts. There are silver pieces, glassware, brass items, dolls, mannequins dressed in lacy Victorian dresses, fancy hats hanging from a tree, gloves, high-top shoes, fans, and jewelry stashed throughout.

Dot Boulware can be blamed—or thanked—for this excess. She started collecting and just couldn't stop. In the purple-and-gold parlors downstairs, heavy drapes are swagged across windows, and fantastic chandeliers illuminate the collections. When I was there one day in late February, the Christmas tree, containing 2,600 tiny lights and probably at least as many ornaments, was still standing, and a photographer had just completed his work for a magazine.

This would be the perfect place to experience a Victorian Christmas.

The guest rooms are as filled with Victoriana as the parlors, prompting one guest to declare, "I had to remove dolls and pillows before I could even see the bed." Nevertheless, once you see the beds you'll never forget them. Victoria, for example, has a magnificent carved burled-walnut 1840s headboard; Lizzie, a massive canopy with lace curtains; Sarah an exceptional 1790 canopy tobacco bed; and Jeb Stuart (who did stop here on his way to Richmond), an 1888 Empire with full curtains. A two-bedroom suite upstairs has iron-and-brass beds. The rooms are filled to the brim with dolls, dolls, and more dolls.

On arrival guests are offered tea, wine, cakes, and coffee. Breakfast will include such delicacies as stuffed French toast or banana-and-walnut pancakes, along with fresh fruit and homemade breads.

Edgewood is located on eight acres that include a creek, a pool surrounded by a white picket fence, and a gazebo. It's popular for weddings and receptions. The estate also includes a 1725 stone gristmill that was used to grind corn for both the Union and Confederate armies.

Dot offers tours of her house daily, and she and Julian sell antiques and gifts from their country store. She also puts on elaborate Victorian tea parties with an array of sandwiches, scones with clotted cream, pastries, and cakes. She is dressed in full Victorian array and she garbs each guest in a Victorian hat for the occasion.

Edgewood is just 20 miles from Williamsburg, so a day trip can easily be accomplished, but there are many things to do close to home also. A visit to Berkeley Plantation, the home of Benjamin Harrison, a signer of the Declaration of Independence, and also of President William Henry Harrison, should not be missed.

How to get there: From the north take I–95 south to exit 84 and travel south on I–295. Take exit 22A to Route 5 east (Virginia Scenic Byway). The inn is on the left in 12½ miles. From the south take I–95 north to exit 46 and travel north on I–295 to exit 22A. Follow directions above.

Innkeepers: Julian and Dot Boulware
Address/Telephone: 4800 John Tyler Highway (Route 5); (804) 829–2962 or (800) 296–3343, fax (804) 829–2962
Rooms: 8, including 2 suites; 7 with private bath, all with air conditioning, 3 with television and fireplace. Smoking in kitchen and outside only.
Rates: $120 to $198, double occupancy, EPB. Two-night minimum holiday weekends.
Open: All year.
Facilities and activities: Pool, gazebo, gardens, historic mill, creek. Nearby: Berkeley Plantation, Shirley Plantation, Evelynton, Sherwood Forest, golf.

Piney Grove at Southall's Plantation
CHARLES CITY, VIRGINIA 23030

It was a sunny winter day when we first drove up to the inn. Joan Gordineer was outside, pulling weeds in anticipation of spring. As she showed us through her inn, she said, "For years my family and I dreamed of restoring a building to its authentic origins. When we purchased this modest 1800s plantation house, it had no roof, and some of the floor had deteriorated, but otherwise it was intact." The house includes the oldest log structure in Tidewater Virginia, and when inside, it's hard to remember that we're actually in the twentieth century. To heighten the sense of an eighteenth century welcome, Joan brought a hot toddy. Had it been summer, we would have been refreshed by a mint julep. As we sipped, we learned more about this remarkable family.

After the restoration of the main house was complete, the family, consisting of Joan and Joe, her husband, their son Brian (who is a historic preservation specialist) and his wife Cindy Rae, saw an offer in *Preservation News* that they couldn't resist. The Ladysmith House, a two-story home built in 1857, was for sale for $1—if the new owners would move it. Today it occupies a spot beyond the gardens and contains four guest rooms.

The main house has four common rooms open to inn guests. The old log-and-chink room is used as a dining room; this is where breakfast is served. It has a huge brick fireplace. The family have dedicated themselves to finding artifacts that have a connection to the house. Old farm implements decorate the walls of one dining room. Another room, added to the house in about 1850 and also used as a dining room, displays maps of the area during the Civil War. There's a display of arrowheads found on the property that were left by the Chickahominy Indians, who had a settlement here in the seventeenth century. A parlor/library contains history books, while a sitting room reveals the Gordineer family history.

The appeal of the entire seven-acre property is the concerted attempt to create an inn that's as historically accurate to its age as it can be and still provide the necessary guest amenities. The guest rooms in the Ladysmith House are simple but charming. Although furnished with period antiques and decorated with stencils, pots of garden-fresh flowers, down comforters, and painted floors, each room has a private bath, fireplace, air conditioning, television, stereo, a refrigerator stocked with Virginia wine, and a coffeemaker. Our Colonial ancestors would love it.

The grounds include a barn that serves as

shelter to the resident ducks, geese, ponies, goats, and sheep. The gardens are gorgeous, and a map describes specimens along a nature trail that meanders through the property. On a slight rise is a freeform pool surrounded by flower gardens and a gazebo.

In the morning we feasted on a plantation breakfast of juice, fresh fruit, Virginia ham, homemade breads and an egg dish—cheddar-cheese strata. Another favorite entree is Joan's Piney Grove Baked French Toast. There are several excellent restaurants nearby that feature fine food in a Colonial setting.

How to get there: From the north take I–95 south to exit 84 and travel south on I–295. Take exit 22A to Route 5 east (Virginia Scenic Byway). In ½ mile after the junction with Route 155, turn left onto Route 615 (watch closely for sign) and continue to the inn, which will be in 7 miles. From the south take I–95 north to exit 46 and travel north on I–295 to exit 22A. Follow remaining directions above.

Innkeepers: The Gordineer Family; Joan Gordineer, manager
Address/Telephone: 16920 Southall Plantation Lane/Route 615 (mailing address: P.O. Box 1359, Williamsburg, VA 23187–1359); (804) 829–2480, fax same
Rooms: 4, including 1 suite; all with private bath, air conditioning, fireplace, stereo, minirefrigerator, coffeemaker, and hair dryer. No smoking inn.
Rates: $125 to $160, double occupancy, EPB. Two-night minimum holiday weekends. No credit cards.
Open: All year.
Facilities and activities: Pool, nature trail, farm animals, bird-watching, croquet, badminton, gardens. Nearby: Colonial Williamsburg, James River Plantations, Jamestown and Yorktown National Parks, Busch Gardens.

Clifton: The Country Inn

CHARLOTTESVILLE, VIRGINIA 22911

We walked down to the lake and then along the wide pathway through the woods. We passed the tennis court and the lap pool. Near the gazebo were eight touring bikes. We saw the map that directs you on a day ride to Monticello, Michie Tavern, and Highland House, once the home of James Monroe. But first we must settle in.

Clifton is a white-columned mansion on the National Register of Historic Places. Secluded among forty acres of woodland, it overlooks the distant Rivana River and a lake. Monticello can be spied in the distance through the trees. This proximity was convenient for Thomas Jefferson, whose daughter, Martha, was the lady of the manor. She had married Thomas Mann Randolph, who, at various times, was governor of Virginia, member of the Virginia House of Delegates, and a U.S. congressman.

You enter a large hallway, and to the left is the small library, where you imagine the household affairs were conducted. Positioned near the fireplace are a pair of green leather wingback chairs; a hunting horn sits on the mantel above the fireplace. Opposite is the large parlor with a grand piano at one end. You like the feel of the place, indoors and out.

Next you're led to your room. On the beds are exquisite cotton fabrics and (in winter) down comforters. Each room has a fireplace and views of trees or the lake.

Among my favorite spots are the picturesque guest rooms in the livery stable. They have their original bead-board walls and are decorated with a splashy cabbage-rose fabric. The rooms are on two levels, have a fireplace in the sitting room, and overlook the lake. Other favorites, however, are the rustic but tender honeymoon cottage, with an exposed-beam ceiling, skylights, and a loft bedroom; and the carriage house, a suite so large it even has a grand piano in the sitting room.

Before dinner guests will have a seat in the large parlor, and Craig may tell the history of the house and describe dinner. On weekends a Celtic harpist or another instrumentalist often plays.

Craig is an outstanding chef who also teaches cooking classes in the large kitchen. A graduate of the Culinary Institute of America, he doesn't just prepare food, he celebrates it. A typical seven-course dinner may start with poached medallions of North Atlantic salmon served over fresh arugula with a sun-dried tomato-pear vinaigrette, then go on to a soup that's an essence of asparagus with watercress oil and fleurons. There will always be two choices of entree. maybe a roasted rack of Summerfield Farms (local) lamb crusted with garlic and served with a sauce Robert or a pan-seared swordfish with a red-bell-pepper coulis and sorrel presto. For dessert a dark chocolate pôt de crème may be served with fresh berries.

You'll be seated in the formal dining room, in a small sunroom, or in the French café–style room that overlooks the trees. After dinner you might walk down to the lake, return to the parlor for a liqueur, or play a game of croquet in the balmy moonlight. You feel like it's your private estate for the weekend.

How to get there: From I–64 east of Charlottesville, exit Route 250 south, go 2 miles, turn right on Route 729, go ¼ mile, and turn left at the discreet sign.

Innkeepers: Craig Hartman; Mitch and Emily Willey, proprietors
Address/Telephone: 1296 Clifton Inn Drive; (804) 971–1800 or (888) 971–1800, fax (804) 971–7098
Rooms: 14, including 7 suites; all with private bath, air conditioning, and fireplace. Wheelchair access. No smoking inn.
Rates: $185 to $245, double occupancy, EPB, and afternoon tea. Two-night minimum weekends.
Open: All year.
Facilities and activities: Prix-fixe dinner Friday and Saturday, $58; Sunday–Thursday, $48. Forty acres, lake, tennis court, bikes. Nearby: Monticello, Ash Lawn, University of Virginia, wineries.
Business travel: Desk in 6 rooms; telephone, dataport, fax, PC, copy machine, laser printer available; meeting rooms.

Silver Thatch Inn

CHARLOTTESVILLE, VIRGINIA 22911-7422

What cadence brings us back to favorite places? Is it the measure of seasons or some inner clock that springs us loose from our pattern and says "time to go"? When a favorite pub and unpretentious innkeepers await, we're off with no hesitation.

How auspicious this return was. We arrived in winter at dusk, when the lights of the inn led us up the path and into the warmth. Rita greeted us at the door and led us to our handsome Washington Room. (Guest rooms are named for U.S. presidents.)

The oldest section of the inn—the gathering room—was built of logs and mortar in 1780 by Hessian soldiers, prisoners during the Revolu-

tionary War. Today it's a cozy area with couch, chairs, and a table. I imagined summer guests having iced tea here before a game of tennis or a swim. The inn's outdoor pool is shared with the neighborhood. It's an arrangement that has worked well for many years.

There are three good-sized dining rooms; one is a sunroom, and the other two have fireplaces. At dinner we perused an estimable wine list. We began the meal with a shared appetizer, a sauté of fresh foie gras with a pear poached in port wine, hazelnuts, and glazed pearl onions. Then we enjoyed grilled rack of lamb with ginger and mint honey and pecan rice pilaf. We toasted transitions, the chef, the innkeepers, and each other.

We pledged we'd defer dessert, but when our waitress appeared with a tray displaying the actual goodies, we succumbed and chose a light strawberry mousse, planning to give the chocolate peanut butter bar a go-round on our next visit.

Rita and Vince appear to have spent their lives innkeeping, even though they have owned the inn only since 1992. They are so easy and comfortable with their guests, unassumingly directing them to Monticello, on mountain drives, to favorite craft shops, and other not-to-be-missed places in and around Charlottesville.

The rooms have crisp linens, down comforters, and handsome antiques. Some rooms have light pine furnishings that coordinate beautifully.

Rita spoke of the coming springtime here and how the soft hills turn green and the dogwood trees and flowers bloom. In April the homes and estates open their garden gates for the annual Virginia Garden Week. Naturally, we love to come then and reacquaint ourselves with the southern plants while strolling through the gardens of Monticello and Ashlawn.

"I live vicariously through my guests," Rita declared the next morning as she visited briefly at the different tables. She was simultaneously fetching freshly squeezed orange juice and hot muffins and pouring hot coffee, while making everyone feel at ease and answering questions about shops and pretty drives and the upcoming art festival.

Charlottesville has an aura: Monticello beckons, and the horse-and-hound crowd sets the pace in this toney area of hills and valleys. But we wanted nothing imposing. We sought comfort, a small pub, a place to talk and feel relaxed, with good food and an inviting room. Someplace that had a gathering room. All those essentials add up to Rita and Vince's authentic country inn.

How to get there: From Washington, D.C., take I–66 west to the Gainsville exit onto Route 29, go 1 mile past the Charlottesville Airport, and turn left at the discreet sign into Hollymead neighborhood. The inn is a short distance on the right.

Innkeepers: Rita and Vince Scoffone
Address/Telephone: 3001 Hollymead Drive; (804) 978–4686, fax (804) 973–6156
Rooms: 7; all with private bath and air conditioning, 4 with fireplace. No smoking inn.
Rates: $110 to $150, double occupancy, continental breakfast. Two-night minimum
    weekends April–June and September–November.
Open: All year.
Facilities and activities: Dinner Tuesday–Saturday ($16 to $25), tavern. Swimming pool
    (shared with neighborhood). Nearby: Monticello, Ashlawn, University of Virginia,
    Blue Ridge Parkway, vineyards, antiquing.
Business travel: Located 1½ miles from downtown. Telephone and desk available;
    conference room.

Olive Metcalf

200 South Street Inn
CHARLOTTESVILLE, VIRGINIA 22902

This in-city inn is located in two gracious town houses—one yellow brick with white trim, the other yellow clapboard with white trim—on a quiet side street in the city of Charlottesville. Although a secondary line of the railroad runs directly behind the inn, trains generally do not operate here at night.

The larger building was built in 1856 for Thomas Jefferson's first librarian at the University of Virginia. It is particularly notable for its stunning wraparound veranda and its solid-walnut, two-story serpentine stairway railing. Both buildings are surrounded by wrought-iron fences. They're separated by a driveway to a private parking lot that's entered between brick pillars.

The inn has been owned by Brendan and Jenny Clancy, expatriate New Yorkers, since 1991, and they've been doing a whirlwind of renovation ever since. Today the inn is a sophisticated blend of interesting colors, fabrics, and furnishings.

When I arrived one afternoon, wine and cheese were set out for guests in the library, which overlooks the gardens. This urbane retreat is painted a deep tomato red and has floor-to-ceiling bookcases. A handsome, walnut, antique gateleg table is a centerpiece. Breakfast is also served here. Or you might prefer to eat on the veranda, which also overlooks the garden. In the summer this is filled with wicker furniture and is a favorite spot to relax. A hideaway study is the perfect retreat for a busy businessperson or just to unwind and watch television. Unusual nineteenth-century oil paintings of exotic animals are on display in the main gallery. A front porch is filled with antique white wicker.

The guest rooms all feature English and Belgian antiques. There are canopy beds, gas fireplaces, fantastically carved armoires, and polished, wide-plank yellow pine floors, topped with brilliant kilims. The baths have tile floors, brass fixtures, and six have Jacuzzis. Several have interesting antiques.

Brendan and Jenny serve a continental breakfast that includes four or five freshly baked breads such as lemon poppy or pumpkin apple, scones, fresh fruit, and juices. One of Charlottesville's finest restaurants, Memory & Company, is just across the street, and my companion and I had an excellent meal there. Other nearby restaurants recommended by Brendan are Metropolitain and the C & O Restaurant and Bistro.

Downtown Charlottesville has an eclectic, artsy population. There are a variety of art galleries, craft shops, bookstores, and boutiques. In addition, Vinegar Hill features art and foreign movies, and the spectacular Charlottesville Ice Park opened in 1995. It offers indoor ice skating, skating lessons, and lots of fun.

Virginia now has more than sixty wineries. It would be a shame to visit Charlottesville and not go to several of the tasting rooms for a sample. They are excellent.

How to get there: From Washington, D.C., take I–66 to U.S. 29 south. Take Route 250 bypass east to the third traffic light. Turn right onto McIntire Road. At the second traffic light, turn left onto South Street. Travel ⅔ block and turn into the driveway on the right between two gateposts. Park in the inn's parking lot and come in the red door in back.

Innkeepers: Brendan and Jenny Clancy

Address/Telephone: 200 South Street; (804) 979–0200 or (800) 964–7008, fax (804) 979–4403

Rooms: 20, including 3 suites; all with private bath, air conditioning, and telephone, 9 with fireplace, 6 with Jacuzzi.

Rates: $100 to $190, double occupancy, continental breakfast. Two-night minimum weekends April, May, and September–November.

Open: All year.

Facilities and activities: Nearby: Monticello, the University of Virginia, Ashlawn, and Montpelier.

Business travel: In-town location, convenient to downtown businesses. Desk in 5 rooms; fax and concierge service available.

The Oaks Victorian Inn
CHRISTIANSBURG, VIRGINIA 24073

The Oaks is named for seven ancient oak trees. Margaret and Tom have received a grant to preserve the trees with the help of experts from the America the Beautiful program. The oldest, a white oak, is estimated to be around 400 years old and has the girth to back up that estimate.

Exteriorwise, the inn's description is simple: It's the queen of Christiansburg. A classic, in fact—a Queen Anne Victorian, now painted buttercup yellow, which was designed by a New York architect in 1889 for Major W. L. Pierce and his wife and seven children. The original beauty of gleaming hardwood floors, stained glass, and trim is intact.

The bedrooms are oases of comfort and style. You might go up to the third floor and select Lulu's Lair, painted in red and cream, or Lady Melodie's Turret, a skylit room with a king-sized canopy bed, gas fireplace, and sunset view. The inn has inviting common areas (which perhaps explains why the inn ended up in a PBS television special). They include the wraparound porch with rocking chairs; the backyard patio with garden and fish pond; a second-story sun deck; and a sunroom with a fireplace, well stocked with books, games, and movies.

When at last you do depart from your oasis for lunch or dinner, Margaret and Tom help you make a wise choice. They might suggest a mountain vineyard, where the vintner is also a French chef and the wine and dining have consistently won awards, or a Brazilian place with exotic international flavors.

One guest once asked, "Margaret, what's your philosophy of art?" It's more a response to beauty than a particular philosophy. Together the Rays select what inherently pleases them. As a result, there's a Joe King above the fireplace that's an evocative depiction of the painter's wife; there are photographs by Darvish and sculptures and prints. "The human spirit needs the sensitivities of the arts," Margaret once said.

Breakfast is served in a style conducive to conversation. The place mats are handmade lace, the china (inherited from Tom's grandmother) is Dresden, and the coffeepot is an unusual heirloom, a silver-over-porcelain piece. You might receive a dish of curried eggs laced with shiitake mushrooms and wine sauce or a broccoli-lemon quiche and apricot-and-pumpkin tea bread or Southern buttermilk biscuits. Meats, if you wish, range from ginger-braised chicken to herbed sausages. One tends to linger over breakfast, even though the patio beckons and the hummingbird feeder is busy.

How to get there: From I–81 take exit 114. Turn left if approaching from the south and right if coming from the north, and you will be on Main Street. Continue for approximately 2 miles to fork at Park and Main streets. Bear right onto Park, then left into The Oaks driveway.

Innkeepers: Margaret and Tom Ray

Address/Telephone: 311 East Main Street; (540) 381–1500 or (800) 336–OAKS, fax (540) 382–1728

Rooms: 7; all with private bath, air conditioning, telephone, and television, 5 with fireplace, 2 with Jacuzzi. No smoking inn.

Rate: $115 to $140, double occupancy, EPB. Additional person $15. Two-night minimum in October and special-event weekends.

Open: All year, except first week in January.

Facilities and activities: Parlor, patio, hot tub. Nearby: 24 miles to Blue Ridge Parkway; Transportation Museum in Roanoke, antiquing, outlet shopping, Long Way Home Outdoor Drama. Bicycling, hiking, Mill Mountain Theatre, Virginia Tech University, Radford University.

Business travel: Telephone with dataport, desk, and minirefrigerator all rooms, valet service, parking on premises; corporate rates.

Fountain Hall Bed & Breakfast

CULPEPER, VIRGINIA 22701

Many things haven't changed. You can still arrive by train as I did every summer as a child, when I'd come to spend a week in Culpeper with my grandparents. You still see the whitewashed railing marking the expansive pastures of the horse breeders, the turn-of-the-century barns and homesteads of farmers, and the freshly turned soil exposing the red clay of Virginia. And the heart of downtown Culpeper retains the integrity of the small Southern town that I remember. At the corner of Main and Davis streets, the corner drugstore still has its soda fountain intact.

From the railroad depot it's only 6 blocks to the Fountain Hall Inn. You walk past historic homes until you reach the inn, named for Foun-

tain Fisher Henry, who once owned this neighborhood. The house was a Victorian that was transformed into a grander Colonial Revival in 1923. Tessa, the inn dog, is likely to greet you at the side entrance. She's amiable and performs her job of emitting two barks; then she returns to a curled position in the hallway.

I especially liked being shown the inn's three common areas and invited to browse among the books or enjoy a cup of tea. If you mention some special interest to Steve, he briefly disappears then returns with a book or a morsel of relevant information to keynote your travels.

The rooms are attractively furnished with a

blend of antiques and comfortable pieces. Steve and Kathi have selected traditional floral prints with an old-fashioned appeal. Three of the rooms have private porches (convenient for storing your bicycles).

Above the wooden table in the sunny breakfast room hangs a map of the United States on which guests have pinpointed their homes. Over a continental breakfast of croissants and freshly baked muffins (the innkeepers' seven-year-old daughter, already an experienced innkeeper, occasionally assists), you can discuss your leisurely agenda with fellow guests.

You might plan a day of country activities that includes a visit to the farmer's market, an orchard tour, golfing at the Meadow Farms Golf Course, bicycling, or horseback riding. For Civil War aficionados the two local battlefields to see are the Brandy Station Battlefield, with its annual reenactment, and the Battlefield of Cedar Mountain, which is located on privately owned land and open during reenactments.

For lunch or dinner you might consider the Prince Michel Vineyard, which serves elegant fixed-price lunches and dinners Thursday through Saturday, or the more casual Davis Street Ordinary, within walking distance of the inn.

Culpeper is as slow paced as it always was; and I still come to visit grandma. She's a healthy ninety-five years of age and keeps up with all of the comings and goings in town. In fact, she told me there was a good little inn in town that I must see. Grandma was right.

How to get there: From the north take Route 29 and exit Route 3 (Fredericksburg/Culpeper). Turn right onto Route 3, go 1 mile to first traffic light, turn right. Rail: Amtrak. Fly-in: Culpeper County Airport.

Innkeepers: Steve and Kathi Walker
Address/Telephone: 609 South East Street; (540) 825–8200 or (800) 298–4748, fax (540) 825–7716
Rooms: 5, including 1 suite; all with private bath, telephone, and air conditioning, 3 with porch, 1 with whirlpool bath, 1 with hydro-tub. Wheelchair accessible. No smoking inn.
Rates: $75 to $125, double occupancy, continental breakfast. Two-night minimum October and some other weekends.
Open: All year.
Facilities and activities: On 1½ acres, gardens. Nearby: vineyards, antiquing, battlefields of Brandy Station and Cedar Mountain, bicycling, annual summer wine-tasting event and horse show, canoeing and tubing on Rapidan, Meadow Farms Golf Course.
Business travel: Telephone with dataport and desk in all rooms; fax and PC available; corporate rates.

The Bailiwick Inn
FAIRFAX, VIRGINIA 22030

We binged on pleasure. But who wouldn't?

In retrospect it was to be expected—a historical restoration of this caliber in this location is deserving of a binge.

One enters the gracious 1820 Federal brick home to a wide center hall with a polished balustrade climbing to the second floor. Double parlors have wide-plank pine floors covered with Oriental rugs, bookshelves filled with books, and wood-burning fireplaces. There are carved wooden garlands over the fireplace, and the quality of the furniture is as fine as when Joshua Gunnell built it. There are Sheraton and Duncan Phyfe pieces, all upholstered in lush raspberry or ivory colors or polished to a gleam.

The dining room is on two levels in the back of the manse and overlooks a brick courtyard with a soothing fountain. Imbued with romance, it's an elegant setting, with candles and fine silver, stemware, and china. We started with a chanterelle mushroom soup with fresh herbs, followed by a duck confit with a warm salad of lentils laced with a balsamic vinegar. Our entree was a filet of beef with Merlot sauce, with a side dish of gratin of rutabagas, but we might also have sampled the saddle of rabbit or the sea bass. I believe I had my all-time favorite dessert that night. It was a surprisingly light but rich custard-with a dense chocolate center garnished with fresh raspberries. I'd love one now.

Selecting a room for the night hadn't been easy; we liked them all. The Thomas Jefferson Room, with its private fireplace, has a desk chair similar to the one Jefferson used at Monticello. A huge, satiny mound of feather comforter tops each bed, along with a bounty of pillows. The Lord Fairfax Room is furnished in English pieces styled after the Fairfax family castle in Leeds, with the family coat of arms on the wall. In the George Washington Room, you find a plethora of green, his favorite color, as well as a four-poster bed and darkly stained woods.

The building is a brick structure dating to 1830. The first skirmish of the Civil War occurred on Main Street on June 1, 1861, says a plaque outside.

For breakfast you are seated privately or you may request to join other guests around a formal dining table. Using a historical recipe modified for contemporary palates, the chef might prepare Robert E. Lee Eggs—an English muffin served with poached eggs laced with mushroom sauce along with Virginia ham. Or perhaps it will be a sausage-and-egg casserole or a crabmeat omelet.

We traveled here from an impressive distance—all of 17 miles—to reach the inn for a birthday celebration of my companion. Regardless of how far guests travel, they feel like they have arrived in another world, and a civilized one at that. They can't resist the lure of splendid cuisine and the knowledge that they will be pampered in such elegant surroundings.

The inn is only 17 miles from Washington, D.C., and its multitude of museums, gardens, and music. It is also within short walking distance of Fairfax's shops and restaurants and is positioned nicely between city and country.

How to get there: From I–66 take Route 123 east toward George Mason University. It's 1½ miles to the inn, which is opposite the old courthouse. Off-street parking behind the inn.

Innkeepers: Bob and Annette Bradley; Stewart Schroeder, manager

Address/Telephone: 4023 Chain Bridge Road; (703) 691–2266 or (800) 366–7666, fax (703) 934–2112

Rooms: 14, including 1 suite; all with private bath, telephone, and air conditioning, television available, 4 with fireplace, 2 with whirlpool bath. Wheelchair access. No smoking inn.

Rates: $130 to $295, double occupancy, EPB and afternoon tea.

Open: All year.

Facilities and activities: Dinner (fixed price) nightly, except Monday and Tuesday, by reservation, helath club available to guests. Nearby: restaurants (within walking distance), Washington, D.C., Manassas Civil War Park, George Mason University, Mount Vernon, swimming, golf, tennis, historic sites.

Business travel: Located 17 miles from Washington, D.C. Telephone in room; desk in 11 rooms; fax and secretarial services available; corporate rates.

Caledonia Farm–1812

FLINT HILL, VIRGINIA 22627

Rappahannock County, population 6,600, has no traffic lights, no towns of more than 280 people, no major highways or waterways, and no shopping center. It's devoted to staying rural.

The drive to Caledonia Farm is through miles of bucolic beauty. Once you've turned down the lane framed by a stone wall on the left and split rail fence on the right, you're on a 52-acre cattle farm, which is protected under Virginia's "Scenic and Open-Space Easement." Black Angus graze amid vistas of rolling hills and ridges. The view out the dining-room window alone is worth the drive.

Since 1985 Phil Irwin, whose announcer days with "Voice of America" are still evident in

his melodic voice, has overseen this country inn. The small farmhouse-inn boasts a peaceful quiet. There's not even a rooster to disturb your morning slumber.

The stone mansion (on the National Register of Historic Places) dates from 1812, and since that beginning several changes have taken place. For instance, two of the doorways have been rounded and attractive additions have been made. What hasn't changed are the fine stonework with perfect ninety-degree angles and the stone fences that meander around the property.

The stone cottage is a two-story building dating from 1807 that's reached through a small porch. If you select this romantic accommodation, you have the entire cottage to yourself. Downstairs is the great cooking fireplace, which is very inviting on a chilly fall evening. Bring champagne and enjoy the view.

You'll have breakfast in the dining room, with its sunny windows on both sides of the dining table. A well-placed antique mirror on the wall gives everyone an equitable look at the view. For your preselected breakfast you may have smoked salmon and bagels, a farm-egg omelet, or Phil's very fine eggs Benedict. You'll hear the hits of the 1700s playing softly in the background.

In the afternoon you might embark on a hike up the hill from the inn or borrow a bicycle for a jaunt down the surrounding country roads.

By reservation Phil takes guests on a hayride through the hills. The inn has three porches, as well as a patio and a hot tub. In the main inn is a living room, where you might pause on a winter's day for a game of chess, to read a book, and to sip a complimentary local wine before stepping out to dinner at one of the many excellent restaurants that Phil can recommend.

How to get there: From Washington, D.C., take I–66 to exit 13. Go south on Route 79 to Route 522 to Flint Hill. Turn west on Fodderstock Road. Go 1½ miles to inn, which will be on the right. From Washington, Virginia, go north on Route 628 4 miles, turn left at inn sign, and proceed to drive on the left.

Innkeeper: Phil Irwin

Address/Telephone: 47 Dearing Road; (540) 675–3693 or (800) BNB–1812, fax same

Rooms: 3, including 1 stone cottage; 1 with private bath,; all with air conditioning, telephone, refrigerator, and working fireplace. No smoking inn.

Rates: $80, rooms; $140, cottage; double occupancy, EPB. Saturday night, surcharge of 50 percent. Two-night minimum all weekends, 3-nights holiday weekends and during October.

Open: All year.

Facilities and activities: On 52 acres, bicycles for guest use, hot tub, balloon rides, hayride ($10 per person). Nearby: restaurant (5-mile drive), hiking, winery tours, Shenandoah National Park, horseback riding, antiquing, Civil War battlefields.

Richard Johnston Inn
FREDERICKSBURG, VIRGINIA 22401

Fredericksburg is a lovely gift from the past. There are more than 350 eighteenth- and nineteenth-century buildings in its 40-block National Historic District. The rosy-brick facades look much as they did when George Washington and James Monroe walked on these streets. You can visit Washington's boyhood home, Ferry Farm, and the home that he later bought for his mother. In addition, you can tour Kenmore, the elaborate and elegant plantation house that his sister occupied, and Rising Sun Tavern, his brother's home. The town was the center of a fierce two-year struggle during the Civil War, and four major battles were fought here. The battlefields are now national park sites.

The Richard Johnston Inn is located in a pair of brick buildings, built between 1754 and 1780, in the heart of the historic district. It's a serene retreat that faithfully re-creates the ambience of the Federal period while offering the amenities we crave today. When we arrived we were glad the inn has its own parking lot, as the town teemed with visitors, all vying for parking places.

Susan Thrush, proprietor and innkeeper since 1992, has thoroughly updated her inn since our last visit. She showed us to Room Number 5, a large, handsome room with an ornately carved, 1830s plantation-style bed, 12-foot ceilings, and a pretty bath. Although every room has a private bath, several are located across the hallway from the rooms. Another of my favorites is Room Number 9, which is located in the original brick-floored kitchen and has two antique double beds. Two suites on the ground floor have their own entrances off the courtyard and contain wet bars, refrigerators, and televisions.

Caroline Street is filled with excellent antiques shops and boutiques; the sidewalks bustled with browsers. Next door to the inn, a charming little warren specializes in teddy bears.

We were eager to visit some of the historic homes, so we walked across the street to the Fredericksburg Visitor Center for assistance. It has excellent walking maps of Fredericksburg that give a brief history of almost every building. We visited Kenmore, the elegant Colonial mansion in the heart of Fredericksburg. The elaborate plaster decor in three of the rooms has earned them a place among "the 100 most beautiful rooms in America" according to a book by the same title. After the tour we sat in the gardens enjoying spiced tea and gingerbread. We also visited the James Monroe Museum, which contains many of the furnishings that Monroe collected while on American service in France and used in the Monroe White House.

Susan directed us to Merriman's, which is next door, for dinner. It was exactly as she described. Excellent fresh ingredients, expertly grilled, prepared by an outstanding chef. Another good choice is Le Lafayette Restaurant, in a handsome, landmarked 1771 Georgian building.

The next morning we enjoyed a continental breakfast of freshly baked muffins and breads, fruit, juice, and coffee in the ornate dining room. The cherry Duncan Phyfe table is set with fine china, silver, and linens. Juice is served in stemmed glasses.

How to get there: From I–95 take exit 130A onto Route 3 east and travel 3 miles to Fredericksburg. Follow the signs to the Fredericksburg Visitor Center. The inn is across the street and has a parking lot just behind, on Sophia Street.

Innkeeper: Susan Thrush
Address/Telephone: 711 Caroline Street; (540) 899–7606
Rooms: 9, including 2 suites; all with private bath and air conditioning, 3 with television and minirefrigerator. No smoking inn.
Rates: $90 to $130, double occupancy, continental breakfast.
Open: All year except one week at Thanksgiving and another at Christmas.
Facilities and activities: Courtyard. Nearby: golf; historic sites include Ferry Farm, Kenmore, James Monroe Museum, Belmont, and Fredericksburg/Spotsylvania National Military Park.

The Joshua Wilton House
HARRISONBURG, VIRGINIA 22801

The lights shimmered through the windows when we arrived on a summer evening. Dinner had begun, and we went upstairs to wash away the travel dust. "This room," smiled my companion, "is precisely my style. It's how I'd want my inn to look." He has always appreciated the finer things in life.

The bed was a queen-sized canopy with chinoiserie trim and French lace curtains; painted shutters covered the turret windows. Craig's mother selected the lace and made the decorative pillows and the rose tablecloth that covered a small table around which white brocaded chairs were paired. Feeling pampered and civilized, this is where later we had our tea.

Craig and Roberta selected beige carpeting, soft rose wallpapers, and dusty rose decor throughout the inn. Roberta made the curtains. Each bedroom has an aura of resplendent comfort. Even the smallest, with its cozy fireplace, is a serious temptation; and all rooms have queen-sized beds.

Here you are settled in a small university town with midway access to the Shenandoah Valley. From the lap of luxury, you can hike or golf in Massanutten, go antiquing, visit New Market Battlefield, go fishing, and still be only two hours from Washington. Most guests who come here forget to leave behind their forwarding number.

"One of the most important aspects of

Joshua Wilton's house is the quality of construction," explained Craig. "The building has all the original faux marble fireplaces and beveled glass; 85 percent of the woodwork, which is original, was stripped, painted, and remounted." The Victorian's exterior is a dusty rose with gingerbread trim and a soaring turret.

The Victorian inn has three dining rooms, two with fireplace and terrace dining, and two menus, one café style, the other more formal. You order with craving; perhaps smoked salmon served on an apple-potato cake topped with dill crème fraîche and caviar. Then roasted venison with sour cherry sauce and cheese-spinach ravioli, or grilled duck breast with plum sauce on a tangle of tart greens. For dessert try the crème brûlée or the white-chocolate hazelnut cheesecake.

In the mornings Craig prepares poached eggs with smoked salmon or a jumbo-lump-crabmeat omelet, or perhaps a prosciutto-and-wild mushroom omelet. During winter you'll have a seat beside the fire; in the summer you can sit in the garden patio, as we did, and enjoy a sumptuous meal.

How to get there: From I–81 take exit 245 and go west on Port Republic Road to Main Street, turn right, and continue approximately 1 mile to the inn on the right.

Innkeeper: Karen Kelly; Craig and Roberta Moore, proprietors; Pat Spicer and Sean Pugh, managers

Address/Telephone: 412 South Main Street; (540) 434–4464, fax (540) 432–9525

Rooms: 5; all with private bath, telephone, and air conditioning, 1 with fireplace. No smoking inn.

Rates: $95 to $105, double occupancy, EPB.

Open: All year.

Facilities and activities: Dinner Tuesday–Saturday (fixed-price menu, $36; café entrees $9 to $19), tavern. Nearby: Massanutten, New Market Battlefield, Shenandoah Valley, fishing, hiking.

Keswick Hall

KESWICK, VIRGINIA 22947

Have you ever turned the pages of a Laura Ashley catalogue, envisioning the fabrics and colors in your own little mansion? Without going abroad you can visit the final word on Laura Ashley—a manor house decorated using fabrics, furniture, and wallpaper from the entire collection.

Sir Bernard Ashley, knighted for his contribution to British textiles, knew England had an abundance of grand country houses, but America is short on great manors. He searched the United States for the perfect property and in 1990 found 600 acres in the rolling hills surrounding the Keswick Hunt Club, northeast of Charlottesville. He expanded the building, which resembles a classic Tuscan villa,

to 60,000 square feet, painted it corn-muffin yellow with hunter-green trim, and provided half the rooms with a view of the course, which was designed by Arnold Palmer.

You enter the Great Hall and, after being cordially met, are led to your room to settle in. BA's philosophy ("BA" is how the staff refers to Lord Ashley) is that you should feel you're going away to a friend's English country home for the weekend—a rather grand one.

We found people playing cards in the card room; others were hard at a game of snooker in the billiards room. In the morning room a couple sipped libations while perusing the lunch menu; and in the music room, furnished in white, a young woman performed a haunting sonata. A few steps down the hillside, others were swimming in the heated pool, enjoying a massage, or lunching in the English pub adjacent to the golf pro shop.

Each bedroom is decorated using the Laura Ashley fabric line that BA and his family originated. You might prefer a bright, French country look with blue-striped wallpaper and brilliant fabrics, or the masculine deep greens and browns found in a room that has hunting and dog prints. There are a Jane Austen room, a rowing room, a sports room, and a game room with an antique toy in the bathroom. Druthers? The rooms with a golf course view. The antiques were also selected and shipped from England.

The chef has a delicious past that includes credentials at three-star Michelin establishments. For Sunday brunch you might begin with oatcakes, a quiche, then roast beef with York-shire pudding and roast potatoes, followed by local and French cheeses, and, finally, a quince and marscapone pie or lemon parfait.

Book a reservation for Wednesday's very fine buffet luncheon or come to Sunday brunch and enjoy the view. Perhaps you'll collect friends and meet for tea on the patio. Perhaps you'll like it so much you'll decide to move here. Approximately seventy-eight homes will be built on the property.

"Spot on," say the English when something is done right, and Keswick Hall is very right.

How to get there: From Washington, D.C., take I–66 west to Route 29. Follow 29 south to eastbound Route 250 bypass to exit Route 22 (only goes south). After 2 miles turn right on Route 744, continue to a stop sign. Keswick is directly ahead beyond trees.

Innkeeper: Stephen Beaumont; Sir Bernard Ashley, proprietor
Address/Telephone: 701 Country Club Drive; (804) 979–3440 or (800) ASHLEY–1
    fax (804) 977–4171
Rooms: 48, including 4 suites; 18 with private balcony or terrace, all with private bath, air conditioning, telephone, television, 17 with decorative fireplace, 4 with whirlpool. Wheelchair accessible.
Rates: $195 to $645, double occupancy, EPB and tea. Murder-mystery, wine-tasting, and winter-interlude weekend packages. Two-night minimum holiday weekends.
Open: All year.
Facilities and activities: Six hundred acres. Lunch, dinner (prix fixe $57.50), Sunday brunch, tea. English pub, Arnold Palmer-designed golf course, clay tennis courts, indoor-outdoor swimming pool, fitness center, sauna, massage therapy, gift shop, garden, croquet lawn. Nearby: Charlottesville, 5 miles, Monticello, Ashlawn, University of Virginia.
Business travel: Telephone and desk in room; conference and meeting facilities including audiovisual, fax, Internet access.

The Inn at Levelfields
LANCASTER, VIRGINIA 22503

The Northern Neck of Virginia is a peaceful historic stretch two and a half hours from Washington, D.C., bounded on the north by the Potomac, on the south by the Rappahannock, and swept to the east by the Chesapeake. The Inn at Levelfields is an eye-catcher. It is reached down a lane bordered by parallel meadows that are neatly framed by trees; along the brick path to the front door, you step between ancient box elder bushes. When Doris and Warren Sadler turned down this lane with the realtor, she instinctively whispered the words "This is it." Today many of their guests stay at the inn while searching for retirement property along the Northern Neck's waterfront. This is a quiet country location.

On a summer's night in the cool living room, we eased into the mood of the place. There's a relaxed pace to the inn, where two chocolate Labradors amble by, finding a kind hand from a receptive guest.

No stately Southern manse dating back to 1857 is complete without intrigue. Notice the blood marks on the stairs; locals say it resulted from a lovers' quarrel that ended in the shooting death of a beautiful young woman. The Sadlers have tried to discover exactly what happened that night, but each time they ask, they hear a unique version of the story.

The inn has expansive rooms cooled with ceiling fans and air conditioning. Women often prefer the yellow room, which is a blaze of brightness. Each room is named for its predominant color: red, blue, green, or yellow, and decorated in fine period antiques. The Green Room has a high-poster queen-sized bed; all the rest have high-poster kings. One room has its own small porch on the inn front that is reached through a half door in the bathroom.

My favorite excursions in this area have included Stratford Hall, Ingleside Winery, George Washington's birthplace, and a day trip to Tangier Island from Reedville. At the inn itself you can swim in the pool, walk to a stream located in the woods, or go into the parlor on an autumn's eve to absorb the warmth from the wood-burning stove.

How to get there: From the north on I–95, exit Bypass Route 17 South to Tappahannock; then go east on U.S. Route 360 to Warsaw. From Warsaw take Route 3 East to Lancaster Courthouse. Levelfields is 2 miles on the left.

Innkeepers: Warren and Doris Sadler

Address/Telephone: Route 3 (mailing address: P.O. Box 216); (804) 435–6887 or (800) 238–5578, fax (804) 435–7440

Rooms: 4; all with private bath, air conditioning, and fireplace. Pets by prior permission. Smoking permitted in some common rooms only.

Rates: $95, double occupancy; $55, single; EPB. Additional person $15. Two-night minimum holiday weekends.

Open: All year.

Facilities and activities: Outdoor swimming pool, 54 acres. Nearby: historic Christ Church, Mary Ball Washington Museum and Library, George Washington's birthplace, Stratford Hall, Ingleside Winery, nature trails, bicycling, Chesapeake Bay island trips.

Lavender Hill Farm
LEXINGTON, VIRGINIA 24450

When Colin taught survival skills for the British military in remote desert and Arctic settings, he'd fantasize about cooking impossibly lavish meals: lamb with red currant sauce, herbed Cornish hen, cream of shiitake mushroom soup, and ornate chocolate and fruit desserts. Now that he's ensconced on a small Virginia farm, Colin's culinary imagination flourishes along with the herb gardens. As he composes the dreamily delicious dishes, Cindy records his creations.

In addition to gastronomic pleasures, Lavender Hill is a good base for outdoor excursions. You can ride through the Blue Ridge Mountains on horses saddled and waiting, following the lead of a trail master who's on inti-

mate terms with horses and the forest. Or you might prefer hiking, canoeing, or bird-watching. If there's time in your schedule, the Smiths will recommend town and country shops throughout the county.

"I never expected to leave banking," admitted Cindy one afternoon. While diving in the Caribbean, she and her instructor—Colin— began a relationship that led to marriage and ultimately a small, rural inn.

"Now I'm the rock," explains Colin, "and Cindy's the imaginative one."

"Except in the kitchen," reminded Cindy, who worked at her spinning wheel, which occupies a corner of the living room, while we visited.

"The touch of the material is very soothing and relaxing." Not unlike sitting on the front porch, sipping your iced tea, and smelling the herbal scents wafting unmistakably from Colin's kitchen.

The rooms are sensibly furnished with queen-sized beds; one pair of twins fits together to form a king. In the parlor a versatile collection of CDs and a television are accessible.

The inn's surrounding twenty acres are pasture to the Smith's organically raised sheep, who graze along with two goats. Fresh lamb is served occasionally.

Consider meeting friends here and booking the entire inn, which has only three bedrooms. You and friends might also ask for cooking lessons. Colin collects everyone in the kitchen after breakfast and describes dinner, demonstrating his techniques for preparing the evening's four-course meal. You go off for your day of pursuits, then return before dinner to observe further preparations. Keep in mind, you select your own menu and he or she who makes the first reservation creates the menu on the phone.

Breakfast selections are made the night before from Colin's menu: French toast made with homemade bread and stuffed with raspberries and cream cheese and the equally excessive herb omelet with cream cheese are possibilities. A homemade, sugar-free muesli without salt or preservatives is also available.

The inn pets, who live outdoors, include Jess, a border collie, and Ocho, the cat.

How to get there: From I–81 take I–64 West at Lexington and proceed to exit 50 (Kerrs Creek, which is second exit). Turn left at end of ramp onto Route 60, turn left again at the stop sign onto Route 60E, and almost immediately take another left onto Route 631 (Big Spring Drive). Go 1³⁄₁₀ miles to inn, which will be on the left before the bridge.

Innkeepers: Colin and Cindy Smith
Address/Telephone: Big Spring Drive, Route 631 (mailing address: RR1, P.O. Box 515); (540) 464–5877 or (800) 446–4240
Rooms: 3, including 1 suite; all with private bath and air conditioning. No smoking inn.
Rates: $65 to $75, double occupancy, EPB. Horseback-riding package of 3 meals, 2 nights lodging, and 2 days of riding, $263 per person. Two-night minimum holidays and special events.
Open: All year.
Facilities and activities: Dinner by reservation only ($24.50 per person), BYOB. On 20 acres. Nearby: Lexington, George C. Marshall Museum, Stonewall Jackson House, Virginia Military Institute, Washington & Lee College, horseback riding, bird-watching, antiquing, theater.

Maple Hall
LEXINGTON, VIRGINIA 24450

Maple Hall is a Greek Revival–style residence built in about 1855 for a wealthy Rockbridge County entrepreneur. The inn is conveniently located near the interstate for travelers wanting a good night's sleep and visitors who've come to explore Lexington and the season's splendors along the Parkway. It's a first-class restoration, well insulated and beautifully decorated. Gas-log fireplaces in the rooms are a comforting touch. There's also an adjacent guest house.

To enter you climb either side of the double staircases up to the second-floor entrance and walk down the hallway of this antebellum inn to a small office, where you are oriented and di-

rected to your room. Most rooms are spacious and have hardwood floors, a good selection of antiques and fine reproductions, wing chairs, desks, reading lamps, and all you'll need for a comfortable stay. Among my favorites are those located on the upstairs entrance level, east side.

Dinner is served in the sunny conservatory and in the English basement dining room. You can select from five or more entrees, including veal Oscar topped with crabmeat and asparagus with béarnaise sauce or a chicken tarragon. Desserts could include deep-dish apple pie served with a scoop of creamy smooth vanilla ice cream.

In your room is an "Inn-formation" book with things to do in and around Lexington. You might want to make your way, as my companion insisted we do, to the V.M.I. Museum.

How to get there: Take exit 195 off I–81; the inn is visible to the east on Route 11. Some interstate noise.

Innkeeper: Don Fredenburg; Peter Meredith family, proprietors

Address/Telephone: 11 North Main Street; (540) 463–2044, fax (540) 463–7262

Rooms: 21, including 6 in guest house and 5 suites; all with private bath, telephone, television, and air conditioning, 16 with gas-log fireplace, most with porch. Wheelchair access. No smoking rooms.

Rates: $95 to $140, double occupancy; $80 to $125, single; continental breakfast. Additional person $15. Children under 12 $5. Two-night minimum some weekends in April, May, September, and October.

Open: All year.

Facilities and activities: Dinner (entrees $15 to $22). Short hiking trail to pond; 56 acres, swimming pool, fishing pond, 3 miles of hiking trails, gardens, and tennis court. Nearby: 6 miles from Lexington, George C. Marshall Museum, Stonewall Jackson House, carriage tours; Blue Ridge Parkway, Virginia Military Institute.

Business travel: Telephone in all rooms; desk in 15 rooms; fax and copier available; conference room; corporate rates.

The Red Fox Inn
MIDDLEBURG, VIRGINIA 22117

A Sunday drive out to The Red Fox Inn and the Stray Fox in Middleburg for dinner is a worthwhile Washington tradition. It can be improved upon by staying the night. It's a hotel-inn 50 miles from the city, yet worlds away.

OLDEST ORIGINAL INN reads the sign outside the stone inn, which dates from 1728. Under various names it has warmed, nourished, and rested guests ever since. It began as a stagecoach stop and was first known as Chinn's Ordinary.

In 1976 Turner Reuter's mother and sister thoroughly researched how an eighteenth-century inn should look in furnishings, fabrics, wallpapers, and bedspreads. Today several rooms and suites have canopy beds, working fireplaces, and desks. They are furnished with antiques and reproductions.

In the nearby Stray Fox, the elegant Belmont Suite has a living room spacious enough to host a large hunt party after the ride. In the small Furness Room upstairs, the floor has been beautifully stenciled. It's difficult to steer you to a favorite room, but you might begin with location. Those in the main inn are on the second and third floors above the restaurant. Those in the McConnell House, a cottage connected to the Red Fox by a pergola walkway, includes the O'Conner Suite, with private brick porch and a queen-sized canopy bed, the bay-windowed McConnell Room, and three other rooms. Four additional rooms are found in the Middleburg Inn nearby.

Dinner at the Red Fox is a la carte from an American menu. Appetizers start at $6, salads at $4, and entrees at $18. You could begin with tasty baked Brie with pistachio-nut butter served in phyllo pastry and move on to Long Island duckling, a crab-cake platter, or an elegantly prepared poached salmon. A light-fare menu is served before 5:00 P.M. midweek.

Middleburg is a treat. The town is small and has antiques shops, clothing boutiques, and a horse-and-bridle shop; the area hosts many posh events. If you've never seen polo or a Middleburg horse race or gone on a stable tour, this is your chance. The inn itself has a fine-arts gallery, which offers shows of nineteenth-century paintings, bronze with sporting themes.

How to get there: From Washington take Route 66 west to the Winchester exit or Route 50 exit near Fair Oaks Mall. Go 26 miles west to Middleburg; the inn is in town on the right.

Innkeeper: F. Turner Reuter, Jr., proprietor; Frank Vitale and Berte Gibson, managers
Address/Telephone: 2 East Washington Street (mailing address: P.O. Box 385); (540) 687–5780; from Washington, D.C., (703) 478–1808; outside Virginia (800) 223–1728; fax (540) 687–6053
Rooms: 23, including 8 suites; all with private bath, air conditioning, television, and telephone, some with fireplace. Wheelchair accessible. Designated no smoking rooms.
Rates: $135 to $245, double occupancy, continental breakfast. Children: cot $25.
Open: All year.
Facilities and activities: Lunch, dinner, tavern. Nearby: Upperville Colt and Horse Show (June), Stable Tour (Memorial Day), Point to Point Races, equestrian meets, polo on Sunday (June–September), vineyard tours, biking.
Business travel: Desk in all rooms; fax available; meeting rooms; corporate rates.

Fort Lewis Lodge
MILLBORO, VIRGINIA 24460

From an enclosed viewing room atop the former grain silo, there's a magnificent 360-degree panorama of the lodge's natural beauty. Fort Lewis's 3,200 acres ascend into the Allegheny Tower Mountain Range and descend to the Cowpasture River valley. It's an inn where birders rise early to walk through the meadows, bicyclers take the bikes on the paved and remote country roads, and hikers head for the inn's private woodland trails. Others walk to the river for fishing or swimming.

John and Caryl moved here from Ohio to farm in 1977. From their hilltop home (above the inn), they and their three children raise Black Angus cattle, pheasants, goats, and chickens.

The inn is composed of the lodge, which is attached to the silo, and the nearby historic gristmill. John built the architectural designed lodge in 1987, incorporating walnut and other timber he cut on the property. The great room's contemporary windows reach the cathedral ceiling opposite a raised stone fireplace.

Forty yards away is the restored gristmill, which dates from the 1850s. Downstairs the open kitchen and dining room form another great room. Buck's Bar, an attached, screened-in porch overlooking the millpond, is where folks gather for cocktails and become acquainted before dinner. This inn accommodates a family reunion or business meeting as smoothly as it does the individual traveler seeking a relaxing evening.

Caryl, who has a background in education, has always enjoyed cooking. Her single-entree diners express a natural love of food. Her food sources couldn't be finer. She uses fresh produce grown on the farm by master gardener Lee Church. At dinner we helped ourselves to a rich creamy chicken divan with cheese and broccoli, herb-flavored carrots, barley, and a superb hot corn bread. Her desserts are delicious American classics: cherry pie, cheesecake, and chocolate four-layer cake. As for breakfast, her blueberry pancakes are divine.

John is a master craftsman. He restored the old gristmill with its 2-foot-wide walls himself, and since the silo was too deteriorated to restore, he rebuilt it to the exact dimensions of the original. There are three guest rooms here that visitors vie for, as they have treetop views across the meadows. City slickers are awed by the deer they see grazing in the morning.

John moved two little mid-1800s log cabins to the farm several years ago and has restored them as well. These are favorites for honeymooners, as they have stone fireplaces, pioneer furnishings, and front porches on which to rock and survey the acreage.

The inn's furniture is Shaker-like in style; the tables, beds, and dressers are original in design and handmade by a local craftswoman from butternut, walnut, and cherry.

When Fort Lewis was established in 1759, this was the edge of the western frontier. Today it's a peaceful frontier that we all need on occasion.

How to get there: From the intersection of Route 42 and Route 39 in Millboro Springs, go 7/10 mile west on Route 39 and turn right onto Route 678. Continue on Route 678 for 10 8/10 miles, turn left on Route 625, and go 2/10 mile to the inn sign on the left.

Innkeepers: John and Caryl Cowden
Address/Telephone: HCR 3, Box 21A; (540) 925–2314, fax (540) 925–2352
Rooms: 17, including 4 (2-room) suites and 2 log cabins; all with private bath, cabins with fireplaces. Smoking limited to some common rooms.
Rates: $135 to $145 per couple; $90, single; $150, suite; $190, log cabin; MAP. Additional person $35. Children 3–12, $20; under 2, free. Two-night minimum weekends.
Open: April through mid-October.
Facilities and activities: Picnic lunches prepared by reservation ($5 to $7), wine and beer service. Guest fridge, playroom, 5 bicycles, 2 canoes, 3,200 acres, swimming, fishing, hiking, biking, birding, spelunking. Nearby: hot springs, golf courses.

The Garden and The Sea Inn
NEW CHURCH, VIRGINIA 23415

On a summer evening you arrive while the sun is still up, and have a seat in one of the parlors. The room is pastel; a large painting of an egret hangs on the wall. Tea is served with thick chocolate brownies. You visit, browse through the French books, and catch the delicious wafts of fine French cooking.

Remove your watch and adjust your mental clock, for time on Virginia's Eastern Shore moves on a seasonal scale. Country roads interlace this peninsula between the Atlantic Ocean to the east and Chesapeake Bay to the west. This is where travelers come to shake off the city; to find remote places; to absorb the sun, wind, and water of Chincoteague; to recompose the senses into a pleasurable state of relaxation in beautiful inn rooms.

En route here you'll pass fields of tomatoes, canteloupes, and beans; if you venture into villages, you'll see the fishing boats of the area. Tom is the accomplished chef. He enhances the local fare through herbs and flowers grown outside the kitchen door. Each year Sara adds another dimension to the patio garden, which is a seasonal composition of camellias, boxwood, tulips, herbs, and flowers.

The menu changes biweekly. You might find fresh grilled drum fish (a regional specialty); Chincoteague oysters magnificently sautéed with local scallops and shrimp in basil butter; a superb chicken (raised nearby); and often Tom's saffron and fennel bouillabaise with fish, scallops, and shrimp. Wine lovers will receive experienced recommendations from Sara, who's very knowledgeable about Virginia's vintners.

The guest rooms are elegant Victorian confections. There are stained-glass windows, Oriental rugs, sumptuous chintzes covering windows, and antique beds of iron and wood. One room even has a wicker sleigh bed.

Chincoteague (pronounced shing-a-tig) is where an annual roundup of wild ponies was begun in 1927 to support the local firemen. The custom flourishes, with the annual roundup and auction every July. You may want to book a year in advance for the event, or you might prefer to come during September or October, when you have the beach to yourselves. The Decoy Museum merits a visit, with its displays of hunting, fishing, and carving. Bring binoculars for traveling on the paved trails of the refuge; we saw wild ponies, Sitka deer, and birds.

How to get there: Two miles south of the Virginia-Maryland border, turn west off the artery, Route 13, onto Route 710. Inn is short distance on the right. It's centrally located on the peninsula, about 12 miles from the ocean and Chesapeake Bay.

Innkeepers: Sara and Tom Baker

Address/Telephone: Route 710 (mailing address: P.O. Box 275); (804) 824–0672 or (800) 824–0672

Rooms: 8, including 3 suites; all with private bath, and air conditioning; with television, telephone; and fireplace, 6 with whirlpool bath. Pets permitted with prior consent and deposit. Wheelchair accessible. No smoking in rooms.

Rates: $75 to $185, double occupancy, hearty continental breakfast; $135 to $245 per couple, MAP. Two-night minimum weekends; 3-night minimum holidays and last week in July.

Open: April–November.

Facilities and activities: Dinner Tuesday–Sunday in July and August; Wednesday–Sunday in June, September, October, and November; Friday–Sunday in April. Four-course fixed price, $25 to $32; also a la carte. Two parlors. Nearby: Chincoteague National Wildlife Refuge, Assateague National Seashore, wildlife, swimming, boating, village touring.

The Page House Inn
NORFOLK, VIRGINIA 23507

"Champagne tastes and jogging shoes," my companion said as Stephanie, wearing an attractive warm-up suit, swung open a highly polished oak door to an elegant foyer. We beheld other guests in the formal dining room; they were laughing, sipping cappuccino, and savoring the cookies. We couldn't believe our good fortune at finding The Page House in Ghent—Norfolk's prestigious historic neighborhood. It is within walking distance of the Chrysler Museum, the opera, and the Hague, a tranquil canal where boats lie at anchor year-round.

Stephanie introduced us to a pair of small black-and-white Boston terriers named Charlie and Tootsie, who went off to their private lodg-ing while we followed her up the wide oak staircase. She presented to us a "definitive" honeymoon suite. We admired the boldly printed wallpaper and window furnishings and the canopied bed with its antique handmade spread and coverlets. We had hardly caught our collective breath when Stephanie opened the door to the commodious sitting room with love seat and bay windows. Here, as in the other rooms of the inn, were lovely antiques.

Returning down the stairs, Stephanie pointed to a basket full of goodies for guests, should hunger strike at any time of the day. A collection of games, books, and magazines were organized beside a rocking chair.

Meanwhile I tried to determine what made the inn's design style so vigorous yet different. "I have an aunt who's a decorator," explained Stephanie. "She helped me arrange our family collection of antiques and art." The result is an inn that's a balanced creation of personal vision. Stephanie's husband, Ezio, a retired contractor and woodworker, renovated the three-story Georgian Revival building. He artfully reworked the interior: new plumbing, wiring, and safety features were part of his masterful transformation, which also included quality oak woodwork installed according to historic preservation guidelines.

Stephanie named the inn for Herman L. Page, the man who first laid out and developed the Ghent area in the late 1800s. But Stephanie is a mover and shaker in her own right. She had to break through the town's codes, which prohibited a historical bed and breakfast, to create her first-class, award-winning restoration.

We rose early for a breakfast of perfectly textured scones and fruit jams, homemade granolas, and bagels served in the formal dining room. (We wore jeans.)

Stephanie's dog, Charlie, wearing a mildly spiked collar befitting his breed, licked my hand when I stooped to pet him as we left.

"Lucky dog," remarked my companion as we said goodbyes.

How to get there: From I–63 East or West take exit for I–264 (toward downtown Norfolk) and follow signs (staying in left lane) to exit 9, Waterside Drive. Continue on Waterside Drive, which curves and becomes Boush Street. Turn left onto Olney Street (after Grace Street). Continue for 2 blocks and turn left onto Mowbray Arch, go 1 block to Fairfax Avenue, and turn right. Inn is on the left; park behind.

Innkeepers: Stephanie and Ezio DeBelardino
Address/Telephone: 323 Fairfax Avenue; (804) 625–5033, fax (804) 623–9451
Rooms: 6, including 2 suites; all with private bath, telephone, television, and air conditioning, 3 with fireplace, 2 with whirlpool bath. No smoking in rooms.
Rates: $85 to $150, double occupancy, continental breakfast and afternoon refreshments. Two-night minimum weekends April–October.
Open: All year.
Facilities and activities: Rooftop garden. Nearby: Chrysler Museum; Virginia Opera, Symphony, and Stage Company; Naval Base Tour; Hampton Roads Naval Museum; Mariner's Museum; Harbor and Sailing Tours; Virginia Beach.
Business travel: Telephone and desk in all rooms; fax and copier available; meeting rooms; corporate rates.

The Hidden Inn

ORANGE, VIRGINIA 22960

It's Friday night. You're about to surprise your lover. You've requested the Candlelight Picnic Basket. He opens the door to your room (the Madison with the fireplace), and there on a blanket beside the fire is a straw hamper filled with wine, pâté, cheeses, and fruits laid out as if it were a holiday for two. It is. You're celebrating togetherness.

Paradoxically located in the middle of Orange, yet tucked away from the town behind trees on eight acres of garden and grounds, is an inn with a large parlor and porches that offers gourmet dining.

The five-course dinner begins with Artichokes Romano, an appetizer baked with Ro-

mano cheese sauce. (This is Barbara's most requested recipe, the one that motivated her to write a country-inn cookbook.) Next Ray (a former corporate executive who retired young) announces the soup, perhaps a light asparagus soup served in antique soup dishes. Dinner resumes with fresh mixed greens followed by a tender filet of beef served with chasseur sauce. The plates are garnished with nasturtium and other edible flowers from the garden. Dessert might include Key lime pie or raspberry cheesecake served with a savory blend of coffee.

The rooms are located in three buildings and one cottage. My preferences are the pretty rooms in the main inn and the adjacent cottage, and always those with a whirlpool bath.

The James Madison Room, with a private veranda that overlooks the trees, is inviting. Several of the bed quilts were handmade by Barbara's mother, and the fine needlework was hand stitched by Barbara. "That was in a former life," she laughs. Now her time is spent more often in the kitchen or garden.

The honeymoon cottage has a private porch and whirlpool bath and is decorated in country pine. It's here that Ray's fine building skills are obvious. From here there's a view of the new garden planted in vegetables, herbs, and edible flowers. Barbara has plans for herb teas, herb vinegars, and other flavorful endeavors.

Ray is very knowledgeable about Virginia wines and will frequently conduct tastings in the afternoons. Dinner will generally be accompa-nied by a Virginia wine as well.

Breakfast occurs at private tables. Barbara whisks up fresh omelets or scrambled eggs using farm-fresh brown eggs to serve with bacon, seasonal raspberries or fruits, and hot carrot muffins. Then you might head off to tour the presidents' mansions and Montpelier or go winery touring, horseback riding, or bicycling. Or you could sit back with a new book and let your mind do the traveling.

If you come for the holidays, there's a Dickensian Christmas dinner every Saturday in December.

How to get there: From the intersection of Route 20 and Route 15 (at light) in Orange, go south on Route 15 for 100 yards and take an immediate left to the inn.

Innkeepers: Ray and Barbara Lonick; Chrys Dermody, manager
Address/Telephone: 249 Caroline Street; (540) 672–3625, fax (540) 672–5029
Rooms: 10, including 1 cottage; all with private bath and air conditioning, 3 with fire-
place, some with porch, telephone, and whirlpool bath. No smoking inn.
Rates: $79 to $159, double occupancy, EPB and afternoon tea. Additional person $20.
Two-night minimum weekends.
Open: All year.
Facilities and activities: Five-course dinner ($35 per person) and gourmet picnics available
by advance reservation. Wine and beer available. Nearby: Monticello, Montpelier,
James Madison Museum, antiquing, Charlottesville, wineries, biking.
Bsuiness travel: Desk in 2 rooms; telephone in 4 rooms; computer and fax available.

*W*illow *G*rove *I*nn
ORANGE, VIRGINIA 22960

Willow Grove is a plantation that existed back in the 1800s. Horse-drawn carriages would turn into the lane and gently ascend to the four-story mansion. Gradually the anticipation of an evening spent dining and dancing mounted, until finally you heard the music from behind the front door.

Inside a pianist playing softly and the sounds of crystal delicately clinking are heard. Dinner is commencing, and you have arrived, in the late 1900s, for a memorable Southern meal in a beautiful location.

Today's Willow Grove is owned by the Mulloy family. The inn is on the National Register of Historic Places. The stately columned mansion, with several smaller buildings, is also a Virginia Historic Landmark.

When furnishing the rooms, Angela selected antiques corresponding to the era of the presidents: Washington, Madison, Taylor–Monroe, Harrison, and Wilson. The lodgings, located on the second and third floors of the inn, are on a grand scale, but don't expect an impeccable restoration. Angela loves and respects her grande dame so much you may see a crack here and there or hear a creak underfoot until she can have it repaired in a historically accurate manner.

Angela is quick to emphasize the inn includes a full-scale restaurant, and you're left to pursue your pleasures privately—to walk over the grounds, explore the garden, and have a drink on the veranda.

The inn actually offers very different dining experiences. The Dolley Madison Dining Room, on the antebellum mansion's second floor, is and elegant room that's enhanced by tables set with antique linens, vintage china, and heirloom silver. Downstairs, Clark's Tavern is a convivial, casual, and cozy pub. Both specialize in Southern dishes. And what could be more appropriate than to sip a mint julep on the veranda before dining?

There are formal gardens to roam thorugh in the moonlight, and three dependencies have recently been converted to guest quarters as well. The summer kitchen, the weaver's cottage, and a former schoolhouse now offer engaging and private rooms. By the way, don't miss looking at the suspended balcony off the second floor of the mansion. Its unique construction was influenced by a Jeffersonian design (and perhaps the great man came here to approve of it himself). From the inn it's a short drive to Montpelier to spend the day in Madison history.

How to get there: From Orange, Virginia, go 1½ miles north on Route 15 to inn on the left. From Washington, D.C., take Route 66, Route 29 (Warrenton), left on Route 15, approximately 20 minutes to the inn on the right.

Innkeepers: Angela Mulloy and Richard Brown; Douglas Gibson, manager
Address/Telephone: 14079 Plantation Way (Route 15 North); (540) 672–5982 or (800) WG9–1778, fax (540) 672–3674
Rooms: 11, including 3 cottages and 3 suites; all with private bath, telephone, and air conditioning, 8 with fireplace, 4 with whirlpool. Wheelchair accessible.
Rates: $175 to $285, per couple, MAP.
Open: All year.
Facilities and activities: Dinner Thursday–Sunday ($20–$23), Sunday brunch ($18), tavern. Located on 37 acres. Nearby: Five minutes to James Madison's Montpelier, antiquing, country-roads touring, 30 minutes to Charlottesville.

The Ashby Inn
PARIS, VIRGINIA 20130

A full moon shone in the sky and a quiet prevailed over the mountain and meadow view the night we arrived. We felt we'd left the week behind and anticipated the pleasures to come.

If you've ever longed for a country inn with a small tavern, dreamed of an outdoor courtyard with the scent of summer blossoms in the air, or imagined a place without contrivance or bustle, then take a drive out to the countryside and abandon your cares at The Ashby.

Paris is a neatly groomed, 1800s-epoch village of fifty residents. The Ashby is a former residence dating from 1829. From the peaceful village you can start out into the surrounding Virginia hunt country, either as a wanderer or with the local vineyards or antiques shops for destinations, and you'll happen upon evocative scenery at every twist and turn—a stone fence, cows grazing in a field, or ducks beside a pond.

Inside the inn, where the local horsey set and escapees from the fast pace gather, there's the easy comfort of a tavern complete with dartboard and a Victorian stuffed carp above the fireplace, both influences from Roma's English heritage.

The experienced chef and the Shermans serve country fare, local game, meats, and fresh fish when available. You might find potato-crusted sea bass with a fricassee of woodland mushrooms, or a succulent beef tenderloin napped with Burgundy sauce and mushrooms.

Another winter selection was the delicious broiled Norwegian salmon fillet with asparagus, leeks, carrots, and fresh dill-shallot butter. Follow that with the richness of the crème caramel, and you're happily reminded that country tastes are sophisticated today.

Upstairs you'll find country antiques and a pleasing simplicity. Spread across the clean, polished wooden floors are softly colored rag rugs. One suite has a Palladian window that looks out to the parklands and the distantly rising hill, where guests like to go hiking.

Downstairs in the inn there's a small parlor with a fireplace and a wall of bookshelves. The evening's entertainment centers on a leisurely candlelit meal, perhaps a game of darts in the tavern, and conversation with soul mates.

How to get there: Take I–66 west from Washington to exit 23, Delaplane/Paris; continue 7 miles north on Route 17; turn left on Route 701 into Paris. The inn is on your immediate left.

Innkeepers: John and Roma Sherman; Debby Cox, maanger
Address/Telephone: 692 Federal Street; (540) 592–3900, fax (540) 592–3781
Rooms: 10, including 4 suites; 8 with private bath, all with air conditioning, 5 with fireplace and balcony, 4 with steeping tub, telephone, and television. Designated no smoking rooms.
Rates: $100 to $150, double occupancy, EPB. Add $20 for Saturday night stay only. Schoolhouse suites $190, EPB.
Open: All year.
Facilities and activities: Dinner Wednesday–Saturday, Sunday brunch, tavern. Nearby: hiking Sky Meadows State Park and Appalachian Trail, Bellegrove Mansion, antiquing, vineyard tours, horse shows, trail rides, Shenandoah River sports.

The Emmanuel Hutzler House
RICHMOND, VIRGINIA 23220

Lyn knew that she would live here one day from the first moment she saw Monument Avenue, Richmond's grand historic boulevard of brick townhouses and Civil War monuments.

When we began corresponding, Lyn wrote, "We underestimated the scope of this project! All is beginning to take shape nicely now—our central air is in, three of the baths have been tiled, the front porch is being repoured and retiled, and I'm still hand-stripping all the mahogany paneling on the whole first floor!" Lyn and John worked longer and harder than they had expected. Twenty thousand pounds of debris exited the building to pave the way for fixing walls, installing bathrooms, sanding floors, and

carpeting, wallpapering, and painting. Finally, in 1990, they opened the double set of great front doors to guests.

When I arrived we walked through the lovely restoration, and I paused in Lyn's office, where several folk art paintings hang. In the living room, I stooped to pet TC, the inn's cat, who was curled contentedly on the sofa near the fire. "I've experienced a change in furniture," Lyn noted. "I love country, but the inn's basic elegance called for more formal furnishings, so we made a transition with the help of antiques auctions."

There's a refined comfort in the 8,000-square-foot inn. The mahogany woodwork has raised paneling and coffered ceilings with dropped beams. A French tapestry hangs above the fireplace, an expanse of original bookcases (I'd like to wish them back home to my house) covers the wall, and a handsome pair of English vases sit on the mantel. It's a place where one feels like sitting in the sun that shines through the leaded-glass front windows and reading between sips of lemonade, or relaxing with TC before the fire on a warm-inside winter's afternoon.

You can expect breakfast, which is served in the pleasant dining room opposite a pier mirror, to be wholesome. You find a variety of natural cereals, home-baked breads, and often scrambled eggs.

As we discussed restaurants, several of which are within walking distance, Lyn suggested music-oriented dining. Choices include country music and places that feature classical music and jazz. She is careful to find something that suits you.

Of the four rooms my favorites are the front room and the back room. The front room has

southern exposure, a fireplace with gas logs, and an enormous whirlpool tub (4 by 6 feet), which you might want to share. The sunny back room is painted Concord red with off-white trim and has a brass-and-iron, queen-sized bed. Lyn explains your choices very clearly.

How to get there: From Washington, D.C., take I–95 and follow signs to Petersburg I–64 east toward Norfolk and Williamsburg (do not follow signs to I–295). Take exit 78, which is the exit for the Travel Information Center and Boulevard Street. Take a right onto Boulevard and follow Boulevard for 1 mile to Broad Street. Turn left onto Broad and go approximatel ½ mile past the Science Museum to Meadow Street. Turn right onto Meadow and go 2 blocks. Turn right onto Monument and drive to Number 2036. You can park in the loading zone to unload, but there is overnight parking in rear.

Innkeepers: Lyn Benson and John Richardson

Address/Telephone: 2036 Monument Avenue; (804) 353–6900 or (804) 355–4885, fax (804) 355–5053

Rooms: 4, including 2 suites; all with private bath, telephone, television, and air conditioning, 2 with whirlpool bath. No smoking inn.

Rates: $89 to $145, double occupancy, EPB. Two-night minimum holiday and special-event weekends.

Open: All year, except Christmas week.

Facilities and activities: Off-street parking. Nearby: restaurants, State Capitol, Science Museum, Battlefield Park, White House of the Confederacy Museum, St. John's Church, Virginia Museum of Fine Arts, Valentine Museum, Agecroft Hall.

Business travel: Telephone in all rooms; desk in 2 rooms; fax available; corporate rates.

The Manor at Taylor's Store
SMITH MOUNTAIN LAKE, VIRGINIA 24184

I spent the pleasantest of days here. Mary Lynn had cheerfully suggested a walk. We passed the paddock—home to two Newfoundland dogs—and traveled down a shady lane. In the pasture a horse grazed. We came to the first of six ponds and met a gaggle of geese, which had been ordered as goslings from the Sears catalog. Next we came to a larger pond, a sunning deck, and, beyond that, two more ponds and a trail that led into the woods.

Within the Colonial mansion dating from 1820 is a full range of opportunities for relaxing. There's the formal Victorian parlor with a double fireplace in the corner; through the dining room is the sunroom, where you can step out onto the brick patio overlooking fields and trees. Downstairs are a pool table, a 55-inch television (with large video collection), the exercise room, and the outdoor hot tub.

Mary Lynn and Lee have made each bedroom as lovely and sunny as the next. The rooms were draped and canopied with the assistance of her aunt, a professional decorator. The Plantation Room has two exquisite double beds and is located on the first floor. There's a sunken whirlpool bath for two in the Castle Suite. The Toy Room is filled with antique toys.

Mary Lynn's breakfasts are healthful and stimulating. As a former public health nurse who loves cooking, she makes low-cholesterol masterpieces: individual fruit tarts in summer, whole-wheat waffles raised with yeast, and whole-grain dill breads adorn her table. Her French toast has the delicate taste of Grand Marnier and is covered with Virginia maple syrup. Supporting these feasts is a Queen Anne table hand made by Lee.

One of the directions some guests go for dinner is toward Smith Mountain Lake for a choice of waterfront restaurants. Lakeside is an airport where you can go for a biplane ride, and there are several marinas offering boat rides and charters. Roanoke is thirty minutes away, and between the inn and the town are antiques shops. If you fly into the Roanoke Airport, Lee will provide limousine service in his 1960 Jaguar. He's a surgical pathologist who finds that the scientific side of his life balances with innkeeping.

The inn was a trading post as early as 1799, later an ordinary, and then a post office in 1818. "In a sense, we are custodians of the land for future generations," said Mary Lynn.

How to get there: From Roanoke take Route 220 South to 122/40 East. Continue on Route 122 North when routes split, and follow signs for Booker T. Washington Monument. The inn is 1⁶/₁₀ miles past the Burnt Chimney intersection on the right.

Innkeepers: Mary Lynn and Lee Tucker
Address/Telephone: Route 122 (mailing address: Route 1, Box 533, Wirtz);
    (540) 721–3951 or (800) 248–6267, fax (540) 721–5243
Rooms: 10, including 16 suites and 1 cottage; all with air conditioning, 8 with private
    bath, 3 with whirlpool bath, 5 with fireplace. No smoking inn.
Rates: $85 to $185, double occupancy, EPB. Corporate rates available.
Open: All year.
Facilities and activities: Game room, exercise room, hot tub, guest kitchen; on 120 acres,
    Colonial garden, walking paths, with ponds for swimming, fishing, and canoeing;
    volleyball, badminton, croquet. Nearby: restaurants and Smith Mountain Lake (5
    miles), antiquing, country roads, state park, plane rides, hot-air balloon rides, golf,
    Blue Ridge Parkway.

The Conyers House
SPERRYVILLE, VIRGINIA 22740

If you've never gone on a dewy morning trail ride with an experienced horsewoman or hiked on Old Rag Mountain, then your holiday awaits.

Two wooden verandas are perfectly positioned—one to capture the sunrise, the other to linger over the sunset. When we arrived the summer flowers were in bloom in the Blue Ridge Mountains; the sounds of water from the fountain played harmoniously in the background. Once again we found the country views beautiful. Two saddles rested on the banister, and riding boots stood at attention in the hallway of this informal English country house. Everywhere we looked objects attracted our eyes.

Sandra rides with the Rappahannock Hunt Club, which departs every fall from the inn. Guests are invited to join the departure ceremony, which occurs around a large hunt breakfast. She's also adept at conveying the principles of riding to the novice. You saddle your horses and leave directly from the inn, then meander up into these lovely hills with your hostess.

The Conyers House, which dates from 1790 with some additions, was Conyers' Old Store. The oldest part of the inn is the book-filled parlor, with a grand piano and comfortable leather couches. It makes an inviting wintertime gathering place.

Most of the bedrooms are named for family members, neighbors, or occurrences. Helen's room is named for Norman's mother, who lives in Yorkshire. This is my favorite room, with its fireplace and small balcony. There are two cottages; the more private one is Hill House, with its Franklin woodburning stove, which is nice for cuddling in the winter.

You dine deliciously at breakfast in the warmth and coziness of the kitchen, in the formal dining room at a great table, or outdoors. The red-pepper jelly is a house delicacy, along with Mrs. Woodard's bread pudding and the cheese strata, a hot, baked, multilayered affair that's scrumptious. On our summer excursion we met on the eastern veranda for breakfast, where we had fresh blueberry pancakes, local sausages, and fruits while discussing the nearby hike up Old Rag, Washington's Blue Book, and Sandra's weekly German club. Norman had just departed for the Court House to become a justice of the peace. He was to preside over a hillside wedding

to be held the following Sunday.

Sandra serves candelit dinner to guests by advance reservation. Among your preset choices are fresh mountain trout, tenderloin of pork braised in cider with sauerkraut and fresh apples, and cheesecake with gooseberry sauce or a savory chocolate cake with raspberry jam. Outstanding restaurants are located nearby.

How to get there: From I–66, exit onto 29S at Gainsville and drive 12 miles to Warrenton. Turn west on Route 211 and go 28 miles to Sperryville. Turn left at the Sperryville Emporium, then left again at the blinking light at Route 522. From 522, turn right on Route 231 (¾ mile). Drive 8 miles to Route 707 (Slate Mills Road) and turn left. Go on Route 707 for ⁶⁄₁₀ mile to the inn on the left.

Innkeepers: Sandra and Norman Cartwright-Brown

Address/Telephone: 3131 Slate Mills Road; (540) 987–8025, fax (540) 987–8709

Rooms: 8, including 2 cottages and 1 suite; all with private bath, air conditioning, and fireplace, 3 with television, 1 with whirlpool. Pets allowed on limited basis. No smoking inn.

Rates: $100 to $150, double occupancy; $165 to $170, cottages; $195, suite; EPB. Two-night minimum in October and on holidays.

Open: All year.

Facilities and activities: Seven-course dinner served by advance reservation weekends ($67.50 per couple, including wine and gratuity). Trail rides ($40 for 2 hours). Nearby: hiking on Old Rag Mountain, antiquing, golf, canoeing, fishing.

Business travel: Telephone and fax available; conference room.

Jordan Hollow Farm Inn
STANLEY, VIRGINIA 22851

Jordan Hollow began as a single log cabin more than 200 years ago. A second cabin was added, and around these hand-hewn gems the inn has grown. It's home to horses, goats, cats, and sheep, who are responsible for greeting and charming the guests. Among the diversions possible in this 150-acre retreat are the horseback riding and hiking on private trails.

The accomplished staff members lead guests on trail rides. Depending on your skills, you can take a gentle beginner ride or join the advanced treks into the mountains. All this activity will undoubtedly make you hungry, but not to worry. The evening often begins in the Watering Trough, a rustic bar that's been carved out of a former stable. Convivial conversation centers on the pool table and other games.

Dinner is not a dress-up affair at Jordan Hollow Farm. The dining rom is located in the original log cabin, which has heart-pine floors and chestnut posts and beams, conveying the rustic simplicity of its origins. The food, just like the furnishings, will be homey and hearty. The menu includes fresh trout, chicken, and pasta dishes. There are house-baked breads, fresh-from-the-garden salads and vegetables, and desserts such as pear crisp and chocolate mousse cake. A complete wine and beer selection is available.

A mere hundred yards from the front porch of the inn is Arbor View Lodge, reached along a wisteria-covered porch, with cozy homespun guest rooms. They are furnished with antiques, country artifacts, quilts, and twiggy headboards. Each holds a small bookshelf, which is selectively filled. The rooms open onto a long wooden deck. My favorites are the south-facing rooms overlooking the Shenandoah Mountains. The newest rooms are in Mare Meadow Lodge, a log cottage with four spacious rooms. The rooms have handsome, hand-hewn pine furniture, fireplaces, and whirlpools.

There are many activities to keep you busy at Jordan Hollow Farm in addition to horseback riding. A swimming pool and Luray Caverns aren't far, and a canoeing outfitter will arrange for a day on the Shenandoah River. Bicycling and hiking (the inn has 5 miles of trail) are also convenient. When I arrived a newly born litter of kittens was being nursed into the world in a box behind the tavern's wood-burning stove.

Jordan Hollow has a comfortable, relaxed atmosphere. It offers plenty of fresh air and beautiful countryside, and I was happy to hear Betsy say, "We are surrounded by national parks; no one can ever take our views away."

How to get there: From Route I–66 exit onto Route 55 to Front Royal, turn south onto Route 340, and continue past Luray for 6 miles to Route 624. Turn left onto Route 624 and the left again onto Route 689. Go over the bridge and turn right onto Route 626. Travel ⁴⁄₁₀ mile to inn.

Innkeepers: Gail Kyle and Betsy Anderson
Address/Telephone: Route 626 (mailing address: Route 2, Box 375); (540) 778–2285, fax (540) 778–1759
Rooms: 21, including 5 suites in lodge; all with private bath, telephone, air conditioning, and porch, 9 with television, some with fireplace and whirlpool bath. Wheelchair accessible. No smoking inn.
Rates: $100 to $140, double occupancy, MAP. Additional person $35. Children 6 and over $15. Two-night minimum holiday weekends.
Open: All year.
Facilities and activities: Breakfast, dinner ($20 for outside guests), tavern, game room, lounge, 150 acres, horseback riding ($20 per hour), horse boarding for guests' horses, hiking trails. Nearby: swimming pool, fishing, golf, tennis, hiking, canoeing, museums, antiques shops.
Business travel: Telephone in all rooms; desk in 5 rooms; fax available; conference center with all facilities.

Belle Grae Inn
STAUNTON, VIRGINIA 24401

High above the street you can sit on the front porch of this Italianate mansion and cast an eye over the Victorian rooftops of Staunton; the distant double mountains are named for the green hills mentioned in a Robert Burns poem, "The Ode to Betsy Belle."

The inn, situated in a historic residential neighborhood called New Town, 4 blocks from downtown shopping, comprises five houses that are peppered with antiques, reproductions, and collectibles. We were led up to the Jefferson House (circa 1865), which has a great front-porch view. Our room had every comfort, from an armoire to a sitting room to a small balcony to welcome the morning sun. But there is a nice se-

lection of rooms from which to choose, so I won't play favorites.

Out you must go to explore. I'd begin with the European influences of Staunton, which are traced at the Museum of American Frontier Culture. There we visited with interpreters and saw cottages that were originally imported from Germany, Ireland, and England. The interpreters explained the lifestyle abroad and how it was adapted locally. Along the path we saw kerry cows, a frisky donkey with braided mane, chickens, geese—and finally a Colonial homestead that demonstrates the evolution from European to settler. There's a canyon of contrast between the accommodations of the English "squatter's cottage" and the luxury of your comfortable bed and the Victorian guest parlor at the Belle Grae. I'm glad we're living in the country inn era.

Next go antiquing (at noncity prices) in the shops 3 blocks from the inn; visit the Woodrow Wilson House, only 7 blocks away; and return in time for an evening aperitif on the patio (also a good spot for summertime reading and sipping tea).

The inn serves continental cuisine with a few Southern specialties. From fresh seafood, lamb, pork, and beef entrees you might choose delicious classics like roast pork tenderloin with an apple glaze or tournedos served with a creamy sherry sauce. The grand finale could be a slice of inn-made peanut butter–chocolate pie or a white-chocolate-macadamia-nut parfait with red raspberry sauce. For the setting you can choose

between the formal Victorian elegance of the historic mansion or the casual contemporary Bistro, with its floor-to-ceiling windows overlooking Victorian rooftops. I like the different moods.

The inn is thirty minutes from the Blue Ridge Parkway and Skyline Drive. But there are many directions to take. Ah, decisions of pleasure, they are my favorite kind.

How to get there: From I–81 exit Route 250 West to Staunton. Follow the signs to the Woodrow Wilson Birthplace, staying on 250. At the corner of Wilson Birthplace, turn left onto West Frederick Street and go past the inn on the right at 515 West Frederick. Turn right onto Jefferson Street, turn right in 1 block onto Baldwin, and park behind the inn.

Innkeeper: Michael Organ; Ronn

Short, manager

Address/Telephone: 515 West Frederick Street; (540) 886–5151, fax (540) 886–6641

Rooms: 14, including 7 suites in cottages and houses; all with private bath and air conditioning, 10 with gas fireplace, telephone, and television. Wheelchair access. No smoking inn.

Rates: $85 to $145, double occupancy; $148 to $208, per couple, MAP. Two-night minimum in May and October if Saturday night included.

Open: All year.

Facilities and activities: Breakfast and dinner daily, Sunday brunch, full beverage license. Nearby: Woodrow Wilson Birthplace, Mary Baldwin College, Trinity Church, antiquing in town, Museum of American Frontier Culture, Garden Week (end of April) and private home tours, Monticello, Ash Lawn, Shenandoah Valley.

Business travel: Desk in all rooms; telephone and fax available; conference room.

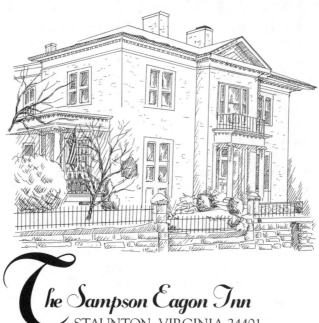

The Sampson Eagon Inn
STAUNTON, VIRGINIA 24401

Do you carry an image of the classic inn, located in a historic town, where welcoming hosts open the front door and cordially suggest tea on the porch? If you wish to explore your dream in an elegant setting or simply want to tour central Virginia from the Shenandoah Valley to Monticello and the Tidewater, then the historic Sampson Eagon is for you.

Frank and Laura long had visions of restoring and creating a country inn. They advanced through several restoration projects, gaining valuable experience, while they continued their passion for antique collecting. Finally, a grand but neglected 1840 Greek Revival mansion in downtown Staunton appeared on the market.

They sold their home in Washington, D.C., quit their administrative jobs, bought the building, and moved south.

The inn, located in the Gospel Hill Virginia Historic Landmark district of Staunton, was the home of a former blacksmith turned preacher, Sampson Eagon. (His sermons inspired the area's name.) It's easy to see how Frank and Laura's marvelous restoration won them a historic preservation award. Laura pointed to architectural features of Empire, Victorian, Egyptian, and Colonial Revival styles as we moved through the inn. Her antiques complement the inn's age, although some, like the Chippendale dining-room chairs, predate the mansion. In a small den she's hung Frank's horse brass collection, and her antique baskets fill a cupboard.

The spacious guest rooms and suites reveal a sensitive attention to luxurious details—three-way lights beside the bed, individual temperature-control nozzles on the steam heaters, love seats and chairs for reading.

We met couples who'd come with distinctly different goals: One came merely to take advantage of the local movie theater, where you can see a film for $2.00 and consume all the popcorn you can eat for $3.00. Another couple joined the neighborhood in sledding; a third pair had elaborate plans for antiquing. The small town of Staunton has more than 200 buildings dating from the Victorian period, a collection of antiques shops, and fine restaurants within walking distance of the inn. Across the street is the Woodrow Wilson Museum, where we found ourselves absorbed in the dramatic life and times of one of the United States' most fascinating presidents. We also spent an afternoon learning from the knowledgeable guides at the American Frontier Museum.

Laura's breakfasts, served on Royal Doulton china, might include a Grand Marnier soufflé pancake or an asparagus omelet. This is not a meal to eat in a hurry. The scent of coffee and baking breads draws you into the dining room, where before the fireplace you begin with fresh juices and seasonal fruits. The fire crackles along with the conversation, and the sun splashes through the windows as it must have when Sampson Eagon joined his family for breakfast.

The inn is a perfect setting for those seeking quality and beauty, rest and romance, or perhaps a provocative beginning to any sojourn.

How to get there: From I–81 take either exit 225 or 222 and follow the signs to Woodrow Wilson Birthplace. Inn is in center of town, opposite Birthplace on the corner of East Beverley and Coalter streets. Enter parking area on Coalter.

Innkeepers: Frank and Laura Mattingly
Address/Telephone: 238 East Beverley Street; (540) 886–8200 or (800) 597–9722, faxsame
Rooms: 5, including 2 suites; all with private bath, air conditioning, telephone, television, and VCR. No smoking inn.
Rates: $85 to $109, double occupancy, EPB. Corporate, AARP, and off-season rates available. Two-night minimum weekends in April–November.
Open: All year.
Facilities and activities: Nearby: Walking distance to good restaurants. Mary Baldwin College, Woodrow Wilson Birthplace, Museum of American Frontier Culture, Statler Brothers Complex, Cyrus McCormick Museum, Blue Ridge Parkway.
Business travel: Desk in all rooms; telephone and fax available; corporate rates.

$\mathcal{P}$rospect $\mathcal{H}$ill

TREVILIANS, VIRGINIA 23093

Michael Sheehan greets you with a firm handshake and ushers you into this former plantation house, which dates back to 1732. This is reputedly the oldest continuously operating plantation in America; it traces its roots to the 1600s. As families grew and plantation activities increased, dependency buildings were added to the grounds: a smokehouse, carriage house, and summer kitchen, to name a few. These structures have been turned into charming guest rooms, all connected to the main house by a stone pathway.

One of my favorites is the Boy's Cabin, a log cabin that dates back to 1699. It has log walls, a brick fireplace, and a simple bed that is covered with a quilt; nevertheless, the bath is large and absolutely modern. Anther favorite is the Overseer's Cottage, which has a four-poster bed, a fireplace, and a step-down sitting room with a private deck. Each of the cottages is impeccably furnished in a style that is appropriate to its original use, but with all the comforts we love today. There are five rooms in the plantation house as well; these are the most elegant.

Bill and Mireille Sheehan created the inn in 1977. Eventually, they eased out of hands-on innkeeping, and their son Michael stepped into the innkeepers' shoes. When I asked if he and his wife, Laura, are training their daughter and son to eventually assume the responsibility, he replied they wear T-shirts that read: "Innkeeper in training."

Behind the inn stretches a lawn shaded with massive old leafy trees. A hammock is suspended between the trees. A pool and cabana entice sun-lovers on warm days. Large white wicker chairs cuddle the afternoon reader on the small porch in back, while the Board Room downstairs, with its soft leather chairs and fireplace, serves the purpose in cool weather. There's also a formal living room with a stereo to listen to classical music.

Dinner at Prospect Hill is an experience that should not be missed. For many years Mireille was the chef, preparing meals inspired by the foods of Provence, where she grew up. Today Michael prepares classically inspired French cuisine spiced up with a bit of Provence, as his mother used to, but with his own twist. He uses herbs from his kitchen garden and garnishes each dish with flowers, making them as pretty as they are delicious.

The dining rooms (there are three separate rooms) are charmingly decorated, as if they were plucked directly from the French countryside. There are wide-plank polished floors, fireplaces in two the rooms, and French antiques and fabrics used throughout.

Dinner begins with a wine reception. The five-course menu changes every night, but typically it will include a creative appetizer, then a soup, followed by a salad. The entree may be a pan-seared tenderloin of veal forestière. For dessert perhaps Michael will have prepared a blackberry-and-Drambuie cheese torte served with a blackberry coulis. All this is accompanied by wines from the extensive slection. It's a wonderfully romantic way to spend an evening.

Prospect Hill is one of my favorite inns—an enchanting getaway in the country, where exceptional food, gracious innkeepers, charming rooms, and a relaxed style blend to create a perfect stay.

How to get there: Take exit 136 from I–64 to Route 15 south to Zion Crossroads. Turn left on Route 250 east. Go 1 mile to Route 613, turn left, and go 3 miles to Prospect Hill on the left. Fly-in: Gordonsville Airport.

Innkeepers: Michael and Laura Sheehan
Address/Telephone: 2887 Poindexter Road; (540) 967–574 or (800) 277–0844, fax (540) 967–0102
Rooms: 13, including 3 suites and 5 cottages; all with private bath, air conditioning, and fireplace, 8 with whirlpool bath. Wheelchair accessible.
Rates: $245 to $325, double occupancy, MAP; 10 percent discount Monday–Thursday. Two-night stay may be required on weekends.
Open: All year.
Facilities and activities: Dinner daily ($35 to $40 for the public), wine served. Swimming pool. On 45 acres. Nearby: carriage rides, fishing, golfing, horseback riding, tennis, winery tours, hot-air ballooning, Monticello, Ash Lawn, antiques shops.
Business travel: Desk, coffeemaker, and minirefrigerator in most rooms; fax and copier available; meeting room.

1763 *Inn*

UPPERVILLE, VIRGINIA 22176

Caun the Lab romped forward to greet me. Two horses grazed behind the inn, and a Canada goose walked alongside the pond; 1763 is a German-influenced inn. Its fifty acres near Upperville are located in the heart of Virginia's horse country.

Upon entering you pass down a hallway where paintings of American military officers are hung opposite those of German officers. "They face one another in peace," says Uta, who is from Germany and has taught English in the United States. The paintings were done by a relative of Don's and lead the way to a pleasant tavern, where two ornate chandeliers draw your attention. One is an antique that Uta found on their travels to Istanbul.

You can dine in one of the four intimate dining rooms. The oldest is the for George Washington Room, with a fireplace, dating from 1763. There's the German Room, where photographs of Uta's family give the room a special warmth. Everyone tries to guess which relative she most resembles. The small French Room has a secluded romantic ambience and lacy lampshades covering the lights.

Our dinner began amiably with German beer and a pâté appetizer. The classic tournedos sautéed with mushrooms, shallots, and flavored delicately with a Burgundy sauce were perfection. The sauerbraten, simpler, was accompanied by pungent red cabbage. Then my companions and

I shared desserts, including chilled chocolate mousse, and finished a bottle of crisp white wine. Contentedly, we stepped out under the stars for a late-night walk.

My favorite rooms are the two authentic log cabins that Don found in West Virginia. They were taken apart, transported, and reassembled in the woods. There's a handsome fireplace room in the main inn that overlooks the pond. In the remodeled barn the Buffalo Room has a small private balcony. From here it's an easy walk to the pool, which is built atop a small hill.

There's a casualness here that's nice. You find balconies, whirlpool baths, fireplaces, and a swimming pool—all the pleasures of a romantic night away from home.

How to get there: From Washington, D.C., take Route 66 west to exit 23 north, also Route 17 North marked Paris/Delaplane. Go 9 miles to the stop sign at Route 50. Turn right; go 1½ miles. The inn is on the right.

Innkeepers: Uta and Don Kirchner

Address/Telephone: 10087 John Mosby Highway; (540) 592–3848 or (800) 669–1763, fax (540) 592–3114

Rooms: 16, including 1 cottage and 2 log cabins; all with private bath, air conditioning, telephone, and television, most with fireplace and whirlpool bath. Wheelchair accessible.

Rates: $95 to $185, double occupancy, EPB. Additional person $35. One box firewood provided, additional is extra. Two-night minimum if Saturday included. Corporate rates.

Open: All year.

Facilities and activities: Lunch Saturday and Sunday, dinner Wednesday–Sunday and holidays ($14 to $22). Tavern, 50 acres in Virginia horse country, pond, swimming pool, tennis, trails through private woods. Nearby: wineries, Middleburg, Winchester.

The Inn at Gristmill Square
WARM SPRINGS, VIRGINIA 24484

Nestled in a quiet village around a brook is the enticing and romantic Inn at Gristmill Square. It's a combination of five buildings that surround a stone-paved square. The flavor is that of a nineteenth-century mill village, with rooms located in a former miller's house, blacksmith shop, hardware store, and town residence.

The inn's romantic Waterwheel Restaurant, located in a stone mill, has a foundation that dates back to 1771. Although the mill subsequently burned, it was rebuilt in 1900 and continued to operate until 1970. The Simon Kenton Pub is named for a boy who once worked here after fleeing his home because he thought he had killed a rival suitor. Before dining you can de-

scend to the wine cellar to select your own wine. Simply cross the brook to reach the swimming pool and three tennis courts.

There is a diversity of rooms to suit every mood, and all are furnished in good taste. The Silo is a round, white, shingle-roofed building. You can sit before the fire in the round room or on the patio. In the Quilt Room, Americana addicts will feel comfortable, and there's a room with an Oriental flavor, with a lovely window that looks out to the brook. The little Miller's House offers its coziness, and the Board Room is spacious, with natural board siding. Continental breakfast is brought to your room in the morning.

For lunch you might try the rich king crab

soufflé or fresh fruit salad. For dinner tournedos or steak au poivre smothered in green peppercorns and served with a brandy-and-cream sauce might tempt you. The fresh mountain trout, grilled and served with black walnuts, is a trusted classic. Don't leave without tasting the caramel custard or chocolate mousse. The chef will share the recipes and even send them upon request, and you'll enjoy the setting as much as the dining experience.

Ask for the trail map to the Cascades, one of the most satisfying hikes in the area. Or you might play one of the outstanding golf courses, as my traveling companion did. His report: "A peak experience." If you browse through the country store in the blacksmith's shop, you're sure to find a treasure to take home. Even driving in these lovely hills is a rewarding pleasure.

I always enjoy returning here. There's an easy comfort.

How to get there: From I–64, take Route 220 North to Warm Springs. In the village, turn left on Route 619 and right on Main Street at the dead end. The inn is on the right in less than a block. Closest airport is at the Homestead.

Innkeepers: The McWilliams Family; Bruce McWilliams, manager

Address/Telephone: Main Street (mailing address: P.O. Box 359); (540) 839–2231, fax (540) 839–5770

Rooms: 17, including 1 suite; all with private bath, air conditioning, television, telephone, and refrigerator, 7 with fireplace, 1 with Jacuzzi.

Rates: $80 to $140, double occupancy, continental breakfast; $155 to $210, per couple, MAP.

Open: All year.

Facilities and activities: Dining room closed Mondays during winter. Full breakfast available, lunch May–October, dinner (entrees $17 to $22), Sunday brunch, pub. Swimming pool, 3 tennis courts, sauna. Nearby: natural hot springs; carriage rides, horseback rides, golfing, fishing, hunting, Garth Newel Music Center, skiing at the Homestead.

Business travel: Telephone in all rooms; desk in 8 rooms; corporate rates; conference room.

Meadow Lane Lodge
WARM SPRINGS, VIRGINIA 24484

Turn down the paved lane bordered by meadow and you're amid the inn's 1,600 acres. It's peaceful and lush, a place to unwind surrounded by natural beauty. The only sounds might come from one of a bevy of animals: goats, sheep, peacocks, chickens and roosters, guinea hens and ducks, dogs, and a pair of donkeys.

You can walk through the meadows, climb mountains, fly-fish in the crystal-clear Jackson River, which flows for 3 miles through the inn's land, play tennis on the Dynaturf court, set up for a croquet game, cozy up to the fireplace, or simply lie back and catch the summer breezes on the porch. Mr. Hirsh has a name for it: "creative loafing."

There are numerous walks to take, but one is

a must. It leads down the lane alongside the barns, out to a cliffside wooden deck where the view stretches to the beaver bog below and far meadows. You can walk along the racehorse route; it's exactly 1 mile and was built by Mr. Hirsh's father to time the thoroughbred horses. A much longer walk is to the oldest slave quarters in Bath County, a log cabin on the former site of Fort Dinwiddie. From this location you can look up to the gap between the hills and see a bushy remnant of the colonists' trail westward. The soil is rich with Indian and Colonial artifacts; a million years from now, they'll wonder what we did for pleasure as they study our artifacts. Will they understand that we found peace and contentment at a country inn in the Alleghenies?

Mr. Hirsh's recipes influence the breakfasts. "Where else," he asks, "can you practice an art that involves all the senses—smell, sight, touch, and taste?" Menus are prepared a week ahead; one morning it might be French toast, bacon, fried grits, scalloped tomatoes, and corn muffins; the next you might sit down to eggs Jackson and hash brown potatoes. His cookbook is a handwritten collection of childhood and traditional Virginia dishes. For dinner, you might have Southern baked chicken and scrumptious pecan pie for dessert.

Among my favorite rooms is the bay-window room in Craig's Cottage; it has a fireplace and a splendid view. All rooms are comfortably furnished, some with antiques, and are clean and simple.

How to get there: From I–81 and Staunton exit onto Route 250 west. Proceed to Churchville. Past village, turn south onto Route 42 to Milboro Springs. At Milboro Springs take Route 39 west. Cross Route 220 and continue 4 miles to lodge entrance.

Innkeepers: Steve and Cheryl Hooley; Philip and Catherine Hirsh, proprietors
Address/Telephone: Route 39 (mailing address: Route 1, Box 110); (540) 839–5959, fax (540) 839–2135
Rooms: 14, including 2 suites and 8 cottages; all with private bath, most with air conditioning, television, telephone, and fireplace. No smoking inn.
Rates: $115 to $145, double occupancy, EPB.
Open: All year.
Facilities and activities: Friday and Saturday dinner by reservation (around $30); service bar for wine and beer. On 1,600 private acres with 3 miles on Jackson River for trout and bass fly-fishing; mountain biking, canoeing, inner-tubing, cross-country skiing, hiking, tennis court, swimming, croquet court approved by U.S. Croquet Association. Nearby: restaurant within 10-minute drive, 3 golf courses.

Bleu Rock Inn
WASHINGTON, VIRGINIA 22747

We came for a quiet, private occasion. While the rest of the world worked, we plotted our escape. The gleefulness of childhood returned. I packed simply, my pearls and a classic black; he carried a suit and his Ferragamos. For traveling comfort we wore jeans.

"You may come early, since it's midweek," offered our hostess on the phone, "and then you'll have time to walk through the vineyard before dinner."

Bleu Rock has grown from a small white farmhouse into today's white-stuccoed inn with robin-egg blue gingerbread trim. We were reminded of inns we've visited in France. The owners are brothers, Bernard and Jean Cam-

pagne, who are from the Basque region of France, and have turned the surrounding eighty acres into vineyard and orchard.

That afternoon we quickly deposited our evening wear in our room and returned outdoors for a walk. But first my companion ran his tennis-shoe toes over the blue slate that names the inn. It's a burgundy shade that you'll have noticed on some of Virginia's paved roads. We headed toward the pond and over to the vineyard where the chardonnay, seyval, and cabernet sauvignon vines grow. At the end of each row, Bernard has planted a rose. We passed the hay, rolled into shredded-wheat shapes, and the horses, then walked among the peach, apricot, and nectarine trees in the lush orchard.

When we returned to the inn, passing more roses, a pretty young woman offered us hot tea in the guest parlor. All the staff were as kind as she. Above the stone fireplace sat a French clock whose time has stopped. We browsed among the paperbacks on a shelf (many were in French) and selected from a collection of recent American magazines. We watched as the sun set between the mountains beyond the pond and vineyard. In the summer, I thought, we would be having our drinks on the lovely terrace.

Our room was the largest. It has small balconies—one facing east, the other west. There is a French dresser, and lace curtains cover the French doors. The walls are white, and the flowered linens contrast with green carpeting. The look is uncomplicated and pretty.

Dinner was served in a small dining room with a stone fireplace and hand-painted walls. The brothers also own a Bergerie restaurant in Alexandria, so the food is excellent.

I began with a creamy split pea soup and had an excellent roasted salmon with a pine nut crust. For dessert we chose an orange-caramel-custard-ruit compote and a warm apple-frangipane tart with caramel sauce. Between delicious bites we promised to escape twice a year like this.

Breakfast began with a lemon poppy-seed muffin that was superb. I applied a bit of lemon curd from the jam tray for even more emphasis. Chef prepared a ham-and-cheese omelet.

We toasted one another with our fresh-squeezed orange juice and agreed that quiet occasions have a secret festiveness when the rest of the world works.

How to get there: From Warrenton proceed 22 miles west on Route 211 (past both exits for village of Washington) to inn on right-hand side of the road. Watch for matching white fences marking entrance.

Innkeepers: Bernard and Jean Campagne
Address/Telephone: 12567 Lee Highway; (540) 987–3190 or (800) 537–3652, fax (540) 987–3193
Rooms: 5; all with private bath and air conditioning. Pets allowed in 1 room by prior permission. Wheelchair accessible.
Rates: $89 to $150, double occupancy, EPB. Request special Wednesday, Thursday rates.
Open: All year, except closed Mondays.
Facilities and activities: Dinner Tuesday–Sunday ($15 to $20), Sunday brunch ($7 to $17). On 80 acres. Nearby: Skyline Drive, antiquing, golf, horseback riding, hiking, and vineyards.

The Inn at Little Washington
WASHINGTON, VIRGINIA 22747

The Inn at Little Washington is so discreet that it does not announce its presence with a sign in the traditional sense. When you arrive in the village, you'll simply perceive the location opposite the church and post office. Dispel any notions of Virginia country-rustic and imagine driving one hour from Washington, D.C., and stepping without passport into a small, opulent European haven with world-class dining. The inn is a member of *Relais et Châteaux*. Craig Claiborne celebrated his sixty-fifth birthday here. He continues to return for the annual occasion. Could a higher honor exist? The accolades continue. The inn's fame is international.

Dinner at the inn is a graceful love affair with perfect foods. Chef Patrick O'Connell's menu reveals imaginative creations. One night you might select a fresh Pine Island oyster glazed in champagne sauce or local trout smoked over apple wood with horseradish-apple cream; an intermezzo of sorbets, perhaps grapefruit or rhubarb; then a shockingly picturesque display of red snapper accompanied by sea scallops, followed by the Seven Deadly Sins: a sampling of seven inn specialties spectacularly served with four sauces. On the evening we dined here, I chose the superlative California foie gras, with smoked goose breast, country ham, and black-eyed peas vinaigrette for an appetizer. Claiborne once said of this dish, "It was one of the best things I ever put in my mouth." Afterward you retire to the garden on a summer's night and listen to the mysterious call of the tree frogs around the gentle waterfall.

O'Connell and partner Reinhardt Lynch have, with the artistic eye of an interior designer, transformed a once ignoble building into a spectacular inn. The designer's sketches for each of the rooms are framed in the upstairs hallway. A gold-leaf wallpaper and silk taffeta lamp suspended over each intimate dining table forms part of the scene. Through the French doors is the landscaped garden, which is groomed by the full-time horticulturist.

Climb the stairs to your room; each one is unusual. There are lushly draped fabrics, stylish chairs and couches, marble bathrooms, and heated towel racks. The suites are the most lavish; several have faux marble trim and leaded-glass double entries, like a London apartment. Some face the garden; others look upon the village side street; still others front Main Street and have small balconies separated with thick draw curtains.

The inn is located in the midst of Virginia's hunt country. A journey here might include the local races, polo and horse events, or a tour of local wineries. The heart of your destination is the gastronomic journey upon which you are about to embark.

How to get there: From Washington, D.C., take I–66 west 22 miles to Exit 43A (Gainsville). Follow Route 29 south for 12 miles to Warrenton and turn right at 211 west. Go 23 miles, turn right at sign for Washington Business Route. Go ½ mile to stop sign; the inn is on the right.

Innkeepers: Patrick O'Connell and Reinhardt Lynch
Address/Telephone: Middle and Main Streets (mailing address: P.O. Box 300); (540) 675–3800, fax (540) 675–3100
Rooms: 12, including 3 suites; all with private bath, telephone, and air conditioning. Pets by prior arrangement. Restaurant wheelchair accessible. No smoking in dining room.
Rates: $250 to $525, double occupancy, Sunday–Thursday; $350 to $625 all Fridays and every day in October, as well as slected holiday weekends; $400 to $675 all Saturdays and Valentine's Day; continental breakfast and afternoon tea.
Open: All year except Tuesdays and Christmas Day.
Facilities and activities: Dinner Wednesday–Monday ($78 per person, 4-course, full-choice menu; Friday evening, $88; Saturday evening, $98 per person, 7-course, full-choice menu; beverages additional). Nearby: vineyard tours, antiquing, horse events, Skyline Drive, Shenandoah National Park.

Middleton Inn

WASHINGTON, VIRGINIA 22747

We love the rural quiet of "Little Washington." The cluster of old houses and the clutch of shops, the old post office and library belie the sophistication beneath the surface. To all outward appearances this is a rural farm village that's changed little since the nineteenth century. But we all know better.

Middleton Inn was created in 1995 by Mary Ann Kuhn, a former *Washington Post* reporter and producer for CBS-TV news. On a 1996 trip through Virginia, I heard persistent reports about her terrific new inn, so I couldn't wait to see it for myself. I was not disappointed.

The 1850s brick Federal manor house sits on a six-acre knoll just outside the town. It was built originally by Middleton Miller, who designed uniforms for the Confederate Army—thus the name.

The inn is a dream. Mary Ann proudly greeted me in the spacious center hall and took me to the living room, where wine and cheese were set out for her guests. (In summer guests relax in the afternoon on one of the spacious porches.) The living room has sunny daffodil yellow walls, plaid sofas, and a floral hassock. A border of magnolia creates a frame for the creamy marble fireplace. Oil paintings and sporting prints of foxhounds, horses, and hunting prints line the walls. The focal point, however, is a magnificent, carved rosewood, square grand pianoforte from the 1830s.

Mary Ann showed me to the Hunt Room, a spacious room with hunter green walls, a beautiful antique carved four-poster bed, with its own steps to reach it, an antique Empire bureau, a French-horn chandelier, and a fireplace. The marble bath is exquisite, with a tiny soaking tub and a full shower. All of the rooms have working fireplaces and either a porch or a veranda.

For those who want total privacy, a charming guest cottage is located nearby. It also has a fireplace, and the living room holds shelves of interesting books. Upstairs a loft bedroom has a sleigh bed and the marble bath contains a Jacuzzi.

For dinner I treated myself to a marvelous dinner at The Inn at Little Washington, where the impressive food never disappoints. When I returned I found a decanter of port and delicious chocolates awaiting me.

In the morning I awoke to the tantalizing smell of hot-from-the-oven muffins. In the elegantly dressed dining room, we savored fresh fruit and eggs Benedict. Mary Ann prepares them with smoked trout instead of Canadian bacon and they were delicious. On other days she might fix raspberry pancakes. This is the perfect place to immerse yourself in Virginia's famed hunt country. The property includes a barn, paddock, and, naturally, horses. The Virginia foxhunting point-to-point races take place near here in both spring and fall. It's a grand tradition, with roots in the steeplechases of England and people come from miles around to watch.

How to get there: From Washington, D.C., take I–66 west for 23 miles to exit 10A (Warrenton). Follow Route 29 south for 12 miles into Warrenton and turn right onto Route 211 West. Go 23 miles and turn right at the sign for the Washington Business District. Turn left at the stop sign and go 2 blocks. The inn is on the left.

Innkeeper: Mary Ann Kuhn

Address/Telephone: 176 Main Street (mailing address: P.O. Box 254); (540) 675–2020 or (800) 816–8157, fax (540) 675–1050

Rooms: 5, including 1 cottage; all with private bath, air conditioning, telephone, television, CD player, balcony or deck, and fireplace, 1 with Jacuzzi. No smoking inn.

Rates: $195 to $285, double occupancy, EPB. Two-night minimum holiday weekends and in October.

Open: All year.

Facilities and activities: Barn, paddock on premise. Nearby: restaurants, Virginia foxhunting point-to-point races, Little Washington theater, antiquing, hiking, Skyline Drive, Montpelier.

Sycamore Hill

WASHINGTON, VIRGINIA 22747

Kerri and Stephen didn't go looking for an inn. On a Sunday afternoon drive, Sycamore Hill claimed them. How could you resist? The road leading here climbs beside a bluebird trail through the inn's private meadows and forest to 1,043 feet, where their spectacular view of the Blue Ridge Mountains beckons. The fifty-two-acre property is a wildlife sanctuary certified by the National Wildlife Federation.

After I walked along the garden path and came inside, other forms of beauty caught my attention. Stephen's intricately composed drawings and airbrush paintings are a pleasure to see. "Love . . . it's never too late" is the title of one of Stephen's linoleum-block prints; it depicts a man walking deep in thought through the snow. Make it a point to see every work of Stephen's that hangs in the inn. An artist is born with a talent like this but must nurture it to become nationally recognized, as he is. You may have seen his work already.

Kerri is a former lobbyist with her own creative arenas, plants and cooking among them. As she led me through the inn, she touched a large dracena plant in passing as one might a friend. Along a shelf are more plants: two rosemary bushes, orchids, edible marigolds and nasturtiums, and miniature eggplant. Outside, beyond the curving veranda, the redbuds and dogwoods form a background for her flower bed.

The morning of your stay, breakfast, which is served promptly at 9 A.M., might include a deep-dish shrimp casserole or fresh pan-fried trout; sample the French toast and Virginia maple syrup served with a hot apricot coffee cake. Then sit on the veranda and listen to the bird songs.

The bedrooms have solid new beds and white walls trimmed in designs coordinated with the fabrics; each has a view. The oak floors gleam. Artwork is found in every room, but no antiques. The Wagners like the contemporary look of floral couches and glass coffee tables in the living room. A stone fireplace warms the room on a cool fall night. Summer is ideal up here; you can sit outdoors and rock up a breeze.

If there is a private symbol for this inn, it may be found in Lakota dream art, a form of In-dian woven art composed in string and encircled in wood, which is designed to catch dreams. Two years before Stephen and Kerri purchased the inn, he drew a sleigh bearing the two of them up a curving road to a hillside house. That house and its location look so much like their inn that I believe the drawing is a work of dream art.

Molly Bean is the inn dog. She appears indoors on request. Watch her sweeping tail near the chess board, unless you are looking for a convenient draw.

How to get there: From Warrenton go 22 miles west on Route 211, turn right toward Little Washington and immediately right again onto Route 638. Follow the road past the library to the white pillars and turn left up the hill.

Innkeepers: Kerri and Stephen Wagner

Address/Telephone: 110 Menefee Mounain Lane; (540) 675–3046

Rooms: 3, including 1 suite; all with private bath, air conditioning, and fan, 1 with television. Wheelchair accessible. No smoking inn.

Rates: $100 to $200, double occupancy, EPB. Two-night minimum weekends in spring, October, and all holidays.

Open: All year.

Facilities and activities: Gardens, 52 acres. Nearby: Inn at Little Washington, other fine restaurants, Skyline Drive, antiquing, auctions, horseback riding, tennis courts, Oasis and Linden Vineyards, hot-air balloonin, hiking, Little Washington Theater, orchards, Shenandoah Valley Golf Course.

Iris Inn
WAYNESBORO, VIRGINIA 22980

Architect designed, the Iris Inn was constructed of wood in 1991 and capped with the traditional Virginia steel roof seen on the cottages and barns throughout the area. The building's signature triangular tower and cupolas are visible from the roadway. "What is that building?" say those who pass. But guests know exactly where they are headed as they leave the interstate and drive toward the mountaintop inn. Stepping out of the car, they pause and absorb the view of the Shenandoah Valley and its surrounding mountains. Either Iris or Wayne welcome them into the great room, its 20-foot-high wall painted with a light, woodland scene. Light floods the spacious room and loft, where reading

or a nap might fill a winter's afternoon.

The inn is located outside the town of Waynesboro, known for the P. Buckley Moss Museum, factory outlets, and the making of ornamental brass and Lycra. It's near the Blue Ridge Parkway, fifteen minutes from Staunton and thirty from Charlottesville. Iris suggests leaving work early, fetching a scrumptious sandwich along the way, and arriving in time to catch the sunset from the inn's hot tub. Or bring along a batch of books and settle in for the weekend.

In the morning descend for coffee and muffins, go for a walk, and by 10 A.M. join everyone for a large breakfast around communal tables. You may enjoy an omelet, a casserole, or a stack of blueberry pancakes. Then you might treat yourself to a soak in the hot tub and the pleasures of a massage (reserve ahead).

The furnishings are new Colonial-style reproductions. Each bedroom has a woodland theme that's even expressed in each shower, where a hand-painted scene spans five or six tiles. Most rooms open directly to wide porches with valley views.

Wayne and Iris enjoy accommodating the comings and goings of their guests. Iris goes to extra effort on holidays, putting a tree in every bedroom at Christmas time. Occasionally she prepares delicious love-bird-shaped yeast rolls for guests. "I can do yeast bread in my sleep," she admits. Her kitchen is visible through the buffet window—she likes to let everyone see how clean she keeps it. Hugging her buffet window are three curious raccoons who were painted on the wall by an artist.

Business guests arrive midweek. Those who can't linger over breakfast are served granola, fruits, and hot breads.

Ninja, the black cat, who sat near the doorway on our arrival, isn't the least bit excited by the number of bird houses and feeders that surround the inn. You might bring your binoculars and make additions to your "life list." Of the inn's twenty-two acres, more than twenty have been designated forever wild and natural.

How to get there: From I–64 take exit 96 (Waynesboro-Lyndhurst), turn south on Route 624, then take the first left onto Chinquapin Drive. The entrance is ³⁄₁₀ mile on the left and climbs the hillside.

Innkeepers: Iris and Wayne Karl
Address/Telephone: 191 Chinquapin Drive; (540) 943–1991
Rooms: 7; all with private bath, telephone, fridge, television, air conditioning, 1 with Jacuzzi. Wheelchair accessible. No smoking inn.
Rates: $75 to $100, double occupancy, EPB. Two-night minimum weekends.
Open: All year.
Facilities and activities: On 21 acres. Hot tub, massage by reservation ($25 for 45 minutes). BYOB (Virginia beverage law permits wine consumption in your private room). Nearby: P. Buckley Moss Museum, Virginia Metalcrafters, Waynesboro Factory Outlet Mall, Fishburne Military School, Skyline Drive, and Blue Ridge Parkway. Vineyard tours, Wintergreen Resort for downhill skiing, golf, and horseback riding.
Business travel: Thirty minutes from Charlottesville. Telephone in room; desk in 4 rooms; corporate rates.

L'Auberge Provençale
WHITE POST, VIRGINIA 22663

It's summer. You step upon the front porch of the little French inn and find large wooden white-and-pink rabbits, turtles, carousel horses, and giraffes, which startle and amuse. They are hand carved in Spain by artisans. Celeste and Alain's art collection grows with each visit I make. Alain Borel is a fourth-generation chef from Avignon. In 1981 he and Celeste sold their Key West business and were flying their small plane to Colorado when they stopped in Virginia. They were charmed by the beauty and the tranquillity here. After a search they found their nineteenth-century stone farmhouse and became its restorers.

Throughout the cozy dining rooms are paintings and artwork. You might arrive early for dinner and browse, then retreat to the outdoor patio for an aperitif.

Alain's menu changes frequently. On the evening we met friends here, we found among the selections a Shenandoah mountain trout with sesame-seed batter and fresh tarragon. I chose the grouper served *en papillote* with vegetable julienne. It was the right blend of color, flavor, and texture. My dinner appetizer was a savory tempura-style shrimp with Thai herb sauce. Often there is fresh rabbit on the menu, along with local lamb and veal napped perhaps in a crème frâiche with mushrooms and Armagnac. For dessert, there was a light mango-and-raspberry crème brûlée. My companion chose a semisweet chocolate miniature work of art (it resembled a paper bag) filled with fresh chocolate-coated fruits. We found ourselves lingering around the dinner table on a fine summer night.

Seven of the rooms are located in two wings that the Borels added to the house. They are country fresh with Provençal wallpapers and fabrics, white eyelet spreads during summer, and wicker and antiques. There are three rooms in the inn itself (upstairs), and each has a fireplace. Celeste decorates with a friendly eye, the same way in which she greets you on arrival.

Alain's breakfasts receive the same attention as his dinners. You might dine on crepes with mango or Norwegian salmon. Afterward it's a short drive to Blandy Farm, a 250-acre arboretum filled with indigenous and exotic plants. Celeste can make advance arrangements for a private horseback-riding experience in Upper-

ville or direct you to the canoeing, which is 9 miles from the inn. Nearby are numerous antiques shops and a popular Thursday auction.

White Post, Virginia, population 200, might be small, but it has distinction. If your Dusenberg is looking shabby or you've just purchased another 1937 Cord, White Post Restorations is where car connoisseurs take their classics for restoration.

L'Auberge Provençale is located on a hillock outside of town where inn connoisseurs take their appetites for French food in a country setting, ninety minutes from Washington, D.C.

How to get there: From Washington, D.C., take I–66 west to exit 23. Follow Route 17 north for 9 miles to Route 50. Turn left onto Route 50 and go to first traffic light. Turn left onto Route 340, proceed south on 340 for 1 mile to the inn.

Innkeepers: Alain and Celeste Borel
Address/Telephone: Route 340 (mailing address: P.O. Box 119); (540) 837–1375 or (800) 638–1702, fax (540) 837–2004
Rooms: 10, including 4 suites; all with private bath and air conditioning, 5 with fireplace. Smoking permitted in sitting room only.
Rates: $150 to $220, double occupancy, EPB. Additional person $25.
Open: All year except January.
Facilities and activities: Dinner Wednesday–Sunday (5 courses: $55). On 9 acres. Gift shop. Nearby: White Post Restorations, winery tours, restored mill, antiques shops, Blandy Farm, Skyline Drive, point-to-point races, horse shows, horseback riding, Apple Blossom Festival.

The Cedars Bed & Breakfast
WILLIAMSBURG, VIRGINIA 23185

The Cedars has been welcoming guests since the 1930s, but when Carol, Jim, and Bróna Malecha purchased it in 1993, they transformed it into a bed and breakfast of the 1990s. Located just across the street from the College of William and Mary and within walking distance of Merchant Square and Colonial Williamsburg, The Cedars is a great choice in its location, style, and friendliness.

Carol greeted me in the gracious sitting room of her home, where guests often relax in the evening before the fireplace. The soul of the inn, however, is the handsome, tile-floored tavern porch. An all-season room filled with sunlight, plants, and flowers, it has eighteenth-century,

scallop-legged tables set with novelty candles in hurricanes. Tea, hot chocolate, and soft drinks are set out in the afternoon. In the evening this is a favorite place to read, play cards, or enjoy one of the many board games.

We were staying in the George Washington Suite, located on the first floor. It's a beauty. The high ceilings give dimension to the carved mahogany canopy bed and antique armoire. A sunny sitting room contains a lovely antique writing desk, and the tile-floored bath has a tile shower.

Upstairs the Plantation Room has an arched bed with a fishnet canopy and a bow-front dresser, while the Christopher Wren Room, on the top floor, has windows on three sides, a four-poster bed draped in a plum floral fabric, and a dormer window with a window seat. A cottage behind the house has two more rooms, both with fireplaces.

Carol suggested dinner at one of the re-created Colonial taverns along the streets of Colonial Williamsburg. The atmosphere is so authentic (no cars are allowed) that, as we walked along the streets, passing shopkeepers in Colonial garb, it was sometimes difficult to realize we weren't back in the eighteenth century—but, of course, that's the idea.

Carol's hobby is food and wine, so breakfast here is one of those "don't miss" affairs. She sets out an assortment of items on a hand-hewn huntboard on the tavern porch. The array is astounding and includes some of the most inventive breakfast items I've encountered. There will always be an assortment of freshly baked breads and muffins as well as a tray of fresh fruit. In addition, she might create an oatmeal-pudding en-tree. This unusual dish is made with oatmeal, eggs, milk, cottage cheese, nutmeg, and cinnamon. Brandied raisins and maple syrup are served on the side. Another specialty is a smoked-salmon flan or sausage-and-egg soufflé. To accompany the entree there will be Virginia ham biscuits or perhaps baked or poached fruit. You definitely will not go away hungry.

Ready to immerse ourselves in the Colonial attractions of Williamsburg, we were glad that we were close enough to walk, allowing some of the bountiful breakfast to settle. There's so much to do and see in and around Williamsburg that several days are necessary to see it all.

How to get there: From I–64 take exit 242A (Busch Gardens) onto Route 199. Follow Route 199 for 4 miles. Turn right onto Route 5 east (Jamestown Road). Go 1⅕ miles to The Cedars, which will be on the right.

Innkeepers: Carol, Jim, and Bróna Malecha
Address/Telephone: 616 Jamestown Road; (757) 229–3591 or (800) 296–3591
Rooms: 9, including 2 suites and 1 cottage; all with private bath and air conditioning, 2 with fireplace. No smoking inn.
Rates: $95 to $165, double occupancy, EPB. Two-night minimum holiday and special-event weekends.
Open: All year.
Facilities and activities: Nearby: golf and beaches, Colonial Williamsburg, Jamestown, Yorktown, James River Plantations, Busch Gardens.

Liberty Rose

WILLIAMSBURG, VIRGINIA 23185

If you feel as if you've been in a Colonial time warp in Williamsburg, the Liberty Rose will be a welcome change. Definitely not Colonial in feel, the inn has an eclectic style that might best be described as Southern Victorian. One thing is for sure, however: Each guest room is a thoroughly romantic retreat—a couple's paradise.

The Liberty Rose is located about a mile from Colonial Williamsburg on the way to Jamestown. On a hill surrounded by venerable beech, oak, and poplar trees, the slate-roofed clapboard inn offers a serene and relaxing retreat after visiting the numerous local historic sites.

Sandi and Brad Hirz have owned Liberty Rose for ten years. Warm and gracious, Sandi

greeted us and immediately offered a plate of freshly- baked cookies. Who could resist?

Sandi is an interior designer and the guest rooms are a reflection of her exuberant personality and eclectic taste. Rose Victoria, for example, where we were staying, has an elaborate cherry French canopy bed swagged in fringed and tasseled bed curtains. It has red damask wall coverings, a tin ceiling, and ivory woodwork. A television is hidden in an exquisite French antique walnut armoire. The bath is incredible. One wall was in a Victorian turn-of-the-century townhouse that was torn down. The wall was saved and installed here. There's an oversized clawfoot tub and a red marble shower.

Suite Williamsburg contains a massive carved ball-and-claw poster bed with bed curtains and valences in copper silk stripes and a bed cover of rose-colored jacquard fabric. A working fireplace and a bath that contains cherry paneling, a clawfoot tub, and a black Italian-tile shower make this a popular sanctuary for honeymooners. The television in this room is cleverly concealed in a swiveled box painted to look like an elaborate doll mansion. Magnolias Peach and Savannah Lace contain similarly romantic decor. The elaborate rosewood tobacco post bed in Savannah Lace is wonderful.

There are a grand parlor with a fireplace and a piano and a morning porch overlooking the gardens. Breakfast is served here. On balmy days breakfast is also served on tables in the courtyard.

Sandi is an incredible cook. One day she fixed a breakfast that included French toast stuffed with cream cheese and marmalade and topped with fresh strawberries. Alongside she served eggs and bacon. Another day she filled a croissant with thinly sliced Virginia ham, Swiss cheese, and honey mustard and heated it. This was served with country-fried potatoes, fresh fruit, and freshly baked muffins. She also makes Granny Smith apple-fritter hotcakes topped with roasted pecans. With this she serves scrambled eggs with cheese-and-sausage patties.

How to get there: From I–64, take exit 242A (Busch Gardens) onto Route 199. Follow Route 199 for 5 miles. Turn right onto Route 5/Route 31 East (Jamestown Road). Go ½ mile to the inn, which will be on the left.

Innkeepers: Brad and Sandi Hirz
Address/Telephone: 1022 Jamestown Road; (757) 253–1260 or (800) 545–1825
Rooms: 4, including 2 suites; all with private bath, air conditioning, telephone, and television, 1 with fireplace. No smoking inn.
Rates: $125 to $195, double occupancy, EPB. Two-night minimum.
Open: All year.
Facilities and activities: Gardens. Nearby: Colonial Williamsburg, Jamestown, Yorktown, Busch Gardens, golf, and beaches.

The Williamsburg Inn and Colonial Houses

WILLIAMSBURG, VIRGINIA 23187

To savor the true flavor of Colonial Williamsburg, I heartily recommend the rooms located in the restored Colonial houses. They are named for the former owners or for their uses. One is so small it's only one room and is called the Lightfoot Laundry. Another is Peter Hays' Kitchen, which honeymooners love.

They are charming, comfortable places amid the historic district and the archeological dig. You may step out the door of your home to see a shepherdess and her flock going down the street or hear the sounds of guinea hens in the yard next door. In Williamsburg, where authenticity is the byword, Colonial life is nurtured and made a modern pleasure.

Williamsburg has stopped in time; to be precise, the year of your visit is 1770, which is the year agreed upon by the Colonial "character interpreters" who've assumed the role of actual eighteenth-century Williamsburg residents and appear at appointed times and places through the village. The Reverend Samuel Henley is erudite and speaks of his students and education; Duncan Steward chats with you before the store while he awaits a shipment; and Mr. Kidd, the upholsterer, tries to sell you his wares on the street and brags about his recent jobs.

No two people experience Colonial Williamsburg in the same way. Everyone questions and listens their way through the eighty-eight buildings, talking with printers, musicians, bakers, cobblers, wig makers, carpenters, jewelers, and jailers. You dash through some and linger in others caught by what sparks your interests. At 5:00 P.M. the Colonial town closes (except for evening hours on some holidays), but the day isn't over; there are films, musical events, plays, and lectures to attend.

The houses are decorated with curtains made from Colonial patterns and filled with reproduction furniture. Wooden window blinds are hung at the windows, and upstairs the latch doors on the closets remind me it's hard to improve on some old but good inventions.

The Orell House has been so well preserved that it remains in its original state. It was here that the prime minister of Italy stayed when he came to town.

When you stay in the Colonial Houses, you should eat in one of the old taverns or the Williamsburg Inn. Everything is within walking distance. Among the former you may choose the King's Arms, Shield's Tavern, or Josiah Chowning's Tavern (on Duke of Gloucester Street), or Christiana Campbell's (a bit more distant, but also within walking distance from the heart of the Colonial restoration, on Waller Street). The decor and ambience are strictly Colonial, and you will be served by waitresses and waiters in Colonial dress. Each restaurant has a different menu, but you might have roasted chicken or perhaps a Colonial game pie, fixed with venison, duck, and rabbit. For dessert you might select a buttered apple pie or a sour-cherry trifle.

How to get there: Directions given by the inn. Fly-in: Williamsburg Airport.

Innkeeper: Brian O'Day; Orene Coffman and Ted Horn, assistant managers
Address/Telephone: Francis Street (mailing address: P.O. Box 1776); (804) 229–1000 or (800) HISTORY, fax (804) 220–7096
Rooms: 82, in 26 houses; all with private bath, telephone, television, and air conditioning, most with fireplace. Wheelchair accessible. Pets allowed on a limited basis. Designated no smoking rooms.
Rates: $129 to $180, Colonial Houses; $129 to $299, inn; double occupancy; EP. Package plans. Four-night minimum at Christmastime.
Open: All year.
Facilities and activities: Breakfast, lunch, afternoon tea, dinner, bar in nearby taverns and inn. All facilities of the Williamsburg Inn: golf, swimming pools, parlors, Sunday recitals, Christmas yulelog ceremonies.
Business travel: Telephone, desk, and dataport all rooms; fax, copier, cellular telephones available; business center with secretarial services, computers; audiovisual equipment; conference center.

Trillium House

WINTERGREEN, VIRGINIA 22958

The flag swayed gently in the summer breeze, the rhododendrons were in bloom, and on the porch a pottery cask of iced tea looked inviting. We had returned to Trillium House, the architect designed four-season inn built by Ed and Betty Dinwiddie in 1983. They named their mountain inn for the spring flowers that blossom in the woods around the inn, and from the beginning they've instilled the place with warm ambience.

The Dinwiddies had wanted a unique way of life and gave up their homes, boat, and previous careers for full-time innkeeping. Their three children (and respective spouses) are occasional inn assistants.

In winter the forest is frosted with snow, and a short distance downhill are the ski slopes. A walk up the hill and you're golfing. Cross the road and you slip into the clear waters of an indoor or outdoor pool. There are 20 miles of trails here and more along nearby Blue Ridge Parkway. Any direction takes you into the natural beauty of rolling hills, mountains, and valleys.

Above the inn's entrance is an exquisite Jefferson Palladian window. You enter a spacious living room, where three golden organ pipes are mounted on the soaring chimney. You circle the wood-burning stove on Oriental carpets near stacks of magazines and Betty's collection of perfume bottles. Surrounding the wide balcony is a 6,000-volume library.

In an alcove is a big-screen television and a collection of movies. There are occasions when guests like to watch a favorite late movie on a winter night. Nearby Ed and Betty have designed a nifty bar—order something and you'll see it appear.

At breakfast you can watch the birds from the windowed dining room while biting into the scrumptious French toast plump with a cheese filling and all the trimmings and think ahead to dinner. Ellen English is a very talented chef whose creations have become deliciously synonymous with Trillium. She serves a four-course meal (single entree) on Friday and Saturday evenings. You happily remember what you've eaten here.

You might have shrimp-filled phyllo purses with hot peanut sauce, spinach-orange salad with curry vinaigrette, lemon-grass beef tenderloin with rice stuffing and soy-scallion beurre blanc, a vegetable medley, and homemade pineapple ice cream. I'd make a reservation and go expecting pleasurable, interesting tastes. Special wine-tasting dinners are occasionally held, showcasing Virginia wines and Ellen's cuisine.

You can sit before the fire, pet the chocolate Lab, Jemimah, and be at ease. Perhaps you've signed up for the Orvis fly-fishing school (Ed is a graduate), horseback riding, or a guided walk in the woods with a naturalist. But that's tomorrow.

How to get there: Directions sent with gate pass.

Innkeepers: Ed and Betty Dinwiddie

Address/Telephone: Wintergreen Drive (mailing address: P.O. Box 280, Nellysford, VA 22958); (804) 325–9126; for reservations (800) 325–9126 (9:00 A.M. to 8:00 P.M.), fax (804) 325–1099

Rooms: 12, including 2 suites; all with private bath, telephone, and air conditioning; television available. No smoking in guest rooms.

Rates: $95 to $160, double occupancy, EPB. Additional person $35. Lower rate midweek. Two-night minimum weekends.

Open: All year.

Facilities and activities: Dinner by reservation Friday and Saturday ($20–$26), full beverage license. Activities at 11,000 acre Wintergreen Resort (additional charge), including skiing, nature trails, indoor swimming pool, outdoor pool, fitness center, whirlpool spa, golf, tennis, horseback riding, picnicking, 16-acre lake for boating and fishing, mountains and valleys. Nearby: restaurants, Monticello, Ash Lawn, Woodrow Wilson Birthplace, antiquing, universities, factory outlets.

Business travel: Desk in 4 rooms; telephone in all rooms; fax and copier available.

The Inn at Narrow Passage
WOODSTOCK, VIRGINIA 22664

Good, clean, old-fashioned comfort abounds here. Step up on the porch and settle into a white cedar chair in the summer or snuggle in before the fire in the winter. A few yards away is the Shenandoah River. You're in the midst of the Shenandoah Valley, and not far are a winery, and a summer music festival, and Orvis fly-fishing instructor Harry Murray, to whom Ed will introduce you on request for instructions.

The log-cabin inn built in 1740 grew in increments, which Ed and Ellen Markel point out while relating the inn's history. It was here that Stonewall Jackson said to Jedediah Hotchkiss in 1862, "Make me a map of the valley." They've created a fresh new inn within the historic Early

American structure. I suspect it's the most inviting of all lives for the inn. Located overlooking the Narrow Passage where colonists forged west, the area was the scene of Indian ambushes and skirmishes. But the log cabin that often protected the westward-bound travelers stood because the Indians themselves liked to retreat inside.

From the inn you can walk casually in five minutes to the banks of the famed Shenandoah River for fishing and swimming. Ed will drive canoers to a nearby departure point that puts you on a three-hour canoe ride back to the inn. In the evening some guests drive to nearby Orkney Springs for the Shenandoah Valley Music Festival. Beginning in July and lasting through Labor

Day, there are weekend outdoor concerts. First you might have a traditional Southern dinner at the Orkney Springs Hotel (dates from the mid-1800s) or bring a picnic supper to enjoy on the lawn.

The rooms are warmly and prettily furnished with antiques, Colonial reproductions, and custom-made beds. Four have nifty trundle beds for the children. In the room where Stonewall Jackson slept, you can sleep under a homemade quilt, covered by a hand-tied fisherman's knot canopy.

Downstairs is a large, paneled dining room where a cheery fire is usually burning. The aroma of Ellen's coffee cakes and sizzling bacon will lure you down the stairs for a full, hearty meal. You might have French toast or a batch of scrambled eggs and fresh blueberry muffins.

Colonial tin lights hang throughout the inn, and the Markels have had so many questions and requests for the fixtures that they've opened a small gift shop.

Occasionally a talented guest will sit down and play Ellen's piano. In the large double-fireplace living room hangs a relief map of the Appalachians; it's with relief you pull off Route 11, to be protected from the skirmishes of life in friendly surroundings.

How to get there: From I–81 take exit 283 toward Route 11 south. The inn is 2 miles south on U.S. 11, on the left side of the road.

Innkeepers: Ed and Ellen Markel

Address/Telephone: Route 11 South at Route 672 (Chapman Landing Road) (mailing address: P.O. Box 608); (540) 459–8000 or (800) 459–8002, fax (540) 459–8001

Rooms: 12; all with private bath and air conditioning, 7 with fireplace and telephone. Wheelchair accessible. No smoking inn.

Rates: $90 to $110, double occupancy, EPB. Two-night minimum weekends in spring, fall, and on holidays.

Open: All year except Christmas and 1 week in winter and 1 week in summer (call for exact dates).

Facilities and activities: On 5 acres. Shenandoah River canoeing and fishing. Nearby: restaurants (within 3 miles), Orkney Springs, New Market Battlefield, Belle Grove Plantation, Shenandoah Caverns, Shenandoah Valley Music Festival, skiing at Bryce Mountain, horseback riding, antiquing.

Business travel: Telephone with dataport and desk in 4 rooms; conference room.

The Kalorama Guest House at Woodley Park

WASHINGTON, D.C. 20008

The Kalorama is a convenient and unusual place for Washington. If you don't mind sharing a bathroom, or funky furnishings, you may feel right at home here. There is a blend of antiques in the parlor and a sunny breakfast room, where everyone seems to gravitate in the morning.

This solidly built brick townhouse dates from 1910; on the walls are old copies of the original real estate advertisements enticing prospective residents to visit this Woodley Park home. Car ads on the wall show a Franklin, a Rambler, and a Peerless—you might have driven one here had you been house-shopping in 1910.

The rooms are furnished with a collection of older pieces; I prefer the rooms on the main and upper levels. All the rooms have a warm, pleasing appeal, thanks to the attentions of Birdie. She opened her inn in 1982. A pleasant staff helps out.

Located several blocks from the zoo and Connecticut Avenue in a residential neighborhood, the inn is less than 3 blocks to the Metro and a thirty-minute ride to the Smithsonian.

The Kalorama provides laundry facilities along with ironing boards and pay phones in the basement for outgoing calls. Messages are taken and left at a central message center. Half a block away is a second townhouse that's part of the inn. You may want to be in the main inn near the breakfast room, although both buildings have nice, old-fashioned, and comfortable parlors.

Munching on croissants, bagels, or English muffins and sipping your morning coffee over a paper, you could meet anyone—an actor in a play at the Kennedy Center, or Australians touring the States. The neighborhood is convenient for walking to restaurants and has a handsome architecture. Several embassies are located throughout the nearby streets.

How to get there: Directions given with reservation.

Innkeepers: Rick Fenstemaker, Mary Ann and Mike Gallagher; Birdie Pieczenick, proprietor

Address/Telephone: 2700 Cathedral Avenue, NW; (202) 328–0860, fax (202) 328–8730

Rooms: 19, including 2 suites; 12 with private bath, all with air conditioning. No smoking inn.

Rates: $50 to $115, single or double occupancy, continental breakfast. Parking, $7 a day. Two-night minimum April–June, September–October, and special events.

Open: All year.

Facilities and activities: Guest refrigerator and laundry facilities. Nearby: Parking lot and Metro (3 blocks away), restaurants, National Zoo. Smithsonian Museums, Kennedy Center, Corcoran Art Gallery, National Arboretum, Folger Theater, Arena Stage, National Portrait Gallery, White House, and many other sites.

Business travel: Ten-minute Metro ride to downtown. Phone, desk, fax, and 24-hour answering service available.

Recommended Country Inns® Traveler's Club Benefit: 10 percent discount, Monday–Thursday, subject to availability.

M orrison-Clark

The word "brunch" dates from 1895—how appropriate that we were having brunch in a Victorian setting. My champagne glass had been filled almost the minute we sat down, and my companion had already polished off his first glass of free-flowing bubbly. The three-course menu tantalized him into negotiating what I might share so that he could sample a spectrum of flavors.

"The vegetables alone," I said, "are reputedly worth coming here for." I had inside knowledge. My friend Adele had been here and raved; Adele is never wrong. Covetously, I think, my companion studied my warm winter-vegetable salad with sherry-shallot vinaigrette, after he'd tasted his pear-and-fig compote. I shared my

vegetables with him and watched his composure return. The first course had been a draw, his as good as mine.

Meanwhile he'd noted the Victorian floor-to-ceiling mirrors that had once been covered with eleven coats of gray paint. From 1923 until the inn was restored a few years ago, this was the Soldiers, Sailors, Marines, and Airmens Club. We learned that a specialist, William Adair, had stripped the mirrors to the natural wood and exposed the original gold-leaf trim.

"Only a specialist could do that," my companion averred. Indeed, Adair had worked his magic on other restorations in town, including the White House.

For the main course I chose a pan-fried rainbow trout with bacon-garlic-parsley sauce; he ordered corn-pecan pancakes with country ham and orange butter. We called a halt to the champagne to clear the palate and the mind. (We did have a museum or two yet to visit that afternoon.)

The inn is named for neighbors, Mr. David L. Morrison and Mr. Reuben B. Clark, who owned the townhouses that form the most elegant part of the inn. An addition came later, in the early 1900s. The inn has a small reception parlor and a vase filled with a large spray of flowers centers the foyer. Above the check-in desk is a turn-of-the-century Sears Kit clock. In the English basement there's a workout room, with weights, an exercise bicycle, and treadmills.

The neighborhood is urban; the inn is located only 4 blocks from the Metro and the convention center. This makes the inn popular with New Yorkers, who find it easy to reach via train and cab.

The rooms have three styles. Small rooms furnished country style with light pine armoires and beds face the courtyard. Contemporary rooms have platform beds. The grander, larger, Victorian rooms overlook Massachusetts Avenue.

In the morning you gather your continental breakfast and have a seat in the formal Club Room Dining Room (named for its former incarnation) or the courtyard patio.

How to get there: From I–95 south take exit 22-B, Baltimore Washington Parkway, to Washington, D.C. Follow signs and exit New York Avenue in 5 miles. Continue 4⁷⁄₁₀ miles on New York Avenue to Sixth Street NW. Cross Sixth Street (you're now on L Street) and continue to Eleventh Street. Inn is on right on corner. Short-term parking in front for unloading. Fly-in from National Airport: take Metro to Metro Center and exit L Street. Inn is 4-block walk.

Innkeeper: Bill Petrella; R.B. Associates, proprietor
Address/Telephone: 1101 Eleventh Street, NW; (202) 861–8200 or (800) 332–7898, fax (202) 289–8576
Rooms: 54, including 13 suites; all with private bath, air conditioning, telephone, refrigerator, and cable television, 3 with fireplace. Wheelchair accessible. Designated no smoking rooms.
Rates: $135 to $185, double occupancy, continental breakfast. Weekend rates, especially during summer. Covered, valet parking, $10 per day.
Open: All year.
Facilities and activities: Dinner served nightly ($18 to $22), lunch Monday–Friday ($11 to $20), and Sunday brunch ($20). Fitness center. Nearby: Metro stop (4 blocks), Smithsonian Museum, Kennedy Center.
Business travel: Five-minute Metro ride to downtown. Telephone with dataport in room; desk in 36 rooms; fax and copier available; meeting room; corporate rates.
Recommended Country Inns® Traveler's Club Benefit: Stay two nights, get third night free, subject to availability.

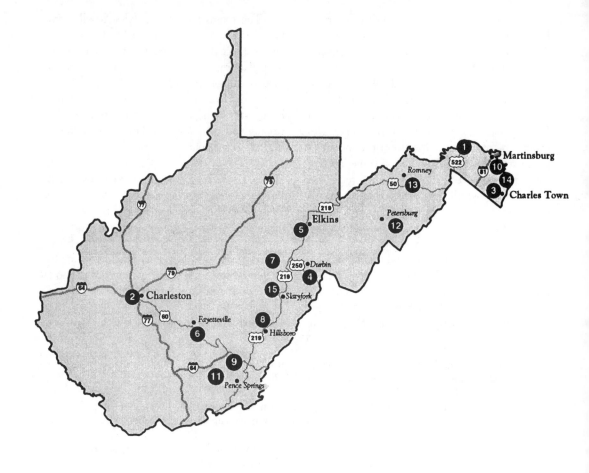

West Virginia

West Virginia

Numbers on map refer to towns numbered below.

The Country Inn
BERKELEY SPRINGS, WEST VIRGINIA 25411

The Country Inn is in town. It's adjacent to the mineral springs and Roman-style baths of Berkeley Springs. Warring Indians laid down their weapons and came to the springs for peace and tranquillity. People now come for massages, facials, and whirlpool baths. The inn's contemporary art gallery is also part of the entertainment.

Several of the rooms are decorated with iron-steel-and-brass beds (a composition) built by a local craftsman. Country Inn West is a large brick building that's more contemporary in style. The newest rooms are suites furnished with the locally made Sealy furniture in cherry.

Wherever you sleep it's only a few steps to the

Renaissance Spa, with contemporary spotless, private whirlpool baths (book the one overlooking the town). You can also have a pedicure, manicure, or facial, or have your hair cut and styled. Afterward you can shop in the posh boutique.

The Country Inn was built of brick in 1932. In 1972 longtime owners Jack and Alice Barker added Country Inn West, which is connected by a covered walkway. Guests are encouraged to wander through the lovely gardens and to put the rockers on the front lawn to good use.

The Garden Room is an indoor dining room with a small sunken dance floor. Saturday night this is the place to trot out your fox trot. First you dine on prime rib of beef, or a steak

Diane prepared tableside. For dessert a cup of coffee and the Kentucky pie are popular. Or a strawberry flambé will give you some dancing energy for the big band sounds. For a good value request a seating for the early-bird dinner.

To inform yourself about the area, request the inn's "Looking for Something to Do?" list. Adjacent to the inn are reasonably priced public spas; up the hill is Berkeley Castle; there's an antiques mall in town; and golfers, like my travel-ing companion, like the local golf course.

On my way back to the gallery, I paused in the lobby. From here I saw the sign above the door: TARRY LONG AT REST AND TABLE, HASTE YE BACK IF YE ARE ABLE.

How to get there: From I–81 take Route 522 north to Berkeley Springs. The inn is on the west side of the road just before the town square.

Innkeepers: Jack and Alice Barker; Sharon Durand, general manager

Address/Telephone: 207 South Washington Street; (304) 258–2210 or (800) 822–6630, fax (304) 258–3986

Rooms: 70, including honeymoon, executive, and family suites; 61 with private bath and telephone, all with air conditioning and television. Wheelchair access. Designated no smoking rooms.

Rates: $40 to $145, double occupancy, EP. Two-night minimum weekends April–October.

Open: All year.

Facilities and activities: Breakfast, lunch, dinner, bar. Art gallery, gift shop, whirlpool baths and health spa, massages ($45, 45 minutes) and facials, public swimming pool adjacent, state park. Nearby: hiking, antiquing, Robert Trent Jones Golf Course, 10 miles.

Business travel: Telephone, fax and copier available; meeting rooms with audiovisual equipment; corporate rates.

Highlawn Inn
BERKELEY SPRINGS, WEST VIRGINIA 25411

Sandra first came to Berkeley Springs to relax. She left her work far behind, took the waters, had a massage, and liked the pleasure of walking along small-town streets. Finally the appeal of the town overcame her. She noticed the house high on the hill was for sale and made Berkeley Springs her home. She still follows a weekly tradition of taking the waters and massage. Most guests take advantage of the same experience.

Berkeley Springs is an affordable holiday. For $25 to $40 you can have a Roman bath and spend twenty minutes in total privacy bathing in 750 gallons of spring water, followed by a half-hour massage. Ten miles away Cacapon State

Park has lovely walking trails, swimming, tennis, a riding stable, and a public Robert Trent Jones Golf Course.

The inn was originally built as a summer house in 1897. The hallways are thickly carpeted, and the rooms are cozy with lace curtains and antique beds. In my comfortable room was a table where I sat in the summer sun and wrote; the massage had given me a burst of energy and clarity of mind. I might have chosen a spot in the garden, however, or maybe on the wraparound porch.

For breakfast we were seated at a small English-pub table. A buffet-style meal upon silver service was arrayed along a side table. You might dip into a hot casserole made with cheeses and herbs from the garden. The fresh fruits include baked apples, strawberries in season, and freshly squeezed orange juice. Pastries range from buttermilk biscuits (a specialty) to chocolate-chip and sour cream coffee cake, wild-blueberry muffins, or Black Forest brownies. A scrumptious baked potato casserole could appear, made with fresh dill, scallions, and lemon and sprinkled with freshly grated cheese.

Every Saturday night May through October, Sandra hosts a five-course dinner party, where she might serve a Cornish game hen with apple dressing topped with lingonberry sauce along with soup, salad, vegetables, and fresh breads.

Each October on Columbus Day Weekend, the town organizes an old-fashioned Apple Butter Festival. Crafts and foods, music, and the scent of homemade apple butter fill the air. A more quiet time at the inn is Thanksgiving Day, when Sandra performs her cooking skills for guests with a traditional dinner that's become popular. Or come for her five-course, candlelit holiday dinners (request menu).

Every February the town hosts an International Water Tasting contest, which my companion and I attended. It was a ball and gave us an appreciation for Berkeley Spring's ever-flowing clean water. Ask Sandra for the brochure that includes this and other special local events, such as concerts, wine tastings, and lecture-discussions at the local café.

How to get there: From north or south take Route 522 into Berkeley Springs. Turn east onto Market Street to the inn at the top of a steep hill. In winter you may want to turn 1 block before or after and climb hill on less steep approach.

Innkeeper: Sandra Kauffman

Address/Telephone: 304 Market Street; (304) 258–5700 or (800) CALLWVA

Rooms: 10, including 1 suite; all with private bath, television, and air conditioning, 2 with whirlpool, 1 with fireplace.

Rates: $85 to $175, double occupancy, EPB. Two-night minimum weekends April–November and holidays December–March.

Open: All year except Christmas Eve and Christmas Day.

Facilities and activities: Dinner Saturdays, May–October, by reservation ($43 per person); Thanksgiving Dinner for guests. Nearby: restaurants, massages, and mineral spring waters of Berkeley Springs State Park; hiking, Robert Trent Jones Golf Course, antiquing mall, historic castle, Cacapon State Park.

Recommended Country Inns® Travelers' Club Benefit: Discounts for certain rooms, Monday–Thursday, December–April, subject to availability.

The Brass Pineapple
CHARLESTON, WEST VIRGINIA 25311

It was so quiet that the ticking of the antique clock on the dining room mantel echoed through the room and across the parlor. The sound momentarily drew attention from the classic, formal warmth. An afghan lay across the love seat beside the unicorn tapestry pillow. The first daffodils of spring filled a vase. We plotted our dinner in advance and studied the menu describing grilled specialties and homemade pastas.

Sue's assistant led us up to our elegant room. We couldn't miss the stained-glass windows on the stairway depicting love birds. When a couple built a house at the turn of the century, it was customary to signify their love in some visual art form.

In our room was an antique bedroom suite and attractive wallpaper. That room also had a beautiful Victorian dresser—one of many striking antiques throughout the inn.

"We should have been born a hundred years ago," Sue said of herself and her husband as she described the restoration puzzles, such as the spindles found in the basement that now fit perfectly into a beautiful railing. Most of the exquisite stained glass is original.

When we went for a walk through Charleston's historic East End, we could see the golden dome of the state capitol building. We passed many Craftsman-influenced designs from the early twentieth century.

Sue is accustomed to hearing people praise the beauty of the inn, a sand-colored brick mansion built in Craftsman style. She also has rural lodgings out in the country called the Benedict Haid Farm, which explains the ostrich egg with a pineapple painted on it sitting beside the front door. On the farm is a pair of ostriches who'd recently gone to Texas to be professionally bred.

Every one of the rooms is handsome; you'll probably select according to bed size and whether you want a private bath directly in the room or a few steps away. The Grandmother's Room, decorated with P. Buckley Moss prints, is located on the third floor, opposite the Hearts and Flowers Room with the king-sized bed. Two baths have marble showers.

At breakfast we feasted on Belgian waffles, selected the night before. Glasses of freshly squeezed orange juice sat at our places and Mozart masked the clock's tick-tock and soft half-hourly chime.

After breakfast Sue led the way to the outdoor patio, where soon the iron tables and chairs would be beckoning. She has found old balusters from another house that was being torn down and saved them to compose a small patio; it suits the inn perfectly.

How to get there: From I–64 take exit 99 (Capitol exit), turn south onto Greenbrier Street, and continue to second light. Turn right onto Kanawha Boulevard, right onto Elizabeth Street, and take another right onto Virginia Street. Look for waving brass pineapple flag and American flag on the right, park behind inn.

Innkeeper: Sue Pepper
Address/Telephone: 1611 Virginia Street East; (304) 344–0748 or (800) CALLWVA, fax (304) 344–0748
Rooms: 6, including 1 suite; all with private bath, telephone, television, VCR, and air conditioning. No smoking inn.
Rates: $70 to $100, double occupancy, EPB and afternoon tea. Additional person, $25.
Open: All year.
Facilities and activities: Bicycles, video library. Nearby: State Capitol, West Virginia Cultural Center, Sunrise: restored mansion, planetarium, and children's museum, cruise aboard *West Virginia Belle*, dog racing, antiques shopping, and seasonal events—Sternwheel Regatta ends Labor Day.
Business travel: Telephone with dataport and desk in room; fax available; guest laundry, valet services, courtesy airport and train pickup service. Corporate apartments available complete with kitchens. Conference facilities at Benedict Haid House, 10 miles away.
Recommended Country Inns® Travelers' Club Benefit: Stay two nights, get third night free, subject to availability.

Hillbrook Inn
CHARLES TOWN, WEST VIRGINIA 25414

Hillbrook is a romantic European hideaway in the lush gentle countryside of West Virginia, where you're smitten by the peace and solitude. After traveling and working around the world and staying in inns, Gretchen Carroll arrived by happenstance one rainy afternoon; the rest is champagne and candlelight.

Hillbrook was built during the Roaring Twenties of stone, timber, and stucco and was terraced with these materials to form a grand country house. Entry is into the living room, with fireplace burning, Oriental rugs, and artworks to be appreciated; an atmosphere of casual elegance reigns. You notice the theme of people's faces in Gretchen's artwork and find interesting books on

foreign travels adjacent to carvings, pottery, and prints.

Two bedrooms are off the living room; one is reached by climbing a stairway, where a private balcony gives you a superior view. The downstairs room has a small private porch and fireplace. A third room is near the library. The rooms are uniquely furnished with antique or brass beds, down comforters, and Gretchen's worldly treasures, such as an antique Vuitton trunk.

Dinner is an absolute affair with flavors. It's served by reservation at a fixed price and set menu; it is a seven-course palatable event. We began with a tasty tapenade artfully arranged, then came a creamy, tangy carrot-and-orange soup, after that an absolutely delicious hot pasta. The entree was veal served with tastefully seasoned broccoli and squash; then a salad arrived, followed by a superb cheese plate with English crackers; last came a perfect chocolate cake. Each table in the room was set differently; ours had black candles that burned exuberantly until after midnight, when we finished our brandies and congratulated the chef for a fine meal.

For daytime excursions Gretchen suggests a route that takes you past several wonderful antiques shops and an excellent winery, where you can have a picnic lunch (conveniently prepared by the first antiques shop). You might prefer to remain at the inn, walk through the garden with Gretchen, to admire the Chippendale bridge with its iron lion's heads, take a nap in the hammock down by the stream, sip a glass of wine on the patio, delve into a basketful of books beside the fireplace, or simply lie back and catch up on your daydreams.

How to get there: From I–270 take I–70 west to Route 340 west. Past Harper's Ferry take Route 51 west to Charles Town. Continue on Route 51 West to Route 13 (Summit Point Road), which bears off to left at west end of town. Go $4\frac{8}{10}$ miles on Route 13 to the inn on your left (past elementary school on right). Watch for stone pillars.

Innkeeper: Gretchen Carroll

Address/Telephone: Route 13 (mailing address: Route 2, Box 152); (304) 725–4223 or (800) 304–4223, fax (304) 725–4455

Rooms: 6; all with private bath, telephone, and air conditioning, 2 with fireplace, 1 with whirlpool.

Rates: $198 to $450, double occupancy, MAP, including wine.

Open: All year.

Facilities and activities: On 17 acres with pond and stream. Dinner (by reservation) for guests not spending the night ($60 to $68). Nearby: antiquing, tour Shepherdstown or Harper's Ferry, Summit Point Raceway, bicycling, and hiking on C & O Canal Towpath.

Business travel: Desk in two rooms; fax and copier available; meeting room.

Recommended Country Inns® Travelers' Club Benefit: Stay two nights, get third night free, Monday–Thursday.

Cheat Mountain Club

DURBIN, WEST VIRGINIA 26264

I care not the season when I come here, since the inherent beauty of pine forest, river, and mountain sunsets dons each seasonal mantle as smoothly as a queen her cape and crown.

My first impression is no less vivid for the lapse of time. We arrived on a hot summer's day amid the lustrous green space and tall trees that surround the inn, then heard the Shavers Fork River tumbling coolly over rocks. We had lunch on the patio, lazing in deep wooden chairs and eating hearty sandwiches, pasta salad, and large chocolate brownies.

If you come in spring, summer, or fall, the hiking and mountain biking are endless: The inn's acreage is contiguous with the 900,000-acre Monongahela National Forest. On a recent visit, though, we'd come to witness the wintry scape. Within minutes of arrival we were clipped into skis and moving upriver. Along the trail the rhododendron stood as tall as 15 feet. Once, while we rested, we listened to cracking river ice and heard a woodpecker hammering; we watched as wood flecks fell from his 60-foot-high perch.

Back at the lodge a fire was burning in the great room's stone fireplace, and several guests were visiting. The lodge was built of spruce and pine a century ago by a German fish biologist. It's located at 3,600 feet, where the climate is reminiscent of Canada. The rooms have pine walls and maple furnishings; they are quite comfortable. Most share the large, clean, health-club–style men's and women's bathrooms.

In summer you might take the canoes on the Shavers Fork for the afternoon, go for a walk along the river to the old fort embankments, or take a fly-fishing lesson.

At dinnertime upon white linen table-cloths are arrayed delicious foods, such as the chicken with Marsala wine sauce that came with fresh vegetables and breads—which fragrantly scent the inn while baking. Near the honor bar Gladys stocks fresh fruits, cookies, and granolas for between-meal snacks. For hikers who are planning to spend the day in the woods, she packs scrumptious lunches. The single-entree dining means the freshest of everything is ex-

pertly prepared. In the summer they often grill steaks, chicken, and occasionally ribs outdoors. Breakfast specialties include buckwheat pancakes and a wonderful sausage grilled on a large coal- and wood-burning stove.

The naturalist John Burroughs gathered Thomas Edison, Henry Ford, and Harvey Firestone for a caravan trip here back in 1918. They called themselves the vagabonds, and they liked this place, too.

How to get there: From the intersection of Route 250 and Route 92 near Monterrey, proceed 12½ miles north on Route 250 to the inn sign on the left. The inn is about 2 miles from the first sign.

Innkeepers: Gladys Boehmer

Address/Telephone: Route 250 (mailing address: P.O. Box 28); (304) 456–4627, fax (304) 456–3192

Rooms: 8, including 1 suite and third floor dormitory; all with sink, 1 with private bath, separate bath facilities for men and women. Cribs and rollaways available. No pets, but boarding facility nearby. No smoking in guest rooms.

Rates: $80 to $150, per person, double occupancy, AP. Children under 5, $25; 6 to 12, half adult rate. Three-night minimum some holiday weekends.

Open: All year.

Facilities and activities: 180 acres; located on Shavers Fork River. Service bar. Cheat Mountain Outfitting and Guide Service, short walk from lodge has mountain bikes, cross-country skis, canoes, and fishing equipment for rent. Funyaks, badminton, softball, croquet, soccer available at lodge. Nearby: Cass Scenic Railroad.

Tunnel Mountain Bed and Breakfast
ELKINS, WEST VIRGINIA 26241

What brings you to Elkins? Small-town life? Quiet woodland walks? A fresh trout dinner served on the patio beside a rushing stream? Or the musical performances that bustle the town during Augusta Days? Perhaps you'll come as I did for a short trip, find it suits you, then happily return to stay at this little inn.

The inn, built in 1939 of stone and wood, has a warm lodge feeling. It's located a mere 2 miles from the entrance to the sixty-five-acre Stuart Recreation Area, which offers hiking, mountain biking, and swimming. In the winter bring cross-country skis; outdoors-lovers Anne and Paul may have already tracked a path into the woods. In the summer you can swim at the lake or drive to the top of Stuart for a terrific Appalachian view.

The Beardslees are former academics who've retreated from university life to the woods. In the living room a former chemistry cabinet stores games for guests. On a shelf above sits Paul's prized collection of well-used iron toys. A pie safe in the foyer is filled with samplers and baskets made by Anne.

Paul once taught mapmaking, so he's composed a map with their favorite places. Anne pointed to Dolly Sods, where I had recently met people catching birds in large nets strung along the mountain's edge for an annual bird count. She also mentioned Augusta Days, an arts-and-music program held at the Elkins & Davis College. I ventured over to the college and entered the first convenient doorway. Rippling through the building were the sounds of banjos and guitars. Evening performances and jam sessions might include Delta blues, Irish reels, or old-time picking. Daytime events run the gamut from poetry writing, herb growing, and storytelling to dancing and woodworking. Reasonable prices and quality entertainment attract sell-out crowds, so guests often book a year in advance.

Book early, whenever you plan to arrive, and you'll get my favorite room—the one with the queen-sized bed on the third floor (garret style) that's paneled in rare wormy chestnut. Another favorite is the room with the antique canopy bed that Anne inherited. The third room has the solidly built maple bed that Paul inherited. It's endowed with a traditional hand-tied mattress.

The tunnel in the inn's name is a railroad tunnel that runs beneath their mountain location. It's buried so deeply that only peace and quiet prevail. One might hear birds and a breeze through the trees or see the winter deer feeding on the lawn. First to greet you might be Jessie or Molly, the golden retrievers.

Downtown Elkins, which was built on timber and railroad wealth, is surprisingly flat for its mountainous surroundings. On a tip from the innkeepers, I visited a bookstore-restaurant combination called the Starr Café. You can browse among the books while you wait for your order, and the food is good. The owner said she came to Elkins and liked it so much that she never left.

How to get there: From I–79 take Weston/Buckhannon exit onto Route 33/119 east (this will become Route 33). Continue on Route 33. Four miles east of Elkins, turn north at the directional sign pointing to Stuart Recreational Area. Go 1/10 mile; inn is on the left.

Innkeepers: Anne and Paul Beardslee
Address/Telephone: Elkins (mailing address: Route 1, Box 59-1); (304) 636–1684
Rooms: 3; all with private bath, air conditioning, and television, 1 with electric fireplace. Designated no smoking room.
Rates: $70 to $75, double occupancy, EPB (continental breakfast during Augusta Days). Two-night minimum holiday and festival weekends. Ten percent off for AARP.
Open: All year.
Facilities and activities: On 5 acres; half-mile private trail, patio. Nearby: restaurants; Stuart Recreation Area for hiking, swimming, mountain biking, fishing, and cross-country skiing; Augusta Heritage Arts and Crafts Workshops; Augusta Heritage Festival.

The White Horse Bed & Breakfast

FAYETTEVILLE, WEST VIRGINIA 25840

"Ooohwee!" Joy, our raft guide, emitted a sound I'd never heard but one that perfectly described our ride through that most recent rapid. We were white-water rafting with Class VI Outfitters on the New River, one of the best rafting-canoeing rivers on the East Coast. Eight novice strangers at 9:00 A.M. had coalesced by noon into an amiable team. We paddled furiously through fifteen rapids, swam or drifted in current, and listened to the history of five mining towns, now ghost towns, that once thrived down the 16-mile-long stretch we traveled. By 4:30 P.M. we were happily on our way to luxury for the evening.

"I always wanted a carousel horse," admitted Jane, "so we asked our seventy-year-old friend who's a bird carver to make one for us. He called other makers, studied horses' gaits and physique, and became as smitten as us in the effort." I appreciate remarkable efforts like this, but no less remarkable is the engaging beauty of Jane and Cleon's restoration project.

After a refreshing shower in our room's grand old tiled bathroom (characteristic throughout), we went on a tour. Jane and Cleon, who have always liked large places, previously owned a home dated from the year 1906; curiously, The White Horse Bed & Breakfast is Gothic Revival in style and also dates from 1906. It was built by the local sheriff and his prisoners.

You can imagine them laying the intricately patterned parquet, applying fabric over the three-plaster walls, or installing the tile work in the bathrooms.

The Voslers first came to this area with their children for the quality of the white-water rafting. They previously lived in other mid-Atlantic cities, where Cleon was a corporate executive. As we visited in the parlor, a masculine room furnished with his collections, including carved birds, we gained insights about the area.

The other guest areas are more feminine in nature and include a wicker-filled sunroom that calls out for you to come with a good book and where you walk on carpeting so thick you think it might touch your ankles. Through the door is the Victorian music room, with a formal sitting library and a piano.

Breakfast, which is served in the ambassado-rial dining room, varies depending on the number of guests. If there are only two at the table, Jane prepares whatever you like, perhaps a light cheese omelet with a rasher of bacon. When there are several guests, she often serves Thomas Jefferson Casserole, an apple-and-egg puff pastry coated lightly with brown sugar, or a delicious crumbled bread-cheese-and-sausage omelet.

The dining-room walls are painted with an exotic and lovely mural; parts of it appear to be scenes of the Argentine, others of Egypt, and some scenes are pure jungle. On the sideboard was a crystal decanter of sherry and a small silver bell. It's a grand setting with informal, fun hosts.

How to get there: From I–77 traveling north, exit onto Route 19 north at Beckley. Fayetteville is 23 miles north. The inn is in residential Fayetteville. Directions given with reservations.

Innkeepers: Jane and Cleon Vosler
Address/Telephone: 120 Fayette Avenue; (304) 574–1400 or (800) CALLWVA
Rooms: 7, including 1 suite and 1 cottage; all with ceiling fan, 3 with private bath. Pets allowed. No smoking inn.
Rates: $80 to $110, double occupancy, EPB. 2-night minimum in cottage. Less off-season; call. Senior citizens or 3-day stay, 10 percent discount. No credit cards.
Open: All year.
Facilities and activities: Located on 27 acres in the village. Hot tub. Nearby: restaurants 5 to 20 minutes away. Rafting center less than 5 miles away. New River Gorge Touring. Mining town tours. Hiking, fishing, boating, and bicycling.
Recommended Country Inns® Travelers' Club Benefit: 10 percent discount, Monday–Thursday. Inquire if active or retired military.

The Beekeeper Inn
HELVETIA, WEST VIRGINIA 26224

Been everywhere? Now looking for someplace unusual?

My sister and I stepped inside The Beekeeper Inn. Blue-and-white tablecloths accented the beauty of flower bouquets. Eleanor Mailloux carried a sign she was hanging. In Swiss German it read, FOOD SERVED HERE WITH LOVE. Enticing gastronomic scents filled the air of this inn, which is a touching personal expression of village life. In the corner sits Ella Betler's mother's hutch, and in another room is Mrs. Karlen's stove and John Martis's cherry brandy jug. The people of Helvetia surround you through their everyday utensils, their photographs, and their mementos. The rooms are old-fashioned, with

antique beds. In the parlor are magazines that reveal the international tastes of the voracious reader.

In October 1869 Swiss folk arrived in this remote wilderness along the headwaters of the Buchanan River. Early settlers included educated people with trades: tailor, baker, musician, doctor, teacher, and cheesemaker, but no farmer. Locals gave encouragement and taught them hunting and fishing. Today more than twenty-five descendants live in Helvetia (including a woodworker and nearby cheesemakers).

Eleanor Mailloux, who grew up here, returned more than twenty years ago. She mentions nothing of what she's accomplished with her fellow Helvetians, not the health clinic, the library. Instead she encourages you to come inside.

We chose a seat near an oil painting of cows and began dinner with savory Helvetia cheese and beer. Homemade bread and applesauce preceded a lovely plateful of scrumptious homemade sausage. The superb Zurich sauerbraten was served with noodles. For dessert a lusciously light peach cobbler was thickly crowned with whipped cream. It was a beautiful evening, rich with wonderful tastes.

Helvetians encourage visitors to join Fastnacht, a Swiss tradition held the Saturday before Ash Wednesday, which frightens away Old Man Winter. Grotesque masks are worn, and a community gathering centers on the inn and lots of very good foods.

Who comes to this out-of-the-way place? People arrive by helicopter. Sierra Club members, cross-country skiers, birders. New Yorkers fly into Elkins, and Eleanor picks them up for the 35-mile ride to Helvetia. Word of mouth brings the romantic, the gourmet, the young, the old, the locals, and *Food & Wine* editors. It's an experience rarely found in the twentieth century.

How to get there: From I–81 take Staunton exit onto Route 250 north. Travel 89 miles to Mill Creek. Turn right at Helvetia sign, and proceed 20 miles to the inn.

Innkeeper: Eleanor Mailloux
Address/Telephone: Swiss Village (mailing address : P.O. Box 42); (304) 924–6435
Rooms: 3; all with private bath.
Rates: $85, double occupancy; $50, single; EPB. No credit cards.
Open: All year.
Facilities and activities: Lunch and dinner served from 12:00 to 7:00 P.M. Beverage license.
    Nearby: walking, hiking, jogging, cross-country skiing, bicycling, birding, photographing; Helvetia Swiss Museum, Holly River State Park, Kumbrado State Forest.

The Current Bed & Breakfast

HILLSBORO, WEST VIRGINIA 24946

West Virginia's Pocahontas County is a place of such diverse natural beauty that one wonders why it was so fortunate. It's known as the birthplace of rivers, because seven of West Virginia's rivers begin here: the Greenbrier, Cherry, Elk, Cheat, Gauley, Tygart Valley, and Williams and Cranberry. Your list of must-sees will depend on your preference for natural landscape. Go to Bear Town State Park and the boardwalk mazes through surrealistic rock formations. At the Falls of the Hills Creek, cascades of 20, 45, and 65 feet form a lush trio. In Cranberry Wilderness, according to the season and whether you're biking, cross-country skiing, or walking, you'll see bogs, vistas, and distinctive vegetation.

Watoga State Park has the beauty of the hardwood forest and river.

To reach The Current, we turned east in Hillsboro and traveled over narrow country roads to the white farmhouse inn with blue shutters. You enter through the large kitchen; in the fall there's a fire in the fireplace, and several breakfast tables are arranged for views of the meadow and forest. The outdoor hot tub is adjacent to the inn deck. From the inn there's direct access to the 72-mile-long Greenbrier River Trail for walking and mountain biking.

Leslee is an articulate hostess and extremely knowledgeable about the area. She was born in West Virginia and has an advanced degree in social work. In the summer Leslee's parents help with breakfasts, gardening, or directing guests to the nearby golf course.

The rooms are furnished with antiques and collectibles; on most beds are quilts; on the floors are small handmade rugs that have been found at country auctions. In our room was a cribful of dolls; Leslee collects them, and they are found throughout the house. This is a kick-back, casual place with shared baths and dogs and cats to visit with on the porch.

We arrived in the spring and walked along the trail to where the trillium, red and scarlet, covered the hillside. I've never seen this many in one place. We passed Canada geese nesting along the riverbank. If you wish to canoe, there's an outfitter in Ronceverte. The Greenbrier is a family river and is best traveled on in the spring; there's an occasional class 3 rapid, but mostly you float pleasantly southward.

Breakfast is simple. We ate a big plateful of blueberry pancakes. No meats are served, since Leslee is vegetarian; the juice is usually orange.

For dinner we drove to Hillsboro's Four Winds. This former general store is open daily and offers a delicious range of food at country prices. Try the French silk pie if you're feeling wicked. It's a wonderful little place; don't miss it.

If you have time after all these treks, there's still more to visit. Hillsboro is the birthplace of Pearl Buck, and a tour through the home is worthwhile, as is an afternoon trip to the town of Cass with its fine lumber museum (offers a steam railroad ride). You can't visit the area without making plans to return.

How to get there: In Hillsboro on Route 219 (south of Four Winds), turn east on Denmar Road. Continue 4 miles (road meanders through hill and dale) to Denmar's green institutional sign and turn left. Continue 2 miles (past little church) and make first left. Inn is short distance on the left.

Innkeepers: Leslee McCarty
Address/Telephone: Hillsboro (mailing address: HC 64, Box 135); (304) 653–4722
E-mail: current@inetone.net
Rooms: 6, including 1 suite; 1 with private bath, 3 with television, 1 with fireplace. Pets allowed on occasion. No smoking inn.
Rates: $55, double occupancy; $40, single; $75, suite; EPB. Two-night minimum holiday weekends.
Open: All year.
Facilities and activities: Outdoor hot tub; Greenbrier River Trail. Nearby: Pearl Buck Birthplace. Bear Town State Park. Watoga State Park. Mountain biking. Canoeing. Cross-country skiing.
Recommended Country Inns® Travelers' Club Benefit: Stay 2 nights, get third night free, Monday–Thursday, subject to availability.

General Lewis Inn

LEWISBURG, WEST VIRGINIA 24901

You register at a desk that's more than two centuries old. The lobby opens into an inviting living room. Around the corner is Memory Hall—a collection of tools, guns, musical instruments, and household utensils used by pioneer families in the area. In every room are substantial wooden beds, antiques, and pretty rose and print wallpapers. A rocker or petite chair sits invitingly to one side of the room.

The General Lewis is an old-fashioned place with big white pillars, rocking chairs, and a carriage out front. A few hundred yards from Lewisburg's main street, the inn exudes a secure and serene sense of the perfect country haven.

Lewisburg deserves its own accolades. At the desk request "A Walking Tour of Historic Lewisburg," and you'll find fifty-four historic buildings within walking distance of the inn.

Part of the General Lewis dates from 1834. Notice the beautifully hewn beams in the dining room. The inn is warm and homey and has a large, comfortable common room from which it's very difficult to move once you're ensconced before the fireplace. Interesting conversations happen here.

If you come for that big event, the West Virginia State Fair in nearby Fairlea, you're going to have a busy holiday seeing the prize farm animals, blue-ribbon cakes, and country entertainers. Off-season touring can be just as much fun. Arrive here on a wintry snowy day, and a warm fire rewards you for the journey. In other seasons you can tour historic Lost World Cavern or spend the afternoon walking or biking on the beautiful Greenbrier River Trail. There's "gorgeous golfing," according to my travel companion, who golfed at the Greenbrier one fall afternoon.

Dinner is delicious Southern cooking. The ham is country cured, the chicken Southern fried, and the pork chops juicy and tender. Perhaps you'd prefer a filet mignon or fresh boneless trout. For dessert the cobblers are served piping hot with a dip of vanilla ice cream.

In the morning over hot coffee and fresh biscuits served with brimming pots of apple butter, preserves, and honey, you'll notice many local businessmen enjoying the same breakfast. There are friendly, softly spoken greetings. Why is it that, in a good inn, everyone is so polite?

How to get there: From I–64 take Route 219 south for 1 mile to Lewisburg. In town turn east (left) onto Route 60 and go 3 blocks to the inn. Fly-in, Greenbrier Valley Airport.

Innkeepers: Mary Noel Hock and Jim Morgan; Nancy Morgan, manager

Address/Telephone: 301 East Washington Street; (304) 645–2600 or (800) 628–4454, fax (304) 645–2600

Rooms: 25, including 2 suites; all with private bath, air conditioning, television, and telephone. Wheelchair accessible. Pets allowed. No smoking inn.

Rates: $64 to $92, double occupancy, EP. Additional guest, $10. Request winter packages. August State Fair week higher.

Open: All year.

Facilities and activities: Breakfast, lunch, dinner (entrees $9.50 to $16.50), wine, beer, and cocktails. Nearby: historic walk through Lewisburg, golf at Greenbrier Hotel and Greenbrier Valley Country Club, fishing, Lost World Cavern, Organ Cave, Greenbrier River Trail, West Virginia State Fair, Greenbrier Valley Theater.

$\mathscr{A}$spen $\mathscr{H}$all $\mathscr{I}$nn

MARTINSBURG, WEST VIRGINIA 25401

During the French and Indian War of the 1750s, when Martinsburg was at the American frontier, Aspen Hall, which had been built by Quakers was part of Fort Mendenhall. The modest home was enlarged to a Georgian-style mansion in the 1770s and during the early 1900s was modified to reflect Victorian tastes. The Clauchertys are experienced restorers who were equal to the task of returning the mansion to its comfortable haven in town.

On a warm afternoon you pass by the porch hammocks into a long, wide foyer that opens to an elegant, three-story staircase. A large folk painting of the town hangs above an Empire sofa.

If you've arrived in time for tea, you've planned smartly. Every afternoon LouAnne reveals her English heritage by serving cake or cookies and tea. She's flexible about where you take tea. Carry it off to the gazebo if you wish, join guests in the inn's library, or relax on the porch swing.

Climb the grand staircase to your lodging. In the bride's room you place your luggage upon an antique child's bed. On the dresser I found a 1905 hatbox and inside it an elaborate black hat that guests may try on. In the bathroom is the original claw-footed tub and pedestal sink. All of the rooms are filled with antiques. The gentleman's room has a queen-sized canopy bed and a fireplace; the mantel is covered with LouAnne's grandfather's apothecary collection. In the Quaker room there's an eighteenth-century spice cabinet. LouAnne explained that spices were traditionally placed under lock at the foot of the bed, which clearly indicates their value to Colonial settlers. The sink in this room has been cleverly installed in an antique sewing-machine cabinet.

Breakfast in the dining room, where I admired the corner cupboard filled with china that LouAnne inherited from her grandmother, might include plantation hotcakes with maple syrup, sausage-and-corn fritters, or challah French toast with strawberries in orange sauce and new potatoes in herb butter. You'll probably linger in this comfortable setting.

Don't overlook the inn's private fort; it resembles a small stone cottage and is several yards from the inn. I had to duck to enter. Inside, daylight streaked through gun slits. The building probably dates to about 1758, when the Quakers who lived here petitioned the Quarterly Quaker Meeting of Pennsylvania for permission to discontinue holding meetings. They explained that they needed to spend their time building a fortification to defend themselves against the "Indian enemy."

In the summertime you might carry a tray of lemonade and cookies out to the gazebo overlooking Tuscarora Creek. A train might pass, if you're lucky, but they rarely do. Meantime be careful not to let the butterflies and birds disturb you.

How to get there: From I–81 take King Street exit and go east, turn left on Raleigh Street, and go 3 blocks north to Race Street. Go 1 block and make a left onto Boyd Street; proceed to the end of the block, where the inn sits on 7½ private acres.

Innkeepers: LouAnne and Gordon Claucherty
Address/Telephone: 405 Boyd Avenue; (304) 263–4385
Rooms: 5; all with private bath and air conditioning, 1 with fireplace, 2 with television. No smoking inn.
Rates: $95 to $110, double occupancy, EPB and afternoon tea. Two-night minimum in October.
Open: Mid-February through mid-December.
Facilities and activities: On 7½ acres; croquet, gazebo, gardens, creek with bridge, walking trails. Nearby: restaurants, Blue Ridge factory outlets, Harper's Ferry, Antietam Battlefield, Berkeley Springs Bathhouse.
Recommended Country Inns® Travelers' Club Benefit: 10 percent discount on stay of three or more nights.

Pence Springs Hotel
PENCE SPRINGS, WEST VIRGINIA 24962

Upon entering I was drawn into the great room, where a fire burned and a cluster of chairs and couches invited companionship. French doors led to a wraparound porch and a pathway to the historic springs. The hotel is an impressive brick building, and out front are the large, raised gardens where Ashby Berkley grows herbs to flavor his meals. Several of the vegetables he serves are also grown here on the inn's 400 acres.

"I wanted the properties and foods to reflect this place," explained Ashby, graduate of the Culinary Institute of America. He refined his palate (and also studied wines in Europe) before returning to Pence Springs. This native son then opened his renowned Riverside Inn, a nineteenth-century log cabin (built expressly by the governor of West Virginia to appear much older). There he serves foods based on the English settlers' traditions that he's adapted to contemporary palates and local bounty. Among his dishes at the Riverside Inn are roast goose, lamb, and venison pie.

With the English gourmet tradition established, Ashby turned to the Pence Springs Hotel to create a country experience. He refers to the evening's chalkboard menu as "country fare"— but it's a savvy country, for we had an outstanding fresh trout (salmon was also on the menu) and an excellent Colonial meat pie that included chunks of venison, beef, duckling, and capon. The dessert was a delicious, hot apple-rhubarb cobbler served with ice cream.

During the Roaring Twenties Pence Springs was renowned for its mineral waters. Bottles were shipped worldwide, and they were served at the nearby Greenbrier Hotel. During Prohibition wealthy clientele partied at this "sanctioned watering hole." By 1926, the Grand Hotel, as it was then known, was one of the most expensive in the country; fourteen trains a day delivered passengers here. The day after the stock market crash in 1929, the hotel closed its doors. From 1947 until 1983 it was a women's prison.

Ashby Berkley came to the rescue when the governor asked him to purchase and save the distinguished building. The restoration was massive. But he says "grand" in 1926 means modest today.

The bedroom doors still have the now-covered openings from which guards could check on the prisoners. The bedrooms are different sizes, carpeted, and simply furnished.

Downstairs is the Cider Press Lounge, whose lovely back bar formed part of the set for the movie *Matewan*, which is based on a coal-min-ing riot that occurred in West Virginia. Ashby Berkley accommodates friends, neighbors, and guests with immediate rapport.

Ashby is restoring the original spring (which still provides excellent water according to contemporary health standards), and the historic building that houses it is now an antiques shop. Every Sunday morning spring through fall, a popular flea market is held here. Many guests come Saturday evening, since the short walk down the hill leads to early bargains.

You might come for any number of reasons—to shop at the flea market, to explore the myriad sights from the Greenbrier, to see Organ Cave, to enjoy family biking or canoeing, or simply to have a delicious meal and savor a country inn with a fascinating history that's now on the National Register of Historic Places.

How to get there: From I–64 take Alta exit 161. Take Route 12 to Alderson, where Route 12 becomes Route 3. Continue approximately 7 miles on Route 3 to the inn. You'll see the FLEA MARKET sign, then the inn.

Innkeepers: Ashby Berkley and Rosalee Berkley Miller
Address/Telephone: Route 3 (mailing address: P.O. Box 90); (304) 445–2606 or (800) 826–1829, fax (304) 445–2204
Rooms: 16, including 3 suite; all with private bath and air conditioning; television available on request. Wheelchair accessible.
Rates: $69.50 to $99.50, double occupancy, EPB and afternoon tea.
Open: Mid-April through December.
Facilities and activities: Lunch; dinner ($26 to $38); tavern. On 400 acres, with fishing, horseback riding, hiking, bicycling, croquet, volleyball. Nearby: Sunday flea market (seasonal), Organ Cave, hiking, white-water rafting, biking, villages for touring.

$\mathcal{S}$moke $\mathcal{H}$ole $\mathcal{L}$odge

PETERSBURG, WEST VIRGINIA 26847

Friends from way back, we congregated on a glorious fall weekend. It took months of planning and negotiating to coordinate all seven schedules. Babysitters had been found, work put aside, and finally we converged in Petersburg in front of Alt's Grocery Store.

My friends had requested adventure in the wilderness, but I understand their tastes as well as my own. They also craved comfort, a lovely view in the evening, long exhilarating walks together, chats beside the fire, and something different.

In front of Alt's Grocery Store a truck lumbered up, canvas over the top, and sides open. Ed Stifle III descended. I clearly remember Ed's long-ago comment, "You probably won't like the place." I had loved it; that was the old lodge, and in the new lodge he achieved a rustic, Spartan beauty.

Ed drove down a paved road for a while and turned off on a single-lane dirt trail, where he opened the first of several gates that permitted us to travel 5 miles into the West Virginia woods and mountains, where there is no electricity or telephones. It's accessible only by four-wheel drive, on foot, horseback, or canoe. Midway into the 1½-hour journey, Ed explained that we would have illumination by a gas lantern system and hot running water for showers. He also referred to the flood that had washed away the first Smoke Hole Lodge that was in his family for a century and in this book for more than a decade.

We arrived before dark, the sun cutting a swathe across the valley. Smoke Hole came into view—a red-cedar lodge with a streamside location. Ducks swam in the river, fish in the pond, drowsy chickens and turkeys paced their steps, and cattle in a corral logged our progress. Ed had an architect design the lodge to curve around the West Virginia mountainside, and the first impression startles the viewer.

Ed is as unique as his property. He reminds me of Midwestern men like my father who are direct, honest, independent spirits with a passion for the land. His 1,500 acres are also working land where he raises cattle. His ecological bent means he's provided for the future, and his land will never be commercially developed.

That night around long, handmade oak tables, we were served huge helpings of roast beef and potatoes, mixed vegetables, and the inn's signature sticky buns. We couldn't pass up the dessert, a rich chocolate pudding laced with pieces of caramel candy and whipped cream.

At 8 A.M. Ed's clanging of pans downstairs announced breakfast. After huge amounts of pancakes, scrambled eggs, and bacon, we helped him feed the animals.

At each lodge meal we met other guests we fancied. Some had come for the fishing, others to get away to a secret place. We had come to celebrate the season and renew our bonds of friendship, to talk of the many subjects, serious and frivolous, that friends do when they are sequestered together in the woods on a beautiful weekend.

How to get there: From I–81 in Middletown, exit onto Route 55 west. Remain on Route 55 for 52 miles to Moorefield. Then take Route 220 south through Petersburg to Pansy, about 19½ miles. Meet Ed at Calhoun's Country Store in Pansy. Fly-in, Petersburg airport; Ed will pick you up. Inn is 12 miles south of Petersburg, reachable only by four-wheel drive. You can also arrive by horseback. Request information.

Innkeeper: Edward W. Stifel III

Address/Telephone: Petersburg (mailing address: P.O. Box 953); (304) 242–8377 (November through April only)

Rooms: 5, all with twin beds and private bath; 2 dormitories—one sleeps 4 and one sleeps 5. Pets allowed with prior permission.

Rates: $90 first person in room or dormitory; additional person (in same room or dormitory) $75; AP. Ten percent discount for groups of 8 or more, 15 percent for 12 or more. Children under age 4 no charge. No credit cards. Two-night minimum.

Open: May through October.

Facilities and activities: Meals for guests only; BYOB. Located on 1,500 acres on south branch of Potomac River. Fishing (West Virginia license required; can be purchased in Petersburg), swimming, hiking, tubing, bird-watching.

Hampshire House 1884
ROMNEY, WEST VIRGINIA 26757

Once, long ago, Scott had a pleasant experience in Romney; it was a fleeting episode that came back to mind when he and Jane chose to escape from the city. They came to Romney to develop a "deeper sense of belonging to a place" and to tackle a major inn restoration. For Jane it was also the opportunity to live among the trees and hills, a dream she formed growing up in the Midwestern plains.

Jane says, "This is a Victorian home that depicts how the average town person lived, and yet we decorated it to please our modern tastes." The inn strikes a balance of beauty and comfort with thick carpeting, fine antiques, and original oil lamps adapted to electricity, which give a soft glow throughout the inn. When it was built in 1884, the style would have been considered old-fashioned for its day.

The restoration of the inn went beyond the call of duty. The woodwork came off so that the rooms could be soundproofed; the exterior bricks were pointed; all twenty-eight doors were removed, stripped, and refinished; and the latest in safety features and new bathrooms were installed.

Scott led me upstairs (a healthy quickness to his step) and into the Whitaker Room, with handsome Eastlake furniture. I settled in with a hot cup of tea, my pen and notebook before me.

Romney is on the south branch of the Potomac River in the Shenandoah Mountains.

Jane suggested to several guests a trip on the Potomac Eagle, an excursion train. To others she described a local canoe trip.

I was directed to an excellent local restaurant for dinner. In the morning the bountiful breakfast inlcuded blueberry muffins, fresh fruit, and whole-grain fruit pancakes, a recipe developed by Jane and one I use now.

Each of the bedrooms has been named for a former resident. I'm partial to the Eastlake furnishings in the Whitaker, which is hung with white lace curtains and has a small soda-fountain writing table from a Nebraska drugstore in the corner. Two rooms have queen-sized beds.

Jane and Scott both have a background in teaching and human relations. They have found the appropriate niche in innkeeping, and when you arrive you know you've found the appropriate inn for your city-break.

"Give us," a reader wrote, "an old-fashioned inn with reasonable prices, delicious food, and some small-town pursuits where we can meet the innkeepers." The search ends here.

How to get there: From I–81 take Route 50 east in Winchester. From Route 50 in Romney, turn north on Grafton and proceed 1½ blocks to the inn on the left.

Innkeepers: Jane and Scott Simmons
Address/Telephone: 165 North Grafton Street; (304) 822–7171
Rooms: 5; all with private bath, air conditioning, and cable television, 3 with fireplace. No smoking inn.
Rates: $65 to $90, double occupancy, EPB.
Open: All year.
Facilities and activities: Dinner occasionally served by reservation. Nearby: restaurants, three wineries, equestrian center, walking, canoeing, antiquing, athletic club.
Recommended Country Inns® Travelers' Club Benefit: 10 percent discount, Monday–Thursday, except October; or stay 2 nights and get third night free, except October.

Bavarian Inn & Lodge

SHEPHERDSTOWN, WEST VIRGINIA 25443

The Bavarian Inn, a gray stone mansion, became an inn in 1977. In the beginning Erwin was chef and Carol the hostess; she also made the strudels and chocolate Bavarian cakes. Today Erwin, impeccably dressed in a suit, often greets his dining guests and oversees the eighty-six-person staff in the seventy-three-room resort inn overlooking the Potomac River. Four riverside chalets, swimming pool, tennis court, three dining rooms, a rathskeller, a conference room, exercise room, and a private golf course compose the German inn. The inn has received the four-diamond award from AAA and four stars from *Mobil Guide* every year since 1984. It's spotlessly clean and comfortable.

There are three rooms in the stone inn; the other rooms are located in five modern chalets, each hand painted with an attractive Bavarian scene. From your canopy bed you can enjoy the tiled fireplace, which is only steps away from the hot tub. Several rooms have a river view and almost all have a private balcony. Hand-painted flowers or subtle wallpapers accent the rooms. The furnishings, including many queen-sized beds, are fine reproductions. The night you arrive at this little Bavaria, a chocolate is laid at the bedside. A couple celebrating an anniversary, honeymooners, or a family traveling together would be equally comfortable in the spacious lodgings.

For dinner, we chose a seat in the dining room lit with deer-horn chandeliers. We admired a lovely Austrian wood-burning stove that sits in the corner for decoration. In season (September to March) game dishes, including venison, pheasant, rabbit, and wild boar, are served. Fresh Maine lobster is available year-round. We had arrived on a spring evening, the season for fresh crabmeat. Mine arrived very hot and flavored with a scrumptiously light cheese sauce. My companion couldn't resist the classic sauerbraten served with potato dumplings and brightly flavored red cabbage. Cheesecake and coffee followed, while we enjoyed the hillside view.

Later we paused in the gift shop, where wines and imported German mugs reminded us of trips to Europe, and just for one night we felt we had returned.

Every fall Shepherdstown, which dates to its German settlement in 1730, and the Bavarian Inn host an Oktoberfest. Rain or shine an Edelweiss band and folk dancers perform, and the inn serves its traditional sausage specialties and fine beers. If you prefer to come during a quieter time, bring your winter snow boots and cross the bridge to the C & O Canal. You can walk in solitude beside the river and return for a soak in the whirlpool bath and warm up before the fire in preparation for a hot meal in the inn's Rathskeller.

How to get there: From Washington, D.C., take I–270 to Frederick bypass, then I–70 to exit 49, turn left onto Alternate 40 to Braddock Heights–Boonsboro. Turn left in Boonsboro onto Maryland 34 to Shepherdstown. The inn is on Route 480 at Potomac River Bridge. From I–81 take exit 16E. Follow Route 45 to Shepherdstown.

Innkeepers: Erwin and Carol Asam; Kevin Danmeyer, manager
Address/Telephone: Route 480 (mailing address: Route 1, Box 30); (304) 876–2551, fax (304) 876–9355
Rooms: 73, including 2 suites; all with private bath, air conditioning, telephone, and television, 37 with whirlpool, 41 with fireplace. Wheelchair accessible. Designated no smoking rooms.
Rates: $85 to $165, double occupancy, EP. Additional person, $10. Two-night minimum holidays and special events. Sunday to Thursday winter packages and seasonal golf packages.
Open: All year.
Facilities and activities: Breakfast, lunch, dinner (entrees $13 to $23). Rathskeller with entertainment on weekends. Outdoor pool, tennis court, golf course, exercise room. Nearby: C & O Towpath, Harper's Ferry, Antietam Battlefield, Charles Town opera, and races.
Business travel: Telephone and desk all rooms, fax connection 32 rooms; fax and copier available; conference room.

Thomas Shepherd Inn
SHEPHERDSTOWN, WEST VIRGINIA 25443

Margaret's inn has two dining rooms, which is not at all surprising when you find out that she has studied at L'Academie de Cuisine in Bethesda, Maryland. Often she waits until she meets all her guests before she composes the breakfast menu.

She might size you up as a traditionalist who longs for a classic eggs Benedict served with her deliciously cured ham; for you daring types she might fix a chilled blueberry soup or an omelet flavored with sun-dried tomatoes and capers and onion; and for those who deny a professed style but want something deliciously homemade, there might appear cheese-stuffed French toast served with orange butter accompanied by thick

slices of Amish-raised bacon. The problem, I suppose, if you could call it that, is what to do with those who roam the gastronomic world and are seated with those of conservative tastes. In those cases she delivers a sauce on the side that will tantalize the traditionalist yet please the exotic palate.

Besides discussing food we talked about walking, which Margaret is fond of. She explained that about a mile from the inn across the Shenandoah River is the C & O Canal and Lock 38, where she walks and directs guests for bike riding. You can fetch a trail map from the National Park office.

Shepherdstown, settled by Germans, has

several antiques shops, a general store, and a German bakery.

The inn is 4 miles from Antietam Battlefield and not far from either Harper's Ferry or the factory outlets (great Ralph Lauren towels) of Martinsburg. Its central location provides access to historic sites and antiquing.

With advance notice Margaret prepares picnic lunches. She might pack a tarragon chicken salad on French bread and a lemon poppy-seed pound cake for dessert. Midweek in wintertime Margaret offers special packages that are worth inquiring about.

This Federal inn dates from the mid-nineteenth century and began as a Lutheran Church parsonage. In 1937 it became the home and office of local physicians. In 1984 it was restored as an inn. The furnishings are Colonial and comfortable. The wooden floors gleam, they're so clean; they are softened by Persian and other carpets. Along with antiques there are comfortable seating areas in most rooms.

In the morning Margaret serves hot coffee in the living room, where the *Washington Post* sits on the sideboard and the fire is burning. Before the inn begins to stir, you have a moment to drink in the inn and savor the setting. As others arrive you abandon the news of the world for the news of people and places more immediate. You meet gentle people from either faraway or nearby places. One couple had come for the Saturday-night folk dance.

How to get there: From I–70 take Alternate Route 40 in Frederick to Boonsboro. Then take Route 34 to Shepherdstown. In Shepherdstown, the inn is located at the intersection of Route 45, Route 480, and Route 230, the main thorough-fares.

Innkeeper: Margaret Perry

Address/Telephone: 300 West German Street (mailing address: P.O. Box 1162); (304) 876–3715, fax (304) 876–1386

E-mail: mrg@intrepid.net

Rooms: 7; all with private bath and air conditioning; telephone available on request. No smoking inn.

Rates: $95 to $125, double occupancy, EPB. AARP and senior-citizen discounts. Two-night minimum on weekends if Saturday included, April–Thanksgiving.

Open: All year.

Facilities and activities: Picnic lunch; dinner served on request midweek ($20 to $30); BYOB. Library with television and VCR. Nearby: restaurants, C & O Canal, antiquing, canoeing, hiking, Harper's Ferry, Antietam Battlefield, Charles Town Races, outlet shopping.

Business travel: Telephone, fax, and desk available; corporate rates; meeting room.

Recommended Country Inns® Travelers' Club Benefit: Stay two nights, get third night free, Sunday–Thursday, excluding holidays.

Elk River Lodge
SLATYFORK, WEST VIRGINIA 26291

"Bhagwan of the Back Country" is how someone once described Gil Willis, who choreographs off-the-beaten-path tours during biking season (April through October). He has created a six-day back-country trek that begins in the nearby Cranberry Glades and ends in the state's northern Canaan Valley; each night bike riders lodge at an inn.

In August Gil and Mary host the annual West Virginia Fat Tire Festival, which encompasses races, beginning through advanced tours, training, and guidance on gaining trail access with mountain bikes.

Gil is equally adept with winter sports and cross-country skiing, whether at the lodge or in the nearby forest (the shop rents bikes and skis). We arrived to find that a 6-inch snowfall had succumbed to sunny fifty-degree weather—but Gil pulled out his guest map; told us where to drive, park, and ski; then described the trail in keen detail. Without his direction we'd never have attempted the route, but it was a north slope and groomed for fine skiing. Whether you're an adventurer or a novice, Gil custom-designs private tours or sends you off to explore the trails, rivers, and forests of Pocahontas County. He knows where the best view can be had, where to fish, and how to reach the little-known waterfalls. There's also downhill skiing at nearby Snowshoe and Silver Creek.

The inn is also oriented toward families; the winter cross-country ski area becomes a series of meadows in summer. We love the sound of water flowing over the rocks as we pass over two single-lane bridges to reach the inn.

From the dining room we watched deer feed one evening; in the winter a fire burns in the stone fireplace and a few skiers might be heading home along the trail. Mary, who has a degree in marine biology, has turned her attentions to the kitchen. She's a gentle young woman—perhaps it was growing up in a family of ten children that gave her such amiable ways. During dinner sons Thurston and Augustus were being looked after by Dad while Mary was in the kitchen.

In the winter dinner is served nightly. Selections are made from a blackboard menu that includes fresh trout, steak, and a spicy blackened red snapper, all accompanied by salads and homemade dressings. We shared an apple-blueberry pie for dessert. During summer dinner is served Wednesday through Saturday (call to confirm).

My favorites among the inn rooms have private baths and are located in the newer part of the inn. Several smaller buildings have more rustic bath-sharing accommodations. There were plenty of extra blankets on our bed, and we slept soundly. Breakfast included a large plateful of buckwheat pancakes that gave us the energy to ski a vigorous 5-mile stretch among cherry and oak trees, with beautiful distant views of mountains. This is an area of five rivers, country stores, endless hiking, the Cass Railroad, and scenic beauty—none of it far from this inn.

How to get there: From I–64 take Route 219 North in Lewisburg. Go 40 miles to Marlinton. From Marlinton, proceed north on Route 219 for 15⁹⁄₁₀ miles. The inn is on the left at sign: ELK RIVER LODGE. Cross one-lane bridge over Elk River.

Innkeepers: Gil and Mary Willis
Address/Telephone: Route 219 (mailing address: HC 69, Box 7); (304) 572–3771
    fax (304) 572–3741
Rooms: 12, including 2 cottages; 7 with private bath. No smoking inn.
Rates: $45 to $90, double occupancy, EPB. Children under 9 free. Additional person, $5.
    Request MAP and midweek rates. Two-night minimum weekends,
Open: All year.
Facilities and activities: Dinner (entrees $9 to $14; $4 for children). Hot tub, immediate access to 150 acres; 25-kilometer cross-country trail, 2 kilometers with night lighting; ski shop, bike shop, mountain bike rental, cross-country ski rental, hiking trails. Adjacent to Monongahela National Forest, Skiing at Snowshoe and Silver Creek (5 miles away).

Indexes
Alphabetical Index to Inns

Mountain Inns

Lakeside Inns

Inns with a River View

Inns at the Seashore

Inns of the New York Finger Lakes

Inns on the Delmarva Peninsula

Inns on the Delmarva Peninsula

Inns of the Brandywine

Inns Especially Suited to Families

Inns with Wheelchair Access

Inns with a Swimming Pool

Cross-Country Skiing Inns
(* designates skiing trails available on site)

Inns for Going Fishing

Inns for White-Water Rafting

Inns for Mountain Biking

Inns for Business Travelers

Inns in or near The City

Inns Offering Travelers' Club Benefits

The Author Speaks

"She's a woman who sleeps around for a living," a very distinguished woman once introduced me as I was about to present a slide show to a group of country inn lovers. That apt description is an honest one, although I prefer to say, "I'm a travel journalist."

My traveling companion is Charlie, my husband, who golfs and skis his way across the Mid-Atlantic during our travels. He's my opinionated consort, who helps research each inn for its maximum comfort level. We live in Arlington, Virginia—a central point for our Mid-Atlantic travels.

I have a degree in English and my words have appeared in print in sundry places—*Harper's Bazaar, House Beautiful, Family Circle, Travel Holiday, Historic Preservation, Mid-Atlantic Country,* and *The Washington Post.*

Happy Innings.